OTHER BOOKS ON AFRICA
BY BASIL DAVIDSON

Report on Southern Africa (1952)

The New West Africa: Problems of Independence (1953)
(edited with Adenekan Ademola)

The African Awakening (1955)

The Lost Cities of Africa (1959)

Black Mother: The African Slave Trade (1961)

Which Way Africa? The Search for a New Society (1964)

A History of West Africa, 1000–1800 (1965)
(with F. K. Buah)

African Kingdoms (1966)
(with the Editors of Time-Life Books)

*A History of East and Central Africa to the
Late 19th Century* (1967)
(with J. E. F. Mhina)

Africa in History: Themes and Outlines (1968)

The Liberation of Guiné (1969)

*The African Genius: An Introduction to African Social
and Cultural History* (1969)

In the Eye of the Storm: Angola's People (1972)

*Black Star: A View of the Life and Times of
Kwame Nkrumah* (1973)

*Can Africa Survive? Arguments Against Growth Without
Development* (1974)

Let Freedom Come: Africa in Modern History (1978)

No Fist Is Big Enough to Hide the Sky (1981)

The People's Cause: A History of Guerrillas in Africa (1981)

The Story of Africa (1984)

The Long Struggle of Eritrea (1988)
(edited with Lionel Cliffe)

The Fortunate Isles (1989)

Modern Africa (1990)

African Civilization Revisited (1991)

*The Black Man's Burden:
Africa and the Curse of the Nation-State* (1992)

Basil Davidson
The Black Man's Burden
Africa & the Curse of the Nation-State

Basil Davidson
The Search for Africa
A History in the Making

'*Basil Davidson is the most effective popularizer of African history and archaeology outside Africa and certainly the best trusted in Africa itself.*' – Roland Oliver in *The New York Review of Books*'

'*It is a great read. His attacking power springs from lucidity, humanity and dramatic artistry... Of the recent general books on nationalism this is the most useful one to recommend to undergraduate historians.*' – John Lonsdale in *The Journal of African History*

'*Africa and indeed the entire international community owe Basil Davidson, the doyen of Africa's pre-colonial history, a gratitude for reopening discussion on this fundamental issue.*' – Adebayo Adedeji

'*In this sustained attack upon nation-statism and its oppressive tendencies, Davidson brings to bear his vast knowledge of both Africa and the Balkans. This is a knowledge born not only of study, but of tramping the bush with the guerrillas of Vojvodina and Angola. Davidson's admiration for the democratizing effects of grass-roots mobilization goes right back to his youthful years with Tito's partisans; and his attack upon rampant nationalism in Africa is equally relevant, as he demonstrates, to the bloody disintegration of Tito's federation....*' – Gerald Moore in *Le Monde Diplomatique*

'*Basil Davidson is thoroughly familiar with the classical sources, and he is also in close touch with the current work and thinking of specialists in contemporary historical and archaeological research in Africa... Not the least of his gifts is his capacity for compelling narrative and clear exposition.*' – John Fage

'*... a poet who writes in prose about the deep emotions that move mankind.*' – Christopher Fyfe

'*Basil Davidson may know as much about modern Black Africa and Black Africans as anyone in the West. As a scholar-journalist, moreover, he has had closer and more intimate contact with people and events in Africa since 1950 than any academic historian. Throughout, he has been the friend of Africans and, in the early days, a hammer of the imperial powers which still dominated them.*' – D.K. Fieldhouse, *The Times Literary Supplement*

'*This is a book of major importance. The Black Man's Burden is not only about Africa, but about ethnicity, nations, and the problem of living together in society everywhere.*' – Eric Hobsbawm

Basil Davidson says '*The arrangement here is partly by theme and partly by time-when-written; there is also, here and there, an underlying "autobiographical" projection, unfolding firstly the development of an African historiography since its academic establishment some forty years ago and, secondly in that context, my own development.*'

'*He addresses the fundamental issues, not the merely topical. He explores the racism inherent in colonial dispossession and the attempted imposition of "categories of systematic inferiority on colonised peoples". He examines the all-too-familiar paradox – the many critics of independent Africa who find the single-party state intolerable and insist on a multi-party state, and are then astonished that the underlying problems remain. He derides the notion of democracy being contained "in some kind of magic bottle from which it can be poured at will".*'.' – Michael Wolfers in *The Guardian*

'*This collection of his essays and articles, written between 1953 and 1993 as he watched Africa break free from the colonial yoke, gathers together the answers – and questions – that have come out of Mr Davidson's lifelong fascination with Africa. His favourite culprit for Africa's troubling post-colonial history is "the curse of the nation state." Although his thesis is by now familiar to many, the bloody feuds newly tearing apart states from Rwanda to South Africa make it all the more pertinent.*' – *The Economist*

'*Despite its terrible difficulties, Davidson's Africa is a continent of hope. In both the customary and the more fashioable sense, his work is affirmative.*' – Jeremy Harding in *The London Review of Books*

THE

SEARCH

FOR AFRICA

A History in the Making

BASIL DAVIDSON

James Currey
LONDON

Published in Britain
and the Commonwealth, excluding Canada,
by James Currey Ltd.
54B Thornhill Square, Islington
London N1 1BE

British Library Cataloguing in Publication Data
Davidson, Basil
Search for Africa: History in the Making
I. Title
960
ISBN 0-85255-714-0 (James Currey Paper)
ISBN 0-85255-719-1 (James Currey Cloth)

Printed by Villiers Publications Ltd London N3

TO MY READERS

Now do not dream
Good patient friend
That you have seen
This search's end

That's beyond me
That's out ahead!
By you—

To be continued ...

Contents

ARGUMENTS   *313*

THE SEARCH FOR AFRICA

THINKING
ABOUT AFRICA

R EADERS HAVE OFTEN ASKED ME OVER THE YEARS, AND ON OCCASIONS
that I like to remember, two questions that bear upon myself and
my work: why you, and why Africa? Now these are pleasant questions that
could, of course, be simply answered in terms of personal biography: this
and this happened to me along the pathways of my life, and in these and
these situations. Yet that kind of answer, as it has seemed to me, could not
satisfy my tolerant readers: their interest in posing these questions, I
think, was much less personal than general. How and why, they were
really asking (as I believe), has the whole matter of history in Africa come
to be of prime importance in this world as we have it now, an importance
upon which you have always insisted?

"History in Africa," they might have said (and sometimes, not unreasonably, did say), "may be useful for passing examinations, or generally
have something to tell about itself as an interesting subject. But the fact
remains that it is far away, and remote from our everyday concerns and
lives." I don't know that I have ever found a convincing denial of the view
that studying history in Africa may act as a kind of escape from present
tragedies and problems. But my own belief is that the study of history in
Africa, with all its implications for people in society, is in fact an indispensable approach to the understanding of present realities—and certainly insofar as one or another implication of race discrimination has
influence among us. And so this volume of essays emerges as the best
answer I can make to the questions, "Why us, and why Africa?"

True enough, the essays and commentaries collected here are of a
nature that is usually labeled "occasional"; and it is also true that they
were written at various times in response to various needs. Yet they are

neither accidental nor in the least unrelated to one another. I have taken
them from their various places of initial publication—some of these
places hard to find, others not at all—because they offer, as I see it, a line
of thought (precisely the line of thought in which I myself have had the
good fortune to be involved) that can illuminate one of the truly liberating achievements, cultural achievements, of the twentieth century: the
reinstallation of Africa's peoples within the culture of the world.

In this task of recovering and reinstalling Africa within what may
reasonably be called "the equalities of world consciousness"—and I think
the term will be accepted—there have been involved a wide range of
scholars in many countries, men and women of many origins and as many
opinions; and the task is by no means near its end. These pioneers have
had to face, sometimes still have to face, the obstacles and hazards natural ·
to their being pioneers. For they have been saying what was generally
disbelieved, what was new and disturbing of customary opinion, what was
hard across the grain of previous teaching, what was either quickly
dismissed or otherwise—as latterly—received with condescension. In my
own case, I will admit, nothing of all that has been more offensive than
this comfortable condescension of the orthodox: "He's an idealist, he's
well-meaning, but you needn't really take him seriously. . . ." What is
unfamiliar or unacceptable is transformed, like this, into the merely
sentimental.

If so, then my early teachers and fellow workers have been at fault, for
it was they who pointed me along the path ahead. But that is not how I
remember them. In the United States, for example, could one really say
of Melville Herskovits or of Leo Hansberry, or of others like them, that
they were sentimentalists? I remember them as intellectually tough char-
acters whose voices, if they ever became stern or shrill, had been made
so by having for so long to override the prejudices of orthodoxy. The
essence of what they taught, in fact, has now become the stuff of everyday
acceptance. And the same has become true of their contemporaries outside the United States.

There are lots of ironies along this trail. One of these is that the Second
World War, a very general misery for countless millions of people, had
for Africa some excellent results in promoting liberation from externally
imposed servitude. The war and its aftermath had powerful antiracist
implications. Among their fruits was the promotion of a harvest of hard-
thinking researchers into Africa's forgotten centuries: some of these in
Europe, others in North America, and then soon in Africa as well. They
worked in the various disciplines that may be gathered, generally, under
the heading of historiography, and the results of their work can now be

said to be far more revealing of general truths about humanity than is as yet widely recognized. That was a time, moreover, when it seemed all-important to throw new bridges of empathy and understanding across the gulfs that lay between "us" and "them"—whichever way you see the difference, on whichever "side" you may feel yourself to be—so that the beetling cliffs of miscomprehension, from contempt at the edge of one precipice to mere ignorance at another, might be scaled or rendered passable. Out of the slave trade and its consequences, or out of colonial dispossessions and their consequences, or out of industrial revolutions and the absence of such revolutions—out of one historical upheaval or another—these cliffs of miscomprehension or contempt had become a huge obstacle to civility, and even to everyday peace and good order.

In dealing with this obstacle, at least in helping to render it passable, the pioneers of African history, especially those of some forty years ago or thereabouts, may now be seen to have done good service. They had to begin somewhat defensively; it could barely have been otherwise. So powerful was the generalized assumption that Africa possessed no history of its own, meaning that the term "Africa in history" could have no real meaning before about 1850, that defensive postures were scarcely avoidable. Melville Herskovits may reasonably be seen as the father of African studies in the United States, at any rate at the level of university teaching (Hansberry at Howard University, for example, was never given a chair), and Herskovits for a long time preferred to speak of African "ethnohistory," by which he meant to defend the project of an African historiography that was bereft of written records; and this somewhat apologetic usage continued for a while through the 1950s. In England, Gervase Mathew, who was for me the first, if now forgotten, sponsor of the notion of Africa's having truly possessed a proper and effective history of its own, had a preference for the term "intuitive history." This meant that we should proceed by supposing historical truths about Africa—the truths that could make sense of the evidence we then had—until such time as hard-and-fast confirmation should come to hand; and in this, it must be said, he was thoroughly supported by what came about in our discipline even before his unfortunately early death. My own early writing was sometimes of this type. One extended what was known into assumptions resting upon what one was convinced would become known, or was about to become known; the result, of course, was open to serious objections among the orthodox. But African historiography was a very young discipline; and perhaps all young disciplines, if they are going to come to any good, have to take risks. The late Sir Mortimer Wheeler, as I recall, thought I was quite wrong, forty years ago, to draw a cultural comparison, as to peripheral influence, between Meroe, the capital of the ancient kingdom of Kush, and Athens; but I do not know if any serious historian would think that today.

It is, of course, a satisfaction that the evidence of history has indeed come handsomely to hand, and that assertions made in the 1950s under the cover of "ethnohistory" or "intuitive history," and defended against much abuse, are now accepted as easily sustainable. This came about from more and better-funded research—or one can merely say "funded research," since in those early years there had been, effectively, no such funds available—and above all from advances in the techniques of archaeology. Professor Willard Libby at the University of Chicago, though not himself much concerned with Africa, was the man who made all the difference. He showed that measurement of the loss of radioactivity in an isotope of carbon could yield, when uncontaminated samples of carbonaceous material were tested, an approximate date or dates. Archaeological sites could thus become datable with a reasonably approximate accuracy even when no other datable artifacts were available.

This betokened a tremendous advance in temporal analysis. An Iron Age in Africa was already thought to have begun (insofar as such "ages" ever actually begin) some two thousand years before the present. Even by the late 1940s the handful of archaeologists then working in Africa had identified dozens of sites which they attributed to an Iron Age, but the evidence for dating them was either very fragile or was simply nonexistent. With the application of Libby's test, this altogether changed. Iron Age dates began to become available in rapidly increasing numbers, and for a diversity of African regions. The "intuitive history" which had supposed a process of many centuries of Iron Age development of African societies, but with no convincing chronological evidence, almost suddenly achieved a deeply impressive solidity of fact and reference. After that, on through the 1960s and later, it became a matter of diligence and accurate collation, for which, happily, funds became available upon a scale never thinkable in earlier times (though nowadays, alas, such largesse is becoming a distant memory).

So history in Africa—history proper, history dated, history displayed—became possible without benefit of intuition or, at least, of having to rely upon the promptings of intuition; and this, naturally, was good news for everyone involved. We had been engaged, or so I seem to remember it, in a kind of intellectual wager, a bet, that what was surely "there" would certainly be found; and now, ever more clearly, it had been found, or else the means of finding it were known and usable. With this, however, another enterprise had now to be tackled. In what ways, and with what ingenuities, and with how much intensity of scholarship, could this history in Africa be arranged and set forth as a narrative—could be offered, that is, as being among those "grand narratives of emancipation and enlightenment," in the recent words of Edward Said, that mobilize people to throw off subjection,[1] and yield liberating power to those who have lacked its spur? Yet the work of historiography, once the relevant facts and relationships are sufficiently known and tested, is to compose these facts and relationships into just such a narrative; otherwise there is no power in historiography save ornamental detail or bodies of information that only their authors read. For the crucial role of this narrative, becoming the historiography whereby the human mind can know and dramatize its primacy, is that it arises from the fact and obligation of human unity—as I ventured to write some years ago: from the sense of human unity that has "geared and driven the wheels of all liberating action since recorded history began." Without this motivating insight, we have mere chronology or propaganda. With it, we have history. This is what I have ventured to call "solidarity"; and this is a usage which I think can be defended.[2]

Advancing along this line of thought, this African historiography born in the early 1950s began to acquire substance, and, with substance, respectability as well. The old defensiveness has dropped away with every new establishment of centers and departments of African studies in an ever-growing number of colleges, and as it did so, and as new generations of students and mature readers arrived with new accessions of curiosity and criticism, there began to be scope for what had been previously thought impossible or useless: I mean the study of comparative history, between Europe and Africa in the first place, and then, more generally, between the "Western world," meaning the more-or-less industrialized world, the world of modern technologies, and all those peoples, including the Africans, to whom industrial revolutions had yet to arrive.

Stages along this developmental route were marked, as we have seen with the application of radiocarbon dating tests, by new advances and ingenuities; and little by little, with all this, the psychological distance between "us" and "them" has begun to narrow. And as this happens, or is gradually perceived to have happened, there arises another issue—the issue of the nature of the relationship between "us" and "them." Now this is a difficult and much-evaded issue. Yet it becomes increasingly hard to evade as our historiography grows richer and stronger and more self-confident.

The problem of "otherness" in cultural history is no doubt as old as Adam and Eve. Yet it must especially interest Africanists who are or try to be both "us" and "them." It is not an easy problem. For if the pursuit of health, wealth, and happiness makes all men brothers (assuming sisters, of course, while the collective noun remains lacking), then where along the resulting relationship continuum, as between one "world" and another, stands person A or person B? Or again, where along that continuum from the merely mystifying to the validly heuristic is the place for objectivity to take its stand—for science, that is, and synthesis? Is there any such place for objectivity, and, if not, what is that subjectivity which can be useful instrumentally, not only to "them" as well as to "us" but also to a collective "them-us"?

Dogmatists have naturally had no difficulty here. For missionaries of whatever faith or denomination, it has been good objective truth that sauce for the goose must be sauce for the gander. The more dogmatic, especially after the 1880s and the onset of a direct imperialism outside Europe, were content to extend that formula to the "civilizing mission" of colonial enclosure, forced labor, mining profits, and the rest. The less dogmatic went less far, as it is pleasant to remember. "What do we mean," asked the awkward Bishop William Tozer of Central Africa in 1870, "when we say that England or France are civilised countries and that the greater part of Africa is uncivilised?" Surely, he went on, "the mere enjoyment of such things as railways and telegraphs and the like do not necessarily prove their possessors to be in the first rank of civilised nations. Nothing can be so false as to suppose that the outward circumstances of a people are the measure of its barbarism or its civilisation."[3]

But that, of course, was just what the vast majority of Bishop Tozer's audience did suppose and meant to continue to suppose. Attachment to a community equipped not only with Christianity but—still more important?—with telegraphs and railways, and above all with cash, was the ground on which every people must stand if they wished to be thought civilized. In a somewhat later world the Marxists have had their corresponding dogmatism; but so have the capitalists. Many have defined this capitalist dogmatism but in recent years, perhaps, none so well as Walt W. Rostow in his famous "five stages" from a "traditional society" (whatever that may be) to one of high mass consumption (unemployed not counted), a progression which, seemingly, assumes that all societies everywhere follow the same track, no matter what their specific and separate history, and terminate somewhere in the Texas of the 1960s.[4] This way of understanding the world, I have suggested, could be called the Church of Fifth Stage Adventism or, vulgarly, the school of whatever is good for "us" is bound to be good for "them." What Marxist dogmatism could imply may be seen in Eastern Europe during these past years.

Yet for nondogmatists, or anyone striving to be such, again the problem is not simple. For history is not a neatly linear progression nicely adjusted to all and sundry. It is a process fractured and confused by an open-ended quantity of differing "stages" and their consequences. Nationalism has shown this well. In Europe nationalism has led to and through the most frightful wars and massacres; and although you may label this nationalism by the name of imperialism if you wish, it remains that imperialism without nationalism is unthinkable. Any further development of civil society must therefore depend on "transcending nationalism"; and yet here in Africa, after the Second World War, the banners of nationalism not only seemed, but really were, the only ones that could promise an end to colonial subjection. The gander might have tired of the sauce, but not the goose; and with good reason.

At this point, in Africa, the "gift" of the nation-state on the British or French model assumed that this was a "gift" which followed, in all good logic (as it was argued), that Europe in any and every case knew best. Nothing showed this more clearly than the British imperial custom, as late as the late 1960s, of continuing to speed suitable wigs and maces to the new parliaments of the ex–colonial states; nor, in its amused irony, than the careful acceptance by African dignitaries of their manifest obligation to conform. The French set a variant example, but theirs was really a distinction without a difference. In 1952, I was touring French West Africa at a time when brand-new parliamentary assemblies (if with strictly limited powers) were being installed as a concession to the "natives." In Bamako, Mali's capital, the brand-new chairman of his territorial assembly was good enough to show me the brand-new chamber. There he pointed with a cautious smile to the plaster-white figure of the French state symbol on the chamber wall above his ceremonial chair. "There is Marianne," said he with another cautious smile but with an echo of laughter in his voice, "and here are we. She so white, and we so black."

A very small anecdote, no doubt; and yet the relationship continuum in this context of "us" and "them" is nothing if not anecdotal, at least in the sense that Marc Bloch, a truly great historian, meant when he suggested that historical facts are psychological facts.[5] If it is true that the facts of history are always psychologically selected, then an approach from history may be greatly helpful in the matter of our relationship continuum, which is one in which all of us, whether as actors or spectators (or supposing ourselves spectators), are necessarily involved.

That was no kind of problem for the imperialists in Africa, of course. For them the populations of Africa were, in their nature, deviant from the developmental potentialities of a "normal rationality." The "natives" might begin as children like other children, but they failed to become adults like other adults. They remained "grown-up children." They were unable to "develop." Such views were generally held. Among many otherwise sensible persons who held them, in my own experience, was Dr. Léopold Mottoulle, the chief social administrator of the Belgian Congo (called Zaire today) copper mines owned by the conglomerate called Union Minière. Writing in 1946, the good Dr. Mottoulle—who repeated these views to me when I met him in 1954—could affirm with a perfect liberal conscience (which he undoubtedly possessed) that

> the colonizer must never lose sight of the fact that the Negroes have the minds of children, minds which are shaped by the methods of the educator: they look and listen, feel and imitate. The European must in all circumstances show himself a calm and thoughtful chief, good without weakness, benevolent without familiarity, active by method and above all just in the repression of faults as in the reward of goodwill.[6]

No relationship continuum, in short, but a total cutoff. One may say: a total alienation. A study of that alienation belongs to the psychopathology of imperialism, but if we were to follow it into a study of this "deviancy of the natives," we should find—as Shula Ramon has brilliantly shown in one of her papers[7]—that "each action against any sort of deviancy strengthens the conformists in their conformity, just as it tends to reinforce those very influences which may deprive the supposed 'deviant' of his or her innate sense of 'normality.' " Behind Dr. Mottoulle's formulations lay a long paternity; and a sense of being inferior begets its own progeny. The colonial years were laden with that lesson.

Was it always so? Perhaps. Humanity seems always to have diminished with distance—distance geographical or social—rather like those African neighbors of the Lugbara who became (for the Lugbara) ever more peculiar and "upside down" as the kilometers clocked up between them.[8] Writing in the fifth century B.C., a notably level-headed Herodotus had evidently to cope with the same phenomenon. The Greeks and their immediate neighbors were obviously all right, and so were the North Africans likewise known to the Greeks, while the "blameless Ethiopians" who lived beyond the reach of Greek travels were still thought to be the best-looking persons anywhere. The trouble began in Asia, for beyond the distant Issedones were the still more distant Arimaspians, each of whom was reported to have only one eye and not therefore satisfactorily human;

while beyond the one-eyed Arimaspians lived the extremely distant griffins who guarded the gold, and nobody was going to think them human.

The mentality of European exploration in Africa has often shown the same tendency to calibrate deviancy with distance. This was not at all the same thing as racism; it was rather a provincialism. Or a storyteller's zest. When Malfante tells an Italian audience in 1447 that the black peoples who live in "innumerable and great territories" south of the Sahara Desert "are in carnal acts like the beasts," with their women "bearing up to five at a birth," and so on, he is doing little more than retelling the travelers' tales of the long-distance caravan trade. Such tales about the black peoples were of a family with those of *The Thousand and One Nights,* of Sindbad or Aladdin, composed for stay-at-homes in Baghdad who "longed to travel for profit and adventure" but, when it came to the point, preferred that others should travel for them; and nobody is taking them seriously. Long after the Middle Ages there is a host of comparable stories and dramas; but when it comes down to business, Othello is no "grown-up child," but the valiant commander of Venetian armies, and prized as such.

The acceptance of a "different but equal" relationship along our continuum was common to the long period of the Middle Ages, and may be seen, most clearly perhaps, in the ways in which European artists painted or sculpted African men or women. What swept away this acceptance, more than anything else, was the huge spread of chattel slavery with the onset and uprush of African captives sent across the Atlantic in the period, chiefly, after 1600 or 1650. An unbiased view of that terrible process has to begin by seeing that this huge spread of chattel slavery had a consistently degrading effect on the nature of servile institutions. Medieval slavery, for the most part, had been a form of servitude among many other such forms in precapitalist modes of production; more often than not, its nature may perhaps be best understood as "wageless labor." It could be exceedingly painful; it could more often be a lucky privilege. It could be "a personal service in the widest sense of the word, which, when the master served was of high rank and wealthy, carried with it great advantages as well as social prestige."[9] A slave within that context was generally better off than most rural producers, if only because slaves were expensive and hard to replace, while "wage workers" need not be either. But the plantation and mining slavery which derived from the Atlantic slave trade, above all in the Americas, was entirely something else. Within that system, slaves became dehumanized chattels whose cost of replacement grew increasingly smaller as the years went by: smaller, that is, in relation to the market value of their product and sometimes to the ease of their

replacement. Along the relationship continuum, the old attitude of "different but equal" vanished from the scene. In its place came the attitude
that has taken the different as being deviant *by nature*, and therefore
necessarily inferior—humanly, that is, and inherently.

The damage is what we have seen. Already by high Victorian times,
Africans have become, to Europeans, those "retarded children" who are
incapable of growing up, and knowing, as Samuel Baker affirmed in his
unpleasant diary of 1863, "neither gratitude, pity, love, nor self-denial."
Having "no idea of duty; no religion; but covetousness, ingratitude, self-
ishness, and cruelty"—how the "deviancy" piles up!—"all are thieves,
idle, envious and ready to plunder and enslave their weaker neigh-
bours."[10] Baker inclined to the view that the climate was the culprit. Only
the temperate latitudes, somewhere around the southern counties of
England as he seems to suggest, could apparently enable humankind to
produce its "highest development."

Much can be said about this European "side" of the relationship
through the years. The African "side" is more difficult for want of copious
written records. So far as those records that we have can say, African
peoples first confronted with the spectacle of white-skinned visitors who
were not albino by nature were struck with amazement, and applied to
their oracles for comfort and enlightenment. Robin Horton has given us
an example. This is how the Kalabari people of the Niger Delta reacted
to their first sight of white men (which, historically, must have been
around the year 1500):

> The first white man, it is said, was seen by a fisherman who had gone
> down to the mouth of the estuary in his canoe. Panic-stricken, he
> raced home and told his people what he had seen: whereupon he
> and the rest of the town set out to purify themselves—that is to say,
> rid themselves of the influence of the strange and monstrous thing
> that had intruded into their world.[11]

Here, as we see, the relationship was between "two worlds" that knew
nothing of each other but suspected the worst. Baker and the Kalabari
fisherman make a pair.

Where the relationship became familiar, even an everyday affair, there
followed an acceptance which naturally varied from the gullible to the
shrewd. Among the gullible, there was that sixteenth-century king of
Kongo (northern Angola now) who persuaded himself that his "royal
brother" of Portugal really would send him some boatbuilders so that he
could break into the Portuguese royal trading monopoly at sea. This kind

of gullibility fared badly. "I hear your countryman done spoil West Indies," a Niger Delta ruler remarked to some British visitors in 1841, speaking to them in the pidgin customary along the coast: "I think he want come spoil we country all same."[12] Or else there was the conclusion of the Ethiopian emperor Tewodros II, who explained in the early 1860s that "I know their game. First traders and missionaries, then ambassadors, then the cannon. It's better to get straight to the cannon."[13] It wasn't, in his case, but one can see his point.

And later? What men like Tewodros argued was almost necessarily forgotten. Latter-day imperialism and its conquests had placed European cultures, or what could be known of them among the conquered, in so unassailable a position of technological superiority, of power superiority over colonized peoples, as practically to extinguish the mere notion of continuum. The cultures of Africa were seen as being utterly closed off in their continental cul-de-sac; and it became a banal assumption, barely questioned anywhere, that whatever good might accrue to Africa's peoples, whether in their ideas or organizations, would and must now be "done *to* them"; they could produce nothing useful of their own.

Here and there this conviction of a necessary and inherent European superiority—of civility as much as of technology—took a little time to get itself established against clearly subversive Tozerisms which continued to hold, if in voices now hard to hear, that there was more to civilization than railways and telegraphs (or, as it transpired more frequently, than mining concessions). But established it became. By about 1900, with colonial enclosure more or less complete and "pacification" of the "natives" getting under way, the assumptions of Fifth Stage Adventism could be said to have carried all before them, even if appropriate Tablets of the Law had yet to be inscribed.

Now this matrix of assumptions, laid down long ago but thickened and compacted by the culture of generations of technologically superior "whites," has been the ideological legacy deriving from the colonial period and decolonization. It is, we have been told, the consistent application of the lessons of *external* culture that will cure the ills of Africa and ensure progress, even while, as we learn painfully in this decade of the 1990s, the plans and projects of the outside world, applied to Africa, seem to achieve so little good. May it not be, just possibly, the lessons of *internal* culture that are required? Gingerly advanced, this thought that Africa's problems need the application of Africa's solutions has seemed, more often than not in the outside world, rather more harebrained than realistic. Yet it is a thought that returns ever more insistently as grim years in the 1990s succeed each other; and it is in consideration of this thought that the evidence of Africa's own historical development acquires new force and value.

If, as seems possible, we live now at the probable ending of the long epoch of classical imperialism and at the conceivable outset of a whole new relationship between "us" and "them"—whichever "side" is yours, whatever your position along the continuum of humanity's experience—then we have to think ourselves forward into a culture that can have no place for racist assumptions in any of their forms. This is difficult to do, as everyone knows. But the force and value of history are there to help: specifically, in this context, the force and value of Africa's history. In this new epoch, perhaps, "their" reality and "ours"—again from whichever side you take it—may begin to converge: not in the singularities of culture, remaining as these will as richly various as human nature, but in their ever more evident requirement of conjoint acceptance. "They" will begin to be "there" as much as "we" are—from whichever way you come—in forms and intensities never before possible in consciousness. And as they take shape there, and as we begin to see them in their reality and all the lineaments of their condition, and as the same perception arises in reverse, so in that measure can we and they approach and stand on common ground, and, in doing that, find the synthesis which can realize conjoint potentials. The moral acceptance of solidarity—the recognition of our shared nature, plight, and possibilities beyond all the alienations of culture or ethnicity—is no longer, if it ever was, an eccentric addition to scholarship, a sentimental icing on the academic cake. It becomes in this realm, if not in others too, the manifest essence of purposive study.

It has been with these thoughts in mind that I offer these various writings, dedicated chiefly to the force and value of history. There is no need to insist that other writers have done more and done better, for this is obvious. Please take these essays, if you will, as a contribution to the building of a postimperialist culture, as, in this context, some of the fruits of a lifetime's effort to think well and write clearly.

CLAIMS

THE FOUR ESSAYS WITH WHICH I BEGIN OUR SEARCH ARE CONCERNED with the problem of writing as well as rescuing Africa's history: with the dependable narrative, *the story*, within which the fact and process of our history—as of any readable history—can take shape. They are concerned with the historiographical structure, however variously built from a multitude and maze of facts and inferences, that is able to make the drift and tumult of the past accessible to readers in the present. They do this, of course, to the extent of the historian's skills, and in accurate reflection of the progress of his or her research.

"The Search for Africa's Past" was written in 1990 for the excellent Nigerian publisher and editor Raph Uwechue, and is designed to address two primary questions: what kind of states did Africans build in early or in later times, and how did these states respond to the needs of those times? The answers are of course much too capacious for any single essay. But a single essay can confront their essential meaning for the peoples who built those states: all these many states, whether kingdoms or not, have been aspects of a process of self-development. And here, in this context of Africa's history, self-development has meant every chief aspect of social and moral process toward a livable and therefore dynamic building of community.

A worldwide process—but in Africa the outcome has been clearly distinct from the outcome in other continents. Developing in their enormous land mass south of the great deserts of the Sahara, Africans over the centuries since "history began"—here, broadly, since the onset of an Iron Age around 600 B.C. (although with the towering pharaonic centuries distantly behind them)—developed in their own ways, mostly with little

input from any outside world, so as to solve their social problems and
arrive at their own forms of civilization—of the humanization of people
in community.

But how different, in fact and practice, was this outcome? Before the
rise of our modern world of industry and applied science, how far had
these African communities really "fallen behind" the outside world,
above all the world of the Europeans? What was the "state of development" of African polities with which African traders and travelers made
contact around or soon after A.D. 1500? Before, that is, there was any
question of European invasion and colonization? My second essay is
concerned with questions, like these, of comparative history.

History without dates, without clear signposts to the passage of the
years, can never make much sense. Up to the 1950s, these signposts were
extremely difficult and often impossible to provide across wide areas of
Africa for want of datable artifacts. Many sites of ancient settlement were
known, many ruins of cities evidently lost in time. But very few had
yielded that kind of evidence—for example, imported pottery—to which
dates could be assigned. Then came some remarkable advances in the
techniques of archaeology. The third essay is concerned with these and
their consequences.

However endlessly diverse within itself, the socializing process in
Africa suggests an underlying unity of culture. All sorts of reasons have
been assigned to the perception of this unity in diversity—this Africanism, discussed here in my fourth essay. Whichever reasons or explanations may be preferred, one thing is now certain: Africanism has become
an absolutely essential part of the study of our world.

THE SEARCH
FOR AFRICA'S PAST

I

THE WISE NORTH AFRICAN HISTORIAN IBN KHALDUN, WRITING SOME six hundred years ago, set down a political maxim which seemed to him an obvious truth. "The authority of kings," he wrote, "is an institution that is natural to mankind"; because, "people not being able to live in anarchy, they need a person to restrain them." Republics there might have been, but the years of warfare and upheaval through which Ibn Khaldun lived had given him no faith in any kingless capacity to impose the law and guard the peace. Yet what he was asserting was less narrow than may appear. He was saying that every viable society has required, and will always require, a structure of authority which is seen and felt by its members to be "right" and "natural." In his experience, this was kingship. The justice of the kingdom of heaven, as Christians would have put it, had its mirror in the justice of the kingdoms of earth.

And kingdoms in Africa are, indeed, among the oldest political institutions anywhere. They emerge in Africa from times even before time began. They loom out of the mists of antiquity like the unknown ghosts of ancestral nations that have no certain place or name, and yet are not to be denied. And the deeper the probings of modern scholarship, the more these "ghosts" of royal authority acquire fact and presence, for we live, happily, in a period when old prejudice begins to give way to new understanding, to an understanding, perhaps above all, that the history of humankind is a single great river into which a myriad tributaries flow.

This essay originally appeared in 1990, written for the Nigerian publisher, Raph Uwechue, and is reprinted with permission.

It used to be thought, for example, that the oldest kingdoms of strength
and stature were those of the Nile Delta and the northern Nile in Egypt.
They emerged around 3400 B.C., two kingdoms until they were joined as
one under the pharaohs of the Double Crown, and on that view they
came, mysteriously, "out of nothing." Having thus arisen from the waters
of myth and legend, they rapidly developed into the most solid and
certain realm of the pharaohs of Egypt, and proceeded to spawn "daughter kingdoms" elsewhere. That is what the Greeks of classical times
believed, and with reason. To the Greeks of antiquity, Egypt of the
pharaohs was the fount and origin of wisdom, venerable in its beliefs and
monuments, amazing in its mathematics and philosophy. Even the names
of nearly all the gods of ancient Greece, Herodotus reminded his readers
in his histories written around 450 B.C., had come to Greece from Egypt;
and, as Homer had said before him, was it not to the lands in Africa south
of Egypt that the gods of Greece flew once a year to feast with the older
gods of inland Africa?

This notion that kingdoms in Africa began in Egypt of the pharaohs
was generally accepted by a later Europe—but with a difference. To this
later Europe, Egypt of the pharaohs became entirely separated from, and
different from, the lands of the black peoples. Egypt ceased to be seen as
being a part of Africa; and whatever ancient Egypt had achieved ceased
to be seen as having been an African achievement. Now this was a
"separation" that was imposed on European minds by the centuries of the
Atlantic slave trade. For if Africans could be seen to be fit for enslavement
by Europeans, because Africans were seen as having no claim to any
civilization of their own, how could the civilization of the pharaohs,
mightiest of antiquity, be accepted as African? In the grand period of
imperialist expansion the question was barely asked, let alone pondered;
Europe's philosophers knew better. So it was that the otherwise pathfinding German philosopher Hegel could blithely comment in 1830—when
almost nothing of the realities and truths of Africa was, as yet, known in
Europe—that "Africa is no historical part of the world," and, "has no
movement or development to show."

Nowadays, when the veils of racism are somewhat lifted, or in any case
are less shrouding than they used to be, Hegel's successors have begun to
put Egypt of the pharaohs back where it belonged: back into its own
continent. Archaeology has produced varied and no longer questioned
evidence to show that the lands of the blacks—of those whom the classical
Greek authors called "Ethiopians," not after the country we know as
Ethiopia but after the Greek word for black persons, *aithíops*—were, in
fact, the lands from which most of the inhabitants of Egypt had originally

come. They had migrated into the valley of the Nile, that is to say, in times before and during the early desiccation of their wide Saharan grassland homes.

The classical Greeks knew this too. Summarizing Greek historical knowledge as it stood in the last century B.C., and by way of many Greek historians whose works are lost to us as well as by Herodotus and other Greek historians whose works have not been lost, Diodorus of Sicily could affirm their consensus on the subject. "The Egyptians," he wrote, "are colonists who were sent out by the Ethiopians"—by the black peoples of the African interior, that is to say, and in times long before. It was an astoundingly modern statement of the case, though written twenty centuries ago. But modern research has begun to go a step further toward putting Egypt back into its own continent, into its own African context. The archaeology of the upper Nile, of the regions of the Nubian, or Kushite, Nile, can now be seen to indicate that recognizable kingdoms emerged here, a long way to the south, even before they took shape in the region of the Delta a long way to the north. We have reason, in other words, to think that the earliest kingdoms loomed out of the mists of an inner-African antiquity.[1]

Does this introduction seem rather distant from our subject? It's not really, for the nature of kingship and of kingdoms has to derive from their origins and early development; and these origins and early development have to be seen within their own context. This context was not only African: more exactly, it was *inner*-African. We shall see that this kingship-producing culture in Africa would have its parallels and comparisons with kingship-producing cultures elsewhere, not least in Europe. Meanwhile, the African evidence goes on to show that the elevation and authority of kings was a gradual crystallization of a pattern of lesser powers: from the secular powers of elders, chiefs of clans, and so on, buttressed by spiritual powers that were ancestral and shrine-inhabiting—in a word, religious. Kings, or queens ruling as monarchs, were the accepted and convenient apex of the pyramid of social cohesion. They might wish to be dictators or tyrants; if so, the checks and balances of custom and ritual would pull them down, or, as the Yoruba of Nigeria used to say, a bad ruler would be sent "the parrot's eggs," and the parrot's eggs spelled dethronement.

Later in pharaonic history, mighty rulers over the Egyptian empire made themselves into gods, or, rather, saw to it that they "became gods" as soon as they had vanished in their tombs. This, no doubt, was an aberration derived from the ambitions of an overweening priesthood eager to expand its power and privilege. Kings in the inner-African tradition were not and could not be divine, no matter how much ordinary mortals might humble themselves in the dust when approaching the royal presence. What was divine, in African belief, was their spiritual authority. They would die, but that could not. The ancient kingdom of the West African Mossi was only one of many in which the king's person was believed to embody the spiritual and, therefore, the material welfare of the Mossi people as a whole. Mossi kings certainly died, as everyone knew, and Mossi people would have thought it ridiculous to suggest anything different. But the spiritual power embodied in the king was quite another matter. If that should die, then general disaster must ensue, for the gods who rule the world would have turned their backs upon the Mossi. So the Mossi, like many or even all African peoples who lived in kingdoms, made a clear distinction between the "body natural" of the king and the king's "body spiritual," and took determined steps to insist upon this distinction in all the ceremonies which accompanied kingship and hedged it around. "The king is dead, long live the king!": the old European cry upon the death of one king and the succession of another was also what the Mossi cried on similar occasions.[2]

The emergence of kingship thus went hand in hand with the development of society from simplicity to complexity: from the "nuclear" or small family units of early times through the material advances—hoe cultivation, metalworking, and so on—which produced ever larger and more powerful settlements, and, with that, the need for more effective and eventually centralized forms of government. It is, consequently, misleading to divide African societies into two distinct categories of "kingdoms" and "nonkingdoms," as anthropologists used to do for reasons of convenience. All these many and even countless societies which evolved from farming cultivation, metalworking, and permanent settlement were actual or potential kingdoms of one kind or another. All of them possessed patterns of self-organization which could, if men so wished, bring forth kings and, therefore, kingdoms.

Some of them found it desirable to make the move into kingship, while others did not. Often the reasons for the move, or the absence of the move, remain beyond our grasp. In southern Nigeria, for example, Yoruba-speaking peoples developed kingdoms in very early times, while neighboring Igbo-speaking peoples seldom wished to have kings. Yet it would be very difficult to show which of these two large groups of Nigerian peoples has been the more enterprising or successful.

Yet kingdoms in Africa have played a large and even brilliant part in the record. In some initial period or another, about which there is no precise evidence and no doubt never will be, they took their first vague shape in that great nursery of early social development which lay in the green Saharan plains before their time of desiccation. This form of government was then given a continuous development and elaboration within the Nile Valley kingdoms, above all in the realm of the pharaohs, and later, within that of the kings and queens of Meroitic Kush. As desiccation continued, reducing the green Sahara into an arid wilderness of sand and rock, there came a serious "cutoff" between the lands to the north and the lands to the south; and the lands to the south increasingly disappeared from the history that was written in or about the lands of the north. But if they vanished from northern consciousness, they by no means vanished from their own.

With no written history until after Islamic literacy had traversed the Sahara around the eighth century, the early development of the lands and peoples of the south can still be studied from their archaeology and other such sources. Fortunately, these combine into a fairly coherent picture which, after the seventh century, is repeatedly enlarged by the writings of North African and Middle Eastern travelers and chroniclers. These began to cross the desert, along the old Berber trails, within less than a century of the Arab conquest of the North African littoral, and to send back fragmentary reports which became ever more complete and interesting with the further growth of Muslim wealth and power. And what was happening in western Africa in this respect was also happening, though by sea, down the long coastland of eastern Africa.

Oral tradition has added to these written records. Sometimes this kind of history rests on the carefully conserved memorials of persons at court designated to remember rulers and their deeds; and so, for example, we have some often quite detailed records of the kings of Nigerian Benin over a period of several centuries. Further insights into the nature of these kingships can be got, moreover, through inspection of their rituals and customs as these too have been remembered or are still practiced. What Michael W. Young found about the kingdom of the Jukun, again in Nigeria, is all the more enlightening because it can help us understand other kingdoms.[3]

Like the king of the Mossi, the king of the Jukun embodied in his person the divine power that came from God by way of the appointed ancestors; having that power, the king of the Jukun was expected "to maintain harmony between society and its natural environment by means of ritual action" such as no other person could perform. "His duties in this sphere," says Young, "were threefold: to perform the daily rites for which he was uniquely qualified by office; to provide for and direct the activities of other cults; and to sustain and control his own spiritual potency." Thus empowered, he had then to govern, but the power of governing remained secondary to the power of ensuring harmony with the rules and wishes of the divinely appointed ancestors.

In what follows we shall look at a number of African kingdoms, many of them famous in their time and place, and at the decisive part that was often played by their rulers. It has seemed useful, first, to say something of their origins and of the ways in which they were created by their peoples, if only to emphasize that these kingdoms belonged to a wide and varying social evolution. Often oppressive of the peoples they subjected, frequently painful to their own peoples in the wars they fomented or provoked, usually an instrument of exploitation of the many by the few, they were an aspect of that often contradictory process whereby, however fallibly, humanity has made its journey through the years. But more than that, these kingdoms were also an invention often as useful and productive as they were hard to bear; and we need to see them not only as salient episodes of individual courage and bravado, as comets in the firmament of individual ambition, but also as effective means of political development. They could be very destructive of life and happiness. But they could also build sound frameworks of law and order. Old Ibn Khaldun may have overenthused on the desirability of kings; his argument for them, nonetheless, was strong.

This is a large subject, reaching across continents. The kingdoms of Africa were the children of their own history, but their origins and nature shared many characteristics with kingdoms elsewhere. Far away in the misty north, for example, the kings of Anglo-Saxon and Norman England were legitimate in the eyes of those they ruled by the same kinds of measure as the kings of Africa were legitimate. They had to stand within the line of succession, and be accepted so to stand, from the earliest divine ancestors who, in turn, derived from God. They had to rule justly, and in England, down to the fourteenth century, they could be thrown out by justified rebellion if they ruled unjustly. That is what the Great Charter of 1215, the Magna Carta as it was called, precisely reaffirmed, even though later kings were able to subvert it.

Like needs, in short, have produced like results. The rights and obligations of European kings, all through medieval times and later, were framed in ideas and beliefs that were familiar in African kingdoms. The kings of East African Ruanda, for another example among many, were thought to be able to do no wrong; embodying divine power, they were necessarily above earthly criticism. And in this the people of Ruanda were at one with English constitutional law in holding, with the great constitutional lawyer Blackstone, writing in the years after the close of the

Middle Ages, that the king "is not only incapable of doing wrong, but even of thinking wrong. He can never do an improper thing: in him is no folly or weakness." When kings in England did, in fact, do wrong, and were seen to have done wrong, they had to be regarded as the innocent victims of wrong or evil advice, as Blackstone well explained. In Ruanda, along the same line of convenient political fiction, the king was provided with an official scapegoat upon whom blame could be laid, so that the king's unblemished reputation might be preserved.

I I

THE TRAVELER CURIOUS TO DISCOVER AFRICA GOES NOWADAYS BY PLANE AND begins the journey with a choice of widely spread airports. But in early times, when the kingdoms of West Africa began to be heard of in the outside world, the traveler from afar went by camel and had to choose, for departure to the south, a starting point in one or other of the cities close to the shores of the Mediterranean Sea.

The greatest of these cities, and the most frequented, was called Fustat. But Fustat was renamed al-Kahira, or Cairo as we know it, by the conquering kings of the Fatimid dynasty after these had moved eastward from Tunisia and taken all Egypt into their dominions. That was in the tenth century A.D. Thanks to this African drive and ambition, Cairo became "the metropolis of the universe," as Ibn Khaldun would sing its praises centuries later: "the garden of the world and the throne of royalty embellished with castles and palaces, and adorned with monasteries and colleges lit by the moons and the stars of erudition."

Some of those splendid buildings remain for our admiration today. None, in my memory, stays more impressive in its power or instructive in its purpose than the Bab Zuweila, a majestic city gate constructed around 1087 for traffic to and from the African west. Gaston Wiet, the French art specialist, was surely right when he affirmed that "one can hardly imagine anything more majestic than this monumental gateway" piercing the ancient walls. "Surmounted by minarets built on twin towers of fine-cut masonry, the mighty portal opens through a high rounded arch." Riding out through the Bab Zuweila, the medieval traveler must have felt that he had all of Africa before him.

Every kind and class of person went that way: caravan leaders bustling along their file of beasts, lean-faced guides heading for the inland trails, wandering scholars bent on joining distant academies, soldiers and com-

manders going on garrison or expedition, pilgrims coming back from
Mecca, and, above all, the masters of the long-distance caravan trade.
Rarely but very usefully for us, there also were men whose aim was to
travel "the roads and kingdoms," *al masalik wa'l-mamalik,* so as to write of
what they saw and heard.

Such chroniclers had been doing this for a long time before the Bab
Zuweila was built. The earliest of value to our story here was Ahmad ben
Abi Yaqub, al-Yaqubi, whose *tarikh,* or chronicle, was composed in A.D. 871,
which was 259 of the Muslim calendar. Whether al-Yaqubi himself had
traveled west through the Cairo gate is not recorded, and he wrote his
tarikh in distant Asia. But he certainly drew on the information of others
who had. His writings give the first clear glimpse of the many kingdoms
of western Africa, south of the desert, which already existed in his time,
the ninth century A.D. or the third century of the Muslim calendar.

The desert highway of greatest use, for the intercontinental markets of
Cairo, passed southward through the city-kingdom of Zuweila. That was
in the Fezzan of Tunisia. Like other city-kingdoms on the northern
"shore" of the Sahara, such as Tahert in central Algeria or Sijilmasa in
Morocco, this little kingdom of Zuweila was a principal northern relay
point for the transdesert trade. Southward beyond it, along the empty
trails that linked one remote oasis with another, the camel caravans at last
reached the region that is nowadays the republic of Niger, and southward
again the northern states of Nigeria; and there, as al-Yaqubi reported,
they began to reach other kingdoms. Some of those mentioned by al-
Yaqubi have long since disappeared. But one of them was the Kanem
which would long be famous in the world of the Middle Ages and for
centuries after. Traveling farther, the voyager came eventually to the
middle Niger River, and reached the comfort of the "kingdom of Kaw-
kaw, which is the greatest of the realms of the Sudan, the most important
and powerful. All the kingdoms obey its king, and al-Kawkaw is the name
of the town."

Al-Kawkaw was the ancient city of Gao, nowadays a provincial town
of the Niger republic but in olden times the best-known "terminal" of the
transdesert trade, together with Awdaghost and Kumbi Saleh to the west,
along the southern "shore" of the Sahara. Much shows that Gao, down-
stream from its much later and more renowned neighbor, Timbuktu,
played a crucial part in the development of trade from the eighth century
on, and that al-Yaqubi's words about it were warranted by its influence
and value. Six centuries after al-Yaqubi, Gao would become the capital
of the vast Songhay empire, but was enclosed, soon after al-Yaqubi's time,
within the power of the empire of Ghana. Westward from Gao, says

al-Yaqubi, "there is the kingdom of Ghana, whose king is also very powerful. The gold mines are in his country, and a number of kings obey his rule."

Information about this old empire of Ghana was still very scarce; later travelers learned more. By the eleventh century these were traversing the desert as much by a major western route, southward from Morocco, as by the route through the Bab Zuweila. This was because the wealth of Muslim Spain, of the splendid caliphate of Cordoba in al-Andalus, was by now a trading power that rivaled even Cairo itself. Anyone who visits Cordoba today can still hear echoes of that famous past. A grand center of scholarship as well as trade, Cordoba in the tenth century was reputed to have thirteen thousand weavers in silk or wool or cotton, while the palaces of its Berber and other Muslim rulers, all of them African by affiliation, were admired as being among the architectural wonders of their world.

Though Muslim and literate in Arabic, this Andalusian state was essentially an African kingdom in Europe, and its contacts with northern and western Africa were many and important. That is why the writers of Cordoba have left us good records of the kingdoms they knew about in Africa. They could draw on firsthand sources of information, for the traders of al-Andalus were great users of the transdesert routes to and from the south. It is thanks to al-Bakri of Cordoba, who wrote in 1067, that we have a detailed insight into the Ghana mentioned two centuries earlier by al-Yaqubi.

"Ghana is the title given to their kings," al-Bakri tells us, "but the name of the kingdom of Awkar. In this year of 1067 [or 460 of the Muslim calendar], their king is Tunka Manin who came to the throne in 1063. He rules an enormous kingdom, and wields strong power." The Andalusian traders who informed al-Bakri would have been men of wide travel and sophistication. But the majesty of the king of Ghana could still impress them.

Giving audience to his subjects and visitors, or hearing complaints against his administration, Tunka Manin "sits in a domed pavilion around which stand ten horses covered with gold-embroidered materials. Behind the king stand ten pages holding shields and swords decorated with gold; and on his right are the sons of his vassal kings, wearing splendid garments and with gold plaited in their hair. The governor of the city sits on the ground before the king, and the king's ministers are likewise seated near him. At the door of the pavilion are dogs of excellent pedigree. They hardly ever leave the place where he is, guarding him. Round their necks they wear collars of gold and silver."

Gold, clearly, was the keynote. But the gold, as visitors soon found, did not come from the kingdom of Ghana itself. It came from another kingdom some way to the south: as later records would explain, this was the rising kingdom of Mali. Its capital city was Niani on the upper Niger River. That city has long since vanished, but this empire of Mali rose to great power in the thirteenth century, following the decline of Ghana, and flourished for long after. This was where the gold came from, whether panned in rivers or mined from seams fifty feet below the surface of the ground. But before we look at the significance of West African gold for the whole world of that time, let us continue along the kingdom-forming trail.

The history of the western and central Sudan tells of half a dozen major kingdoms or empires, mostly in succession to one another. The first in time was Ghana, from about the sixth century until the thirteenth; next was Mali, larger still, from the thirteenth to the fifteenth; after Mali came Songhay, based on the ancient city of Gao, in the fifteenth and sixteenth centuries; and, eastward from Songhay, the venerable kingdom of Kanem, afterward joined with Borno. As well as these kingdoms of the grassland plains—of the Sahel, or southern "shore" of the desert—there were numerous others, notably those of the Hausa people of northern Nigeria and, later on, of the Fulani. Southward in the near-forest and forest belt, toward the coastland of the Atlantic Ocean, another range of peoples had begun to form impressive kingdoms at least by the eleventh century, and probably earlier. Among these were the kingdoms of the Yoruba in what is now western Nigeria. These and their various neighbors shone especially in their trading enterprise, their farming wealth, and their arts of sculpture in terra-cotta and bronze.

By at least the thirteenth century the artists of the Yoruba kingdom of Ife were producing some of the best sculpture the world has ever seen. So fine were their heads and busts of kings and leading persons that European critics of the twentieth century, when first seeing them, were unwilling to believe that this sculpture was not the product or inspiration of European teaching. Better understanding has confirmed that this sculpture was entirely African, and that the artists of Ife belonged to an ancient Nigerian tradition which had produced its first known works of art in the last centuries before the onset of the Christian era. Well dated by archaeological means, these earliest sculptors of Nigeria in the fifth or fourth century B.C. were those of village cultures in the region of the confluence of the Niger and Benue rivers.

Not long after royal Ife flourished, the sculptural tradition passed onward to the notable city of Benin (not to be confused with the modern republic of Benin), also in western Nigeria, where it is still alive to this day. And with Benin, capital of the powerful kingdom of that name, we reach new sources of written information. European mariners came to Benin late in the fifteenth century, and European traders afterward became frequent visitors to that abundant city. Among these traders were the Dutch who, at that time, were ahead of all other Europeans in trade and trading information. Like the desert crossers from al-Andalus long before, these ocean-crossing Dutch were trained to investigate and write about what they saw.

The city of Benin, wrote one of these Dutchmen in about 1600, "looks very big when you go into it. You enter by a great broad street, not paved, which seems to be seven or eight times broader than the Warmoes-street in Amsterdam. This street goes right through, not bending; and the place where I was lodged with Mattheus Cornelison was at least a quarter of an hour's going from the gate, and yet I could not see the other end of it.

"The houses in the town stand in good order, one close and even with the next as our Dutch houses are . . . while the king's palace is very large, having within it many four-square plains [squares], each surrounded by galleries which are always guarded. I went as far into the palace as to cross four of these squares; but wherever I looked I saw gate after gate for entry into other squares; and in this manner I went in as far as any Dutchman had been permitted."

Though access to the king (the oba of Benin) was usually denied to visitors, the Dutch reported that they were well received by the people, whom they found to be hospitable and honest trading partners. The Dutch in that period were probably the cleanest people in Europe, but they were still impressed by Benin household manners, reporting that "these people are in no way inferior to the Dutch in cleanliness. They wash and scrub their houses so well that these are as polished as a looking glass."

III

THERE IS NO WAY HERE TO LIST AND LOOK AT ALL THE KINGDOMS OF western Africa, whether large and famous or small and little known. But the progress of our investigation calls for a special mention of one of these: that of Asante (or Ashanti, as it is often written), a kingdom which took shape during the seventeenth century and became a powerful empire.

This is where gold again appears. By about 1400 the gold of Mali, of the region of the upper Niger now in the republic of Guinea, began to run short. New and rich deposits were happily available in the forest country to the east—in the country of the Akan, or of modern Ghana—and gold from there was soon being traded from the forest-fringe city of Begho. This place became an important center of regional trade. Most of the Akan country at that time was under the suzerainty of another Akan kingdom, that of Denkyira, but the leaders of the Asante clans decided that the time had come to recover their independence. This was achieved by successful warfare in the wake of an Asante confederation formed in about 1695 by a chief who became the king of Asante, Osei Tutu, assisted by his leading shrine priest, Okomfo Anokye. The successors of Osei Tutu went on to extend their rule over neighboring clans, and finally over all the country which is Ghana today. Only repeated British invasions during the nineteenth century proved able to subdue Asante. Meanwhile, the regional trade in Asante gold had acquired, as had that of Mali before it, a continental dimension by means of the trans-Saharan caravans.

Much else could be added to this brief outline of the kingly records of western Africa, whether looking westward in Senegal or northward across the Maghrib of North Africa. Yet this outline may be enough to indicate that the organization of states and nations often took the same general course as in Europe or Asia, even if the cultures within which kingdoms took shape in Africa were very different from European or Asian cultures. Inquiry at this point, therefore, prompts a number of questions about why this was so. What were the driving motives behind this development of kingdoms? What purposes did these kingdoms serve? What were the social and economic powers which raised men to the dignity of thrones or cast them down again?

That same al-Bakri of Cordoba, who wrote about ancient Ghana nine hundred years ago, helps us to begin to answer such questions. And what he has to tell on this subject is confirmed by the oral and written records of West Africa itself: notably, for example, by the two great chronicle-histories of seventeenth-century Timbuktu, the *Tarikh al-Fattash* of Mahmud Kati, and the *Tarikh al-Sudan* of Abd al-Rahman al-Sadi, both of whom were authentic natives and citizens of Timbuktu or its environs, West Africans by birth and loyalty, but writing in Arabic.

Al-Bakri gets to the nub of the matter with his record of the import-export trade of Ghana and its kings. "On every donkey-load of salt the

king levies one gold dinar when it is brought into the country, and two
dinars when a load of salt is sent out of the country. From a load of
imported copper the king's revenue in tax is five mitcals, and ten mitcals
on every load of other goods." As to gold, "all nuggets found in any of the
mines of his country are reserved to the king, only gold dust being left
to the people." But for this measure, explains al-Bakri in terms of monop-
olist organization that we today can easily recognize, "the people would
accumulate gold until it lost its value." Thus, the import-export trade
provided the king with a substantial revenue; and with this revenue he
was able to finance his government and support his army.

These monetary terms, such as *mitcal*, call for a little explanation. The
dinar known to al-Bakri was a gold coin, a famous standard of value.
Throughout the Middle Ages, the dinar represented what the American
dollar has represented in our own time. This Muslim dinar was the
successor, in fact, of the *dinarius aureus*, the golden dinar of Byzantium,
when Muslim dynasties in the Middle East arose to outshine Byzantium,
and when all Middle Eastern sources of gold had been exhausted. This
was when the gold reserves of West Africa acquired their worldwide
importance by way of the Fatimid dinar and then the Almoravid dinar,
minted from West African gold in the cities of the northern "shore" of the
Sahara, notably Sijilmasa in Morocco. The standard weight of this Muslim dinar was 4.233 grams, and was well maintained at that weight for
centuries. This weight of a dinar was called a mitcal; and the mitcal, as
a weight rather than as a coin, became a universal measure of exchange
throughout these regional and continental systems, and, not least,
throughout West Africa.

How much was the royal dinar worth in terms of what it could buy?
The records give us some information. In eleventh-century Cairo, for
example, it appears that two dinars could support a fairly humble family
for one month.[4] A domestic servant in the same city could be bought—in
those days of "wageless labor," bought as a slave but by no means as a
mere chattel—for 20 dinars; and this is a price which says a good deal
about the high cost of domestic servants. For it seems to have been a price
equal to some ten months' subsistence of a humble family. Elsewhere, the
price could be much higher, depending upon the skills of the purchased
workers and the available quantity of such workers. Again, in the eleventh
century, al-Bakri found that the purchase price of one of the famous
women cooks of the West African city of Awdaghost was as much as 100
dinars, an almost princely sum. A house in the grand Andalusian capital
of Cordoba, at about the same time, went for 160 mitcals (effectively, the
equivalent of 160 dinars, or about 676 grams of fine gold), while a black

"wageless worker" in the same city cost the same high price in the year
1065.[5] On this scale of values, the tax revenues of the king of Ghana were
clearly not small.

But the lords of these savannah realms of West Africa had another
economic reason for pushing out their boundaries as far as they could—
and Mali and Songhay, at the height of their power, were geographically
about as large as most of Western Europe. Imperial extension gave them
a second source of wealth. This was in tribute paid by subject peoples. In
this important respect, though in a different context of ownership and tax
extraction, these West African kingdoms shared characteristics with the
feudal systems of western Europe. Their interest lay in securing services,
whether in labor or the products of labor. So we find in the *Tarikh
al-Fattash*, Mahmud Kati's chronicle of the western Sudan completed in
Timbuktu in about A.D. 1665, that vassal peoples of the Mali emperor were
obliged to cut fodder for the royal stables. Others had to deliver fixed
quantities of fish, or, if they were blacksmiths, provide spears and ma-
chetes for the emperor's servants and soldiers.

From this aspect, these systems were as oppressive of ordinary people
as any other system of feudal or authoritarian government. Courts and
cavalry, royal hospitality and waste, princely power and its assertion, the
support of scholars and the advance of learning: all this and much else
gave glory to these rulers. But it had to be paid for, and the labouring
masses were those who paid for it. Other painful costs had to be similarly
met. Whenever one great dynasty or system declined and fell to rising
rivals, the price paid by the defeated was seldom small. "God having
overthrown the emperor of Mali to the benefit of the emperor of Songhay"—to borrow again from the *Tarikh al-Fattash*—"the latter ravaged
the empire of Mali, carried off its children into captivity, and seized all
the goods of the vassal peoples."

Yet to see only this side of the story is to miss another side; and it was
this other side which gave these overarching systems their resonance and
fame, and which endured in the minds of men long after the kingdoms
had vanished from the scene, so that even today the exploits of their
statesmen and heroes live vividly in the songs and ballads of the old
Sudan. Within their frontiers, which enclosed wide zones of tax and
tribute, there could be long periods of peace when oppression would
seem a merely necessary price for everyday security.

Consider only these comments by the shrewdly observant Ibn Battuta
of Tangier, who sojourned in Mali during 1352 as an emissary of the king
of Morocco. "One of their good features," he reported about the government and people of Mali, "is their lack of oppression. They are the

farthest removed from it, and their king does not allow anyone to practise it. Another of their good features"—on certain other points of behavior, Ibn Battuta was sharply critical—"is the security which embraces the whole country. Neither the traveller nor the man who stays at home has anything to fear from thief or from usurper." Justice and peace: these were benefits, now as then, which men have seen as standing at the heart of civilization.

One further fact, and the central one, about these West African kingdoms, whether in the savannah plains or near the coastland forests, is that they promoted wide systems of regional trade, and of production for trade, from which the whole subcontinent could benefit. Through these immense regions a common currency unit was created, for the use of regional and internal trade, in the form of the imported cowrie shell. Along with some other forms of nonnumismatic currency, such as rolls of cotton cloth or bars of copper, cowries provided a standard of exchange across many frontiers. It is in these systems of regional exchange that one may see the truly expansive influence of the old kingdoms. They could provide an extensive "common market." As late as the middle of the nineteenth century, a European traveler in Hausaland could find that the woolen cloths of Kano were being sold as far as the coasts of Senegal or the cities of the Mediterranean seaboard.

Based on large political and economic unities, the old empires of West Africa developed a further projection of their influence and wealth. As we have seen, they provided the gold that was indispensable to the intercontinental trading system of the Middle Ages, centered on that "metropolis of the world" which was the Cairo of Fatimid and later times. Of course, they provided other useful goods as well, while offering a valued market to the exports of the Middle East, often as luxury items such as the fine swords of Damascus or the tableware of Cairo and Baghdad. But it was the gold of West Africa that fueled the whole wide system and made it work.

This intercontinental system became much more than a Muslim achievement. It extended into Europe as well. It extended into a Europe still emerging from the poverty and confusion that followed on the collapse of the western Roman Empire. Here too the sources of gold for coins were long exhausted. If a few ambitious European kings—the eighth-century Anglo-Saxon Offa of Mercia was one of them—nonetheless minted coins in gold, they did it only for reasons of prestige, and by dint of melting down and reminting old gold coins of the late Roman period that they happened to possess.[6]

By the thirteenth century, however, this long-impoverished Europe was beginning to recover itself and emerge from its provincial obscurity. Europe could once again export manufactures, whereas for many earlier years it had exported little but European slaves. With this ability Europe's rulers began to buy gold so as to create a new monetary standard of exchange such as their rising enterprises now required. This imported gold had to come from Africa, for no other source existed. The newly rich city-states of Florence and Genoa led the way in 1252. Others followed.

This appearance of the golden *fiorentino,* or florin, of Florence and the ducats of Genoa and Venice, all of them minted in gold from West Africa, signaled a major advance for the economies of Europe. With expanding arteries of trade that were lubricated by the new gold coins, Europe could now lay the foundations of its future supremacy. So it may be said, without exaggeration, that this new prosperity of late-medieval Europe, with its first steps toward the development of capitalism, was another consequence, however indirect, of the achievements of Africa, and of Africa's miners, merchants, and entrepreneurs.

IV

THE IBN BATTUTA OF MOROCCO WHOM WE HAVE MET IN MALI, TRAVELING to discover "the realities of the world," had also journeyed elsewhere. In fact, he traveled tirelessly. He set out for Egypt and the Middle East and India when he was young, went on to Indonesia and finally, taking his time, arrived in China from where he safely returned several years after first setting out. But in the course of this long eastern journey he also traveled along the coastland of East Africa. That was in 1332.

Twenty years later, upon returning from his visit to Mali, our Moroccan globe-trotter retired from the road and dictated his memoirs to a friend. Recalling his trip to East Africa, he revived a vivid memory of the city-kingdom of Kilwa, today in southern Tanzania. He had greatly admired its king at the time of his visit in 1332, and remembered him as "noted for gifts and generosity," for "I have seen him give the clothes off his back to a beggar who asked him for them." He had also admired the city itself: Kilwa, he recalled, "is a very fine and substantial place." He thought Kilwa one of the most handsome cities he had seen in all his travels.

That was a generous opinion, because Kilwa could certainly not have rivaled imperial Peking or other great capitals where Ibn Battuta had sojourned. Yet if Kilwa in our own day is only a humble village of thatch and clay which nestles amid ruins of its stone-built past, the Kilwa that Ibn Battuta saw was undoubtedly a city of some splendor. Now long reduced to an obscure ruin known as Husuni Kubwa, Great Husuni, the king's palace was once a capacious complex of courtyards and dwellings, rooms both public and private, effective indoor sanitation and even, admirably placed on the brow of a cliff to catch the breezes of the Indian Ocean, a large eight-sided bathing pool. Here came merchants and envoys from every leading country of the East, and even, briefly in the early fifteenth century, the great ocean-sailing ships of imperial China.

Arriving soon after in small vessels bent on piracy and exploration, the mariners of Portugal were understandably impressed by East African city-states and ports such as Kilwa, of whose existence they had known nothing. They thought that the inhabitants were "Moors," their name for the Muslims of North Africa, whereas, in fact, the inhabitants were Swahili, as African as the Muslims of Mali or the Hausa kingdoms. But the Portuguese did not mistake the wealth of these Swahili cities, and lost no time in looting it. At the same time their literate supercargos had occasion to describe Swahili urbanism.

The city of Kilwa, recorded Duarte Barbosa, "has many handsome houses of stone and mortar, with many windows such as our own houses have, and very well arranged in streets." He likewise found Mombasa, another Swahili city a little to the north, "a very handsome place, with tall stone and mortar houses well aligned in streets as they are at Kilwa, as well as being a place of much traffic with a good harbor where are always moored boats of many kinds, and also great ships" which come and go across the Indian Ocean.

What explained this prosperity and sophistication? What was the role and place of these coastal cities in the mercantile world of their time? Little but ruins can speak of them today, but the old records are sufficiently ample; or one can visit old Swahili houses in one or two old towns such as Lamu on the Kenya coast, merchants' houses for the most part, and stand in some awe at the comfort of those who had desired and built them.

The historical parallel they display with the old cities of West Africa in the same epoch is one way of understanding their importance and development. Even the name of their people, then as now, speaks in the same sense. For the word Swahili derives from the same Arabic word as Sahel or Saheli, meaning "shore" or "people of the shore." So here was another great intercontinental trading system of medieval times, the difference from West Africa and its Sahel being that this is the shore of an ocean of water and not of an ocean of sand.

Across the Indian Ocean to the east lay the commercial centers of near and further Asia, eager for the gold and ivory of East Africa. To the west were the kingdoms and peoples of the African interior, well known to the Swahili even while still unknown to the outside world. And here along the coastland, linking these two great regions of production and of trade, were the Swahili middlemen who could connect them. This entire pattern of production and exchange, in short, formed an eastern counterpart to the regional and intercontinental systems of western and northern Africa. Like circumstances again produced like results: inland kingdoms of resilience and strength, far-ranging arteries of trade, middleman ports and cities, a myriad of useful contacts outside Africa.

A principal inland and regional system, in this eastern counterpart, lay in what today are Mozambique and Zimbabwe. Abu al-Hasan al-Masudi, another early writer, gives us a valuable glimpse. He sailed down the East African coast on "the sea of the Zanj"—the sea of the black people—in about A.D. 925, and left in his only surviving book, entitled *The Meadows of Gold and Mines of Gems*, a brief but vivid description of a kingdom of the Zanj that was ruled by a "king of kings" whose title was Waqlimi, "which means supreme lord." The Zanj "give this title to their sovereign because he has been chosen to govern them with equity. But once he becomes tyrannical and departs from the rules of justice, they cause him to die and exclude his posterity from succession to the throne, for they claim that in behaving thus he ceases to be the son of the Master, that is to say, of the king of heaven and earth." Other Africans will quickly recognize the echoes of their own attitudes to good rulers, as well as to bad rulers who depart from the ways of God and the wisdom of the ancestors; the English of the time of the Magna Carta, as we have seen, would have recognized this as well.

This kingdom of the Waqlimi, adds al-Masudi, reaches as far as the country of Sofala, the coastland of Mozambique, where gold could be had in abundance. Ivory was another valued export. Tusks from there "go generally to Oman [in Arabia] and then to China and India. That is the way they go, and if it were otherwise, ivory would be abundant in Muslim countries." Iron for forging was a third export. In A.D. 1154, some two centuries after al-Masudi, the Andalusian chronicler al-Idrisi, living then in Sicily, compiled a copious record of the international trade of his period. He says that the people of Indonesia were in the habit of visiting that same East African land of Sofala in order to buy smelted iron, "which they carry to the continent of India and sell it there at a good price, for this iron is a material of big trade and consumption in India."

And what did the Zanj and their neighbors buy in return? One answer comes from a Chinese inspector of customs, writing in Fukien (in southern China) during the thirteenth century A.D. Every year, he records, the maritime kingdoms of northwestern India and of southern Arabia, "send ships to this country [of the Zanj] with white cottons, porcelain, copper, red cottons, and sell them there." Even today one may stroll along Swahili beaches and pick up fragments of fine porcelain and pottery from medieval China and Iraq, the "kitchen waste" of broken tableware. And the same shards even make a trail to the kingdoms of the interior, and above all to the stone-built *zimbabwes* from which the rulers of those inland kingdoms ruled in western Mozambique and across the plateau of what is now the republic of Zimbabwe. These were the inland kingdoms that shaped and developed another wide regional network of trade and tribute, and promoted, in time, its extension into intercontinental trade by way of the Swahili coastal cities.

Visitors to the major stone-built sites of the Zimbabwe Culture have wondered what power and ambition could have raised these structures, the largest of which, at Great Zimbabwe, has enclosing walls rising to thirty feet, and twenty feet thick at the base. This power and ambition were of the same order as those embodied in the capitals and governments of old West Africa in the same period. They were the outward and visible signs of a political and economic organization which had developed regional production and exchange, and then enlarged this system by ample international contacts. Recent archaeology has even shown us that the *zimbabwe* nearest to the East African coast—at Manikweni in central Mozambique—had almost direct access to the Swahili "shore." And in conducting this trade between the interior and the coastland, the traders of the inland kingdoms and the traders of the Swahili appear to have worked in cooperation.

News of all this whetted the appetite of the early Portuguese mariners who came to this coastland around 1500. "Beyond this coast country toward the interior," Duarte Barbosa writes in 1518, "there lies the great kingdom of Benemetapa [that is, of the Mwene-Mutapha, or Lord of Zimbabwe]" whose leaders are "warlike men, and some too are great traders in gold and other goods." By that time, as was found out later, the inland kingdoms had been trading to the coastland for more than half a millennium. Lured by the hope of gold, Portuguese expeditions set out from the coast for the interior, but found the inland kingdoms, generally, too strong for them. Not until the nineteenth century were the Zimbabwe kingdoms to be overthrown, and then, initially, by other African hands.

But the East had long known of this inland wealth by way of the coastal intermediaries. Contacts as far as China had been made by at least the

eleventh century A.D. Ambassadors went back and forth. Gifts were ex-
changed. In 1414, for example, the emperor of China was delighted to
receive the gift of a giraffe from the Swahili city of Malindi (now in
Kenya). Previously considered by the Chinese to be a mythical creature,
a living giraffe had been delivered to them. There has even survived a
Chinese painting of this giraffe together with its keeper. It looks as
bewildered by its travels as the Chinese were no doubt puzzled at seeing
in reality what had hitherto existed for them only in legend. The emperor, for his part, was so impressed by this Swahili gift that he ordered
his ocean-sailing fleet to convey the ambassadors from Malindi back to
their own city. This was done by Admiral Cheng-Ho, commanding big
ships, in 1417. And Cheng-Ho made six other long voyages, the last of
which reached East Africa in 1431. It proved to mark the end of one epoch.
Sixty years later the Portuguese arrived and opened another. This was to
be the epoch of European piracy and dispossession.

V

I HAVE DEVOTED MOST OF THIS ESSAY TO AFRICA'S TWO LARGEST INTERNAL
systems of economic and political development between roughly the
sixth and sixteenth centuries: regional systems, one in the west and the
other in the east, each of which developed an intercontinental dimension.
Not only do the strength and age of these systems give them a leading
place in the continent's history—beyond that, and beyond their promotion of a wider progress in the outside world—these systems also imply
an unfolding process in many other polities and kingdoms. Even within
the limits of my essay here, the picture calls for a little rounding out.

A first point to keep in mind is that this unfolding process of development was first and foremost a process internal to the old societies of
Africa. A notion in Europe and North America used to be common, and
may still be found here and there, to the effect that some outside stimulus
or guidance was indispensable to any "forward movement" among African peoples. "Development" had to come from outside; otherwise, it was
alleged, there could only be stagnation. A later derivative of this same
complacent Eurocentrism has argued that the development of African
kingdoms was by diffusion of ideas and structures from an outside source.
This "Hamitic hypothesis"—the legendary "Hamites" being supposed to
have supplied a necessary "outside stimulus" from somewhere initially in

Europe—had in fact no scientific basis and was simply another Eurocentrism. We see better today.

That the outside world brought much to old Africa goes without saying. Even the earliest forms of forced-draft smelter adopted by tropical Africans around the sixth century B.C. may well have derived from technologies developed somewhat earlier by Indo-European peoples. Even the alphabetical script invented by the Kushite kingdom of Meroe in the eastern Sudan during the third century B.C.—one of the first such scripts invented anywhere—may possibly have taken its inspiration from the "cursive" Greek script in use in Greek-ruled Egypt since the fourth century B.C. Even a number of Africa's favorite food crops, such as cassava and sweet potatoes, came from America in the sailing ships of the sixteenth century. No continent, in this sense, can claim any all-embracing primacy of invention or development.

It remains that the invention and development of the unfolding process of kingship and kingly forms of government in Africa was persistently an internal process. If this had not been the case, indeed, there would be no way of explaining many of its features. Alongside and in counterpoint with the major systems I have mentioned in this essay, there appeared, for example, other systems of more or less importance, each with its place and part in the developmental dynamics of its time. The Horn of Africa saw the rise of Somali and Ethiopian kingdoms. The big kingdoms of the western and central Sudan may have stood in the center of their West African scene, but they were not alone. Aside from the major forest-country kingdoms, such as those of the Yoruba, of the Edo of Benin, of the Akan to the west of them, of the Mossi to the north of the Akan in the grasslands of the forest fringe, there were others of weight and influence.

Among the latter was a cluster of states in the region of Senegambia—the far west of West Africa—of which the most successful were the various kingdoms of the Wolof. When the Portuguese at last got down this coast in their caravels, after 1430, they were no little surprised to find themselves confronted by these powerful kingships. Thus the strongest of the Wolof states, they found (no doubt with a large exaggeration), "puts 10,000 cavalry and 100,000 infantry into the field whenever he [the king] goes on campaign"; and they hastened to make alliance with this power so as to develop a profitable trade. Again, one needs to see these Wolof kingdoms, and those of their neighbors, as part of a process of state formation which arose, primarily, from the *internal* dynamics of the region.

Much has been written in recent years of the trans-Saharan traders who linked North Africa with the regions south of the desert. Yet in this developmental process these trans-desert contacts were of secondary importance when compared with the intraregional trading systems developed, for example, by the Dyula companies of the Mandinka—the Wangarawa, as their Hausa competitors called them—or by the Hausa themselves and others in the forest and near-coastal belt. And we find the same complex and self-enlarging system when we turn to eastern and central Africa. If the Zimbabwe kingdoms stand out by reason of their building in stone and their exports of gold and ivory, such features were not the only ones in this kind of developmental enterprise. Regional trade in salt, for example, led early to the opening of trans-African trails through the whole eastern and southern periphery of the Congo Basin.

Responding to the same process of state formation and economic enlargement, the traditions of Central Africa show that the fifteenth and sixteenth centuries brought the emergence of a series of Luba and Lunda kingdoms right across the southern Congo Basin periphery to the frontiers of other kingdoms in western Angola. At least by the eighteenth century all these internal regions were under the government of polities in which kingship was usually prominent. Some of them, such as that of the Muata Yamvo of the Lunda empire or the Kazembe line of kings who ruled over what afterward became the Katanga province of Zaire, were of considerable power and prestige.

"King Kazembe," wrote a European visitor in 1832, "was seated on the lefthand side of the gate of his royal residence" when the visitors arrived. "Many leopard skins served him as a carpet, the tails pointing outwards to form a star. Over these was an enormous lion skin, and on this a stool covered with a big green cloth. On this throne the *mwata* [king] was seated: in greater elegance and style than any other African king whom I have seen."

About fifty years old, the king "has a long beard already turning grey. He is well built and tall, and has a robustness and agility which promise a long life. His look is pleasant and majestic, and his style is splendid in its fashion. We certainly never expected to find so much ceremony, pomp and ostentation in a potentate of a region so remote from the seacoast." Yet by 1832 the times were changing, and this new chapter told the long and violent story of European invasion. The unfolding process internal to the continent was now to be distracted and obstructed by the European colonial dispossessions with these upsets and upheavals. No region was to feel this more than the far southern countries which were to become South Africa.

Here in the far south, very much earlier, the same process of state formation had produced a large range of polities among Bantu-language groups, notably those of the Nguni and Sotho peoples. They had formed their earliest polities, south of the Limpopo River, as long ago as the fourth or fifth century A.D. They took shape in the grasslands and hills to the east of the wilderness of the Kalahari, and in what were to become the countries of Natal, the Transvaal, and the Orange Free State, as well as in the Cape Province as far as the Great Fish River. By the eighteenth century, however, incoming European settlers had begun to clash with the Africans in a Dutch (Boer) search for land and slave labor. This northward-shoving pressure continued. The wars of the invaders, now with the British taking a hand, were many. One after another African polity found itself attacked and dispossessed.

As these pressures continued northward, various disasters came. Battling for better means of self-defense, African peoples formed themselves into kingdoms so as to win greater strength. Among these were the Swazi to the north of Natal, the Zulu in Natal itself, and the Basuto in the mountains of the Drakensberg, two of them being the forerunners of the modern kingdoms of Swaziland and Lesotho.

But these were peoples and states that stood upon the verge of huge change and upheaval. Their story belongs to the colonial period of external domination and dispossession, rather than to the age-old process of internal African development. In this essay we could have looked at many other aspects of that manifold process, and in much greater detail. But "the wise reader"—to borrow from the comment of a West African historian of long ago—"will understand that beyond the river there is the ocean."

AFRICA AND THE INVENTION OF RACISM

THIS ESSAY SETS OUT TO THROW LIGHT UPON THE ANSWERS TO SOME central questions about the relationship between Europe and Africa in the broad period of A.D. 1500 to 1600—that is, after the European discovery of large sectors of the African coastland and its peoples, but before any systematic European attempt, save fragmentarily on the part of the Portuguese, to impose a political or economic domination.[1]

What was the nature of the principal African polities with which Europeans made contact in that period? How were those polities perceived, and, summarily at least, how did they perceive themselves? With the hindsight of modern historiography, what contrasts and comparisons may be made between those polities and their European contemporaries? And how is this period of Euro-African contact—essentially, one of mutual discovery and often of partnership—to be measured in light of the sharply different period of expansive European domination that came later?

One can introduce this difficult, dense, and sometimes contradictory material by looking at a far easier question: what did the early European travelers and mariners find? Happily, their memoirs or reports are numerous in several European languages, and most usefully in Portuguese, Dutch, and English. As in Asia and the Americas, they found much to astonish them in custom and belief: that kings, and even citizens, could have the possession of many wives; that shrines were raised to ancestors

This essay originally appeared in 1987, commissioned by the Italian publishers Unione Tipografico–Editrice Torinese, in *La Storia*, volume 3, *The Modern Age* (Turin, 1987), and is reprinted with permission.

who were revered as gods; that human sacrifice could be practiced on certain though few occasions of ritual solemnity; and much else besides. Essentially, however, if with exceptions here and there (such as Dutch reactions to the Stone Age people of the Cape of Good Hope in the 1650s), these mariners, traders, and adventurers found what appeared to them neither strange nor perverse, but natural and even familiar. They found polities whose concern for trade appeared much the same as their own, whose laws were seen to be generally respected, and whose sense of independence, as well as their will and ability to defend that independence, were never in serious doubt. They found kings who were held to be divine—sanctioned, that is, by spiritual as well as temporal authority—in much the same meaning or degree as their own kings in Europe. In a number of polities they perceived a hierarchy of power, descending from the monarch through nobles and notables, which they wrongly but understandably considered to be comparable with the feudal structures they knew at home: as witness, in one well-known example, the famous *regimento* of the king of Portugal in 1512, recommending his "royal brother" of Kongo (afterward, northern Angola) to adopt the whole range of Portuguese titles of nobility from duke to viscount to marquis and so on.

In short, and again with the exceptions that so vast a subject must allow, the Europeans of the sixteenth century believed that they had found forms of civilization which were often comparable with their own, however differently and variously dressed or mannered. A later age would prefer to forget this, and would roundly state that Africa knew nothing but a savage and indeed a hopeless barbarism. We shall do well to remember that a familiar European contempt for Africans—and I will return to this aspect at the end of my essay—was an attitude born of the Atlantic slave trade after about 1650, and, later, of the cultures of European capitalism. It had no instrumental existence before, at any rate, the middle of the seventeenth century, and became generally accepted only in the eighteenth. To glimpse the relationship which preceded an instrumental racism, we need to think ourselves back into earlier times.

I

THE EARLY RECORDS, ONWARD FROM THE 1460S, SPEAK OFTEN OF "DIFFERence"; they do not speak of "inferiority."

In 1603 the captain of a Dutch ship trading to Guinea—broadly, the West African coastland from Senegambia (as it would become) to the mouth of the Congo River (which the Portuguese, first among Europeans, had reached in 1483)—decided to investigate the prospects offered by the kingdom of Benin, already believed to be a powerful coastal state (in what was to become western Nigeria). So he detached a boat, oared and sailed, with fourteen well-armed men under the command of a German called Andreas Josua Ultzheimer, who afterward wrote his memoirs. This small craft went safely eastward from the Gold Coast to the island of Lagos, then within the kingdom of Benin. They found a welcome there as traders, and the welcome was increased after this little force of soldier-mariners had helped the local authorities to reduce a "rebellious city" whose name, unfortunately, Ultzheimer afterward forgot.

Ultzheimer and his men thereupon proceeded into the Benin River where they disembarked, and, leaving their boat (presumably at Ugwato, the regular port of Benin), made the day's journey to the capital city of the kingdom. At this point Ultzheimer becomes short on detail, having lost his notes before writing his book; but one may reasonably look to contemporary Dutch accounts and find, in the memoirs of "D R" (thought to be Diereck Ruiters) and other Dutchmen of the same period, graphic accounts of a strong and prosperous city, with its main street "seven or eight times broader than the Warmoes-street in Amsterdam." Arriving shortly afterward, Ultzheimer and his men stayed there for three months as guests of the court.

"D R," with his fellow traveler Mattheus Cornelison, and somewhat later Dutch travelers have left us much precise and interesting detail about the trade and customs of Benin and its kingship. They fared well there, and were impressed by its civic stability and peace. But Ultzheimer's account, though far less rich in detail than later accounts, has a particular interest in the comparisons that he drew. These were decidedly partial, but not in the ways that a later Europe would expect and accept. Ultzheimer himself was a strongly Protestant product of the German conflicts of religion as well as having served as *Landsknecht* in battles against the Turks in Hungary. He tended to see matters in western Europe in terms of a Protestant-Catholic conflict, which he interpreted as a holy war between God and the Devil, just as the German Catholics did the same in reverse; and his reactions to what he found in Benin were framed in the same perspective. What distressed him about the manners and beliefs in Benin was not their exoticism, or little so, nor of course their nonliteracy (among the last of facts that could have distressed a former *Landsknecht* of 1603); it was their similarity, as he saw it, with attitudes which he deplored as "Roman Catholic."

When he describes the pomp and isolation surrounding the ruler of

Benin, he finds them sadly reminiscent: "This king allows himself to be seen in public only once a year, and that is on his birthday when he rides in progress round his city's walls, clad in scarlet cloth and bejewelled with beads of coral." The people crowd to see him with the awe of obedient submission:

> Everyone wants to see the king, just as in Rome when the Pope celebrates his "Jubilee." Six thousand people press towards him, and when he comes they all go down on their knees and clap their hands in greeting. For his part he waves his hand back and forth, just as does the Pope in Rome when he blesses the people.

I mention this little-known and clearly very personal account only in order to illustrate the need to "think ourselves back" into the minds of those who made the early journeys from Europe to Africa. Like his coevals, Ultzheimer saw Africa in the light of the Europe that he knew, and found there nothing to induce the mythologies of racism that were to engulf later European minds. And one can draw much the same comparative picture in other accounts of kingdoms that these Europeans came to know: from those of the Wolof in Senegal to their contemporaries along the Atlantic coastlands, and again up the eastern African coastlands to the city-kingdoms of the Swahili.

Can one find corresponding aids to thinking back in contemporary African accounts? What did the ambassadors of Benin or Kongo think about Lisbon and the Portuguese when they were royally entertained there? Unhappily, the records are lacking. Yet the implications of what we nonetheless know, largely from the European accounts, will be found to confirm a general conclusion: these were African states and citizens who learned to know European states and citizens as being clearly different from themselves in custom and belief, and yet with no inherent superiority of power or civic achievement. They recognized a European technological superiority, for example in ships and firearms, and became interested in certain European solutions to political and military problems, being sometimes glad to investigate the teachings of Christian missionaries and the value of European mercenaries. But there is no suggestion of any acceptance of a gap in capacity for whatever anyone then might understand by the word "civilization."

Thus the oral record of the kings of Benin, quite reasonably complete back to about A.D. 1400, makes mention in due course of the arrival of Europeans, but finds it unnecessary to say more about them. Court sculptors of the period were regularly engaged in decorating the royal palace with descriptive brass-bronze plaques in high relief; among much else they show us Portuguese soldiers, some of whom certainly served in the king's army, but these are no more than exotic visitors, strangely clad, whose presence is worth recording because it is rare. There developed a relationship which may be measured in the reports of diplomatic agents as well as Portuguese missionaries. In 1516 Duarte Pires writes to his royal master in Lisbon that:

> The favor shown us by the king of Benin is due to his love of your Highness; and thus he pays us high honor and sets us at table to dine with his son, and no part of his court is hidden from us but all the doors are open.

A self-serving exaggeration, no doubt, and yet one can see that relations more often than not were stable, peaceful, and of a kind which states observe when mutual respect reigns between them. Even the early English mariners, tough captains such as Wyndham and Towerson who had to fight their passage through the monopoly claimed by the Portuguese or battle with their French rivals, and did so with a ready and ruthless violence, had no impression of being superior in power to the African authorities whom they encountered. On the contrary, they were well enough content to ship in peace their cargos of ivory and gold and malagueta pepper, and then fight their long way home against European rivals at sea.

How wide, then, was the effective "technological gap" in 1600? Before looking at this question, it will be helpful to reconstruct, at least in summary outline, the lineage of these states and polities found by early Europeans. They were already the outcome of a long indigenous development.

II

THE EARLIEST STATES OF WHICH WE HAVE RECORD BEYOND THE SAHARA—south, that is, of the great desert and the valley of the Nile—became known to the Arabs soon after A.D. 700, and with increasing detail after about 900. Pre-Muslim Berber caravans had traversed the desert for many centuries before that, but little had become known of their enterprise. Then those who led the Arab conquest of North Africa rapidly developed a new interest in the trans-Saharan trade. There were two central reasons for this. The first of these was an increasingly felt need for a new gold standard such as could take the place of the Byzantine *dinarius aureus*, given the enormous expansion of Muslim power after 650 and the exhaustion of known gold deposits. Strongly desirable by 800, notably with the growth of Tulunid power in Egypt, this need was again increased—and here we have the second reason—after the Tunisian Fatimids had enclosed Egypt in the tenth century, and, with their surging initiative, had transposed the "central core" of world trade westward from the Persian Gulf to the Red Sea and the Mediterranean.

Then it was that Cairo, overtaking Baghdad or Damascus, became the hub and center of an international system of exchange that reached from Muslim Spain and Morocco in the west to the ports of southern China by way of India, Ceylon, and Indonesia; and this system, in turn, depended on a monetary gold standard—primarily, the early Fatimid and then the Almoravid dinar—whose metal came, and indeed had to come, entirely from West Africa. Minted in several North African cities, these coins and various derivatives remained the stable measure of exchange for all the centuries of the Late Middle Ages and even some time after. Along with ivory and slaves (the latter being a regular but, compared with the volume of the later transatlantic slave trade, a relatively small trans-Saharan component), gold became and stayed an indispensable import from West Africa; and this helped to fuel an already intricate network of communications across the desert.

What the Arabs and their Berber intermediaries found, south of the desert, was a number of market cities and kingdoms whose foundation certainly predated, and sometimes by a long period, the development of Muslim power north of the desert. In these savannahs, which the Arabs called the Sahel, the earliest of note seems to have been Aoukar (or ancient Ghana, the land of the "lord of the gold"), possibly taking some form of organized shape around A.D. 500. For a thousand years and more after that, West Africa knew a series of occasionally huge and always impressively powerful polities—Mali, Songhay, Kanem-Borno, with some others, such as Benin and Oyo, in the forest belt—while other regions added more achievements of the same kind. Most of these old empires can be reasonably seen as systems of military control modified by the lineage structures within which the rulers had to function. Enduring for centuries, "the phase of domination by the medieval states of the Sahel corresponded to that of the constitution and domination of a military class which grew out of plundering warfare" (Meillassoux, p. 82).[2] The central aims of this "class" changed little over time: they were to establish over wide regions a control sufficient to the extraction of taxes on long-distance trade—within the regions so controlled, as well as with regard to export and import of goods to and from neighboring regions—and of tribute from subjected peoples. The vivid details assembled from travelers by the Cordoban chronicler, al-Bakri, and published by him in A.D. 1068, show how the warrior rulers of Ghana, lineage chiefs of the Soninke people, led the way. They imposed taxes on imported salt and copper as well as on exported gold, while their royal and military expenses were further sustained by tribute in kind from vassals within their empire. Later rulers followed suit, if with innovations of their own.

Yet these military systems, later strengthened further by the development of stirruped cavalry and professional soldiers, were more than a means of exploitation by successful kings and generals, although, as on other continents, they were certainly that. Their unification of wide regions within an overall if generally loose control both helped the development of mercantile enterprise and enabled it to expand across much of western Africa. There emerged, to quote from Meillassoux again, "the presence of merchants, markets, towns or quarters peopled by traders, organized networks, commercial circuits, money (cowries, pieces of copper, or money-of-account commodities)"; and all these were continuously reinforced by new methods of exchange and communication such as those evolved by the Dyula or Wangarawa "companies" after about A.D. 1300. Long before our comparative "benchmark" date of A.D. 1000, accordingly, the sinews of production for trade and of trading exchange could nourish a complex and effective body of wealth formation, and on a semicontinental scale.

The Hausa states (now within northern Nigeria) demonstrate this well. As a people and culture, the Hausa appear mistily in the first millennium as cultivators of the central Sudanese savannahs. Gradually, they develop village systems, and, as early divisions of labor become possible, they embark on various forms of artisanal production. By the period of the European Middle Ages, they are already building walled towns, *birane*, which acquire political importance soon after about A.D. 1000 as the residence of kings. The function of these kings—who for a long time remain no more than *primi inter pares* with other lineage chiefs—is twofold. They are expected whenever necessary to defend the region they command while in return they enjoy the prestige and privilege which come from tax and tribute paid by the *talakawa* or "common people."

Placed in a fertile land at a crossroads of trade, the Hausa flourish. They produce food in abundance. They develop a skilled artisanal production, chiefly in textiles, which find an ever wider market. By 1500, as shown in such works as the writings of the Andalusian traveler al-Wazzan al-Zayyati (the "Leo Africanus" whose work will be published in 1550 by the Venetian Giovanni-Battista Ramusio, and will at once grip the imagination of literate Europe), the Hausa states, each centered on its walled city, are enviably rich and even comfortable. By this time, in a parallel political development, the kings are no longer *primi inter pares;* they have become rulers in their own right. Yet they are not tyrants. Their power is hedged around with constitutional checks and balances, so that a king can act only by playing off one set of officials or titleholders against another. Here we find another characteristic evolution, whether in the savannahs or the forest belt. At least from 1300, the kings develop early forms of administrative service—that is, they rule through their own appointees, as well as through titleholders whose authority comes by inheritance. Usually, the appointees derive from subject or servile origins outside the lineage loyalties of the ruling system in question. They are men of humble status, or prisoners of war deprived by capture of their civic rights as free men, or men castrated and therefore incapable of organizing power through family connections. They serve the king only and, in serving him, help him to curb or outmaneuver the power of hereditary nobles.

To these complex systems, Islam adds a large contribution of ideas and techniques. Reaching West Africa in the ninth century, Islam fails to make any profound impression in the Hausa states until a good deal later, and, decisively, only in the fifteenth century. Then, toward the end of that century, we find a king of Kano, Muhammad Rumfa, soliciting advice from a North African jurist, al-Maghili, who writes for him a book called *The Obligations of Princes;* a little later the same pundit goes on to give advice on similar subjects to the powerful emperor of Songhay, Askia Muhammad the Great. By this time, in short, literacy and its civic uses have found an important place in everyday life, and "Leo Africanus," writing of Timbuktu and the cities of the western Sudan soon after 1500, can justifiably emphasize the role of scholarship and the value placed on libraries. How little there was of exaggeration in Leo's well-known affirmation about the book trade's high value in these old cities of the western Sudan has been amply shown by modern scholarship. Mahmoud Abdu Zouber has lately given us the list of required reading for students in higher studies at Timbuktu in the second half of the sixteenth century, as recorded at the time by the most eminent of their teachers, the redoubtable Ahmad Baba. These twenty-five works (whether in *fiqh, hadith, tafsir,* or other disciplines) include "almost all the works that constituted the basis of classical Islamic studies. The libraries of Timbuktu had practically the whole of Arabic literature. Works produced in Spain and

the Maghrib stood alongside those of Egypt and Iraq." No doubt, adds
Zouber, the learning thus available in Timbuktu may have failed to reach
the levels achieved in centers such as Cordoba and Fez, let alone Cairo.
"However that may be, Timbuktu was the greatest intellectual center of
the Sudan in the fifteenth and sixteenth centuries. It was, moreover, one
of the great scientific centers of the Muslim world of that time" (Zouber,
p. 55). There were corresponding advances in the organization and functioning of the markets of the Sahel, in expansion of the long-distance
caravan trade, and in the use and deployment of currency and credit.

III

OUTSIDE THE CITIES AND THEIR PERIPHERALLY ORGANIZED STATES, THERE
was a large number of rural communities without kingships or their
equivalent, and whose economy consisted more or less entirely of semi-
subsistence systems of production supplemented by purely local trade.
Yet they too were drawn increasingly into the patterns of a regional
economy steered by a variety of political systems but otherwise united,
save for the interruptions of dynastic warfare and the search for plunder,
by the trails and needs of the long-distance trade. This emergence of a
wide regional unity had continuous development. Two and a half centuries after our comparative date, for example, we have the precise evidence
of Heinrich Barth, intellectually the best equipped of all the European
travelers in Africa during the nineteenth century. He reaches the Hausa
city of Kano in 1851, and finds it prosperous from the local manufacture
and export of textiles:

> The great advantage of Kano [and he means its village economy,
> rather than the market city itself] is that commerce and manufac-
> tures go hand in hand, and that almost every family has its share in
> them. There is really something grand in this kind of industry,
> which spreads to the North as far as Murzuq, Ghat and even Trip-
> oli; to the West not only to Timbuktu, but in some degree as far as
> the shores of the Atlantic, the very inhabitants of Arguin [off the far
> western coast] dressing in the cloth woven and dyed in Kano; to the
> East all over Borno ... [while] to the South it invades the whole of
> Adamawa.

Now we do not know the exact trading position in 1600, but one
important fact appears beyond dispute: however considerable was the

value of gold, ivory, and salt in the long-distance trade (that is, feeding the trans-Saharan trade), this value was still less in its influence for economic life, year by year, than the internal trade in food and manufactures produced within the wide West African region. The very patchy information assembled by Europeans in the coastland, whether in 1600 or long after, could provide no understanding of this regional economy, and, indeed, only in recent years have historians been able to come to grips with it and with its implications for the societies that developed it.

It has accordingly been usual to understate or even ignore the inherent capacity of these Iron Age systems to develop their own modalities of economic growth, no matter by what mode of production one may prefer to label them, and on this last point there is much debate. Not only the Sahelian and Muslim states reveal this capacity. Southward from Hausaland, for example, the Yoruba empire of Oyo acquired after about 1550 a primary importance in the region that is now, broadly, western Nigeria and eastern Benin (the former Dahomey, that is, and not the Nigerian city of the same name); by the seventeenth century Oyo was a leading commercial power in eastern Guinea. Growing from ancient roots, some of which had produced the remarkable culture of royal Ile-Ife and its world-famous sculpture (dated now to ca. A.D. 1000–1300), Oyo held to the ancestral gods and beliefs of the Yoruba. It developed its own hierarchies of counterpoised nobles and titleholders, but without the influence of Islam, and still was able to exploit its own production and trade, profiting in this respect from its position across the trade routes between the coastland and the states of the Sahel. The equally non-Muslim kingdom of Benin makes the same point even more clearly. The prosperity that Ultzheimer and his Dutch companions so much admired around 1600 appears to have depended little on long-distance trade, but much on trade within its own subregion.

The same inherent capacity for self-development was demonstrated in other regions far outside West Africa. It had long been at work, of course, in the states of the middle and upper valley of the Nile: from Meroitic Kush and Christian Nubia to Axum and the early states of Ethiopia. Far south again and later, there is the imposing evidence of the states of the Zimbabwe Culture on the central-southern plateau (forming, today, Zimbabwe and Mozambique). There, from about A.D. 1300, kings and leading lineage nobles built fine stone dwellings for themselves, the largest of which, at Great Zimbabwe, remains awe-inspiring in its powerful ruin, and says much about the majesty of a kingship whose wealth likewise had come from regional production and trade and, to a lesser degree, from long-distance trade with the city-states of the eastern coast. Here we have a reasonably clear picture-in-outline of a very long process of development which began (in the sense that such a process ever actually begins) with the evolution of Bantu-speaking communities capable of growing food, raising cattle, and mining, smelting, and forging iron, copper, tin, and gold with a manifestly cumulative technological skill; and, in parallel, of moving from simple to more complex forms of cultural and political self-organization.

IV

To this nexus of purely internal and regional factors of development, the long-distance and external trade added a sometimes decisively useful contribution. Here we may turn again to eastern Africa. By the eleventh century, and in some cases earlier, the steady expansion of Muslim maritime trade across the Indian Ocean had fastened itself securely into a series of city-ports all the way down the long eastern coast from what is now Somalia in the north to what is now Mozambique in the south. Developed and dwelt in by a Bantu-speaking people who accepted Islam, progressively after about A.D. 800 these city-ports became crucially significant intermediaries between the gold and ivory producers of the Zimbabwe Culture on one side, and, on the other, the maritime networks of the world of the Indian Ocean from the Red Sea to Indonesia. As early as A.D. 943, the Cairene traveler and historian al-Masudi is telling us of the great value of gold and ivory exported from eastern Africa to Arabia, India, and China. In 1154 the Andalusian chronicler al-Idrisi, writing in Norman Palermo, records the export of iron and other goods to India from what is today the coast of Mozambique. In 1228 a Chinese inspector of customs in Fukien, Chao Ju-kua, tells of the annual departure of many ships from northwestern India, carrying textiles to the East African coast; and in 1332 the youthful Ibn Battuta, then on his travels in the East, visits Kilwa, the richest of the East African city-ports of his day, and even long afterward remembers it as one of the finest towns he saw in all his journeys.

Here we find another synthesis of indigenous African culture and Islam, just as in the West African Sahel; and this one, like its western counterpart in a later period, will continue to develop its potentials until wrecked by European piracy after 1498. Pushing up this coast, Vasco da Gama and his crews are astonished to come upon wealthy ports whose inhabitants, as da Gama's logbook records, "valued nothing that we gave them," and who had "already seen big ships like ours." Writing a few years later, another Portuguese eyewitness, Duarte Barbosa, notes:

> Going along this coast from the town of Mozambique [he means the town on the island of that name], there is an island hard by the mainland called Kilwa; and this is a Moorish [he means Muslim] town with many handsome houses of stone and mortar, with many windows after our fashion, very well arranged in streets, with many flat roofs. The doors are of well-carved wood and of excellent joinery. Around the town are streams and orchards and fruit-gardens with many channels of fresh water.

Farther north there was Mombasa, "a very handsome place with lofty stone and mortar houses, well aligned in streets after the fashion of Kilwa . . . a place of great commerce with a good harbor where are moored craft of many kinds and great ships." Barbosa and his companions even caught a glimpse of emissaries from the inland country of the Zimbabwe kingdoms, "who carry swords thrust into wooden scabbards bound with much gold and other metals, worn on the left side as we wear them. . . . These are warlike men, and some of them are great traders."

Here, in brief, was the socioeconomic counterpart in eastern Africa of the regional trading network of western Africa, with the ocean of Saharan wasteland, so far as the long-distance trade was concerned, replaced by the waters of the Indian Ocean. Even terminology can show this. Just as the western savannahs acquired the Arabic name of Sahel, meaning "shore," so did the Bantu-speaking builders of the East African city-ports become the Swahili, after *swahil,* or "shore," in a variant of the same term. Both became literate in Arabic, and later in some of their own languages written with an Arabic script.

V

LET US NOW TRY TO RESUME THE PRINCIPAL TECHNOLOGICAL COMPONENTS in this capacity for self-development. Three of these were essential, and had been at work for many centuries before A.D. 1600. The first had consisted in the development of effective techniques of tropical agriculture, determined by the often hostile ecologies of those regions. This assurance of a slow but continuous expansion in available food may be taken as the central factor in enabling sparse early peoples to grow in number and populate vast areas hitherto occupied only by handfuls of Stone Age hunters and food gatherers. Characteristic techniques of hoe cultivation; a regular rotation of village settlement so as to allow land to lie fallow after a number of years of cropping; primitive but sufficiently effective forms of soil nourishment by fertilizers such as wood ash; a variety of types of irrigation using canals and terraces; and an evident readiness to experiment with new plants—these were among the inventions and adaptations that enabled early settlements to become stable, grow in size, and master the local environment. Their consequences in African farming systems may reasonably be accepted as among the grand successes in humankind's conquest of nature.

A second component lay in the development of adequate techniques for the winning of metals—above all, from a developmental standpoint, of iron. Where did these techniques come from? Or were they separately invented? Much ink has been spilled on the possible answers. What appears probable at the present stage of research is that the techniques of winning iron began to be developed in the sub-Saharan savannahs around 400 B.C., or perhaps a little earlier, and that they were so developed, locally, from a trans-Saharan and ultimately Celtic (or at any rate Indo-European) technology. The Kushite city of Meroe (lying about 130 kilometers north of modern Khartoum in the Democratic Republic of the Sudan) was smelting iron by about 500 B.C., and corresponding techniques developed a little later in what is now northwestern Ethiopia; but there is no evidence, as yet, to show that Kushite or Ethiopian technology penetrated much to the south of those lands. On the other hand, the sure evidence of early trans-Saharan trade and travel by the middle of the first millennium B.C., together with some artifactual hints of Indo-European influence in certain West African types of iron-smelting furnaces, lend weight to the opinion I have offered here.

However that may be, the capacity to win iron from Africa's abundant deposits of the ore passed southward with an impressive speed. The earliest Iron Age cultures of western Africa identified by archaeology—for example, at Nok, Jenne-Jeno, and Daboya—date from the last centuries B.C. By about A.D. 100 they were being certainly replicated in eastern Africa (with Kenyan "Kaole Ware" among the evidence for this), thence spreading southward to reach, by about A.D. 300, as far as the Transvaal of modern South Africa. The bulk of continental Africa, in other words, had moved from a Stone Age into an Iron Age at least one thousand years before our comparative date of 1600. And this Iron Age, by then, had passed through perceptible stages of socioeconomic development, while its leading cultures had long ceased, in any meaningful sense, to be primitive cultures.

A third component in development consisted in the social relations of production by which these inventions and adaptations were deployed. The subject is as large as it is controversial, and cannot here be more than sketched. Essentially, it takes us back to all those lines of political evolution that produced the kings and kingships, or their equivalents, which our early European travelers admired. Here one may merely note, perhaps, that the basic advance came with conquest of the means of settlement and the production of a food surplus that could support divisions of labor, and, with these, the growth of non-food-producing activities, whether in a material dimension with blacksmiths, weavers, boat builders, and so on, or, in a political dimension, with shrine priests, oracle-diviners, secular rulers and their henchmen, all of whom and their kind combined to promote what humanity has recognized as civilization.

At this point our "thinking back" must allow for great changes of scale between "then and now." An average African ironsmith, working with his furnace of ant-heap earth and his bellows, could produce no more than a handful of hoe blades in several days of work; as likely as not, he would then abandon his furnace and wait until another round of smithing was required. The work was slow and arduous, but "the important conclusion is that iron was produced in quantities large enough to satisfy the local markets, and that its quality was often of quite high standard" (Kjekshus, p. 91). Changes of scale were similarly slow, though faster in western Africa after 1550 when European sea trade could deliver the raw material of iron and copper in the shape of bars and bowls, and thus provide smiths and sculptors with relatively large supplies of metal for the embellishment of royal palaces and the like. Even so, no present evidence suggests that a shortage of available metals held back the further evolution of Iron Age structures, or of the trading networks that could support them. This might indeed have become the case if the nature of European contact had been such as to begin to encourage early forms of industrial transition instead, as was actually going to happen later, of making any such transition absolutely impossible.

VI

WHATEVER WAS GOING TO HAPPEN LATER—AND THE CHANGE WOULD BE enormous—up to about 1650 the general nature of European contact was to encourage a mutually profitable partnership which rested, emphatically, on a mutually accepted equality of power. Generally, the Africa found by Europeans seemed to them to possess, along with much mystery and strangeness of behavior, a productive capacity that was in most ways not greatly different from their own, save notably in respect of firearms and long-distance shipping. For many years, as one example of this, Europeans continued to buy fast-dyed West African textiles, for sale in Europe, that were superior to anything Europe then produced. Even Europe's maritime skills were equaled in the Indian Ocean, where Swahili sailors and pilots shared in the Arab, Indian, and Chinese ability to sail by compass and stellar reckoning, and by ships that could make head against the wind. Indeed, it was not until Indian Ocean rigs had been assimilated by the Portuguese that the latter became able to embark, onward from the 1430s, on their great voyages of discovery. As late as 1505, when the Portuguese admiral d'Almeida sacked Kilwa and Mombasa, he could count on only two advantages apart from the element of surprise: one of these was a better ability to mount cannon on shipboard, while the other, very much a product of European history, was a far greater aggressiveness than anything then practiced in the East. These advantages proved decisive; technologically, they were scarcely wide ones.

This acceptance of an equality of power, and even of capacity, rested on a long history. Here again one needs to think back to the structural characteristics of international trade in medieval times. At least until the thirteenth century this trade was dominated by the circuits of North Africa and Muslim Spain, exploiting their markets from Morocco to China and their control of a unique gold standard based on West African supplies of the metal. The monumental mosques and walls of old Cairo remain, even today, the outward and visible sign of that old dominion. Only in the thirteenth century could West European exports begin to reach a volume and value capable of paying for the import of African gold. True enough, Castilians in Toledo and Normans in Sicily had made earlier attempts at minting new gold currencies. But these had done nothing, as Marc Bloch pointed out long ago, to change the monetary map. "The real revolution," Bloch observed in 1933, "came when the European countries which until that moment in the High Middle Ages had minted nothing, officially, except silver, returned to gold" (Bloch, p. 189).

Genoa and Florence opened the new chapter in 1252, with Perugia, Lucca, and Milan following with various gold coins until, in 1284, the ducats of Venice appeared upon the scene. After that, as everyone knows, brilliant development rapidly took shape. Yet it needs to be remembered that this monetary and financial revolution always depended on imports of the African metal; even Spanish imports from the Americas could not sustain it. And this remained the situation for long after. European development continued to depend on African producers, but, in contrast with later times, the relationship was one of mutual acceptance of equality, as may be seen—and how convincingly!—in the portraits of Africans in Europe that were painted by Velázquez, Rembrandt, and other masters.

Just how great was this European dependence, and how penetrating its consequences, is shown repeatedly in the history of the sixteenth century—perhaps never more persuasively than in Spain's imperial reliance on Italian bankers for an exchange of American silver for African gold, given that Spain's troops in the Netherlands, as Fernand Braudel has explained, insisted on being paid in gold that Spain could not supply from her own resources (Braudel, I, pp. 448ff). The men of those days were acutely aware, even if we have forgotten it, that it was an African partnership in trade—whether between the galleys of Venice or Genoa and the markets of Barbary, or the caravels of Portugal and the markets of Guinea—that opened the gate to new forms of economic expansion.

Not surprisingly, the fact and meaning of this partnership entered profoundly into the culture of the times, a point to which I will return. Only after the middle of the seventeenth century, with a tremendous expansion in the purchase of African captives for enslavement in the Americas, did the old concept of equality begin to vanish. That slave trade, of course, was another kind of partnership: between "kings, rich men and prime merchants," as was remarked in the 1680s; but now it was one that supposed, on the European side, and morally was bound to suppose, a natural African inferiority. Now, increasingly, Africans came to be seen as mere savages whom it was legitimate and even laudable to enslave, whereas the enslavement of Europeans, by this time, had become an abomination. With this new attitude we have entered the period of modern racism; and the colonial conquests, accompanied by the same instrumental justifications of a "natural white superiority," will follow in due and dismal course.

Yet the effective gap in technological capacity, as between Africans and Europeans, could nonetheless remain narrow. There are some startling fragments of evidence from a little-studied subject. In 1818, for example, a German mining engineer published in Weimar a memoir of years spent in the great mining province of Brazil, the Minas Geráis. "The Captaincy of the Minas Geráis," he wrote, "seems to have been the last in which the use of iron ore and the extraction from it of iron was learned from African slaves" (von Eschwege, I, p. 234); and he went on to describe the smelting methods he had seen in use until about 1800, chiefly by small furnaces with a bellows-induced draft, the typical method of tropical Africa. Only after 1800, in other words, did mining entrepreneurs in Brazil become dissatisfied with a technology imported from Africa (together with the skilled African labor to use it), and move over, gradually, to an entirely new technology now available from Europe. Could there be a more illuminating demonstration of the great divide thrust through the world by the growth and impact of industrial capitalism?

VII

CLEARLY, THERE IS MORE TO SAY. A REAL AND WIDE DIFFERENCE IN TECHNO-logical capacity, if largely still potential, existed between the leading polities of Europe around 1600 and those of Africa, and this was a differ-ence already pregnant with future consequences. Although it had little cultural influence, as yet, on the ways in which Europeans conceived their relationship to Africans, we need to take it into account. For the differ-ence was to weigh heavily, even tragically, in the balance of all that unfolded later.

However fast the minds of European orthodoxy might still be chained to myth and fantasy, the sixteenth century saw Europe, or at any rate some parts of Europe, already far along the road of technological initia-tive and scientific inquiry. The last year of that century, precisely 1600, might see Bruno at the stake and Galileo awaiting persecution, but the technological advances of the Late Middle Ages were nonetheless achiev-ing their irreversible effect. It had required five hundred years for the humble waterwheel to arrive in Britain, during the ninth century, from nearby France, but the pace since then had enormously quickened. And when industrialism appeared at last upon the scene, initially in England around 1775, all the necessary inventions came rapidly—and, as it were, logically—to hand.

Hindsight can see all this, and that the trends of 1600 were bound to carry Europe into an incomparable lead through new technology and science. But we should also remember, when setting out to measure the realities of the Euro-African relationship before the onset of the modern age, that remarkably few saw it at the time, even if they were not among the crowd who gathered to watch the blasphemous Bruno burning at a divinely punitive stake. And they saw it all the less because the actual gap in technological capacity remained small or insignificant so far as everyday life was concerned. Soon after 1500 we find the king of Spain sending mining equipment to Hispaniola, yet nearly three centuries later the miners of Brazil are still using the mining equipment of Africa. In that same period the king of Benin feels rich enough to embellish his palace with splendid bronze plaques in high relief, but no smith or sculptor in Europe is working to a higher standard then.

Only the habits and attitudes induced in Europeans by the Atlantic slave trade and American slavery can explain the coexistence of this actual near-equality of effective technology with, at the same time, a deepening European conviction of "natural superiority," such as became widespread after 1700. Later, of course, the immense achievements of the industrial revolution would provide an everyday demonstration of the superiority of European power. By 1900 the difference would be enormous and would be used as an easy justification for every dispossession of Africans, who, as the ideologists of a new European imperialism would brashly affirm, had "invented nothing."

The reasons why industrial capitalism developed in Western Europe long before it developed elsewhere cannot be rehearsed here. Only in recent years, by contrast, has the study of African economic history begun to free itself from the constricting orthodoxies of the colonial period, when it could be held that no such history was to be found or that, if any were discoverable, it must be of the crudest kind. We see now that the understanding of economic realities in vast African regions, such as these had developed by the sixteenth century, demands an analysis of modes and relations of production and exchange whose evolution was long and complex. Broadly, however, it may be no great oversimplification if we say that leading regions of Africa—for example, the western and southeastern regions—were still in the process of realizing the full potentials that remained available to them within socioeconomic and cultural structures whose erection had begun, long before, with the deployment of technological components such as I have discussed earlier in this essay. Those potentials continued to induce organizational and productive developments: the further growth of regional economies; the spread of various forms of money-of-account; and the opening of new sources of wealth or avenues of trade. But they induced no technological revolution.

Why, for example, did countries south of the Sahara see no adoption of the wheel? The simple answer is that necessity is the mother of adoption as well as of invention. Much more than two thousand years ago the trans-Saharan trade, however small in value then, was conducted by men with wheeled carts and donkeys or horses; and this we know full well from graffiti they left behind them on surfaces of rock along their principal north-south trails. So we may take it for granted that no few West Africans became aware of the wheel in times of remote antiquity. It remains just as sure that no West Africans adopted the wheel, and there need be no mystery why this was so. Like the Berbers of the great desert, they preferred to use the camel as soon as the camel became available— probably coming from the valley of the Nile in middle Roman times— because the camel, in their circumstances, was superior to the wheel as a means of transport. Farther south, in the forest zone where camels were unhandy and where, in any case, tsetse flies made their breeding and even their survival more than difficult, head-porterage could have no economic rival, and indeed it still often has no such rival save for four-wheel-geared trucks or cars. The horse, by contrast, was welcomed and rapidly developed in the savannahs, notably for the cavalry of kings, and was used even in the forest zones for ceremonial or luxurious purposes. At any rate, by 1400 the import of equine breeding stock southward across the Sahara had become a valuable item of long-distance trade.

The history of metallic currencies teaches the same lesson: here as elsewhere, innovations were accepted and developed only where they could find a social application. Although the standard gold coins of medieval Islam were minted from African gold in North African cities such as Sijilmasa, they continued to have little or no currency south of the desert. There it was found sufficient to use weights of gold dust adjusted to the values of the trans-Saharan trade, and chiefly to the mitcal (the notional weight of a dinar) and its lesser values; otherwise moneys of account were adequate to trade above the level of intervillage barter. True, the leading Swahili city-ports opened their own mints soon after A.D. 1000; but these mints produced no more than copper coins and some silver coins. Although the gold of the inland country passed through the hands of the merchants of Kilwa, those entrepreneurs struck no gold coins—at least no single specimen has yet been found. Just as instructively, very few gold coins of non-African minting have come to light in these city-ports.

The Swahili cities were rich and powerful, as their ruins and records amply testify, but their phase of development still required no more than base-metal currencies or none at all; while the inland polities of the

Zimbabwe Culture, great producers of copper and gold, struck no coins of any kind, and their principal money of account for transactions large in value seems to have consisted of copper ingots. These east-central economies, one sees, were largely comparable with those of western Africa: they were mercantile economies rooted into modes and relations of production which were still held firmly, for the most part, within structures of family lineage and tribute. Any transition of these structures would have to depend upon a demand for change; and this was a demand that either was weak or was contained within ingenious adjustment to new needs. The evolution of new forms of exchange during the West African slave-trading period before 1800 displays this from another angle. Here the coastal partnership called for agreement on terms of sale and purchase. This agreement was found in the famous "trade ounce" along the Guinea coast or in the "India piece" farther south; but it was still not found in coins or ratings of purely monetary value.

European traders would have thought a coin-based standard of exchange convenient to their requirements. That being impossible, they and their African partners evolved a complex system of ratings according to the bargained value of leading items of trade. On the European side the "trade ounce" consisted of an assemblage of goods—guns, gunpowder, iron and copper bars, alcohol in bottles, rolls of manufactured cotton—that was reckoned to be worth double the purchasing power of an ounce of gold in western Europe, this 100 percent "markup" being justified by costs and risks. On the African side the same "ounce" consisted of the assumed value, at the point of trade in West Africa, of a different assemblage in which human captives were the most valuable item. The trading trick on either side consisted, by argument or fraud, in getting more for one's "ounce" than the other partner wished to concede. However clumsy and time-consuming such transactions might be, they proved an adequate means of relating two economies, in Europe and Africa, that were by now increasingly remote from each other.

Much more could be added without changing the essential picture. After 1600 it was not simply that progress in Europe called in no way for the progress of its overseas suppliers: it was also, increasingly, that the progress of Europe called for the enclosure of those suppliers within a system of European domination, itself increasingly supported by assumptions of inherent European superiority. Yet to the Europeans of 1600 the reckoning of profit and loss had no such systemic implications. They had no need to assume and assert that distant peoples were naturally inferior, and therefore ripe for enclosure within a system of spoliation. I should like to emphasize the point in concluding this brief essay in comparative history, for it is a point of altogether comprehensive importance in measuring the cultural relationship that governed the Euro-African connection in those times that heralded, however blindly or unintentionally, the later onset of outright conquest and dispossession.

Writing of West Africa in 1610, with the worst of the wars of religion still to be endured, an Ultzheimer could well enough find a Protestant audience willing to accept that the pomp of a "Devil-worshiping" king of Benin might be comparable with that of the "great enemy in Rome." Yet, however deplorable any such comparison would then seem to a Catholic audience, cultural factors of a racist nature will have had no part in the reasons why. Outside the promptings of an age-old xenophobia or the superstitions of provincialism, no such cultural factors, as yet, entered into the question. Only a few years earlier, Shakespeare had dramatized this truth in his tragedy of *Othello*, written between 1602 and 1604.

Later generations have often seen Othello as the victim of Venetian racism, or more exactly of English Elizabethan racism. That has been a misinterpretation, because no such racism yet existed. The play is motivated by quite other feelings and prejudices which were, indeed, acutely alive for Elizabethan playgoers: by resentment of strangers, by rivalry for careers, by plots of the mean against the great or of the cowardly against the brave. Listen to the judgment offered by an outstanding Caribbean political thinker of our own time, the Trinidadian C. L. R. James, whose understanding of what is racism and what is not can be scarcely called into question:

> I say with the fullest confidence that you could strike out every single reference to [Othello's] black skin and the play would be essentially the same. Othello's trouble is that he is an outsider. He is not a Venetian. He is a military bureaucrat, a technician, hired to fight for Venice, a foreign country. The Senate has no consciousness whatever of his color. That is a startling fact but true. They haven't to make allowances for it. It simply has no place in their minds (James, p. 141).

And James goes on to insist with a wealth of critical perception, and I am sure wisely, that Othello's person—his being and significance—is not to be seen in that great captain's magnificence but in his limitations, no matter how otherwise extraordinary the man may be. "He is a soldier and sees everything and everybody in military terms—duty first, and when duty fails it must be paid for in military terms, that is to say, by death." Desdemona must die because she has failed in her duty; and then Othello

himself, censured by the Senate, his commanders, must do the same.
Thereupon he kills himself to words that once again rehearse the essence
of his character and standpoint:

> *Speak of me as I am; nothing extenuate*
> *Nor set down aught in malice . . .*
> *And say besides that in Aleppo once*
> *Where a malignant and a turban'd Turk*
> *Beat a Venetian and traduc'd the state*
> *I took by the throat the circumciséd dog*
> *And smote him*—thus.

It is a world far distant from us now in which the natural equalities of
humankind were still the ground of everyday acceptance and behavior.
Sure enough, that ground was already beginning to shift and slide toward
an assertion of natural inequalities among peoples, even if the shift and
slide are one of those transitions never fully perceived, let alone explained, till after they are made. Working within the structures of development were all those drives that would crystallize in the expansion of
Europe and Europe's eventual subjection of the peoples of Africa and of
many more. By 1750 the forced migration of millions of African captives
sold into American slavery will approach its peak. By fifty years later the
English will be well advanced into their industrial revolution. By 1831,
along with others, Hegel will duly offer—and as though it were a statement of the merely obvious—his summary dismissal of Africans from
having any conceivable claim to civilized achievement of any kind whatever:

> The Negro exhibits the natural man in his completely wild and
> untamed state. We must lay aside all thought of reverence and
> morality—all that we call feeling—if we would rightly comprehend
> him: there is nothing harmonious with humanity to be found in this
> type of character. . . . [Africa] is no historical part of the world; it has
> no movement or development to show.

And after that dismissal, as the new imperialist decades open and demand
their moral legitimation for committing in Africa—rampant ravage and
invasion—what no right-minded European could think it legitimate to
commit in Europe, there is need only to embellish and enlarge a corresponding mythology of natural white supremacy over blacks incapable of
"movement or development." And this will duly reach its full-blown

arrogance above all in Victorian England, with the pseudoscientific rav-
ings of vulgar Darwinists at home and of explorers such as Burton and
Baker abroad.

All this, in the sixteenth century, was still to come. Yet even then, as
we probe back into that time, we come up against the initiation of
tremendous contrasts. Let me conclude with one of them, on this occasion
from the archives of old Scotland and old Spain. Early in 1506 a Scottish
vessel, probably a privateer come home from preying on the Portuguese
and Spanish ocean trade, lands "a black lady" in a Scottish port. News of
her exotic distinction is quick to reach the court of King James IV, and
the Scottish king proceeds to organize a ceremonial jousting, in Edinburgh, of all knights, whether from near or far, who may wish and be able
to compete. The honors of that brave day are given to "the black lady":
she presides as its ceremonial sovereign over the brilliant jousting, with
King James himself in the lists, and afterward she is installed as a luminary
of the Scottish court. That is one scene.

Another opens only four years later. The Spanish imperial government
issues its first orders regulating the transport of captured Africans directly
from Africa for sale as slaves in the Americas. Branded like beasts but
treated worse than cattle, millions will duly follow. I think that anyone
who ponders on the contrast of those two scenes, as an old era gives way
to a new, may well pause in amazement, and breathless with the shock of
their clash of values.

RESCUING AFRICA'S HISTORY

IN OFFERING WHAT IS HERE ESSENTIALLY A WRITER'S CONTRIBUTION TO the solving of certain major problems of form in writing African history, I stand with some assurance on the belief that history, whether or not it be a branch of science, is certainly a branch of literature. Not the least of our problems, after all, is that of ordering an already large but rapidly growing body of material into an acceptably readable framework; after several efforts of various kinds it now seems to me that this simply cannot be done without the aid of some broad scheme of periodization. For otherwise, without this aid, one is forced either to plod from region to region, more or less confusingly and repetitively, or else to abandon all hope of providing a continental view of the African past: one is obliged, in short, to abandon the hope of writing precisely that kind of regionally integrated history which seems increasingly possible, useful, and imposed by the facts. In what follows, accordingly, I propose a scheme of periodization which seems to me both sufficient to meet the facts—or, rather, to enable the facts to be met—and to enable us to advance through our material phase by phase, detaching the general movement of history as it unfolds, relating one region to another (or noting the reasons for a lack of relationship), and helpfully pausing at a few clear "points of continental change."

The question of periodization has been discussed before. It was argued,

This essay was originally delivered in 1965 as a lecture at the University of California at Los Angeles and Berkeley. Published as Occasional Paper No. 1, November 1965, entitled "Can We Write African History?" by the African Studies Center, University of California, Los Angeles. Reprinted with permission.

for example, at the Fourth Seminar of the International African Institute in 1961. Although no new solutions were proposed there, the assembled historians found the application to Africa of familiar European periods—antiquity, the Middle Ages, and so forth—of little or no value, although they were generally at one in thinking that such tentative terms as had appeared in previous years—Pre-Islamic, Period of the Great Discoveries, Period of the Slave Trade, to mention only three—belonged to the colonial past when history in Africa was considered possible, or at any rate desirable, only from a non-African standpoint. Failing any new proposals, the distinguished editors of the Seminar Proceedings fell back gracefully, if, as one may think, a trifle cautiously, upon the agreeable formula that unanimity in this delicate matter of periodization would be surely reached one fine day by "the wisdom of men struggling for the triumph of truth."[1]

This left the question pretty much where it had been before. Yet the question has become a good deal more pressing since then, for the simple reason that the problems of writing coherent African history, narrative history, have since then become a good deal greater, and this for two reasons: first, from the continued and continuing accumulation of new interpretations, facts, and probable facts; and, second, from the need to fit these not solely into their local or regional setting, but also into a wider continental framework. And so it becomes increasingly obvious from a practical point of view—in this respect, from a writer's point of view—that no lucid or meaningful approach to this towering mass of material is any longer feasible without the help of a system of interpretive periods, even if this system has to be revised, as no doubt it will be, by the larger wisdom of the future. And why, indeed, be afraid of interpretation? "The attempt to distinguish periods in history is a mark of advanced and mature historical thought, not afraid to interpret facts instead of merely ascertaining them."[2] When R. G. Collingwood wrote those words some thirty years ago, nobody was thinking very much, if they were thinking at all, about the possibility of writing African history. Today we have a different situation. Today the only real question in this matter is whether or not we are sufficiently far advanced as to justify attempting the step toward "advanced and mature historical thought." How far, in other words, can we now write African history—as distinct from accumulating facts and listing hypotheses? What follows here is nothing very original, but rather an attempt to consider these questions in the light of recent experiments, including, if I may, some of my own.

I

THE STARTING POINT IS THAT THE CONDITION OF AFRICAN HISTORY NOW yields a picture of long, continuous, and broadly definable movement from one phase of sociopolitical relationships to another; and that this picture is generally valid, if with many partial modifications, for every large region of the continent. Thirty years ago, or even less, this kind of statement would have seemed perfectly absurd. Our predecessors generally saw nothing in the African past that was remotely like this. Whenever they cared to look, which was seldom enough, all they could discern was stagnation quickened only by the advent of European contact and conquest. Characteristic of their attitude was that of Hugh Edward Egerton, sometime professor of colonial history at Oxford. "What had happened" with the coming of the Europeans, Egerton believed (and in believing it he was anything but eccentric), was "the introduction of order into blank, uninteresting, brutal barbarism."[3] Sir Reginald Coupland, eminent teacher of colonial history at the same university somewhat later, thought the same. African history, he expounded, had begun in the middle of the nineteenth century. Before then there had been nothing, or nothing worthy of attention. The "main body of the Africans . . . had stayed, for untold centuries, sunk in barbarism . . . stagnant, neither going forward nor going back."[4] There is no need here to comment further on such views; later learning has effectively disposed of them. What has been less noticed, perhaps, is that the picture we are now getting is not merely one of sociopolitical movement over a long period of time—something which might have been inferred in any case, even without new facts—but, much more interestingly, one of definable phases of growth: not only process, in short, but also progress.

Regional periodization has already gone quite far. In Kushite studies, for example, the marked contrast in political and cultural organization and content between Napatan and Meroitic Kush, noted early in the twentieth century, is now modified and further explained by the introduction of a number of subperiods for each of them. Thus W. Y. Adams has lately proposed three main subperiods for Napatan Kush, and has underlined the cultural change and advance which began with what he has called the Meroitic renaissance in the fourth century B.C.[5] He has likewise given us a tentative periodization for Christian Nubia.[6] Much the same kind of sharper definition is becoming available for Axumite origins and growth in the wake of the French archaeological discoveries of the

1950s.[7] Westward through the northern Sahara and littoral the growth of Berber Bronze Age culture is now seen to have held a place of special importance not only in itself, but also in relation to the origins and early development of the trans-Saharan caravan trade of western Phoenicia and, in later Iron Age times, of Roman Africa as well.[8]

Southward across the Sahara the beginnings of an Iron Age some two thousand years ago are fixed, with reasonable certitude, as marking the foundation of new types of social system which spread and enclosed more and more peoples not only of the grassland country, but also of the rain-forest regions and the plateau lands beyond. For some of these it is already possible to detect phases of growth in terms of greater centralization of political power: the forming of state bureaucracies, the adoption of literacy, and the elaboration of more effective techniques of commodity production and exchange. And all this, we may note, is increasingly the case not merely with the familiar cases, such as those of Mali and Songhay, but also with other systems where the written documentation is either negligible or altogether lacking. At the historians' seminar mentioned above, M. G. Smith, for example, was able to devote a paper to "an outline of Hausa development during the 'Dark Age of Hausaland' which may be said to end with the fifteenth century," while he could conclude by showing how reforms such as those of Muhamad Rumfa of Kano (1463–99) introduced "a medieval society of city-states."[9] Even for the interior of a territory as obscure and apparently baffling in its historical outline as the Ivory Coast, Yves Person on the same occasion could offer a broad periodization from the fourteenth century, linking this to the whole development of central Guinea, to the foundation of the Bono and Dagomba states, to the opening of new trade routes between the central forest area and the markets of the middle Niger, and, foreshadowed by all this, to the subsequent emergence of a most powerful state system, that of Asante, in a region which was now of great potential wealth and power.[10]

In other regions, it has been much the same, though with varying degrees of clarity and certainty. The historical states of the Congo Basin may now be seen to have developed from a few main centers of sociopolitical growth. In Uganda we have imposing if as yet largely unexplained archaeological evidence for Iron Age systems of the same general period, as well as unusually good oral tradition for different and more centralized states during a later period. Recent excavation by H. Neville Chittick along the East Coast has begun to yield a sound chronological framework after the twelfth century for city-states such as Kilwa. Farther south the archaeologists have again led the way with a periodized scheme of Iron Age development for the stone-building cultures of the central plateau and even for the lands to the south of the Limpopo. And Desmond Clark, opening a still wider perspective, has told us that "in another decade it is certain that a firm chronology will have become available" for the "history of the spread of Negroid and Bantu culture into the subcontinent."[11]

In terms of this same wide perspective, reaching far back into an absolutely nonliterate past, the linguists likewise have new and interesting things to say. They appear to be finding more and more reason to emphasize what R. G. Armstrong has lately called "the immense antiquity of West African languages and therefore of West African culture"—a statement which need not, of course, be limited to West Africa—and to emphasize the profound unities which seem to underlie the cultures of the greater part of the continent.[12]

II

AS A FURTHER ARGUMENT FOR SOME AGREEMENT ON PERIODIZATION AT THIS stage, there is the fact that many scholars now seem agreed that the old and rigid dividing line between what was considered to be history and what otherwise belonged to prehistory should be abandoned as obscuring more than it can possibly reveal. Here too one may see an evolution of thought. When they first began challenging the widespread notion that history began with the coming of the Europeans, Africanists were still pretty much on the defensive. Knowing that they must rely largely on nonliterate evidence, they tended to speak not of history but of ethnohistory, inviting us to enter, as it were, a sort of antechamber of the subject, an antechamber that was under the same roof as history itself, but was not really endowed with the same historical status or equipped with as good a kind of historical furniture. This understandably defensive approach was abandoned by the historians at Dakar in 1961. Yet the real coup de grâce, it seems to me, was delivered not by a historian, but by an anthropologist, and as long ago as 1950. Then it was that E. E. Evans-Pritchard, in a celebrated Marett Lecture, declared that "social anthropology is a kind of historiography," and that "social anthropologists can provide the historian of the future with some of his best records . . . and they can shed on history, by their discovery of latent structural forms, the light of universals."[13] He carried this Collingwood-like pronouncement a good deal further in 1961 by agreeing with F. W. Maitland's dictum that "anthropology must choose between being history and being nothing," duly qualifying this with a dictum of his own that "history must choose between being social anthropology or being nothing."[14] The writing of history, in other words, could only be the outcome of a creative combina-tion of all those disciplines which can reveal the process and the progress of human society since the earliest times, and can therefore build for any given generation what Carr has described as "a coherent relation between past and future,"[15] or display, as Africans may be more inclined to see it, the true community and continuity of man within his threefold condition of ancestor, man alive, and babe as yet unborn.

But even though one rubs out the arbitrary line between prehistory and history, one still has to begin somewhere. And here the difficulty is manifestly much greater than in Europe. The literacy of the Greeks offered a pleasantly helpful starting point for European history. But once you accept that literacy in itself is no adequate guide to social develop-ment—to the stuff of history—where do you begin in Africa? The very fact that nearly all books of general African history make at least a bow in the direction of Stone Age origins reflects the fluidity of a situation where there seems no good reason, once the test of written documents is given up, why history should not go back if it can to those little furry creatures, the Australopithecines, who seem to have been so much more ingenious than we thought they were, a point of view extremely well and authoritatively illustrated only the other day when the *Journal of African History* published a survey by Desmond Clark of the "prehistoric origins of African culture."[16]

If the term "prehistory" is to go the way of "ethnohistory"—and this is what seems to be happening—there remains the general plan of period-ization already in use or evolution by the prehistorians, a plan that does in fact yield the two desiderata necessary for historical periodization: process and progress, or sociocultural movement by reference to the inherent but ceaselessly changing relationship between material culture and social organization. This, of course, lies outside my argument here; I bring it in only as a prelude to arguing that, having accepted this kind of plan (however presently obscured by the jungle of its terminology) as an organic part of history, it can become relatively easy to fit subsequent phases into an extension and cultural enlargement of the same kind of plan. From the late Neolithic, that is to say, we pass into metal-using cultures which, partly but essentially because they *are* metal using, become progressively more and more different, definably different, from their Stone Age predecessors. We pass, in short, into an age of increasing social production, a production which leads for the first time to a surplus of food and other goods, a surplus which cumulatively promotes a whole series of new departures associated in one form or another with metal-working and metal-using, departures which include an early stratification of societies into rulers and ruled, the emergence of primitive state systems, the projection of kings into gods, the crystallization of craftsman castes, the early growth of production for exchange, trade in these commodities, and, generally, the routing of African peoples onto that particular course of social movement which has continued through the centuries to the present day.

With all this, it seems evident that future histories of Africa must begin with at least some account of the origins of *Homo sapiens* and his diversification, and pass from there to that sinuous complex of development associated with the shift to Mesolithic and Neolithic cultures in the valley of the Nile and the green Sahara; with the emergence of dynastic Egypt and its history; with the Saharan diaspora as the Makalian Wet phase comes to an end after about 2000 B.C.; with the Bronze Age of the Berbers; with the growth of Kush, Axum, and comparable "post-Egyptian" cultures; and with the Neolithic in the western and central Sudan. But for Africa south of the Sahara, or at any rate south of the Sudan, the crucial point of change clearly occurs with the earliest metal-using cultures—effectively, iron-using cultures—about two thousand years ago; and it is with this shift that another main period can be seen to begin. The using and making of iron tools and weapons emerge with remarkable rapidity in one region after another, opening up new land, carrying Bantu-speaking and other peoples into a vast unfurling of new populations, pushing cultivation and stock raising far into the southland, generally laying foundations for all those phases of change which historians now increasingly reveal. Even so, just where and at what approximate date can the starting point of this Iron Age be most helpfully placed? Perhaps the best answer to this may turn out to be the reign of Nastasen of Kush (335–315 B.C. by Hintze's dating);[17] for it is with Nastasen that the Meroitic renaissance may be said to begin, or at any rate to get into its stride. Kush becomes a distinctively non-Egyptian system and culture. It develops its own alphabet and cursive script, extends its international trade, and, what matters most of all in this connection, builds a large iron-making industry.

Then we have several transitional cultures to the west and south. Of these, the most revealing, in its evidence for western Africa, is at present that of the Nok Culture of the Niger-Benue confluence region. Another carbon date has lately confirmed the view that iron making began here around 250 B.C., and it may be supposed with some confidence that traces of other such early "siderolithic" cultures will be found in this wide region.* Comparable transitional cultures appear well established in the southern Congo Basin and across the central plateau as far south as the Limpopo within another five hundred years or less. And by the end of the first millennium, if not before, early Iron Age cultures have spread beyond the Limpopo into the northern and central parts of modern South Africa, as well as far to the east and west.[18]

By the eighth century or thereabout, we have clear evidence, in several large regions, of socioeconomic growth associated with the emergence of early state systems which already possess a growing if still marginal interest in commodity production and exchange. The gold traders of the western Sudan are identified by North Africans as belonging to the powerful state we now call Ancient Ghana. A probably Bantu speaking polity in Katanga is producing copper on no mean scale, and trading in it as well. And then, with the middle of the tenth century, we have al-Masudi's celebrated description of the kingdom of the Waqlimi somewhere around the lower Zambezi Basin, while the gold trade with the Indian Ocean traders has undoubtedly begun. Within something like a thousand years, that is to say, the greater part of this vast and varied continent has passed from Late Stone Age cultures to farming and metal-using systems which contain within themselves the seeds of very fruitful growth.

III

IF WE CAN ACCEPT AN EARLY IRON AGE BEGINNING WITH MEROITIC KUSH in the fourth century B.C., where should we draw the next big line? Where should we mark the transition to mature Iron Age cultures; to all those systems and polities which signal the flowering and full realization of the potentials of growth inherent in the seeds of Early Iron Age development? There will never be, one feels, any more exact answer to this than to a similar question directed at the beginning of the European Middle Ages. But do we need an exact answer? All we need, surely, is a date, an approximate date, which can notify the onset of another broad phase of significant change in a sufficiently large number of regions. This looks something like A.D. 1000.

Not, admittedly, if we apply it to North Africa. So far as the Muslim

---

*And this, of course, is what has happened with more and wider excavation.

systems of North Africa are concerned, there seems no good reason for picking on the years around A.D. 1000 as particularly meaningful. True enough, we have the coming of the Bani Hilal devastations around 1050, but these affect only the eastern and central Maghrib; Morocco, by contrast, acquires a new extension and deepening of Muslim culture with the almost contemporary rise of the Almoravid reformers, and this is carried still further by the Almohads, who do not end their dynasty until 1289. Nor is it sensible to think of the Christian kingdoms of the eastern Sudan, which reach their zenith in the eleventh century, as belonging to an Early Iron Age; and one can think of other such difficulties in the way of making this date a "line of pause."

All the same, elsewhere on the continent—and precisely in the nonliterate sub-Saharan regions where the movement of history remains most difficult to fix—this terminal line of about A.D. 1000 does offer some advantages. By this time there are at least two large Iron Age systems in the western Sudan, Ghana and Kanem-Borno, whose organization may reasonably be said to have passed beyond the phase of primitive experiment. There are several large market centers or incipient cities, such as Awdaghost, Gao, and probably Kumbi, where techniques of trading exchange are relatively advanced, and may even be connected with early credit systems. And, as we may safely infer from what was to happen next, there is also a number, perhaps quite a large number, of smaller systems poised on the brink of vigorous development. Kangaba is one of these; Tekrur is another. To this period, likewise, there may possibly be attributed some notable trends such as the spread of Mande and Hausa systems out of their respective homelands to west and east of the middle Niger region; moreover, linked with all this, there will have been the emergence of the earliest Yoruba polities. For some of these new systems, Islam now begins to grow attractive as an ideology for central government and for providing new techniques for long-range trade. At the outset of the twelfth century, as the tombstones show, the kings of Gao have accepted Islam at least as one of their state religions, while tradition gives 1086 as the first Muslim king of Kanem-Borno. The early twelfth century similarly brings a new stone-building culture into existence on the southern plateau between the Zambezi and the Limpopo, while other evidence of various kinds, though often rather fragile, indicates that many small Iron Age polities are now established in the Rift Valley highlands of the east. Along the East Coast, at the same time, city-states like Kilwa have become important in the expanding network of the Indian Ocean trade. Writing in the mid–twelfth century, al-Idrisi hears that Javanese sailors regularly visit the southeastern coast of Africa and carry its iron to India.[19] The influence of long-range trade on the development, if not on the formation, of a number of important states is already clear.

If the term "Early Iron Age," at least for sub-Saharan Africa, may be defined as the period of emergence and establishment of metalworking, agriculture, and associated adaptation to new forms of community life and government, then it does seem reasonable to bring this Early Iron Age to an end around A.D. 1000. If we do so, however, it becomes clear that this Early Iron Age is not immediately or even quickly followed by anything that resembles a mature development of its sociopolitical potentialities. There follows, on the contrary, an intermediate period of about three centuries before we get a much greater extension of Iron Age structures.

IV

THIS INTERMEDIATE PERIOD AFTER A.D. 1000 VARIES IN LENGTH. FOR THE western Sudan, there is a time of confusion after the collapse of the Ghana system, involving a number of wars of succession between contending rivals, before the firm grip of Mali, under Sundiata and Mansa Musa, takes hold at the end of the thirteenth and beginning of the fourteenth centuries. When it does take hold, however, Mali appears to display a notable advance on Ghana. I say "appears" because pitifully little is known of twelfth-century Ghana; yet Mali of the fourteenth century is undoubtedly a much more successful and coherent—and even, to some extent, bureaucratic—effort at enclosing a wide area of the western Sudan within a single system of revenue and centralized power. The mere fact, at least in al-Omari's hearsay, that Musa used literate clerks makes only one piece of evidence to suggest that Islam has now begun to have its sophisticating effect on the towns where the kings rule, even though the everyday life of the peasants has changed but little. One suspects, however, that the everyday life of the peasants has changed a good deal: by all the signs, there is a considerable extension of tribute or servile labor—the "wageless labor" of a precash economy—and a correspondingly greater surplus for kings and city folk who know how to secure and organize this labor. The history of the Muslim states has to a large extent become the history of city governments which have learned how to exploit peasant labor power and to defend their exploitation by armed force. Elsewhere, there are comparable changes. Toward 1400, for example, the Mossi states emerge under their early warrior chiefs. In the Akan country the gold trade begins to be organized and extended by new methods: Bono comes into being, and the Dyula traders from the northeast establish themselves at Begho so as to link this trade with Jenne and other entrepôts of the middle Niger. A new line of rulers appears in Yorubaland. Benin acquires a fully historical dynasty of kings and grows more powerful.

All this, and much else, reveals a greatly different situation from the period around A.D. 1000. From about 1300 onward, this new situation continues to evolve: there is the steady movement into more tightly organized forms of state structure, the growth in Muslim areas of literate bureaucracies, and the gradual emergence of long-service armies as rulers come increasingly to rely upon their Muslim townsmen and upon their capacity to impose tribute services and to mobilize labor power, increasingly employing for these purposes a corps of soldiers who stand outside the traditional lineage loyalties of old. Large regions are increasingly linked by commercial and political ties in a way that is much more systematic than before. One good example is the Karanga empire of the Monomotapa. Emerging in the fourteenth century, this empire was clearly established by reference to principles and motives that are comparable to those of the Sudanese imperial systems: typologically they belong together, although the impact of Islam remains insignificant in the south. For, just as the empires of the western Sudan had a major interest in extending their control over a wide area of tribute and production for exchange, depending for their outlets on the Berber traders of the north, so did the Karanga and their neighbors have a major interest in a similarly large area of tribute and production for exchange, relying for their outlets on the Muslim Swahili traders—the "Moors" of the Portuguese records—of the southeastern seaboard.

Our Early Iron Age, then, begins about 350 B.C. and comes to an end about A.D. 1000, being followed by an intermediate period of some three centuries which form the prelude or first phase of a Mature Iron Age that will carry African society to its peak of "pre-European" development. If this seems reasonable—and I am conscious, of course, of the need for a closer definition of a kind that must remain impossible within the limits of a brief statement—where does the next dividing line occur? Here we are on less controversial ground. Most practitioners seem to agree that A.D. 1600 marks some kind of turning point in the history of the African past.

This is not to say that Iron Age structures characteristic of Africa everywhere realize their inherent potentials of growth by 1600, nor that the following years witness only the decline of "classical structures" until, with the 1950s, Africa can at least break through colonial doors toward a total reconstruction.

This African "Middle Ages"—this Mature Iron Age, as I should prefer to call it—comes to an end around 1600. There now begins an equally long period, essentially an age of transition, which must itself be subdivided into a number of lesser periods. These include, for example, the post-Songhay reorganization of power in the central and western regions of the western Sudan; the Muslim revival movement; the growth of new polities in Guinea, such as Oyo, Abomey, and Asante; in East Africa, the partial revival of the Swahili cities and then the extension and crises of the coastal slave trade; European encroachment along the seaboard in the seventeenth century; conquest and the colonial period; and, lastly, the present phase of postcolonial reconstruction. The actual "point of change," if any such neat moment of chronological break can be sensibly extracted from a process so very complex, occurs at different times in different places. For the western Sudan it falls in 1591 with the Songhay disaster at Tondibi and Moroccan conquest. For the Guinea seaboard it comes a little later with the tremendous expansion of the Atlantic slave trade. For the East Coast it strikes as early as 1498, with the arrival of da Gama and the years of ruin that immediately follow. For North Africa, less identifiable than elsewhere, this "point of change" may lie with the Ottoman advances of the early and middle sixteenth century; for southernmost Africa it can be fixed as late as 1652, when van Riebeeck goes fatefully ashore on the Cape of Good Hope. Yet 1600 seems a reasonable compromise among these regional dates.

V

FROM ABOUT 1600, THEN, A NEW SITUATION BEGINS TO UNFOLD. IT IS ANYthing but simple, and yet it seems to be concerned with two principal trends.

First, there is the continued growth and evolution of a large number, perhaps a very large number, of political systems; but for a long time—indeed, with a few notable exceptions, right up till colonial times—this growth and evolution take place predominantly within the framework of existing structures: within the framework, that is, of Iron Age subsistence economies modified marginally by production for exchange. There are many revolutions, but they always fail to change the basic order of society; more exactly, they are not revolutions, but reforms or attempts at reform. In the western Sudan, for example, the fall of the Songhay system is followed by the revolt of the peasants against the towns. The servile peoples throw off their tribute obligations. The Muslim traders and rulers fail in strength and influence. There comes the rise of pagan peasant systems such as those of Segu and Kaarta, already prefigured, indeed, by the overthrow of the Soninke Muslims of Tekrur in the middle of the sixteenth century.

Yet these peasant pagan systems may be seen, if we follow the same regional example a little further, to march the same road as their predecessors. They too adapt to urban life, go in for trade, reforge the old caravan links, and settle themselves into another variant of the old "city-empire" structure. And this recurs in still another form. After 1725, with the formation of the imamate of Futa Jallon, there opens the long and vivid period of Muslim revival. Here the intention of "going back to the past" is frankly avowed. "In their search for the ideal society and the just ruler," as Charles Smith has written, "they looked back to a previous golden age in the history of the dar al-Islam, and their aim was to re-create in the western Sudan the society of the Rightly-Guided Caliphate."[20] In this, of course, they and those whom they inspired were embraced by an illusion: they looked back to a "just society" whose real strength had lain precisely in a deepening social stratification which presupposed and reinforced the great privilege of rulers over ruled, rich over poor, and strong over weak. In another way, the new systems of the Forest Belt were likewise, in their essence, a repetition of the past—or, rather, an evolution from the basis of the past: though immensely more powerful and impressively successful, Asante can reasonably be seen as Bono writ large, while the Fon system in Dahomey, even if it does introduce new elements of rule and order, is little different in kind from the Yoruba empire of Oyo. In short, there is important and intelligent elaboration and internal growth, and there is a great and interesting variation of basic structure; but there is no essentially new departure.

Yet new departures were greatly needed now. For after 1600 there is a second trend, and it is this second trend, more and more insistently, which supplies the factor of disturbance, the factor of transition. Often hard to isolate, it is constantly at work, subtly and indirectly eating at the foundations of established order and nagging at the certainties of accepted tradition. Iron Age Africa wrestles with its problems. New patterns are forged. New kinds of leaders appear. New imperatives are faced. Yet Iron Age Africa falls more and more behind a Euro-American world that is now moving rapidly into an age of science, mechanical invention, and

early industrialism. No doubt, as S. J. Patel has argued,[21] the actual
difference in average standards of living does not greatly widen; what
undoubtedly does widen, and widen enormously, is the potential of
economic and technological growth. During this age of transition, the
opening impacts of a widening power differential between Africa and
Europe may be small and local, but they ruthlessly expand and spread. If
they can be seen to begin with the Portuguese ravages along the East
Coast or in Angola during the sixteenth century, or with the rise of the
Niger Delta city-states in the seventeenth, they gradually impinge on
other regions. Late in the eighteenth century, the Atlantic trade has
become a major shaping factor along much of the western littoral, while,
with the nineteenth century, it seems not too much to say that the greater
part of Africa is plunged ever more deeply into crisis, a crisis that comes
partly from the incapacity of Iron Age ideologies and modes of action to
cope with the problems of future growth, and partly from the pressures
of European action. Applied though they often are by men of outstanding
courage and intelligence, the old solutions will no longer work.

My point here, briefly, is that after about 1600 the greater part of Africa
moves out of its customary certainties and modes of organization into a
long transitional grapple with the challenges and problems of adjustment
posed by what we may call modern society. During the nineteenth century this rises to a power and violence whose impact may be seen on
many sides. It may be seen, for example, in the starting and the spread of
the East Coast slave trade or in the ending of the West Coast slave trade.
It may be seen in the wars of wandering of southeastern Africa, in the
Yoruba conflicts of succession after the evacuation of Old Oyo, or in the
harsh and weary battles of the western Sudan. It may be seen in the steady
encroachment of Europeans along the seaboard as well as in their final
invasion and conquest. Upon all this there follows a prolonged interlude
of destructive subjection and foreign occupation whose main achievement was not to carry Africa into a new world, for any such service lay
beyond its purpose or capacity, but merely to complete the dismantlement of the old. And what we are witnessing today, in all its inevitably
contradictory questioning and confusion, is the last great phase in this
often tumultuous and always dramatic age of transition: the attempt by
one means or another, under one guise or another, to establish African
society upon the foundations of industry and science, to place Africans
upon a footing of manifest equality with all their fellow men, and to finish,
once and for all, with the ideological servitudes of our racialist past.

AFRICANISM AND ITS MEANINGS

I

THE WORD "AFRICANISM" ITSELF IS OLD, AND OVER A PROLONGED period has possessed different but more or less consecutive meanings. Its earliest known use in English referred in 1641 to "the Africanisms" of the early Church fathers, and had to do, as in other contemporary usage, with scriptural exegesis. This meaning persisted until at least late in the nineteenth century; an 1882 dictionary of Christian biography is thus found explaining that the principles affirmed by Origen correct "the Africanism which, since the time of Augustine, has dominated Western theology." By then the word was also being used by European travelers, though rarely, to label African cultural features taken to be unusually exotic; and this meaning acquired a brief currency in North America when describing the linguistic "Africanisms" of black slaves.

New and again various meanings began to emerge by the end of the nineteenth century. By 1900, Africanism reappears as Pan-Africanism, derived from the need for a substantive of "Pan-African," then being adjectivally applied to the idea and program of an envisioned continental unity. The term will also persist and develop in this sense. Increasingly heard after about 1920, one of the new meanings refers to the study of Africa by "Africanists," another neologism; and this meaning will have a long and fruitful evolution. A further meaning had brief usage in the 1950s, as when Lord Hailey, in the 1957 revision of his survey of 1938, oddly

This essay originally appeared in 1991, written for the *Enciclopedia della Scienze Sociali*, published by the Instituto della Enciclopedia Italiana, Rome. Reprinted with permission.

advised the use of "Africanism" for "nationalism" in an African context. But the concept of a humanist study of Africa, as of the idea of a continental unity, would thereafter carry the whole sense of the word which, however, has been increasingly overtaken by the name for a person, an Africanist, and the fruits of his or her work. A further meaning of Africanist, rather than Africanism, has lately emerged in the black politics of South Africa, as someone who rejects political cooperation with whites in the black struggle against racism; this meaning may very well prove ephemeral.

Lord Hailey, the distinguished British imperial administrator, in 1957 had some justification for equating Africanism with nationalism in Africa, since this nationalism has proved inseparable from that whole range of ideas and inspirations joined in the drive to transform African colonies into nation-states, and hence to bring about a new evaluation of their cultures and sociologies. But the early evolution of the term can in practice be followed only through the history of the ideas and inspirations of Pan-Africanism. The latter was born in North America and the Caribbean, not in Africa itself, and in its early phases could better be called Pan-Negroism or Pan-Blackism. Yet the early Pan-Africanists were concerned to claim for the blacks of Africa, as well as of the Americas, the same real equality of human value with other peoples, which was precisely what the culture of enslavement and imperialism had denied to all black peoples. And this, in turn, was to energize the development of modern African studies, of Africanism in its currently largest meaning.

The trends of thought and attitude which led to Africanism in an older meaning, today still current and of some importance, may be traced to remote conceptions of a continent peculiar to itself and therefore, in an ideal or mystical sense, unified within itself—the Africa of antiquity from which came "always something new." Such conceptions had survived all through the centuries since the first teachings of the historians of classical Greece. The latter had affirmed that "the land of the blacks" had fathered the civilization of pharaonic Egypt, and that Egypt, in turn, had helped to father the civilization of Greece—succintly, as Herodotus put it in ca. 450 B.C., "the names of nearly all the gods came to Greece from Egypt." This was a view which remained in wide European acceptance until the early years of the nineteenth century, more exactly the years after 1830, when it was abruptly displaced by the rise of imperialist ideologies of racist hierarchy, within which the blacks were reduced to a low and even subhuman level of capacity. Hegel's famous teaching of 1830, affirming that "Africa is no historical part of the world, having no movement or development to exhibit, and still involved in the condition of mere nature" coincided, as by unconscious logic, with that very moment when France was invading Algeria; that is, when Europeans began doing to Africans, in the way of large-scale dispossession, what no extant morality could justify Europeans doing to other Europeans. The blacks, by consequent agreement, could not be admitted to be fully human; nor, by extension of the same attitude, could Africa have produced a civilization of its own.

Among those protesting this racism of conquest, there were some in Europe and America who, as well as denying its assertions, reached toward mystical or messianic forecasts of Africa's "special destiny." Thus a poem by James Montgomery written in 1841:

> *Unutterable mysteries of fate*
> *Involve, O Africa, thy future state ...*
> *Dim through the night of these tempestuous years*
> *A Sabbath dawn o'er Africa appears:*
> *Then shall her neck from Europe's yoke be freed,*
> *And healing arts to hideous arms succeed ...*

Few outside Africa, much less inside the continent, will have glimpsed any such vision. But the note now continued to be struck in the transatlantic diaspora, and was heard with greater vehemence toward the end of the century with the spread in Africa itself of Ethiopianist and other separatist Christian communities, holding out the prophecy that God would endow the land of the blacks (conceived of as "Ethiopia," although not meaning the country which we now know by that name) with blessings which it specially deserved.

These ideas at the root of what was to become Pan-Africanism were essentially chiliastic. They looked forward to a divine dispensation whereby Africa should be redeemed from miseries judged, not unreasonably, to be of recent and external origin. Nineteenth-century mythologies of the "noble savage" added their own romantic overtones. But after the colonial conquests and the installation of colonial systems, all such notions began to acquire a much more political guise. This "Africa of special destinies," very much the Africa of the diaspora and of Western-educated groups in western and southern Africa, was seen as needing the united strength of its peoples if justice and therefore equality were to become possible. By 1920, for example, the four colonies of British West Africa (Nigeria, Gold Coast, Sierra Leone, Gambia) saw the launching of the National Council of British West Africa on a program, nebulous and yet significant, designed to prepare the way for a four-colony federation as a step toward some form of continental unity. In a characteristic statement of 1921 its president, the Gold Coast lawyer J. E. Casely Hayford, affirmed that "as there is an international feeling among all white men, among all brown men, among all yellow men, so must there be an international feeling among all black folk."

The theme acquired momentum. Writing to the black American thinker W. E. B. Du Bois in 1929, the (western) Sudanese Tiémoko Garan Kouyaté explained that the aim of a newly formed League Against Imperialism, active in London and Paris, was no less than the "political, economic, moral and intellectual emancipation of the whole Negro race," with the eventual program of "setting up in Africa a great Negro state." Already by that time, in other words, there was in motion a synthesis of previous ideas and attitudes concerning a "special destiny"; and it was out of this movement that the political concept of Africanism, as a framework for agitation and the beacon for a liberated future, would gradually be born.

These were the beliefs which enabled their devotees to set aside all evidence concerning the real and actual diversities and conflicts of Africa's constituent peoples. Their own experience had taught them, often bitterly, that what joined them inseparably together, the blackness of their skins, was far more potent in the world they knew than anything which might divide them. And this meaning of Africanism, as a shield for the persecuted and a guerdon of hope, would in fact persist against every discouragement or defeat. It would gain, as Africanist scholarship proceeded, from every new perception of the underlying unities of Africa's cultural development through history, whether in terms of Africa's religious or sociopolitical structures, as well as from the almost universal African experience of colonial dispossession. It would give impetus to the early nationalists of the 1950s, and lead thereafter to the founding of the Organization of African Unity in 1963. Pan-Africanism may thus be seen as one of the creative ideologies of the twentieth century.

∴

II

PAN-AFRICANISM IN THIS GUISE TOOK SHAPE AND GAINED NOTICE THROUGH a series of conferences between 1900 and 1945. Organized by a barrister of Trinidad, Henry Sylvester-Williams, the first of these meetings assembled in London in 1900 with some thirty-two black persons of whom only four appear to have been born in Africa. Its deliberations created a

Pan-African Association and a journal, *Pan-African,* of which only one issue seems to have been published. The meeting's wind-up address "to the nations of the world" was written by an African-American spokesman and historian who was to become a figure of worldwide fame, William Edward Burghardt Du Bois (1868–1963), and opened with a passage that was to make its mark. "The problem of the twentieth century," it declared, "is the problem of the color-line, the question of how far differences of race . . . will hereafter be made the basis of denying to over half the world the right of sharing to their utmost ability the opportunities and privileges of modern civilization."

Du Bois called a second conference in Paris in 1919, hoping to exploit the occasion of the (First World War) Peace Conference for publicity on the movement's aims. These were now summarized in a resolution of the approximately fifty-seven participants as being the protection and advancement of "the natives of Africa and the peoples of African descent"; but this call for justice, insofar as it was as much as heard by the Great Powers then assembled in Paris, was in no way heeded. A third conference followed in London and Brussels during 1921, and a fourth congress ending in Lisbon in 1923 reiterated the demand "that black folk be treated as men. We can see no other road to peace and progress."

Meanwhile, another and distinctive strand of the same movement emerged with the Universal Negro Improvement Association (UNIA) and its International Convention of the Negro Peoples of the World, held in New York in 1920. Powered by the flamboyant Marcus Moziah Garvey (1887–1940, of Jamaican origin), it raised the slogan of "Africa for the Africans, those at home and those abroad," and for some years gained a popular audience in Africa as well as in the Americas. As Garvey's natural rival in character as in policy, Du Bois persisted with the holding of another Pan-African Congress in New York in 1927, but the onward drive of colonialism, then at full flood, drowned any influence it might have had.

The last of the Pan-African congresses, held in Manchester, England, during October 1945 and attended by ninety delegates and other persons, broke entirely new ground. It carried Pan-Africanism, for the first time but decisively, from the black diaspora to the continental source. Du Bois was present, as were leading Caribbean activists such as George Padmore (1902–59, of Guyanese origin) and the always remarkable C. L. R. James (1901–91, of Trinidadian origin), but so were leading political figures from Africa, including two who were to become presidents of independent republics: Kwame Nkrumah (1909–72) from the Gold Coast (Ghana after 1956), and Jomo Kenyatta (ca. 1889–1978) from Kenya, as well as the veteran Sierra Leonian nationalist I. T. A. Wallace-Johnson (1895–1965), and a strong Nigerian presence. With this congress in Manchester, the demand for anticolonial independence and nationalism merged clearly for the first time: "We are determined to be free," the delegates affirmed. "If the Western world is still determined to rule Mankind by force, then Africans, as a last resort, may have to appeal to force in the effort to achieve freedom."

I I I

THE ESTABLISHMENT OF STABLE COLONIAL SYSTEMS IN THE YEARS BETWEEN the two world wars had meanwhile begun to produce a less crudely dismissive attitude on the part of the conquerors toward the peoples they had enclosed within imperial frontiers. This owed its inspiration partly to the requirements of scientific study, chiefly then in the field of social anthropology, and partly to a small but influential group of senior colonial officials of various empires; in these men a long contact with African peoples had stimulated an interest in, and even a respect for, indigenous cultures. Thanks to them, in large measure, the study of Africa's history and sociopolitical institutions began to seem possible and even, conceivably, desirable.

Important in forwarding or confirming these influences was the foundation in London of an International African Institute in 1927, financed generously by the Rockefeller Foundation and under the administrative guidance of the British Colonial Office. In 1928 its journal *Africa* was created in order to provide a home for discussion of and reporting on research into social-anthropological, linguistic, and some other aspects of African cultures which now, with the needs of colonial administration, clearly demanded better understanding. A corresponding initiative in France was launched in 1931 by the ethnologist Marcel Griaule. This was the Société des Africanistes, soon to be followed, in 1936, by the foundation in Dakar of the Institut Français de l'Afrique Noire (IFAN) which would achieve major scholarly importance. Parallel concerns were evident in Belgium, but the serious study of Africa was cut short in Italy, Portugal, and Germany by the rise of fascism in its various forms of racist prejudice.

But generally, when the consequences of the Second World War opened a perspective of decolonization early in the 1950s, the ground for scientific study of Africa was well marked and to some extent cleared for cultivation. A first step toward incorporating Africanist studies in a university curriculum in the United States came in 1947 with the institution of an interdisciplinary program of such studies at Northwestern University, and comparable centers of Africanist studies soon followed at Boston University and elsewhere. The same process was vigorously initiated at the University of London, where the existing school of oriental studies became a school of African as well as oriental studies. Pioneering works conceived from an Africa-centered rather than a Europe-centered approach were soon among the fruits of these departures. Now too these began to be the work of African scholars; mention in this respect should be made of the Nigerian K. Onwuka Dike's study of the trade and politics of the Niger Delta, in which Africanism received, as it were, its first modern historiographical recognition from a native of the continent.

By the 1950s, in short, the familiar Europe-centered approach to African research was greatly undermined. Understandably, this undermining was largely the work of historians, since it was above all in the field of history that African culture had been denied all development in the past. The project they embraced was not to attempt to argue, futilely, that European and African history stood upon the same ground, but to affirm that the study of African history could rely upon values and sources which were, or could be, as valid as those that underpinned the study of European history. With the gathering of all these strands of interest and effort, Africanism may be seen to have reached maturity, whether in concept or project, with the First International Congress of Africanists in 1962.

IV

AS WE HAVE SEEN, AFRICANISTS HAD EXISTED FOR SEVERAL DECADES BEFORE this congress met in Accra, the capital of Ghana, between December 11 and 18, 1962. Those earlier Africanists had generally defined themselves as students of a range of disciplines that were humanist rather than scientific, it being held that the latter could not be purely African in content or nature, whereas humanist disciplines might well be concerned with phenomena peculiar to Africa. More loosely, they had simply wished to mark off territories and subjects from their more confident and, at that time, somewhat patronizing colleagues, the Orientalists. The latter had enjoyed academic respect for many decades, as had their periodical congresses, and had taken under their wing any studies concerned, broadly, with non-European cultures east of the Atlantic. Orientalism had thus become an established category of scholarship, even while the substantive word was as little used as its later companion, Africanism, was going to be.

By the 1960s, however, it was widely felt that Africanism must cease to be a mere branch of Orientalism. For with more than twenty colonies now advanced to independence, and the general status of Africa and its cultures considerably improved in the minds of those who made world opinion, the quest for exact or at least for reliable knowledge of Africa had become a powerful impetus in Europe and North America, and now in Africa itself. The Africanists, it was felt, should now make their own bid for independence.

This conviction was well projected at the opening plenary session of the Accra congress by the veteran Africanist of the United States, the late Professor Melville J. Herskovits, long a driving influence behind North American scholarly concerns with Africa. He insisted that "African studies must no longer remain as an adjunct of Orientalist studies. Historically, our presence there represented a survival, in the strict sense of the word [since] the designation 'Orientalist' was used for all humanistic researches not concerned with European or Europe-derived cultures, or with the aboriginal societies of the Americas—which are carried on by Americanists—and of the islands of the Pacific. It was the same complex of ideas that made for the opposition of 'East' and 'West,' something that today in discussions of the relationship of African peoples with those of the northern hemisphere, renders this common phraseology a geographical absurdity."

Herskovits went on to emphasize what was to be a principal concern in the proceedings of the congress: that Africanism, as matters now stood, must liberate itself from the Eurocentric attitudes and approaches of the colonial period. "The fact of the matter," he continued, "is that the Africanist section of the Orientalists for most of its existence limited its interest to North Africa and Ethiopia. Except for the Egyptologists, it was concerned chiefly with African linguistics, and neither the history, languages nor cultures of sub-Saharan Africa figures until the Moscow meeting [of Orientalists] in 1960." Now that the vast majority of all Africans, with advancing decolonization, were or were about to become the subjects of their own history and culture, rather than the objects of colonial patronage or domination, the relegation of African studies to a dependency on Orientalist studies could no longer be accepted.

This had in fact been evident for some time. Much had been achieved even in the few years since the end of the Second World War. "New concepts of African resources, human and material, were being forged,"

Herskovits pointed out. "The African was now an active factor in the direction of his political destinies"; even while, as one may comment, many Europeans and Americans had yet to assimilate the fact. In scholarly research, African scholars had become colleagues, as never before, and this had greatly quickened the movement of research in Africa itself. "Before the Second World War," the same speaker reminded his audience, "a number of Africans had gone overseas for higher education, usually to the universities of their own metropole, or, in a few cases, of the United States and Canada; but this was a fraction of the hundreds and then thousands that later poured into the universities and technical schools of England and France, the colleges and universities of the United States, and, with the passage of time, of other Western European countries, of Czechoslovakia and East Germany and the Soviet Union, of Israel, India and China."

The international status of this modern Africanism was signaled by the congress in the membership of its organizing committee. With Herskovits himself, there was the late Professor Ivan Potekhine of the Africa Institute of the USSR Academy of Sciences, leading Africanists from Britain and Belgium, and delegates and observers from many other countries with, for example, the prominent Ethiopianist Enrico Cerulli representing Italy. Yet the outstanding characteristic of this newly independent Africanism was formed at the congress by its African location, chairmanship, and composition.

It met in Accra with the energetic support of the government of Ghana, now in its sixth year of independence. Its opening session was addressed by President Nkrumah, who took care to link the congress to its indigenous tradition. To that end he recalled the words of a Zulu (South African) student in New York, fifty-seven years earlier, when receiving an award from Columbia University. "The African," Isaka Seme had said in 1906, "already recognizes his anomalous position and desires a change. The brighter day is rising upon Africa. Already I seem to see her chains dissolved. . . . The regeneration of Africa means that a new and unique civilization is soon to be added to the world." It might be visionary and was certainly far too optimistic; yet in Nkrumah's mouth, addressing the assembled Africanists of 1962, it could seem appropriate to the tasks ahead.

The congress was chaired by the Nigerian historian K. Onwuka Dike, then vice-chancellor of black Africa's senior university, that of Ibadan. He was flanked by African scholars whose names were becoming known or who would shortly lead their chosen field. Dike argued the need for a broadening of the scope of African studies. "In my view," he said, "no subject vital to the understanding of our culture or necessary to the

development of our resources, human and material, should be excluded
from our discussions. Thus the delegates from my own country reflect
this wider approach to African studies and include a bio-chemist, a
paediatrician, historians, agriculturalists, economists and political scientists"; and he expressed the hope that the congress would "try and bridge
the traditional division between the humanities and the pure sciences."

Behind these sentiments there lay an acceptance of the need to break
finally from the underlying mental atmosphere, and its stereotypes, which
had for so long hampered approaches to the realities of the continent. If
Africanism—but, again, one should stress that the substantive was rarely
used—was to perform its proper task, then it must dismiss, once more in
Dike's words when speaking of history, the "outmoded and untenable
myths" which "continued to dominate the interpretation of the African
past": as, for example, the then widely current "Hamitic hypothesis,"
according to which "Negroes have made no contribution to human progress," and that the civilizations of Africa have been the civilizations of the
"Hamites." The *locus classicus* of this since exploded "theory" may be
found in C. G. Seligman, writing in 1930, but was still much canvassed at
the time of the congress. Seligman believed that "it would not be very
wide of the mark to say that the history of Africa south of the Sahara is
no more than the story of the permeation through the ages, in different
degrees and at various times, of the Negro and Bushman aborigines by
Hamitic blood and culture," it being *sous entendu* that this Hamitic influence, however evidently mysterious, had originated outside Africa and
probably in Europe. Such myths, affirmed Dike, must now be finally set
aside; and he mentioned others of the same nature.

The same "very Africanist" theme was touched on in another way by
the Nigerian psychologist T. Adeoye Lambo, whose clinical successes in
Nigeria had already won him international recognition. His lecture, entitled "Important Areas of Ignorance and Doubt in the Psychology of the
African," is another indicator of the intellectual climate in which this
liberating Africanism came to maturity. He expressed dissatisfaction with
the intellectual poverty of recent work by a wide range of non-African
researchers, while, like other African contributors, emphasizing at the
same time that the study of Africa must become a fully international
concern. Some recent exponents of psychological and sociological research on African subjects, he claimed, "have produced works which, at
their worst"—and he mentioned several by name—"are but glorified
pseudo-scientific novels or anecdotes with manifest ethnocentricity; at
their best"—and he mentioned several more—"they are abridged ency-
clopaedias of misleading information . . . containing so many obvious gaps

and inconsistencies that they can no longer be seriously presented as valid observations of scientific merit." Western civilization, he suggested, showed an immense interest in exotic cultural and social institutions, and their psychological implications, while displaying a profound ignorance of the same subject. A British study of only eleven years earlier, he recalled, had been able to reach the remarkable conclusion that "normal African mentality closely resembles the mentality of a section of the European population which is commonly entitled psychopathic or socio-pathic," while "the resemblance of the leukotomized European patient to the primitive African is, in many places, complete." A true social science must clear away all such absurd fantasies. To that end Lambo pleaded for more and better research across the whole spectrum of psychological and social research; and in this he struck one of the keynotes of the congress. The following years would see a response to it.

V

SUCH CONDEMNATION OF ETHNOCENTRIC MYTHS AND SUPERSTITIONS WAS A powerful element in the development of modern Africanism. If this should seem strangely irrelevant in these closing years of the twentieth century, that is no doubt because the mentality of the colonial period has begun to be remote. In between, too, lies the engendering of a mentality very different from that of the colonial period, but also, beyond that, a vast quantity of new scholarly work and nonracist education.

Within a few years of the Africanists' congress of 1962, the humanist and scientific study of the continent had expanded enormously in all the major countries of the world, and in no small number of the minor countries. This was above all the case in Africa itself. There the handful of secondary schools and one or two university colleges which had come into colonial existence by the outset of the 1960s now multiplied rapidly and, for the most part, effectively. Their courses of study gave a large but entirely new place to Africa-centered interests. New textbooks were written for the humanities and, progressively, for the sciences as well; a large number of corresponding faculties were created. This development expanded in line with the further decolonization of the continent and, by the 1980s, had reached and more or less deeply influenced every African country, except for the Republic of South Africa where sharply racist prejudice still greatly infected the whole educational system, whether for whites or for blacks.

Outside Africa there was something of the same useful development. An advancement of Centers of African Study, as they were often known, could draw largely on official funds, whether in North America, Western Europe, or Eastern Europe and the USSR, so long as the stimulus of political and ideological rivalry—felt by governments and institutions if not by pedagogues and students—remained sharp; and this was especially the case during the decade of the 1960s. That was a period in which one may even think that Africanism outgrew itself, in that the need to assert the uniqueness and value of African cultures seemed no longer an urgent concern, whether to Africans in their demand for self-respect or to non-Africans in their effort to free themselves from racist myths. There had been, no doubt unavoidably, a certain note of defensiveness in the work of the earlier Africanists. Their Africanism, in other words, had been obliged to traverse a phase which may now be regarded, if with indulgence, as having a strongly political edge to its argument. The banality of having to respond to common external assumptions—such as that history must demonstrate lists of "kings and queens and battles"—had imposed limits which must now be transcended.

A number of methodological issues combined with growing knowledge and self-confidence to deepen and confirm this process. One of these issues concerned the nature of the sources and records of African history. It had been well understood, even in the 1950s, that the written records of Africa were richer than had been generally supposed, notably for the period which saw the rise of literacy in Arabic to the south as well as to the north of the Sahara, a rise which coincided broadly with the European medieval period. This enlightenment had come as early as the 1850s with the publication in London of the travels of Heinrich Barth and the subsequent recovery, for European use, of major historical texts such as the *Tarikh al-Sudan*, composed in Timbuktu around 1660 but for long unknown in Europe. The new Africanism hoped for more such texts, whether in Arabic or in *ajami* scripts (in which indigenous languages are written in Arabic script); and this hope was not disappointed. At the same time, attention was given to unused European sources in the archives of missionary societies, of trading corporations, and, as archives were gradually opened, of colonial administrations. Here, too, the harvest proved a rich one.

Yet it was already clear that research could not be satisfied to rely only upon written sources. It had to extend itself to whatever could be learned from oral history and tradition. What could be done with that had been demonstrated by Samuel Johnson, a Yoruba clergyman from Oyo, Nigeria, with his 1921 *History of the Yorubas from the Earliest Times*, and by an Edo chief, J. U. Egharevba, who had done the same with the oral history of the kings of the ancient city and state of Benin (not to be confused, geographically or otherwise, with the modern republic of Benin). While calling for use perhaps even more prudent than that applied to medieval European written records, these oral histories were found to throw light into many obscure places.

What remained to be shown was that peoples without kingships, and thus without any established community of official documenters, could also yield oral records of value. To that end an effective methodology was proposed by the Belgian historian Jan Vansina, in a work of seminal importance first published in 1961. Others followed with work in the field, as has Vansina himself. Notable in this respect is a history of a Luo people, drawn largely from oral sources, which began to be published in 1967 by the Kenyan historian B. A. Ogot. Since then the examination of oral history has become a wide-ranging and fruitful addition to historical and sociological knowledge in Africa. It has greatly deepened the understanding of institutional and cultural change and evolution among nonliterate peoples.

VI

THIS AFRICANISM HAD ALWAYS TO INSIST THAT ITS SCOPE MUST COVER THE whole continent, north as well as south of the Sahara; and in this respect too there were adjustments to be made. Generally, the study of Africa north of the Sahara had been awarded to Islamic and Arabist studies, to Egyptologists, or to Ethiopianists. All these had tended to see their various parts of North Africa as possessing cultures somehow isolated from other cultures in Africa, or cultures that were mere adjuncts of Asian cultures. But Africanist meditation on the interplay between cultures north and south of the great desert had produced the conviction that neither could be understood without the other. Africanism would give due weight to the non-African sources and influences of Islam and Arab culture, but it would also insist on the process of initiative and development that owed its strength and flexibility to all the peoples of the region, including those of the oases of the Sahara itself. This conviction was fueled by new studies, notably in the fields of law and institutions, which emphasized the mutual debt of peoples on either shore (*sahel*) of the desert. Africanist contributions to Berber studies, to the recovery of Islamic texts in West Africa and to a smaller but still important extent in

East Africa, as well as some notable translations of classical Arab sources, have been among the fruits of this approach. Africanism and Arabism have been able to march usefully together.

Egyptology has proved a more difficult partner. Was the Egypt of the pharaohs to be regarded as belonging to Africa? Hitherto the question has barely arisen, and in spite of the evidence of all the Greek authors of antiquity, for example Diodorus of Sicily, Egyptologists had generally answered with a curt and condescending negative: either Egypt of the pharaohs had evolved out of its own genius or had derived from the cultures of Mesopotamia; black Africa, in any case, had none but the smallest peripheral relevance. This attitude came under increasingly effective attack by the Africanism of the 1960s; and this attack, being duly repulsed, has continued, as may be seen, for example, in the second volume of the UNESCO *General History of Africa* published during the 1980s. Cooperation with the Ethiopianists has proved happier, although here too the tradition of a non-African "Ethiopianism" has by no means passed away.

Generally, students of Africa appear to have found more to unite than to divide them, however various their origins and approaches may have been. Africanist archaeology has made tremendous strides over the past twenty-five years, thanks in no small part to the application of new dating techniques for organic materials, above all by the testing of radioactivity in the carbon-14 isotope; and the findings of this archaeology have become an integral part of humanist studies. Much the same may be said of Africanist linguistics, where the work of J. H. Greenberg and others has laid foundations for a comprehensive grasp of major linguistic origins and paths of development.

Political science has combined with social anthropology to give depth and perspective to systems and structures of society and government which hitherto had been said to possess no developmental process of their own. So has the study of African law. Building on this work, T. Olawale Elias in his important book, *The Nature of African Customary Law*, published in 1956, was able to dispose of previous European assumptions that law in Africa, properly speaking, arrived with the colonial period, before which there had only been a congeries of customs that, somehow, had not been law; and other specialists have followed in his enlightening wake.

In the years since the congress of 1962, Africanism as a critical means of asserting the study of Africa as a fully legitimate aspect of the study of humankind has probably fulfilled its purpose. All that now seems to remain of it, in the field of scholarship, refers to the useful companionship of Africanists or a convenient label for their concerns. It may be, however, that the earlier political applications still have an unused potential. For while the early nationalist interest in Pan-Africanist objectives has lost its drive, even while the Organization of African Unity (founded in 1963) continues as an intergovernmental forum of discussion or, more often, of rhetoric, the underlying concept of an African unity across the whole or most of the continent has stubbornly survived. The prudent scholarship of these years has tended to reinforce the emotive claims of earlier years, notably in perceiving and portraying essential similarities of cultural and institutional development. The African peoples, in this still unfolding view, have indeed evolved forms of civilization which, while bearing comparative examination with other forms elsewhere, derive from a remote African past and are clothed in an ethos specifically African. There is much more than an intuition, in short, to argue that Africa's manifold diversities and contrasts arise from essential unities of thought and experience. In this elusive but persistent sense, Africanism may still have a purpose to complete. This purpose may be found to arise from the need, very evident in recent years, for an institutional reorganization of the territorial and political partitions imposed by the colonial period. At least in this respect, the energies of a specific Africanism may still be in demand.[1]

ANTIPATHIES

I BEGAN IN 1950 TO THINK ABOUT AFRICA AND ITS AFFAIRS, AND SET OUT a year later upon what were going to be annual travels there. These became the years of my apprenticeship, lived then as a freelance journalist with an eye to becoming, in a chosen field of Africa's history, what a generous friend, Professor David Fieldhouse at Cambridge University, has lately called a "scholar-journalist." It would be nice to think that I have succeeded in becoming that; what in any case is certain is that emerging from the steamy toils of journalism into the pleasing realms of academe was going to take, even if it were possible, a long time. The trail would be difficult, and meanwhile, in those early years (and indeed for some time after), there was the need to come to terms with what was then, stiffly guarding itself, a closed colonial Africa or, in South Africa, an all-white-ruled fortress of prejudice where independent inquiry, not to speak of critical dissent, was going to meet with reprisals both personal and professional. Though of a naturally peaceful temperament, I was going to have to be contentious, as others in my case had already found to their discomfort.

So it proved. And so I have labeled this second part "Antipathies"—not because in my apprenticeship I looked for sorry things and situations, but because these came unasked and sat upon my doorstep, or rather my typewriter, with the evident intention of staying there. In short, I set out upon my travels with a visit to South Africa; and if South Africa gets the lion's share of attention in this part, this is because the fact and ideology of racist South Africa, directly or indirectly, exercised a kind of cultural dominance in those times, perhaps hard to imagine today, over much of the colonized continent. Invited to see some of the realities of South

Africa by what was then the only trade union in the country that actively
opposed racist segregation and its consequences, the Garment Workers'
Union, whose members were women from the white as well as the black
and colored communities, I found some freelance-journalistic support to
pay the airfare and went to South Africa after a little, a very little,
preparatory reading. That might now seem small preparation for penetrating the drama of a large and complex land, and yet there was scarcely
need for more; I found that the drama stood on the surface, could be
found in every street, thundered its messages in a babel of angry voices.
So in the first place it was through the women of the Garment Workers'
Union that I was introduced to Africa at one of its sharpest areas of
contention; but Africa then took me firmly by the hand and so far (I am
happy to report) has not let me go again.

Those splendid women have been unforgettable. They had come out
of harsh rural poverty and cultural starvation. They had come together
in their union with the help of another hero, the late Solly Sachs, against
every sort of discouragement, fighting for above-wretchedness wages,
braving official scorn and contempt, raising their families in the midst of
their daily struggles, and trying all the while—especially those of them
who were of Afrikaner (Boer) origin—to clear their minds of the racist
prejudice in which they had been raised. Just what this mind clearing had
to mean was explained to me by one of their gallant Afrikaner spokesper
sons, Mrs. Johanna Cornelius, whose background was an impoverished
farm in the Transvaal. Johanna, like others of that background, had come
to the vast and sorely dangerous city of Johannesburg as a girl fleeing from
the rural hunger of which, in those days, there was much among the "poor
whites" of Afrikaner parenthood. Courage and a sterling character had
saved her from sinking in the slums of the city. She found others who
thought and fought as she did. A little before the outbreak of the Second
World War, she was already a valiant trade unionist, rough of voice but
none the worse for that. This brought her new experiences. Among these,
a very unexpected thing, was a trip to Europe at the invitation of a trade
union there, she and a handful of others.

"So I went to Europe," Johanna told me, and was suddenly brimming
with laughter. "Because when I got there, you see, they asked me if I was
a native of South Africa. A *native,* can you imagine! I burst out on them:
'Can't you see, I'm *white?*' Of course, they only meant, was I born in South
Africa? But I didn't understand that—I was still stuck in our racist ideas
according to which a black person isn't a person, she's a *native.*" The
women's union taught them differently. And this was a lesson they
learned to good purpose. In 1951, when I met Johanna and her friends in

Johannesburg, they were (and would long be forced by racist legislation to remain) unable to combine all their garment-making members in a single organization, no matter what their skin color. But they had at any rate succeeded in doing the next best thing. They had kept all their members in the same union while accepting a division into white, colored, and black sections (colored in this context meaning of mixed origin). For me, as you can easily imagine, the garment workers provided an ideal introduction to the complexities and lunacies of South African society.

More generally, at this stage of apprenticeship, I was traveling every year to one or another region of the continent. In 1952 to West Africa; in 1953 to the two Rhodesian colonies north of South Africa as well as to Swaziland (then a "High Commission Territory" within the British Commonwealth system); in 1954 to the Belgian Congo and Angola; reading all the while whatever I could find that could be useful. I was already in contention with the South African system, and in 1952 the racist government of Dr. Daniel Malan declared me a "prohibited immigrant" in that country—a prohibition which, officially at least, has so far remained in force—but I outwitted them in 1953 by insisting on going to Swaziland, not part of South Africa but reachable in those times only by land across South Africa. They had to let me in, and they were not pleased. Returning from Swaziland, I stayed in Johannesburg for a few useful days, meeting Nelson Mandela among others in his lawyer's office, until the police caught up with me. Now I will return there when they invite me; not before.

But more generally, outside South Africa, I was becoming ever more deeply impressed with the facts and implications of the colonialist dispossession of African life and thought, whether in the British or French or other colonies. Just what this all-penetrating dispossession must really mean in practice took some time to perceive and absorb. But it became fairly apparent, in general outline, as soon as one raised the question of history. I began, for myself, to raise this question in 1953, and ran at once into one of the intellectual, or rather cultural, oddities of the African situation. This "collision" came about quite simply. If Africans were going to achieve postcolonial independence—and there was some talk of this by now—they would have to be treated as people. Where, in that case, had they come from? What had they done, or not done, before the colonial invasions of the 1850s and later? What, in a word, had been their history? Officially, one was then told, there was no such thing as African history "before the coming of the whites." That was around the 1840s. Before then, the books seemed to agree with a loud chorus of white voices in Africa that Africa had possessed no history of its own development because there had been no such development: Africa had stayed, through countless forgotten centuries, in featureless stagnation, lost to every stirring of the human mind, bereft of the merest hope of self-salvation. And so on.

Now even on the face of it this seemed to me improbable. I looked around for others in Africa with whom to share my doubt, and in those times I found them, more than anywhere else, among the ranks of the archaeologists. These men and women were not, as it soon transpired, all that easy to find. They worked in remote and awkward places where any kind of transport was a rarity; and perhaps as a result of the habit of isolation in the huge wilderness of Africa, as well as by the obscurities of their scientific discipline, they tended somewhat to eccentricity, or what passed for such among nonarchaeologists. If one persisted patiently, however, they came wonderfully alive as soon as they were sure of one's scholarly intentions, and then, as I discovered, they threw wide the gates to a flood of information about Africa's lost history. And this they would do with gusts of excitement and enthusiasm. The archaeologists in those times were my best teachers. They took me to their remote sites of excavation. They sheltered me in their tents. They led me to fields of broken pottery and laid bare the secrets these could reveal. As a little later with the social anthropologists, another solitary species slowly willing to yield to a friendly voice posing questions, I was led to the splendors of archaeological and anthropological literature; and my apprenticeship—we are now in the early 1960s—seemed to be coming to an end.

Meanwhile, with all this, I came to know African people, and to feel at home with them. This was a process of self-liberation already begun in London—meeting African students who were there, sharing discussions with them, adjusting to their concerns and interests, and, soon enough, finding their friends and families during my travels in the continent. As early as 1950, we were even able to mount a little weekend conference to talk about the prospects for postcolonial liberation. The opportunities for becoming less ignorant were beginning to multiply. So these were good years, however fraught with moments of obstruction; above all, they were years of solid self-education. Here in this part I offer some journalistic fragments, rescued from a raft of others written in that time, as samples of what it was like to penetrate that closed-in world of colonial Africa, including South Africa, before beginning to get "beyond the veil."

Among my travels, after southern Africa, were the Belgian Congo (Zaire today) and Portuguese Angola, two huge countries in central and southwestern Africa where, in the 1950s, independent journalists seldom traveled and were far from welcome. Much had been written about the Belgian Congo before it became a Belgian colony in 1908, and when, before that, it had acquired a terrible notoriety as the so-called Congo Free State, where the forced collection of rubber had led to ferocious scandals and oppressions. Since then, a great deal of silence had prevailed. What was going on there, or not going on? Besides, the place was challenging in its sheer enormity of size, enclosing as it does most of the vast central basin of the continent and a wonderful variety of peoples. With much of the continent beginning to buzz with news of possible emancipations from colonial rule—and in 1954, when I went to the Belgian Congo, three years had already passed since Kwame Nkrumah won internal self-government for the Gold Coast that would become Ghana in 1957— there must surely be interesting stirrings in the Congo. Much of my book of 1955—*The African Awakening*—is concerned with what I saw and heard there in 1954; but I have to say that meeting Congolese Africans, and finding out what they thought about their future, proved very difficult. A piece I wrote in that year, offered below, tells some of the reasons why.

Then there was Angola, an even bigger question mark. About Angola there had been some excellent writing in the past, in the fairly recent past notably by Henry W. Nevinson (1856–1941), whose book *A Modern Slavery*, published initially by Harper and Brothers in 1906, remains an enduring classic of its kind. I read that work in 1949 and found in it a prime example to all who practice the craft of telling the truth about things as they happen, or at least of trying to tell it. So half a century after Nevinson wrote his harrowing book about Angola, I decided to try going there too. Being in the Katanga region of the Belgian Congo, I boarded the trans-African train at Elisabethville (now Lubumbashi), and rode it down to the Atlantic coast at Lobito, a long and boring journey which led, however, to far from boring discoveries. My last journalistic extract tells how and why.

By the outset of the 1960s I had published my first history books and had found a wide audience. In reaching this firm ground, there came the welcome of many friends and allies who stood at new gates of learning and opened these for me. In the United States, for example, it was thanks to the late James Coleman, when director of the Center of African Studies at the University of California at Los Angeles, that I was able to learn and teach for a while at that extraordinary campus on which, as it was said, "the cement never sets," even if some of the biggest new buildings were high-rise parking garages and potent laboratories. This began, for me, an

"American dimension" of study and discussion; it is one to which I owe a lot. And this leads me here to introduce the last of my offerings in this part, the fruit of a symposium at UCLA in 1967 on pluralism in Africa.

I chose to examine the colony that became Northern Rhodesia and then, in 1964, the independent republic of Zambia. It was a region of Africa that had been settled, though very sparsely, by agents and followers of the British imperial magnate Cecil Rhodes; a variety of African peoples had lived there since very ancient times. Like the Portuguese next door in Angola, but unlike the Belgians in the Congo to the north, these British agents and settlers (almost all of them were British, being mainly immigrants from South Africa) wrote rather little about the land they had taken; and so here too was clearly a place to be inquired about and examined. Practically, this had to be done almost entirely on the spot. Before first going there in 1951, I did examine what books I could find in London, and these were few. Only one book about the politics of Northern Rhodesia, it appeared, was available. This was a brief study of the work and workings of the colony's all-white legislative council; as might be expected, this said almost nothing about the "natives," and nothing at all about what the "natives" said; none of them, after all, could pass through the portals of the legislative council except as menials. But by 1951, fortunately, these "natives" were beginning to have a good deal to say among themselves about how they saw the future. Shortly thereafter, they would launch into congress-style nationalist politics, the fruits of which would lead to independence thirteen years later. So my last offering in this part is a discussion of political realities in this Northern Rhodesia which was to become Zambia; it is a paper that has retained, I think, some useful relevance to current debates about the deeper meaning of colonial dispossession.

RACE AND RESISTANCE

I

THE DAY BEFORE I LEFT JOHANNESBURG THIS TIME, A FLYING SQUAD OF police went to a beer hall in van Wielligh Street because they had "received a report that a Native there had firearms." In the process of entering the beer hall and throwing their weight around, they encountered resistance, withdrew under a pelting of stones, and opened fire. Five natives, adds the newspaper account, were taken to hospital with bullet wounds. After the brief distractions of last April's general election, the Transvaal has lost no time in getting back to normalcy.

It is normalcy with a difference. Africans and policemen have been exchanging stones and bullets for a good many years, off and on; and most whites in South Africa will think it invidious, and certainly in poor taste, to draw attention to the fact. But latterly the stones have tended to be sharper and the bullets more frequent; and the sense of a fatal dynamism in the course of events, of a flood tide leading on not to fortune but disaster, erupts through the surface of a daily life which is still—for the whites—luxurious and easygoing.

A stray visitor can see this quickly enough, because the skin that covers the inner conflicts and revolts of South African life is now very thin, and getting quickly thinner. In practice, there is little in daily life that remains outside the grasp of a legal system whose nature tends more and more to

This essay originally appeared as two separate articles in 1953 in the *New Statesman and Nation;* the first under the title "Trigger-happy Transvaal," and the second called "Resistance in South Africa." Reprinted with permission.

make a mockery of law. Every trivial fall from grace may open an offender to dire penalties. I noticed one of these the other day when glancing through a recent volume of Appeal Court records; and I give it here as a potent and reasonably typical comment on a country where legalism now tends to usurp the place of every sane and decent regulator of human behavior.

> Case of R. *v.* B. and H. (Cape Province Division) February, 1953: van Wissen J.—The accused in this case were charged with a contravention of Section One of Act 5 of 1927 as amended by Act 21 of 1950, in that accused No. 1, being a male European person, had intercourse with accused No. 2, being a non-European female person. . . . The accused both pleaded not guilty, but were found guilty by the magistrate of Wynberg and each were sentenced to four months' imprisonment with hard labour. . . .
>
> "Briefly," the learned judge continued, "the evidence adduced on behalf of the Crown was to the effect that at 12.30 on the morning of August 16 last year, Constable van Wyk, with Native Constable Sikolo, went to a tea-room called the Green Lawn Restaurant at Hout Bay. They went to a room which both claim was lit by an electric light, and they looked through the window of this room and saw the two accused having intercourse with each other. . . ."

Now the issue which was really at stake in this appeal—which failed— was not whether the law should punish fornication, nor whether the police were justified in collecting their evidence by sneaking and peeping, but whether or not the woman in the case was in fact a non-European. She was able, during appeal, to show that she was by birth a European (and the law, of course, only punishes intercourse between white and non-white); but that availed her nothing. For some time before her arrest she was shown to have been living "as a non-European"—a circumstance which caused the magistrate to rule that she was legally a non-European in spite of having two white parents, since she "appeared" to be a non-European. The Appeal Court found that the magistrate might well have moderated his penalty, but, as it was bound to do, confirmed the sentence. Your "race" in South Africa is what it seems to be, not what it is.

This matter of "race"—and the quotation marks are necessary, since in South Africa the notion of race has become identical with language difference—is nothing academic. Always corrupting and cruel, racial segregation has become ferocious in its consequences. One of the measures enacted by the last Nationalist government, and now about to be applied by the new Nationalist government, is the Group Areas Act, a measure designed to annihilate the last formal possibilities of residential integration in a country where white and nonwhite are thrown more and more closely together by economic pressures, and cannot live without each other. Even if this act is applied with the usual "tolerance" allowable in South Africa for inefficiency—or the very general recognition that many laws cannot possibly be enforced to the letter—it will mean the shifting of big urban populations from one area to another, and the loss of livelihood for many nonwhites who have managed to open shops or conduct small businesses in areas declared to be "white."

For those few whites prepared to make a stand against this rising flood of racialism, and, a fortiori, for all nonwhites, the law comes straight out of *Mein Kampf.* You are guilty under the Suppression of Communism Act if you further any of the "objects of Communism," now statutorily registered as the furtherance of "any political, industrial, social or economic change by disturbance, disorder, or unlawful acts or omissions"—a definition, as a little thought will show, which includes everything but the kitchen stove. As defense counsel have argued, this "statutory Communism" applies to any group of men protesting about anything by marching in the street without a permit (or, given the atmosphere of the lower courts, of *seeming* to march in the street), and, indeed, to the Nationalist Government itself—for passing the Separate Representation of Colored Voters Act which the Appeal Court subsequently declared to be illegal.

Most of the nonwhite leaders can now be seen only by breaking the law—by inviting them, that is, to meet you and thus attend what the law may well interpret, if it pleases, as a "gathering." Most of them are prohibited from attending any gathering of any kind; and the law leaves it to the magistrate—who is usually a crusading Nationalist—to interpret the word "gathering." African leaders like Walter Sisulu, for example, cannot enter a crowded shop, or take a haircut during the busy hours of the day, without opening themselves to the risk of arrest. This means that they can be arrested whenever it suits the police.

All this, though, is small beer when set beside the acts of last February. Designed to crush the passive-resistance movement against racial discrimination, which the nonwhite congresses had conducted with great and growing success, the Criminal Law Amendment Act and the Public Safety Act raise the furies of dictatorship to a level hitherto excelled only by Hitler. The second act makes it possible for the government to declare a state of emergency in the Union or any part of the Union at any time, and to enact emergency regulations designed to cope with almost any conceivable situation; the first act needs to be read to be believed. Two main provisions deserve quoting in full:

1. Whenever any person is convicted of an offence which is proved to have been committed by way of protest, or in support of any campaign against any law or in support of any campaign for the repeal or modification of any law, or the variation or limitation of the application or administration of any law, the court convicting him may, notwithstanding anything to the contrary in any other law contained, sentence him to

(a) a fine not exceeding three hundred pounds; or
(b) imprisonment for a period not exceeding three years; or
(c) a whipping not exceeding ten strokes; or
(d) both such fine and such imprisonment; or
(e) both such fine and such a whipping; or
(f) both such imprisonment and such a whipping.

But this is not the whole story. Supposing you simply *suggest* a protest against the pass laws and their like? The next section takes care of that:

2. Any person who

(a) in any manner whatsoever advises, encourages, incites, commands, aids or procures any other person or persons in general; or
(b) uses any language or does any act or thing calculated to cause any person or persons in general,

to commit an offence by way of protest against a law or in support of any campaign against any law . . . etc., etc. . . .

shall receive penalties set forth in Section One, except that the fine may rise to £500, and the length of imprisonment to five years (the maximum of lashes remaining generously at ten). Furthermore, you are guilty under Section Two if you solicit, accept, receive, offer, or give "any money or other article" for the purpose of assisting any campaign or act of protest involving breach of the law.

The first prosecution under this act was of a certain Arthur Matlala, an African of Johannesburg, who was prosecuted for acts allegedly committed on February 26, or six days *before* this law was gazetted by the government. He was found guilty of "incitement" (fined £50 or six months' hard labor), and guilty of soliciting money for the passive resistance campaign; sentence: one year's imprisonment and eight strokes.

Wherein lay the alleged incitement? In Matlala's possession the police found a copy of Fowler and Smit's *New History for Senior Certificate for Matriculation*. "Certain passages in the book that deal with the French Revolution had been marked in red and blue pencil. Among these were passages describing how the people of Paris had attacked the Bastille." Can you blame the magistrate, staunch defender of white civilization and Western values, for fining the man £50, with the option of six months' hard?

II

A TAXI TOOK ME DOWN JOHANNESBURG'S COMMISSIONER STREET AS FAR AS End Street. I stopped the driver at the corner, and walked along to where a little group of Indians was idling on the pavement. They stared at me as I stopped outside the office marked SURGERY. I asked for Dr. Dadoo and gave them my name; they shook their heads and turned away. A wall of suspicion shuts away the nonwhite man from the white man; and the wall is friezed with the jagged glass of evil things remembered and expected. Then I had a stroke of luck. An Indian in a long white coat, loosely buttoned, came out on the pavement. He had a pipe in one hand and with the other was fiddling in his pockets for matches: he hadn't any matches, and someone in the crowd would go and buy some for him. He gave me a hard, questioning look and suddenly relaxed, for we'd met in this city two years before. This was Yusuf Dadoo, leader of the South African Indian Congress and one of half a dozen nonwhites who have given supremely good leadership to the organization of passive resistance to racialist laws and regulations in this country.

They are marked men, hemmed around with prohibitions and restrictions so all-invading that the police, in practice, could arrest them at any time they choose. They are watched, followed, spied on, prevented from attending meetings or even gatherings of the most innocently social character, forbidden outside their houses after curfew. I am told that the African National Congress was given an office telephone with quite unprecedented speed, and that its telephone bill is never pressed for payment. Over the twenty principal leaders of the African National

Congress and the South African Indian Congress there hangs a suspended
sentence of nine months' imprisonment, automatically applicable in the
event of a second "offense."

Their nerves remain good. Few of them show any signs of flinching or
regretting the leadership they have given. There seems to be a complete
agreement and understanding between the African and Indian leaders;
and a growing cohesion with the Colored leaders from the Cape. This
solidarity was reflected throughout the months of passive resistance by
the masses of their followers; and the evidence shows that cooperation
between Africans and Indians is present in Natal just as it is certainly
present in the Cape and the Transvaal. This interracial solidarity among
the nonwhites is a new thing; and the nonwhite leaders have firm ground
for confidence. In spite of every frantic effort by the government (in this
matter backed unconditionally by the United Party, the official white
opposition party) to frustrate it, nonviolent resistance by thousands of
nonwhites in the second part of 1952 and the early weeks of 1953 was able
to achieve its main objectives—to unify the nonwhite communities in
resistance to racialism, to show that this resistance was possible, and to
educate many thousands of nonwhites, and perhaps tens of thousands as
it turned out, in ways and means of resistance.

This is clear from the unexpectedly large numbers of volunteers who
came forward from the African, Colored, and Indian communities to join
small groups who deliberately and pacifically courted arrest by breaking
one or another petty rule or regulation. Eight thousand of these volunteers were arrested. I am told that many more were available, but only the
most suited were allowed to join the groups, and only those with relatively minor family obligations. But the success of the campaign can also
be measured by the failure of the government to build up separatist
nonwhite organizations.

This failure is not for want of trying. Several of these separatist organizations now exist. Among the Africans there is Bhangu's Bantu National
Congress; among the Indians the South African Indian Organization; and
among the Coloreds the so-called Unity Movement. Bhangu is a herbalist
from Ladysmith; his Bantu National Congress, openly subsidized by the
government, is thought by reliable observers to count no more than two
or three hundred members; and his program is directed against the
African National Congress, but more especially against the Indians. He
wrote a letter to Pandit Nehru lately—it was published in Johannesburg—offering him £20 million for the repatriation to India of all South
African Indians; but even in Natal, where African feeling against Indians
has been intense in the past, he has made no headway. He has earned, if

my observations count for anything, only derision and contempt. The South African Indian Organization, another government-sponsored separatist body, is an even worse case; and, in spite of government instructions, none of its handful of members has dared to oppose the resistance campaign. Among the Coloreds, the Unity Movement consists of a group of teachers and other "intellectuals" whose inspiration appears to derive about equally from Trotsky and others.

What happens next? The restrictive proclamation of November and the Criminal Law Amendment Act and Public Safety Act of February have made it impossible to prolong a campaign of nonviolent regulation breaking by individuals and small groups, for the penalties are crushingly high. "The principle of nonviolence will remain with us," Dr. Dadoo told me, "but we shall change our tactics." Walter Sisulu, secretary-general of the African National Congress, told me the same thing.

They did not tell me what their new tactics will be; and it may be that they have yet to select them. Now that the Nationalists are back in power—and, according to Dr. Dadoo, the nonwhite organizations deliberately curbed their campaign for some time before the general election, from fear of driving whites into the Nationalist camp—they can afford to take their time. The struggle must in any case be long and painful. They have apparently learned a great deal. Nonviolence was most successful in Port Elizabeth, for instance, whence came nearly half of the 8,000 volunteers; and this seems to have derived from a better type of organization than existed in the Transvaal and elsewhere in the Cape. When the African National Congress began its part in the campaign, it had only 5,000 dues-paying members; today, according to Walter Sisulu, it has 60,000. Although four-fifths of these are probably in the towns, the last weeks of nonviolent resistance began to penetrate deeply into the Transkei and some of the bigger native reserves. When the next round starts, the nonwhite organizations will have a far firmer and broader basis among masses of people.

Will it remain nonviolent? Here one enters a more speculative field. So long as the present leaders retain control, it will: they are men of moderate, liberal, or left-wing views who are known to condemn violence on political but also on religious grounds. The influence of *satyagraha* is paramount among the Indians, and is said to be spreading fast among the Africans. But the Nationalist government has shown that there is nothing it dislikes more than *nonviolent* resistance, for its customary method of repression—violence—is then inhibited (though not by any means forgotten). The government has done its best to corrupt or intimidate the present leaders of the nonwhites; so far, it has failed in this. The influence of these leaders has probably never stood so high as it does today. In a literal sense they have been responsible for keeping the peace at a time when the government—through a notoriously provocative police force—has done its best to break it.

The government in its blindness may yet coercively deprive the nonwhites of this sane and thoughtful leadership. Obedient to its racialist doctrine, it may yet drive nonwhites to a point where anything would be better than acceptance. And it would be foolish, I suspect, to imagine that events in Kenya and in other parts of white-settler Africa will appear to South Africans (or to Indians) in the same light as they appear to others. Stray conversations with stray Africans rather give the impression that these events appear in a quite different light. However that may be—and it is exceedingly difficult for a white man here to know what nonwhite men are really thinking—there is a certainty that the Nationalist government (and the great majority of whites who, at least in racialist attitudes, support it) will have only itself to blame if things get out of hand. While stoking the fires of race hatred, this government goes about its business of reducing and if possible destroying every sound, peaceful, and progressive influence upon the nonwhites. So far, as I say, it has not succeeded; and perhaps it will never succeed. But no one should underestimate this government's lunatic determination, nor the abhorrence in which racial cooperation is held by nine whites out of ten

Abandoned to their fate by all but a handful of whites, the nonwhites have at last found strong and honest leaders. They have combined in struggle against their status of permanent inferiority. This combination is likely to prove of high importance in the history of Africa.

THE ROOTS OF
ANTIAPARTHEID

I

LIKE THE GREAT DEPRESSION OF THE 1930S, OF WHICH INDEED IT MUST BE considered something of a natural sequel, the Second World War can be seen in certain important ways as a turning point in the history of South Africa, as in that of other territories deriving from or belonging to the imperialist systems of Western Europe. But the overall consequences of the Second World War in South Africa—again, as elsewhere—were far more ambiguous. So it was that the events and developments of 1939 to 1945 immensely tightened all those economic, social, cultural, and political conflicts already on the South African scene.

These events and developments gave the English-speaking and overseas owners of South African capital and economic power a means of increasing their wealth and influence. At the same time, they offered the Afrikaans-speaking (Afrikaner) section of the white minority a first real chance of preparing a serious challenge to the English minority's predominance in manufacturing, industry, and administrative control. Carried on by governments in which the interests of the English minority were generally paramount, or were politically accepted to be such (even if with Afrikaner participation), the war nonetheless worked to produce the conditions that were to undermine that paramountcy in the political field, but also, increasingly, in the economic field as well. Reduced to a weak and divided opposition in those years, the party of extreme Afri-

This essay was originally prepared for a UNESCO symposium held in Benghazi, Libya, in November 1980.

kaner nationalism suffered severe defeats, including the arrest and internment on charges of sabotage or subversion of some of its most notable
leaders, but then emerged in 1948 with the tools of electoral victory
already to hand.

Once again it was shown, as in 1902 at the end of the Anglo-Boer War,
that the interests of English capital and commerce were ready and even
eager to concede political primacy to the ideas and attitudes of their white
rivals, provided always that the system from which they drew their wealth
was thereby guaranteed. And although the processes that were hastened
by the war gave the non-European majority—whether African, Colored,
or Asian—a new militancy and a new sense of unity, or at least of the need
for unity, seeming by 1944 to promise some relief from systemic discrimination, still the war years ended with their position prospectively worse
than before, and with full-scale apartheid only a few years ahead.

Even a brief analysis can help to explain this apparent dislocation of
cause and effect. It needs to be remembered that the Union of South
Africa, as an autonomous country and then Dominion of the British
Commonwealth, was less than thirty years old at the outset of the Second
World War. Although from the very beginning a system of planned
exploitation of nonwhite labor and land, with racism as its operative
instrument, this was still a society whose capitalist structures were far
from mature. Its ruling white minority—or rather minorities, English and
Afrikaner—possessed a political independence within the wider British
system, as well as all local powers of decision and execution; but theirs
was still a society whose structures were largely dependent on external
interests centered chiefly in London. Its economy had already moved a
long way from the condition of a purely colonial exporter of cash crops
and raw materials, as had been the case at the time of union in 1910; but
it was still economically weak and financially vulnerable.

Much of this began to change during the war years. Let us first look at
a comparison of the population censuses of 1936 and 1946. These show:

	Numbers in Thousands		Percentages of Totals	
	1936	1946	1936	1946
Whites	2,003	2,372	20.9	20.8
Africans	6,596	7,831	68.8	68.6
Coloreds	769	928	8.0	8.1
Asians	220	285	2.3	2.5

The figures seem at first sight to suggest little proportionate change. Yet
they conceal at least two significant trends. In the first place, the annual

rate of increase of the Afrikaner minority was markedly larger than that of the English-speaking minority, including immigrants from Britain. Second, although the African proportion of the whole population actually fell by one-fifth of 1 percent (always supposing, which is much, that the counting of Africans was done with accuracy), the rate of African urbanization rose steeply in these years, chiefly in the war years and more and more as the war proceeded. Thus the proportion of Africans registered as "urban" (a notably loose term but still one that we must use) had stood, in 1936, at 19 percent of the whole urban population, but was 24.3 percent by 1946, while, in absolute figures, the number of Africans living more or less permanently in towns in 1946 was rather more than half as large again as the total for 1936. Seen from another angle, the number of Africans employed in manufacturing rose by 57 percent between 1939 and 1945, or from 156,500 to 245,400; and these totals may be taken as more or less accurate ones. This flow of African workers into industry continued, so that by 1948, when the fuller effects of wartime expansion could begin to be measured, urbanized Africans accounted for 80.8 percent of unskilled employees, for 34.2 percent of semiskilled employees, and for 5.8 percent of skilled employees in all urban occupations subject to wage regulation, and, therefore, capable of yielding accessible data.

Now this, as may easily be seen, constituted a large structural change; and it is in this change that one may seek the reasons for much that happened then and since. Within the ruling ethos of racist segregation, this very marked trend toward African urban employment called for a reorganization and reinforcement of its legal and customary basis. Logically for that ethos and system, the year 1948 accordingly brought in a government vowed to the installation of a full-scale system of apartheid. Though euphemistically called "separate development," "apartheid" was and is a term better understood, in fact, by translating it as the development of the white minority at the cost of regression for the nonwhite majority. This was a structural change, in other words, which, along with parallel expansion in accumulation of capital, could lay foundations for the postwar processes whereby South Africa has developed into a markedly indigenous capitalist system, far less dependent than before, and, from the 1950s on, could evolve its own subimperialist policies toward the rest of the subcontinent. Always important to the system, the urban employment of cheap nonwhite labor and above all of African labor had become a vital element. The system now could no longer manage without more and more of that cheap urban labor (and with this, of course, I include labor in segregated mining "compounds").

There is space here to say little of the detailed consequences of this and

parallel structural changes promoted by the Second World War. Generally, however, it can be said that the effective rate of exploitation of
nonwhite labor was never lessened during the war years, but rather the
reverse, whether by means of low-wage policies, a refusal to develop
nonwhite social services, or any relief in the pass laws and other instrumental regulations. In all its essentials the existing system of segregation
held firm, and was even strengthened. When the Purified National Party
(Herenigde Nasionale Volksparty) came to power in 1948 on a program
of full-blooded apartheid, its task accordingly was in no way to install
systemic discrimination, but only to complete what already existed of that
kind, while taking additional measures to repress a growing volume of
nonwhite protest. A view that is sometimes heard, to the effect that this
pattern of apartheid is a product of the postwar years, can find no support
in the evidence. The nature of the pattern had long been clear by 1948,
just as the means of imposing it were plentiful.

II

THE UNITED PARTY, LED BY GENERAL J. B. M. HERTZOG, HAD EASILY WON
the general election of 1930, with the National Party securing only 17 seats
in a lower house of 153 seats. The fact at that time was that Hertzog's
political views were sufficiently extreme to undermine opponents in his
own Afrikaner community. True to his racist loyalties, he had revealed
obvious sympathies with Hitler and the German National Socialists (who
had taken over the government of Germany in 1933), and had welcomed
Hitler's campaign to revise the 1919 Treaty of Versailles, notably in regard
to the matter of Germany's lost African colonies. While some members
of the National Party were soon to call for the return of South-West
Africa (Namibia) to Germany, Hertzog preferred to look elsewhere, and
in 1935 was credibly reported to have suggested that Germany should be
given Liberia as a substitute. Aware by 1938 of the likelihood of world war,
he hoped to keep South Africa neutral. Events turned out otherwise.

   When war broke out early in September 1939, Hertzog found his
cabinet divided. He and five other ministers were for neutrality, but seven
others, including the very influential General J. C. Smuts, were for declar-
ing war alongside Britain. Hertzog might still have managed to maintain
his view, or at least have long delayed a declaration of war on Germany,
but unhappily for him he had called the South African parliament into
session on another issue. He was obliged to submit to a parliamentary

debate. In a session full of drama Hertzog's colleague Smuts argued the case for an immediate declaration of war and carried it by a majority of eighty votes to forty-seven. Hertzog at once resigned and Smuts formed a new government, while the former prime minister and his followers joined the opposition represented by the National Party under Dr. D. F. Malan.

Although sixty-nine years of age, Smuts thereafter dominated the political scene. Backed by a solid majority, and with his opponents split, demoralized, or under arrest for subversion, Smuts prosecuted the war with vigor while, thanks to his old connections, he at the same time achieved a place of influence on the world scene as one of Prime Minister Winston Churchill's most valued advisers. Though weak and ill-prepared, the South African armed forces (Union Defense Force or UDF) were rapidly expanded to some 137,000 men within a year of the war's declaration. Two fighting divisions were assembled and a small but useful air force. Troops were sent to help the British in their campaigns against Mussolini's armies in the Horn of Africa, thus liberating Somalia and Ethiopia, and then in North Africa. Conscription was avoided, but volunteers came forward from all communities. Some 80,000 African and 40,000 Colored volunteers served in many departments, and also on the field of battle, but were never allowed to carry arms. It was necessary to win the war but never, in Smuts's mind, at the price of admitting any racial equality among the peoples of South Africa.

The National Party, meanwhile, was sorely in crisis. Outmaneuvered by the wily Malan, Hertzog soon retired from the scene (and died in 1941). Yet Malan had other difficulties. The centenary year of the Great Trek, 1938, had witnessed the formation of the Ossewabrandwag (Ox-Wagon Sentry) as an extraparliamentary "action movement" of Afrikaners modeled more or less deliberately on the National Socialist storm troops of Germany. Notably under the leadership of J. F. J. van Rensburg, the Ossewabrandwag and smaller extremist groups developed a campaign of antiwar activity which ranged from political demonstrations to outright acts of sabotage. Malan himself was probably as pro-Nazi as his more outspoken colleagues, yet was careful to leave himself room for maneuver in case his early hopes of Nazi victory should not be realized. Others had no such prudence, at least until 1943. Whether from ideological sympathy with Nazi racism or from the calculation that a Nazi victory must carry them to power—and the two considerations were after all inseparable— these all spoke strongly for the Nazi cause. Thus B. J. Schoeman, a future cabinet minister, affirmed in November 1940 that "the whole future of Afrikanerdom is dependent upon a German victory"; while another future minister, Eric Louw, could say as late as August 1942 that "if Germany wins, Dr. Malan will have the majority, and Hitler will negotiate with the one who has the majority." A future prime minister, Dr. Hendrik Verwoerd, was found guilty in a court judgment of aiding and abetting Nazi propaganda in South Africa; and another future prime minister, B. J. Vorster, was among those arrested under wartime emergency regulations in September 1942 and held in internment until January 1944. Among other things, Vorster had told the public in 1942 that "we stand for Christian Nationalism which is an ally of National Socialism. You can call this anti-democratic principle dictatorship if you wish. In Italy it is called Fascism, in Germany German National-Socialism, and in South Africa Christian Nationalism." Such were the men who were to rule the apartheid state.

Yet the frankly racist nature of these Afrikaner National Party spokesmen, shared as it was during the Second World War by all those who were to govern South Africa after 1948, should not suggest that the party of white "moderation," the United Party, was in reality any less racist. The United Party's slogan, true enough, was "In War or Peace the United Party for a United Nation," and much was said to the same effect in party documents and manifestos. But the "United Nation" had to be all white. A *Guide to Politics for Young and Old*, issued in 1943 over the signature of the United Party's secretary-general, O. A. Oosthuisen, was careful to insist on that. "The paramount object of the United Party," said this pamphlet,

> is the development of South African national unity ... [and] we can claim to have made sufficient progress towards national unity to give us encouragement for the future: A practical demonstration is that the cabinet is composed of Afrikaans and English speaking members. The two races share the governing power of the country. ... The two races within the United Party recognize each other's distinctive cultures and inherent national sentiments.

As to the nonwhite majority who were not within the United Party, there should be moderation and common sense. In this respect

> the United Party standpoint is that, even apart from any humanitarian sentiments or sense of justice, it is only sound common sense to safeguard the rights of the natives, coloured and Asiatic people who live in the Union. The natives in particular are at least a great economic asset, and the rest have their place in our economy.

The "natives," one should perhaps explain, meant the Africans; and we have seen just what kind of an economic asset they had become by 1943. As to "safeguarding their rights," the United Party had already given an unambiguous example of what it meant by that when removing Cape Africans from the electoral roll (of the Cape Province) a few years earlier. But in case this was not enough for its readers, Oosthuizen's *Guide to Politics* hastened to add that this wish to "safeguard native rights"

> does not mean that it is our intention or policy to extend, hastily and indiscriminately, the political institutions that we have built up in many generations to native races on the same terms as apply to Europeans. . . . Our policy is gradually to extend political rights to those capable of carrying out the corresponding duties.

The Africans of the Cape, as it happened, had carried out "corresponding duties" for "many generations," and in 1936 they had suddenly been found incapable of doing so. But Oosthuizen found it unnecessary to say anything about that.

Antiracist gestures by the United Party, in short, were no more than electoral eyewash aimed at appeasing a small but useful white liberal vote in Cape Town and Johannesburg. The historical evidence can in fact reveal no difference of substance between the domestic policies of the two principal white parties. If the National Party's sounded far more severe during the Second World War, this was largely because the United Party had yet to come to grips with the threat to effective segregation presented by the wartime influx into nonwhite urban employment. When the National Party duly came to grips with that threat, and responded to it by a more severe system of segregation, the leaders of the United Party invariably found themselves in substantial agreement. Apartheid, in its various forms, was always an all-white weapon in South Africa.

III

THE HISTORY OF SOUTH AFRICA SINCE THE 1890s—WITH THE GLEN GREY Act of 1894 as the symbolic "starting point," even if the process had been already long in the making—is that of the dispossession and eventual destruction of ancient and stable rural communities, and the transformation of their peoples into the helots and servants of a white minority, whether English speaking or Afrikaner.

This process was far advanced by the onset of the Great Depression of the 1930s; and the Second World War, hauling the white economy out of that depression, carried it considerably further. Even by 1930 there had been 361,000 African laborers on white farms, but by 1946 there were as many as 568,000, with the figure still rising year by year. We have noted the sharp rise in wartime urbanization, whether of whites (chiefly rural Afrikaners) or of nonwhites, but it may be well at this point to offer the detailed proportions as set forth in a series of censuses:

URBAN POPULATIONS AS PERCENTAGES
OF VARIOUS COMMUNITIES

	Census Years				
	1904	*1921*	*1936*	*1946*	*1951*
Whites	53	55.8	65.2	74.5	78.4
Africans	13	12.5	17.3	23.7	27.2
Coloreds	46	45.8	53.9	60.9	64.7

By 1946, in absolute figures, over one-third of all Africans were more or less permanently urbanized or were working on white farms. The remaining African population was confined to that small area of the land surface of the Union—about 11 percent during the Second World War—to which the Land Act of 1913 had "allocated" them. This area had long been divided into a number of "native reserves." And here the process had just as long been one of steady impoverishment of zones, such as the Transkei and Ciskei, whose climatic and other natural advantages had traditionally assured their populations of a relatively ample standard of living. In these "reserves"—the "Bantu homelands" of the future—the general condition was recognized during the Second World War as reaching one of near-disaster because of overcrowding and erosion. It is a point worth dwelling on for a moment.

Thus the Native Mine Wages Commission of 1944 took evidence from many witnesses who dwelt on the impoverishment of the "reserves." Among these witnesses was one Dr. Smit, the chief medical officer for the Transkeian territories. Dr. Smit produced figures for seven districts which he considered to be representative of the whole "reserve." Conservatively estimating an average family as being composed of five persons, he reported that 36 percent of all families had five or more head of cattle, 20 percent had five or less, but 44 percent had no cattle at all. So that some 60 percent of all families in this supposedly flourishing Transkei, by 1944, could be reckoned as deriving negligible or no benefits from livestock on the hoof, traditionally the mainstay of this population. Such cattle as there were, added Dr. Smit, "are for the greater part undernourished, stunted, sub-economic creatures." Another witness before the same official commission, again reporting on the Transkei, computed in that same year of 1944 that a selected group of 8,000 families with arable allotments had an income of 7 shillings (about $1.50 in the exchange values of 1944) per family per month, while a second group of 10,000 families without arable allotments had only 4 shillings (about $1.00) per family per month.

"In other words," this witness explained to the commissioners, "it is erroneous to regard a Native Reserve as an agricultural area. It would be more accurate to speak of it as a well spread out residential area, where the average family unit makes no more out of its land than the average city dweller pottering around in the backyard garden." The "native reserves," in short, had long since ceased to be areas of "native development," and had become what had been intended in white legislation from the first: mere "holding zones" for cheap black labor used in the "white areas" which composed some 90 percent of the land surface. These "holding zones," of course, had been supposed to be able to maintain the families of male migrants while the latter were absent at work in the "white areas"; but by 1944 the time when they had been able to do this was long since gone. Making this point once more, another official commission, the Native Laws Commission of 1948, took evidence which largely referred to trends that became dominant during the Second World War. It found that nearly one-third of all families in the "reserves" possessed no land, and that in any case, beyond this, about one-fifth of all land in the "reserves" was or had become unfit for cultivation. And so it came about, around 1945, that nearly two-thirds of the South African black population was in possession of cultivable land amounting only to about 8 percent of the country.

In theory, this situation was supposed to be relieved by a steady and sufficient flow of urban wages back to families in these "reserves." A certain flow did of course take place, for widespread starvation must otherwise have been unavoidable. It was and is hard to measure. How little sufficient it might be, however, was indicated by the level of wages. Leaving aside the question of wages paid to migrant mining labor, where the level was admitted to be singularly low, one may consider the findings of an official report of 1941 to the prime minister, dealing with "the social, health and economic condition of urban natives." This report found an alarming situation. The following lines say a good deal about the condition of nonwhites during the Second World War:

Recent investigations by the Wage Board into the earnings of unskilled workers in thirty-five industries, including municipal employees, show that in Johannesburg 27,994 adult labourers receive an
average wage of £1 1s. 9d. per week, which with the government cost
of living allowance of 8s. 8d. per month brings the figure to £1 3s. 9d.
per week or £5 2s. 11d. per month.*

An official estimate of two years earlier had put the cost of housing,
feeding, and clothing an average family at £6 10s. 0d., while an estimate
put forward in the same report of 1941 argued that it could not be less than
£7 14s. 6d., or about £2 per week more than the wages actually quoted as
being paid. Several experts in any case doubted that the "minimum
decent standard" of rather more than £7 was in any way meaningful in
its own terms. Such a standard of living, commented one of them in the
same report,

> is perhaps more remarkable for what it omits than for what it
> includes. It does not allow a penny for amusements, for sport, for
> medicine, for education, for saving, for hire purchase, for holidays,
> for odd bus rides, for newspapers, stationery, tobacco, sweets, hob-
> bies, gifts. . . . It does not allow a penny for replacements of blankets,
> furniture, or crockery.

One may note that most Asians suffered as badly as most Africans, or
worse, and that although some Coloreds suffered less, and even considerably less, the trend for them was essentially no different.

IV

NONWHITE PROTEST BECAME MORE EFFECTIVE THAN BEFORE, DURING THE
Second World War, partly under Asian leadership and partly under that
of radicals in the African, Colored, and white communities. Broadly, this
trend toward more effective protest produced a new militancy, and, in
measure with that, the perspective of a new unity of nonwhite action.
Political manifestations of this trend were various and important, both at
the time and for what would follow later. But they have to be seen against

---

*20 shillings = 1 dollar, the rate of exchange at that time being 5 dollars to 1 pound sterling.

the background of growing mass protest against specific forms of discrimination and impoverishment. This too was various in form and often
unexpected. While all nonwhite labor organizations continued to be
severely harassed or banned, the years of war nonetheless saw many
attempts to secure an improvement in wages and conditions. In 1939–45,
for example, there were as many as 304 strikes, however illegal, compared
with a total of 197 in the previous fifteen years, or about sixty a year
compared with about thirteen a year; and these wartime strikes involved
some 58,000 Africans, Coloreds, and Asians (as well as some 6,000 whites).
Labor militancy continued to grow in size and confidence until the great
African miners' stoppage of 1946, when 75,000 Rand mineworkers demanded a better wage, only to be driven back to work by Smuts's police.

This new urban militancy followed a long history of rural protest and
counterviolence to the violence of the system, and was met, as before, by
an increasing repressiveness that was soon to be systematized in the
severely racist laws of the apartheid state after 1948. In retrospect, it may
be seen to have signaled two aspects of response: on the one hand, a mere
reaction to a poverty now felt to be acute and becoming worse, but also,
on the other, a growing if still confused awareness of the operative
structures of the system in which all nonwhites were enclosed. This
growing awareness may in turn be seen as the spur to the emergence of
a new political consciousness. But it came with difficulty. Against it was
another long tradition, that of "reasonable compromise" by nonwhite
leaderships who had hoped, and still to some extent continued to hope,
that black "cooperation" with the system would bring its due reward in
relief from the worst aspects of the system. It was a hope which had
invariably proved, so far, to be a will-o'-the-wisp, leading nowhere, but
it still had its followers. Beyond such influences, there was the fractured
nature of the nonwhite experience. Divisions by community, region,
religion, or even occupation were deepened by illiteracy, rural isolation,
and the many confusions of the time. Yet the outline of a new political
consciousness could still make headway in this period. Decisive in promoting it was the influence of a small but determined South African
Communist Party (outlawed only in 1950) and some other left-wing
groups. All these had greatly quarreled and split among themselves and
even within themselves (perhaps above all within themselves); but on the
central point—that militancy and unity could alone turn protest into
useful change—they were generally solid, often courageous, and sometimes effective.

The history of nonwhite political organization during the Second
World War is no less complex than in earlier or later years, but may be

sketched in essential outline. Briefly, this is the period in which the ideas of black nationalism—more accurately, of nonwhite nationalism (for the Asians share in it, and so, to some extent, do the Coloreds)—grow out of their elitist limits and develop, if slowly and with many setbacks, into a rallying ideology for wide masses of people. It is also the period in which the assumptions of reformism—that the system of oppression is not only susceptible of reform, but that suitably patient pressure from below can actually reform it—begin to lose ground and gradually to sink beneath the rigidities of a system which repeatedly denies all such assumptions, or makes a patent mockery of them.

Taking inspiration partly from the Indian National Congress in India, and partly from the South African Communist Party and other left-wing groups, the leaders of the Asian community developed ideas of militancy and unity somewhat earlier than those of the Africans; or at least their ideas on the subject became effective somewhat earlier. The Coloreds, for their part, suffered more than the others from an internal split between those who still believed that "reasonable compromise" and "patient pressure" would carry them into a privileged position alongside the whites, and those against them who developed a strongly leftist analysis and practice. Even when forms of common action between Africans and Asians began to appear on the scene, unity of the Coloreds and with the Coloreds continued to be problematical. It would remain so

For the Africans, the old National Congress of 1912 (ANC) had gone into a virtual eclipse during the 1930s, and had proved perfectly incapable of reacting effectively to the removal of the Cape Africans from the provincial electoral roll in 1936. Its central frailty lay in its almost exclusively urban leadership by a small educated group whose ideas had barely evolved in thirty years of experience. Its consequent influence in most rural areas was accordingly small in practice, and often nonexistent. Though calling itself a *national* congress, its nationalism was confused and hesitant, while its overall analysis of what to do was still, essentially, that of D. D. T. Jabavu, a leading African spokesman, in the 1910s. If Africans would only prove sufficiently convenient and patient, then the sheer pressures of history, Christianity, economic growth, and even common sense would eventually reward them with "the kingdom of equality." It was the same will-o'-the-wisp that we have noted earlier.

But with the Second World War came a change in this analysis. An initial sign of new ideas, partly from left-wing political work, came in December 1940 with the election as president of the ANC of Dr. A. B. Xuma. Though Xuma was no firebrand, he nonetheless believed strongly in organization; and it was under his presidency, maintained till 1949, that the ANC began to grow out of its constrictive elitism. Another sign of changing times came with the movement's annual conference of 1943. Held in Bloemfontein in the Orange Free State, this reacted to the politics of the Second World War, and above all to the promises of the Churchill-Roosevelt "Atlantic Charter" of 1941. Four years earlier, in December 1939, another annual conference had "respectfully requested the Union Government to repeal all differential legislation," a merely routine appeal in the wake of many others, and as completely futile. Now, in 1943, the tone was different, and so was the content.

The Atlantic Charter had stated that the Allies, when victorious, would "respect the right of all peoples to choose the form of government under which they will live." Meanwhile, with great victories in Russia and North Africa in 1942, it had become clear that the war was being won; and 1942 was also the year, one may add in passing, when the Afrikaner National Party leaders began to change their pro-Nazi tune and sing a different one instead. None of this went unnoticed by the ANC. In a document of some historical importance, entitled *Africans' Claims in South Africa*, the Bloemfontein conference insisted that the words "all peoples" in the Atlantic Charter must apply to colonial peoples as much as to those whose territory had been occupied by the Nazi-Fascist-Japanese "Axis." The following passages from *Africans' Claims* are characteristic of the new state of mind now making itself felt:

We know that the Prime Minister of the Union of South Africa and his delegation to the Peace Conference will represent the interests of the people of our country. We want the government and the people of South Africa to know the full aspirations of the African peoples so that their point of view will also be presented at the Peace Conference. . . . This is our way of conveying to them our indisputed claim to full citizenship. We desire them to realise once and for all that a just and permanent peace will be possible only if the claims of all classes, colours and races for sharing and for full participation in the educational, political and economic activities are granted and recognised. . . .

As African leaders we are not so foolish as to believe that because we have made these declarations that our government will grant us our claims for the mere asking. We realise that for the African this is only a beginning of a long struggle entailing great sacrifices of time, means and even life itself. To the African people the declaration is a challenge to organize and unite themselves under the mass liberation movement, the African National Congress. The struggle is on right now and it must be persistent and insistent.

The language of the old reformism, as may be seen, still had its place in supposing that a system built on cheap nonwhite labor could in fact allow the "sharing and full participation" of those who provided that labor. But the demand was no longer "respectful": it was made as of right, and it was coupled with a clear statement that harsh struggle must lie ahead. Detailed demands were set forth, moreover, in these documents of 1943, and were coupled with a clause-by-clause examination of the Atlantic Charter and its implications for the nonwhites of South Africa; specifically, beyond that, there was also a bill of rights concerned with the meaning of full citizenship. The latter was the work of a committee whose names included all the prominent Africans of that time, from the "old leaders" such as Dr. Pixley Ka I. Seme to new ones such as Dr. Z. K. Matthews and J. S. Moroka, together with Communist spokesmen such as Moses Kotane and some of his colleagues.

Here was the beginning of a new maturity. Many pressures had promoted it. Significant among them, as already indicated, were left-wing influences which had already, in April 1939, taken initial steps toward organizational unity. At Cape Town in April of that year, left-wing representatives of all the communities had sat together in a Non-European United Front conference. Splits and dissensions duly followed. Yet political sociologist H. G. Simons, much later, could rightly recall that "the seed of a grand non-racial alliance had been planted," even if another seventeen years had still to pass before it could produce any useful fruit. An immediate outcome of 1943 was the organization of most activist Coloreds in a Non-European Unity Movement (NEUM) which called for nonwhite unity but proved able to do little about achieving that result. A more important development, also in 1943, once again foretold the future. A group of young African intellectuals and activists, confident of their ability to lead beyond the hesitations of the prudent Xuma and his kind, came together and founded the Youth League of the ANC. And here indeed the historian is tempted to pause, for in the founding names of the Youth League we find all those that were to resound across the years ahead: Nelson Mandela, Oliver Tambo, Govan Mbeki, Walter Sisulu, and others who were to lead the ANC into the bitter years after 1948 and the political victories of the late 1980s and early 1990s.

V

THESE YOUNG MEN RESPONDED TO THEIR OWN PERCEPTIONS, BUT ALSO TO the growing militancy of the urban masses which signaled the wartime years. Notably in the Johannesburg peri-urban "townships" of the Africans, there were protests of a new kind. Some of these took shape in "bus boycotts," protesting against the cost of fares, in which thousands of men and women walked many miles to work and back, week after week, rather than submit to an increase in those fares. Others emerged in a broad campaign of 1944 against the pass laws. And in these same midwar years there came another phenomenon. This was a vast influx of "squatters" onto land around the great white cities, and above all around Johannesburg. Driven by unemployment and hunger from the countryside, but drawn on equally by the cities' call for more cheap labor, tens of thousands of Africans poured in. There was of course no provision for housing them: "of course" because according to the laws they should not have come at all, or, if they came, they should not stay. But according to the needs of the economy, they were urgently wanted. In this characteristic contradiction, the white municipal councils passed strong resolutions but did nothing to alleviate the situation. Doing something would cost money, and this was money they did not wish to subtract from their own comfort.

Countless families or individuals had to live how and where they could, but many decided to take land and build huts. New "squatters' townships" spread across the veld. Perhaps the most famous of them was the one founded on vacant land adjoining the Johannesburg African township of Orlando. Here it was that a huge concourse of rural immigrants built their own "township" of canvas, flattened paraffin tins, packing cases, or whatever they could use, and, under the leadership of James Mpanza, followed his slogan of *Sofazonke*—Let us all die together—rather than surrender to the police who came to remove them. Mpanza's "township" was joined by others, and in this way the foundations of the great legalized peri-urban settlements of the future, such as Soweto (South-West Township) were laid. But these foundations were also, if indirectly, those of a new militancy of protest. And this was the militancy that was to be forged into the basis for a new unity, in the years ahead, by the leaders of the Youth League and their like.

In all these ways, and in others that a fuller record would describe, the years of 1939 to 1945 proved highly influential for the underlying conflicts

of this society. On one side, as we have seen, they enormously strengthened the white economy. They gave this economy the means of developing from a largely colonial structure into one with the power to achieve
its own indigenous capitalism and, with that, its own policy and practice
of a subimperialism in southern Africa. All this would be the work of the
long postwar boom, especially after 1950; and yet it remains true that the
structural origins of this boom lay in the steady shift to urbanization and
manufacturing during the wartime years.

On the other side, there came a clearer consciousness of their condition
among nonwhites, and, in the greatest of their communities, a fresh
leadership among Africans for whom the implications of struggle had
begun to be understood and measured. All this too would mature only
after the war was over; yet once again its origins were in the struggles of
the wartime period. Much at that time remained tentative, confused,
always subject to doctrinal or regional disputes and dissensions, while the
"great divide" between countryside and city—between the "reserves"
(afterward called the "Bantustans") and the peri-urban townships—
continued to wield a powerful influence. But the burden of the evidence
suggests that an underlying drive for militancy and unity stayed in the
center of the picture in spite of all distractions. And indeed, if this had not
been so, it would be difficult to explain the great campaigns of protest of
the early 1950s.

One may suggest, too, that the more percipient leaders of each side
came out of these wartime years with few illusions left to them of the
nature of the contest that must lie ahead. On their side the leaders of the
whites were ready by 1945, as their reaction to the African mineworkers'
strike of 1946 amply indicated, for a major reinforcement in their apparatus of control. No matter that liberal interpretations might continue to
argue that the system would reform itself through the blind pressures of
economic expansion: the facts showed otherwise. The system would not
reform itself: even could not reform itself.* The proof was provided in
1948 and after by the governments of the Purified National Party and their
legislation. Yet there is much to suggest that the same proof would have
come in any case. Governments of the United Party might have strengthened the apparatus of control by means less apparently abrasive, less
patently crude, less obviously repressive, than those adopted by Malan
and his successors. But there is nothing in the evidence to suggest that
the net result would have been essentially different. The election of the

---

*The reforms of the 1990s would all be taken by nonwhite initiative and pressure from
outside the apartheid system.

Purified National Party in 1948 can be seen as little more, in fact, than the logical development of the racist system as it had matured during the Second World War. The United Party could have prevented that election by a reorganization of voting constituencies, for the election was won by the National Party with a minority of votes on an all-white electoral roll weighted in favor of rural constituencies where the Afrikaner extremists had their big battalions. But Smuts and his United Party government did nothing to revise the electoral roll. The United Party may be said to have allowed the Purified National Party to have its victory, and then to have been well enough content.

Few illusions, on the other side, could any longer distract the leaders of the nonwhites. There might be many individuals among the nonwhite communities for whom the future as a "black bourgeoisie" still seemed possible, and if possible then desirable. That was true of petty-bourgeois shopkeepers, traders, urban landlords who squeezed their tenants, and some of those who had managed to gain a higher education at Fort Hare or in other colleges which admitted nonwhites in those days. Yet these were few, and their voices carried no weight among the harried masses. In this respect, as in others, the experience of the war years confirmed the leadership of men such as Mandela and Tambo, Kotane and J. B. Marks, or Dadoo in the Indian community, for whom the prospects of a business-as-usual reformism had become manifestly small or nonexistent. Of what the real alternative to that kind of reformism must consist there might as yet be little clarity. All that now seemed certain in this direction was that a real alternative must be found.[1]

SOUTH AFRICA:
A SYSTEM OF
LEGALIZED SERVITUDE

THE HISTORY OF APARTHEID IS THE RECORD OF A RACISM CONCEIVED and used by small white minorities in South Africa in order to dominate a large black majority, deprive this majority of its land, and maximize the exploitation of its labor for the benefit of the whites and their foreign partners. As such, it is a record which begins very soon after the arrival of the earliest Dutch settlers at the Cape of Good Hope in 1652: almost from the first these settlers and all other settlers who followed them from Holland, Britain, France, or elsewhere considered that they had the right to dispossess the African inhabitants in any way and to any degree that could be profitable and convenient.

In no essentials, since those early years, has anything changed in the relationship between "whites" and "blacks" (the latter being taken to include Asians, and Coloreds of a mixed origin) except the "language of legality" and a vast increase of actual dispossession. Crude forms of outright enslavement have developed, step-by-step, into the sophisticated laws and regulations of a racism whose instrumental force, for those who apply it and those who have to suffer it, is in everyday reality no different from a legalized servitude.

The squalid politics of an "interwhite" rivalry for the fruits of this instrumental racism may often fill our newspapers, as the Afrikaans-speaking minority plays out a charade of parliamentary conflict with the English-speaking minority: they remain, as in the past, only a mask for the solid unity of interest and intention, between these two white minorities, that joins them in exploitation of the black majority.

This essay originally appeared, in slightly different form, in 1983 in *The UNESCO Courier*.

There are other masks to be thrust aside. Apartheid is sometimes portrayed, all over the world, as an invention of the Afrikaans-speaking minority—or by its first elected parliamentary majority of 1948—as a means of realizing its own peculiar doctrine of Calvinist belief. But that is to misrepresent the meaning of the system, or rather to "theorize" that meaning in terms of a subjectivity that certainly exists but which covers an objective meaning of infinitely greater force. This objective meaning differs, in truth, only in degree from any other form of colonial racism, always the instrument of a *mise en valeur*, of "getting out the profits," whether in the British, French, or any other colonial system. Apartheid is colonial racism carried to an extreme.

These may sound like harsh conclusions, but they are what the history of South Africa must teach us.

Up to 1899 the white politics of all the lands south of the Limpopo River—the lands that form modern South Africa—were largely those of military power used to defeat black resistance. Broadly, those politics were contained within two areas of competition. As soon as the British were established securely at the Cape of Good Hope—following victory over the French fleet at Trafalgar in 1805—they embarked on a long series of what were euphemistically called "frontier wars." Against continuous black resistance, not always defeated, British forces pushed north and northeastward from their little colony at the Cape, invading and dispossessing one African community after another until their final conquest of the Zulu kingdom in 1879.

The descendants of the Dutch settlers (enlarged by immigration from Holland but still more by unadmitted unions with black women) had meanwhile gone some way toward forming themselves into a distinctive nation—the Afrikaner *volk*—and by this time spoke a variant of Dutch which was already beginning to be a distinctive language—Afrikaans. They were far too weak in numbers and technology to tackle strong African communities such as the Xhosa and the Zulu, whose destruction as independent entities was left to the British, but were strong enough to dispossess a wide range of small African communities. These lived to the west of the areas of British conquest, and were duly enclosed in the Afrikaner (or Boer, a term simply meaning "farmer") republics of the Orange Free State and the Transvaal.

By the 1880s, accordingly, there were four white political units: the two British colonies of the Cape and Natal, and the two Afrikaner republics in the north and west. All were farming communities, each of them practically without the beginnings of any industrial production, and lived in a typical colonial fashion by exporting wool and other products of the land in exchange for such manufactured imports as they could afford. Diamonds had been discovered in quantity at Kimberley as early as 1867, and in 1871 the British duly annexed these diamond fields which became, a little later, the scene of a veritable "diamond rush," with a railway completed from the Cape to Kimberley in 1885. But even this new source of wealth could change little in the general picture. What changed everything, and soon with violent drama, was the proving in 1884–86 of the great goldfields of the Witwatersrand in the Transvaal Republic.

These goldfields promised the wealth of Croesus to anyone who could exploit them, but, being deep seams with a relatively low gold content per ton of ore, they demanded an intensive capitalization. For reasons widely imperialist and narrowly economic, major British interests now saw that they must secure political control of a Transvaal governed by farmers with little or no interest in large-scale capitalist development. After many skirmishes there followed the Anglo-Boer War of 1899, provoked by the British and won by the British, though at sorry cost in lives, two years later. This victory marked the beginning of modern South Africa.

Having won the war, the British were quick to reassure their defeated Afrikaner opponents that systematic discrimination against the black majority would nonetheless be written into the foundation of the Union of South Africa (that is, the union of Cape Colony, Natal, Transvaal, and the Orange Free State) which followed in 1910. For thirty-eight years after that, the English-speaking minority generally dominated the all-white parliament of a now independent Union, but invariably on apartheid lines. The new Union parliament—all white, of course—lost no time in guaranteeing this. In 1911 the Native Labour Regulation Act provided for the legalization—much elaborated and tightened up in later years—of an all-embracing discrimination against black wage earners. In 1913 the parliament went much further. It passed a Land Act which reserved some 90 percent of the total land surface of the Union for white ownership, and reduced the area available for black ownership to the remaining 10 percent (less at the beginning, today about 13 percent). These small areas where Africans could own land were named native reserves, and rapidly became what they were intended to be: destitute reservoirs of black labor for the "white areas." Within the latter, affecting some 90 percent of the land surface, new laws restricted black rights of residence, movement, employment, and even leisure.

In 1923 came the Natives (Urban Areas) Act which was to remain, with the Native Land Act of 1913, the foundation of all white policy toward blacks, and so remains to this day. Essentially, it was a weapon of physical segregation within the "white areas," and the policy which was held to justify it was called "separate development." The effective meaning of this policy was defined by the African scholar Z. K. Matthews in 1944, when he described this Act of 1923 as providing for "the separation of black and white, not with the idea of protecting each group in regard to its basic interests, but the separation of the groups in order to facilitate the subordination of one group to the other—the exploitation of one group by the other."

But an official and of course all-white government commission of 1921, two years before the act became law, had already put the matter more clearly. It laid down the basic principle of white supremacy. This was that "the native [a term invariably meaning the black or nonwhite inhabitant] should only be allowed to enter urban areas, which are essentially the white man's creation, when he is willing to enter and to minister to the needs of the white man, and he should depart therefrom when he ceases so to minister." What "minister" meant, very precisely, was that the black man should work for the white man at whatever level of wages, and under whatever conditions of work, that the white man might concede. George Bernard Shaw, visiting South Africa soon after, called that country a slave state; and it is really quite hard to think that he was wrong.

This dispensation, ensuring cheap and captive black labor in 90 percent of the land surface, was further protected by "pass laws" which required detailed police supervision of any black employment or shift of residence, and much else besides, and, beyond these pass laws, by customs and regulations designed to prevent or punish any black-white "commingling"—except, naturally, whenever convenient to whites, as in the case of black nannies for white children, or black cooks for white ladies.

Such was the system by which the parliament of South Africa ruled the country so long as the English-speaking minority retained control of the laws. In erecting it the British had fully realized their aims in conquering the Afrikaner republics: they had provided an "ideal structure" for the development of a specific capitalism fueled by British capital, which entered the country increasingly after 1920 and which ensured the English-speaking minority of a uniquely high standard of living while, at the same time, ensuring a uniquely high rate of profit for British investors.

None of all this was to undergo any substantial change until long after the Second World War. But that war did change the underlying positions of the opposing sides, and forecast an eventual end to the system.

AFRICAN SAGA

I

I T IS DAYS SINCE WE CAST OFF MOORINGS AT PONTHIERVILLE AND PUSHED
away upstream. It seems like weeks. Hour after hour the *Baron Delbeck,*
venerable stern-wheeler, flaps his water-jeweled paddle into this dreaming sepia flood, while on either side and behind us and ahead of us the
equatorial forest totters to the riverbank in gray-green fungold decay, and
makes our only horizon. We are miles and miles from the Atlantic Ocean,
as many miles from the Indian. Take a pencil and point it at the middle
of Africa. That is where we are.

Rarely do we pass bankside villages; but then the excitement is all the
greater, because each is full of fifty people or so, and kids leap into the
river and swim out shouting into our wake. The two nuns who are going
to Lokandu to help with an outbreak of meningitis watch them approv-
ingly. Arkady Platonovich, who likes children, comes out of his cabin and
cries encouragement, and even the railway engineer, a sad Ligurian from
Sestri, brightens a little. Now and then the *Baron* lets forth four short,
sharp hoots as we near a couple of European bungalows and a warehouse.
Now and then we stop for timber fuel, because the *Baron* uses no other.
"We're going to have an oil-fired engine soon," the Flemish captain has
explained. "Our Congo's going ahead."

Delightful is this river journey. . . . Around eleven, when the sun begins

This essay originally appeared as two separate articles in 1954 in the *New Statesman and
Nation;* the first was entitled "Congo Saga," and the second was called "A Little Corner
of Paradise." Reprinted with permission.

to burn more fiercely (for we are five degrees off the Equator), Arkady Platonovich arrives with a cheerful apology and wants to know whether it wouldn't be right to break a bottle. And that is when, idly in a row beneath the canvas awning, with our feet on the *Baron*'s smart white rail (for he keeps himself up, despite his advanced years), we call for iced Congo beer and begin talking. We go on talking, Arkady and the Italian and the Settler and the Sociologist and me, all day and all evening; and the end of this conversation is nowhere in sight. I do not think it has an end.

By this time we are beyond personalities and are deep into philosophy. Africa is strong for philosophy. Yesterday the Italian from Sestri was telling us why. He is livid with malaria, and his blue eyes have the pallid stare, not quite focusing, of those who suffer from that sickness. He has malaria because everyone along the river has it, but more especially because his contract with the Congo government takes him on long surveying trips into the forest. There he lives in the company of a dozen Africans whose language he cannot understand; and all this makes him think. "What about? I think how I'm going to pull through. I think about the goal I've got ahead of me. You see, I've got something to live for." He is putting every hard-won penny into the money box of his dreams, which include a little cottage near the beach at Nervi, beside the Mediterranean, and messing about in boats and strolling through summer evenings, and forgetting this equatorial nightmare.

Arkady Platonovich is also strong for philosophy, but of a purer, less personal kind. We met on the train from Ponthierville—Chemin de Fer de la Lualaba et des Grands Lacs Africains—when his book, rather oddly, was Ilf and Petrov's *Little Golden America*. He is a sturdy old man with glinting eyes and a healthy happiness in adversity: one of the things he wanted to know about was the Red Army during the war. He was contentedly proud of the Red Army. "I'm a mortal enemy of the regime, you know," he offered gently, "but I'm a Russian. *Rrr-rien à faire!*" He left Russia with Denikin in 1923 and arrived in the Congo a year or so later. "Go back to Europe?" His stubby fingers spread quickly and relaxed: "And live in an attic?" I do not know exactly what Arkady Platonovich is dreaming about as the endless river swings impassively by. Just when you think you are getting to the point, he is up and away, elusive, lost. He is also sorrowing over his only daughter, whose mother is one of those physically unmatched Watutsi from Ruanda Urundi, because she would not go back with him to their bush home but insisted on remaining in town. "A half-caste girl in town, you know, and one who's handsome, *bien faite. . . .*"

Unique in not dreaming is the Settler, a Belgian who is longing to get back to Kivu, where the blue eastern lakes lie among clean mountains. The Settler is political: that is to say, he would like to be political, but the Congo government will not let him. The Congo government is paternalist, refusing all political rights both to Africans and to Europeans with a resolute determination not to have any nonsense. The Settler is discontented with the Congo government. "They're going too fast with the native out here," he says and keeps on saying. "They're ruining this colony." That is the extent of his philosophy; we know it backwards.

We might have less of the Settler's philosophy if it weren't for the Sociologist, who takes frantic issue with him. The Sociologist is also a lost soul, sunk in singular erotic meditations; but he clings to his duty. He knows so much about the tribal habits of the eastern Baluba that he no longer believes anything general to be knowable, or worth knowing; in moments of lucidity he remains a warm upholder of the Congo government. "As for you," he says to me, "everyone writes books about Africa. Mostly very bad ones. And they never ask the interesting questions, let alone trying to answer them."

"What are the interesting questions?"

"I'll tell you," he says, and surprisingly, they are general questions.

"There's only two that matter. But after all," he checks suspiciously, "you've already been to West Africa and South Africa and God knows where, and you still ask me that? These two questions—they're not peculiar to the Congo. They're the questions which the whole of Black Africa has to answer. They're the common denominator—the substratum, the foundation, the basis of any intelligent opinion." Solitude has made the Sociologist a little pugnacious with his fellow men, whom he rarely sees. "First of all, if it's any good telling you, why did the Congo peoples [since we're in the Congo] stay in a late Stone Age culture—all right, early Copper Age here and there—while the rest of the world moved on? Secondly, what happens *now*—when they've understood where they are and where we are, when they're convinced they've got to catch up? Those are the interesting questions, but you won't answer them because you can't. You've never thought about them."

I am saved by the Settler, who can't resist this opening. "*C'est fou.* They stayed in the Stone Age because they're children. Because they're a lazy, useless branch of the human race that never grew up. Couldn't grow up. As for catching up"—he waves his glass so that drops of beer spatter upon Arkady Platonovich, fortunately thinking of something else, of something quite his own. "It'll take them generations."

"You say that," returns the Sociologist rudely, "because that's your interest as a settler. Well, I've known settlers who've lived for twenty years in the Congo without ever having a serious conversation with a native. And then they talk about natives as though they actually knew anything! Just look at Kenya." He sweeps aside the Settler's retort, for these are fighting words, and goes on: "The point today, in this year and age, is that the African peoples of the Congo—everywhere else too, I dare say—can't stay in their tribalism, their Stone Age—because they're up against the machine age. Right up against it. Aren't we industrializing the Congo? Bringing in machines, building factories? Yes, and if there's anything utterly amazing about our Congo peoples, it's their fantastic power of adjusting themselves, adapting themselves. It's not intelligence they lack, it's opportunity. . . ."

The Sociologist is right about his questions. In repair shops at Jadotville, Africans are using machine tools precise to one-hundredth of a millimeter; between Jadotville and Kolwezi they are driving the latest type of electric locomotives; on the Kasai and the Congo they command tugs and barges and passenger steamers. . . . And I also think of these great Congo cities which pullulate with village Africans learning to live urban lives, of the bars of Leopoldville, of the fun and games and dancing, the astonishing absence of violent crime for all the somersaults in ways of life and family loyalty, the order and upward striving for all the downward influence of those naughty girls associated in *La Joie Kinoise, La Rose, La Délicatesse.* . . .

"Still," I am rash enough to say, "you've put a stopper on all political development. Now we, for instance—I mean, look at the Gold Coast—"

The Sociologist and the Settler take a quick look at one another, and by mutual consent fall upon me in a heap. On this they are emphatically agreed: the Gold Coast is going *much too fast.* I am hauled out from under by Arkady Platonovich, who takes me aside and gives me a drink. He gestures vaguely at the wilted forest. "The Congo. There's nowhere like it. I've lived here for thirty years. I shall leave my bones here." Then he chuckles and goes on: "You know, I've never made a penny, but . . . tell me, did you ever read *Dead Souls?* Do you remember Chichikov, who made a fortune out of nothing, absolutely nothing?" His malarial eyes are staring at the dense green emptiness along the bank. "Just think what Chichikov mightn't have done with the Congo."

II

ANGOLA IS A PORTUGUESE COLONY AS BIG AS HALF OF EUROPE. IT MATTERS
to the world at large in the exact proportion that the persistence of slavery
matters.

To the seafaring voyager this African country is a long, lifting coast of
gray and silver hills behind the line of Atlantic surf some days of southward sailing from the Gulf of Guinea. Here and there along this coast old
slaving forts squat in primrose shadows above the blue sea; the towns lie
half-asleep beneath their fronded palms; and the Banco de Angola, cap-
ping this medieval outpost with a usurious caution which even the Fug-
gers had left behind, refuses to pay interest on deposits and makes no
loans.

I came in myself by the back door, apprehensive of not coming in at
all, and crossed the country by slow railway stages. Seen from the interior,
Angola is a wide wilderness of empty plains and tormented hills apparently without population; in fact, about 4 million people live here. It is
so wide that the rolling stock of the Benguela Railway takes three days
and nights to cross it. More properly, this rolling stock ought to be called
reeling stock, for much of the permanent way is laid on sand and loose
earth; moreover, some of the gradients are best not known about before-
hand. Yet it would be miserly to grudge a word of praise to the Benguela
Railway, for it has two claims on our respect. The first is that its engineer-
ing achievement is amazing, for it crosses not only the savage plateau of
inland Angola but also the tooth-edged mountains which make a belt of
desert along the coast; and it does all this with a fine old pioneering
unconcern for its own or anybody else's comfort. The second is that it is
the only British-owned railway in this day and age, I think, in whose
working forced labor is employed.

It is not entirely or even mainly worked by such labor. Exactly how
many forced workers it employs I discovered only when I could reach
Senhor Escudero, down at Lobito, where the long Atlantic waves reach
over to Brazil. Senhor Escudero is the general manager of the Benguela
Railway, 90 percent of whose stock is held by a British company, Tanganyika Concessions. A gentle Portuguese upon whom a call for courtesy
is happily irresistible, he occupies a modest little wooden bungalow, set
among tall flowers, where the seaward-reaching spit of Lobito's harbor
narrows to a strand between the ocean on either side. He is strongly of
the opinion that there is no such thing as labor trouble in Angola, nor

indeed any sort of trouble, and he was happy to tell me anything I would like to know.

I would like to know how many forced workers he has. Senhor Escudero calls for the files: altogether, we find—examining the files with the curiosity of visitors to a collection of rare stamps—that Senhor Escudero has 13,453 *voluntarios* and 2,018 *contradados*. Not a bad proportion: most companies have a much higher proportion of *contradados*. *Contradados* are really slaves. Senhor Escudero is much too polite for any name as crude as that: all the same, that is what they are. That is what makes Angola rather more than an insignificant wilderness: this is the only colony in Africa where theory and practice combine to operate what Henry Nevinson, looking at the place fifty years ago, called a "modern slavery."

What I saw this winter shows that the system is more humane than it was in Nevinson's day, but is otherwise unchanged. In those old-fashioned times they brought down the *contradados* (who were called *serviçaes*) by foot, marching them crazily across the Hungry Country beyond Silva Porto and down through the mountains along the still older slave trails of the splendid days before full-blown slavery was abolished. "The whole length of the path [into the interior]," Nevinson recorded of his journey from the coast, "was strewn with white bones—the bones of slaves." The British shareholders of Benguela Railway stock will be relieved to hear that nowadays their slaves are brought down in trucks and railway wagons, and almost always survive the experience. Furthermore, they are even paid a small wage, because it is in fashion nowadays to cosset Africans; and the food and medical services are often quite good.

Yet it is still a little breathtaking to travel through a country that is run quite largely on forced labor. The Portuguese Constitution, of course, says that forced labor is abolished, impossible, and generally out of the question; but no one in Angola seems to know about this constitution. Perhaps it got lost in Dr. Salazar's desk: what happens in Angola is that local authority insists that every male African must show proof of having worked for six months in the year previous to inquiry, or of being in work at the time of inquiry. Otherwise (but I fear one should write "in any case") the adult male African—though not if he is less than about ten years old—who falls into the hands of any investigating inquiry, from the cashier's mistress up to the governor-general himself, is likely to find himself "on contract."

So thoughtful is this system that every employer of voluntary labor has to sign his employees' "personal books" every evening; otherwise, as a young Portuguese engineer in charge of a textile mill outside Luanda explained to me, "the men may be taken by the police for forced labor."

Officials defend this system as a means of protecting the women and of educating the idle African to be a breadwinner. A recent Portuguese apologist, Senhor da Silva Cunha, has argued cogently that the system sanctifies "the salutory principle of obligation to labor." Dr. Pereira, who is head of the Department of Native Affairs in Angola, told me that the estimates for all Angola at the moment give a total of about 400,000 *voluntarios* and 379,000 *contradados*. "We do it," he said, "to protect the women." Certainly, the women are profoundly affected. Absence of men on forced labor elsewhere often causes local chiefs and headmen (respon-sible for the unpaid upkeep of rural roads) to call up women and quite small children for compulsory work. Until lately, chiefs and headmen who failed in this duty were mercilessly flogged; but I am assured there is now much less flogging than a couple of years ago.

Employers who need forced labor apply for it from the government-general. The government-general allocates *contradados* according to a theoretical calculation of the probable number of adult males available. Approved demands for forced labor are sent to local administrators; and the *chefe de posto*, through his chief or headman, is then obliged to provide the stated number of men. Thus it happens that forced workers complet-ing one "contract" may be straightaway taken for another, because the demand for forced labor apparently always exceeds the supply. These forced workers pass their lives in intermittent slavery, the only differences between "contract labor" and institutional slavery being precisely that "contract labor" is intermittent, and that it is paid a small wage. This wage may be a pound a month; but the *contradado* receives no more than a third or a quarter of this during his conscripted period, and is generally thought to be extremely fortunate if he afterward sees much of the balance, for the balance passes at the end of his service through the impoverished hands of the local *chefe* and his own headman.

All reliable witnesses whom I was able to consult—and they were not few, because Angola gathers the political opponents of Dr. Salazar as well as many decent foreigners—were agreed that the amount of forced labor had steadily increased over the past twenty years: indeed, ever since this colony climbed out of the Depression of the thirties. At the same time, they agreed, they had witnessed a steady narrowing of the difference which separates free from forced labor. It is apparently beyond question that free workers in the interior are often paid less and treated worse than forced workers. What this means can be watched on plantations up country and at the diamond mines of the Lunda Province. These dia-mond mines belong to the good old days of primitive "pioneering," and I was unable to visit them. Owned mainly by British, American, and

Belgian diamond interests, they possess a prospecting monopoly over five-sixths of the country, and, to quote the limpid words of Skinner's *Mining Yearbook,* the Angola Diamond Company "is exempt from taxation both as to import duties on plant and materials and export duties on diamonds." It may be noted in passing that medical missionaries in Angola are not only not exempt from import duties on such things as steel window frames for hospitals, but have to pay duty even on drugs and medical equipment.

Another right this company possesses is an absolute monopoly on all labor recruitment over most of the Lunda Province, which is about half the size of England. According to Captain Mario Costa, its agent in Luanda, the company now has about 11,000 "free workers" and about 4,000 "forced workers," although other reports give a higher figure for the latter. Other reports also say that forced workers theoretically conscripted for one year's service must often remain at the mines for much longer than that. At these mines, clearly, the difference between free and forced is little more than verbal. Africans who have to pay money taxes have to earn money; in practice, they can usually do that only by seeking wage employment. In most of the Lunda Province they can find employment only at the mines. Perhaps that is why the diamond company's free workers are paid less than its forced workers. However, Captain Costa says on this point that the forced workers are paid a little more because they are *"un petit peu forcés, n'est-ce pas?"* They are indeed.

Captain Costa was unable to come down to sordid detail from the lofty levels of diplomacy which he inhabits in his eighteenth-century office in Luanda, and saw me out with a few well-chosen words. Outside his door, however, the company has erected a number of painted posters on which it advertises the splendors of its "social policy." I quote from these. In 1947 the company had 17,500 workers, of whom 5,500 were provided "by intervention of the authorities"—that is, were forced workers. All these African employees received 10,050,000 angolars in wages and rations, and a further 4,450,000 angolars in "various goods." This gives an average money-kind wage of 830 angolars for each worker in 1947, or about £10 10s. a year. In 1947 the company paid about 32 percent a share.

There is some improvement in the territory to be noted over the past few years. The administration is said to be getting less careless and corrupt: it seems that food and medical services are generally better. About 20,000 people in the African quarter of Lobito now have as many as sixteen water taps among them. Up country, though, things remain much as they were. "Improvement in the general condition of rural Africans? I see none," a doctor with long years in the country told me.

"Nutritionally, they are worse off on the whole than they were when there was more forest and wildlife. The mosquitoes, ticks, flies are the same as ever. Tuberculosis must have increased tenfold in the last twenty years."

Among the gardens of Lobito, Senhor Escudero turned to me with quietly meditative eyes. "Angola," he said dreamily; "it's a little corner of Paradise in Africa, I always say."

PLURALISM IN COLONIAL AFRICAN SOCIETIES

I

THERE ARE FEW COUNTRIES IN COLONIAL AND EX-COLONIAL AFRICA, OR at any rate within Africa south of the Sahara, where the concepts of pluralism may be more helpful to analytical understanding than the British Protectorate of Northern Rhodesia (including Barotseland), which has since become the independent republic of Zambia. For it is here that a process of pluralism—a movement through several types of plural- ist society or pluralist structures, as these are defined in the frameworks set up by Leo Kuper and M. G. Smith in their introductory papers to this colloquium[1]—can be more fully and, as it were, neatly seen than in most other territories of the same type. Northern Rhodesia/Zambia seems repeatedly to offer a stimulating field for reflection on the whole regulation-integration pattern of pressure which underlies the dynamic of pluralism, and whose varying configuration motivates the direction of any pluralist society, toward more conflict or less conflict, at any given time.

There would appear to be three reasons why Northern Rhodesia/ Zambia is particularly helpful in this respect. In the first place, this is a country where a good deal is known about at least two precolonial societies which were pluralist in a sense that was fairly characteristic of many precolonial structures in central-southern Africa, and to much the same extent in western Africa as well. Second, this was a colony (a term which may be taken to include the imperial-administrative sense of

This essay originally appeared in 1969 in Leo Kuper and M. G. Smith (eds.), *Pluralism in Africa*, published by the University of California Press. Reprinted with permission.

"protectorate") where European settlement developed a pluralism of
conflict, in the sense proposed by J. S. Furnivall,[2] and further developed
by Smith, which lay somewhere between the "extremes" represented in
central Africa by Southern Rhodesia at one end of the "white settlement
spectrum" and Tanganyika at the other. Here it was not taken for granted
from the earliest moment of European arrival, in contrast with Kenya and
Southern Rhodesia,[3] that this was to be a "white man's country" where
the newcomers would install themselves as permanent and exclusive
rulers, and where the scene was accordingly set, almost from the outset,
for a racial separatism so acute and inflexible as practically to deny the
existence of any organic community of Europeans and Africans. Such
tendencies developed with the improvement of antimalarial medicine,
and were afterward enlarged to a point at which they could be dominant
for many years; yet even during those years the relatively low degree of
settler density made an important differential between Northern
Rhodesia and Southern Rhodesia or Kenya. On the other hand, European
settler power in Northern Rhodesia was generally stronger, as well as less
confined by theoretical safeguards on the eventual rights of Africans, than
in the Mandated (later Trusteeship) Territory of Tanganyika.

Evolving somewhere between these two, Northern Rhodesia was always a country where the drive for entrenched white supremacy had
powerful but never completely effective influence, and where, because of
this and other factors, the concept of a Northern Rhodesian society as
possibly including all the inhabitants remained at least admissible (though
very seldom admitted) within the practical framework of public (that is
to say, of European) debate. Even through what may be regarded as the
most sterile years of the colonial epoch—the period between the respective ends of the two world wars, but especially for Northern Rhodesia, up
to the middle 1930s—this racially separatist society generally held within
itself at least a few of the seeds of pluralism by consensus, by equilibrium,
and by democratization. And this relative mobility (a very limited mobility, as will be seen, and yet one that was never quite reduced to a
standstill) may not be the least reason why Northern Rhodesia seems
attractive to inquiry.

Third, with Northern Rhodesia becoming Zambia there is the possibility of examining in fairly good detail how a pluralism of embittered
conflict can become, even at the early stages of resolution, a pluralism of
less acute conflict, and can even move toward that kind of pluralism of
equilibrium which supposes the growth of a consensus. It may be that
Nyasaland/Malawi next door would provide as good an example of this
structural series, yet the pattern has been simpler there (if only because

of the absence of a Copperbelt, with its provision of urbanized industrial employment for Africans), and to the extent that it has been simpler, it may be less instructive. Then, in terms of studying "transition from pluralism to heterogeneity,"[4] Zambia has very clear advantages over Kenya, a good deal less resolved today in terms of its basic problems, and even more over Southern Rhodesia, where the resolution of acute conflict has yet to begin. Moreover, it appears to me, as I shall try to show, that forms of resolution in Zambia have interesting parallels in other parts of Africa where the white settler problem has been unimportant or altogether absent.

This essay accordingly looks at several main configurations through which the pluralist process has passed in recent historical times—since, that is, the eighteenth century—and offers a few tentative conclusions in comparison with some other African territories. One should perhaps begin by noting that the sources are of very unequal value. Up to the middle of the nineteenth century, written accounts are limited to the reports of a handful of Portuguese travelers. Some of these, notably Dos Santos[5] at the end of the sixteenth and Gamitto[6] in the first half of the nineteenth, were remarkably good observers, but their travels seldom took them far from the Zambezi, although Gamitto traveled to the lands of Kazembe (approximately eastern Katanga) through what afterward became the northeastern segment of our territory. Oral traditions are somewhat stronger for a few of the peoples concerned, yet still leave much to be desired. The archaeology of this whole region remains at an early stage of research, though the last few years have brought important advances in the understanding of early Iron Age systems here.[7]

Written sources for Northern Rhodesia are good, even very good, for the Europeans, thanks partly to the lively settlers' newspaper founded by Leopold Moore at Livingstone in 1906,[8] and partly to the well-recorded debates of the Legislative Council formed in 1924. After the end of the Second World War these sources become still more copious with the launching of more newspapers and a great deal of political, social, and cultural argument recorded outside the scope of the Legislative Council. An additional advantage here is that the settlers' struggle for federation, and the wider interest stimulated by federation itself (1953–63), set going a movement to write books about the country. When I first went there in 1951, there was only one book of any analytical value on the politics of Northern Rhodesia[9]; today there are at least twelve or fourteen, and two or three of these are likely to be of lasting value.

Against all this on the European side, there is practically nothing before the 1940s to record the opinions of Africans. Northern Rhodesia produced neither a Chilembwe[10] nor a Clements Kadalie[11] in the period prior to the rise of congress and trade-union politics at the end of the 1940s; and the little we know of African opinion comes mainly, though very sparsely even at that, through the mouth of one or other of the more liberal spokesmen in the all-white Legislative Council, notably Sir Stewart Gore-Browne. To these stray allusions, the rise of separatist Christianity, especially in its local form of Watch Tower, adds a useful if somewhat indirect addendum, while missionary records[12] can sometimes be a valuable, though also secondary, source. Seldom does one find an opinion spoken by an African himself.

This alters wonderfully in the late 1940s. At least from 1948 there is a growing volume of African publications which bear directly on many aspects of daily life. And with the later stages of the campaign against federation, with rapid political advance after 1959, and with independence itself, the African voice is continuously and ever more widely heard.

II

WHEN EUROPEANS FIRST CROSSED THE ZAMBEZI IN ANY NUMBERS DURING the last years of the nineteenth century,[13] they found peoples of the Bantu language group. Many of them had been there for the better part of two thousand years, had developed considerable immunity against the malarial mosquito which infested the greater part of the country, and had evolved an indigenous agriculture and a premechanical mining industry, the latter from about A.D. 300. Theirs was a subsistence economy modified marginally by a small amount of internal trade. They had the use of various kinds of primitive money but knew no cash economy. They were entirely nonliterate.

Europeans unhesitatingly called them "tribes" in a sense that was explicitly pejorative and meant everything opposed to any development of the means of material progress or even, with the more extreme interpretations, opposed to any form of juridical and moral order. This term "tribe" has stayed with us because it is convenient; yet even without its subjective overtones it may at best be misleading. These peoples were not nations in the sense of possessing hard-and-fast frontiers, customs posts, or other attributes of what is usually understood by nationalism. If they had not formed nations, however, they had certainly formed states. Some of these states, like those of the Ila and the Tonga, were of a type that allowed little or no central government. Others, like those of the Bemba and the Lozi, were of a type that allowed much. Within these states, simple or complex, they possessed distinctive cultures, whether socio-political, religious, or linguistic; and their respective jural communities were undoubtedly framed by approximate territorial limits—frontiers of a sort—which were customarily recognized by their neighbors as well as by themselves.

The larger of these states were plural societies: in varying ways, that is, they displayed a "political pluralism, with a corresponding social pluralism, in which the units [were] bound together by crosscutting loyalties and by common values or a competitive balance of power."[14] While long-indigenous peoples such as the Tonga had achieved since ancient times a high degree of homogeneity, others, such as the Bemba and the Lozi, looked back to incoming ancestors who had arrived in the country during the eighteenth century, established local dominance, and ruled over many different elements more or less imperfectly welded together. Being little stratified in the horizontal sense of caste (and even less in that of class), these peoples with incoming ancestors were organized on a pluralist model which made for the growth of consensus rather than of conflict. Initially, no doubt, these incoming groups had imposed their authority on local peoples by war and repression, but it would seem that the kinship structure of their societies, having a highly absorptive mechanism, made this conflict period a relatively brief one. By the nineteenth century, if not before, Bemba-speaking people had become a homogeneous group. Between themselves and their outlying vassals to the north and south, however, the process was still at a relatively early stage; it is this that helps to explain how the Bemba empire could and did collapse so rapidly on the appearance of European overlordship. It collapsed, that is to say, not from inner conflict, from a failure of its consensus mechanism, but from the pressure of outside strains.[15]

The Kololo settlement in Barotseland during the 1820s offers another example of precolonial pluralism. These Kololo were formidable Sotho migrants from the great military upheavals south of the Limpopo which had begun with the rise of the Mtetwa under Dingiswayo and exploded with the Zulu under Shaka. They moved into the country of the Lozi, whose local political system was at that time rather more than a century old, and imposed their own rule. This imposition was violent, but Sebetwane, who carried it through, tried almost at once for a consensus. He "discouraged the Kololo from adopting the attitudes of a dominant aristocracy, and consciously strove to fuse the two groups into a single people.... His policy of fusion was embodied in the decree that 'all are children of the chief.'" This policy was successful during his lifetime to a point where "the Lozi and even the river peoples [over whom the Lozi had ruled] adopted the name Kololo and took pride in the daring military exploits with which it was associated."[16] When his successor rejected fusion, the results proved disastrous for Kololo overlordship.

It would not be hard to make comparisons with other large African societies in the precolonial period. Some, like Asante, were able to achieve a marked degree of consensus among peoples of different traditional loyalties, moving toward this by various routes and maintaining it for more or less long periods. Others, like Songhay in its great imperial period of the sixteenth century, were never able to become more than "a characteristically oligarchic regime based on systematic political and social inequality and designed to preserve and perpetuate the institutional conditions essential for . . . sectional dominance."[17] One is reminded in this context of the famous rejoinder of Askia Dawud, one of Songhay's most illustrious rulers, when criticized by a Muslim dignitary for allowing pagan customs at his court. "I am not a fool for doing this," the emperor is said to have replied with a laugh, "but I rule over fools who are both arrogant and impious, and that is why I must pretend to be a fool myself."[18] In fact, the emperor's tolerance of pagan customs at his Muslim court reflected the greatest of his problems, which was how to reconcile the Muslim people of his trading cities with the pagan people of his countryside, never resolved by more than partial compromise; this was the conflict that rapidly undermined the Songhay empire once its main cities were captured by the invaders of 1591.

Acute conflicts such as these were absent among the precolonial peoples of Northern Rhodesia. If they accepted European government with little protest or with none, this was not because their societies could easily be split along the grain of inner conflict as the Moroccans were able to split the Songhay system, but because they needed allies and protectors and saw these in European shape. The so-called stateless peoples like the Tonga were simply incorporated into a European-dominated system without their having so much as understood, perhaps, what was really going on. But the Lozi and Bemba rulers had felt the edge of danger from strong African neighbors, and not unreasonably believed that future risks they might incur from a powerful ally whose homeland was evidently very distant must be preferable to the immediate risks they ran from enemies nearby. Only the Nguni in the eastern part of the country resisted the European takeover, and they were soon defeated.

III

IF CONCEPTS OF PLURALISM SEEM USEFUL OVER A LONG PERSPECTIVE, THERE remain periods in Northern Rhodesia history, and especially up to the middle 1940s when, by seeming to imply some form of consensus, such concepts may risk obscuring more than they reveal. There was, indeed, a pluralist system of acute conflict at work here. But in order to describe it I myself prefer, as I shall indicate, a sharper and more brutal term, if only to emphasize, in Smith's terminology, that "modes of subjugation" are by no means necessarily tantamount (and certainly were not here) to modes of "willing submission." Here there existed no normative consensual basis, no "common value system," so that authority derived its strength, right up till the middle 1940s, only from an increasingly dense "regulation by force."[19]

In contrast with the Kololo, who had preceded them by about seventy years, the incoming Europeans within ten years or so had so completely embraced the attitudes of domination that to speak of "a Northern Rhodesian society," even acutely divided, is really to speak of what did not exist; then, and for some time afterward, the Africans were no more members of Northern Rhodesian society, as recognized and constituted by duly enshrined authority, than the cattle and the game for whom "reserves" were also soon marked out. This apart, the Europeans were extremely scarce. Here the fond old tag about Southern Rhodesia—"Fair and fine, fair and fine, fifty farms and a railway line"—had even better application. Apart from a few hundred settlers living along a narrow strip northward from Livingstone on the Zambezi, and another small group around Fort Jameson, there were no Europeans in Northern Rhodesia except for a handful of missionaries and administrators, and one or two individual settlers who lived far out in the bush, until well on into the 1930s. Few though they were, however, these Europeans constituted "Northern Rhodesia," and they constituted it separately from the Africans.

The actual process of installation was completed by the last years of the nineteenth century and needs little description here. Armed with his letters patent of 1889, Cecil Rhodes had at once dispatched agents across the Zambezi into country then believed to contain great mineral wealth, though not in copper but in gold. Lochner went to Barotseland and secured from the Lozi king, Lewanika, a concession of far-reaching commercial and mining rights across a vast territory between the Zambezi-

Congo watershed and the Kafue River. While it must be clear that
Lewanika would not have grasped the fuller implications of this, it is also
clear that Lochner was perfectly ready to mislead him as to the status of
the treaty he was proffering. One of its clauses stated that "this agreement
shall be considered in the light of a treaty between my said Barotse nation
and the government of Her Britannic Majesty Queen Victoria,"[20]
whereas, in truth, it was nothing of the kind. Lewanika thought that he
was dealing with another sovereign power of status comparable in kind,
if not in degree, with his own; in fact, he was dealing with Rhodes's
Chartered Company, a very different kettle of fish. Thus trickery and
contempt for African opinion prevailed from the outset.

It prevailed elsewhere as well, and notably in the similar concession
treaties obtained in the northeastern part of the country by Joseph
Thompson.[21] With or without deliberate misrepresentation, the Chartered Company, in any case, possessed itself of scraps of paper which it
could present in London as good titles to "effective occupation" of the
lands in question. Having such titles, it proceeded to act upon them. But
it acted with the most slender means. The whole country was divided, at
any rate nominally, into two separate administrations, one in the north-
west and comprising the Barotse concession, and the other in the northeast, based on the Sharpe, Buchanan, and Thompson treaties. Yet for
some time there were no administrative stations of any kind in northwestern Rhodesia, while control remained only partially effective elsewhere.
At the same time, the principles of installation were now perfectly valid
in British eyes and were seen as giving full right to government. This
right was to be exercised by the company subject in its main lines to
British governmental approval (exercised either through the high commissioner for British Central Africa stationed in Nyasaland or through the
British high commissioner in Cape Town); and here the effective instrument was the Northeastern Rhodesia Order in Council of 1899, modeled
on the precedent for Southern Rhodesia of the year before. This gave the
company administrative power to make regulations for "the administration of justice, the raising of revenue, and generally for . . . peace and order
and good government."[22]

These were somewhat greater powers than were granted to the company in northwestern Rhodesia, "where the imperial Government was
more anxious to have a greater say by reason of the unresolved Portuguese boundary dispute and the existence of a relatively strong native
kingdom with recognized treaty rights."[23] Out of this, in later years, came
the limited separatism of the Barotseland Protectorate. The rest of the
country, however, went the way of the Northeastern Order in Council;

and it was not long before the concession treaties were made into a foundation for complete dominance over all Africans except within the "home territory" of Barotseland. With the latter exception, the two territories were fully amalgamated after 1911; an all-European Advisory Council was formed in 1918; and in 1924, after the European community had voted (in 1922) by 1,417 to 317 against amalgamation with Southern Rhodesia[24] (an ironical verdict in view of what was to happen thirty years later), company rule came to an end and the Colonial Office took over.

Yet the Colonial Office was distant, local revenues were extremely meager, and it was the settlers who continued to stamp their attitudes on daily life. Nothing so organic even as a society of "conflict pluralism" now appeared. Except in occasional policy documents issued in faraway London, all of which remained at this stage without the slightest practical effect, no intention can be discerned of any wish to build a single society consisting of different communities. What the settlers had in mind was to impose a fully integrated but entirely separate European society upon a congeries of African societies. What mattered in their eyes was the speed and completeness with which this European society could be crystallized, made conscious of itself as an entity, and pointed firmly toward permanent rule over the rest of the inhabitants. Against this the Colonial Office had little but empty words and a few local but very partial administrative palliatives.

One may note, however, that this evolving European community was itself a pluralism. If the earliest arrivals were mostly Englishmen, others soon came from elsewhere. Of a European population totalling 1,484 according to the census of 1911, 16.7 percent were members of the Dutch Reformed Churches (were Afrikaans-speaking people, that is, from South Africa), while 4.6 percent were practicing Jews. There were also 39 Indians—and soon there would be more—to complicate the non-African pattern, while the number of Coloreds (fruit of irregular unions between European men and African women) grew rapidly from the handful signaled in the 1911 census, which also helpfully explained that the territory held only 376 European women to its 1,118 European men.[25]

What passed for political life right up until the 1940s was the strife and rivalry between these segments of the non-African community, but especially between the majority of the settlers and the company (or later the Colonial Office), as well as between the settlers north and south of the Zambezi. Of African politics there was none at all, or none that was recognized as more than an occasion for calling out the police. The notion of settlers' self-rule was present almost from the beginning, yet not at all, as it would be half a century later, as a means of "keeping the Africans out." Only one or two settlers at this time seem to have thought that a time could come when the Africans might threaten to be "in." The enemy was first the company and then the Colonial Office, each of which was successively condemned as somehow depriving the settlers of their birthright or the fruits of their labor.

This feeling among men who had gone to "build a new home for themselves" may have existed among a few individuals from the earliest pioneering days, but it first became vocal in 1908 when the proprietor and editor of the *Livingstone Mail* put in the earliest of many claims to settler independence north of the Zambezi[26]—at a time, one may wryly note, when the Europeans in the territory still numbered fewer than a thousand. Yet the claim, however derisory it may seem today, nonetheless made its mark and became the theme song for nearly half a century of settler politics.

One reason why it came so early was an accident of personality. The founder of the *Livingstone Mail*, Leopold Moore, happened to be a rare bird among his fellows in possessing no mean share of intellectual capacity, political talent, and dry abrasive wit. Moore had originally come from England as a settler in Southern Rhodesia, where he opened a pharmacy in the little town of Bulawayo. His ideology is revealed in many editorials and speeches as being a very simple one even in those days of simplified revolution; regarding the Africans as a necessary evil, but not as a danger because they were well kept under, he was mainly concerned at the beginning of his colonial career with what he called the Asiatic menace. He made himself a nuisance to the Chartered Company in Southern Rhodesia, then casting around for means of importing Chinese labor in the hope that it would be more efficient, or at any rate more willing, than African labor; and the company, it is said, placed a boycott on his shop by way of reprisal. "He was unable to hold out and in the end he left Bulawayo, defeated and penniless, filled with hatred against the Chartered Company."[27] He moved to Livingstone, north of the Zambezi, where he started his little newssheet, first as an editorial scourge of the company's agents in Northern Rhodesia and afterward of those of Whitehall.

Yet Moore and his readers and friends initially welcomed Whitehall: better the distant devil, they thought, than the one next door. They voted in 1922 against amalgamation with Southern Rhodesia not, as we have seen, because they disagreed with the objectives of the Southern Rhodesian settlers, but because they hoped that a period of Colonial Office rule could win them time to acquire their own separate independence. The southern settlers were more numerous, after all, and likely to remain so;

amalgamated with the north, sooner or later they would put their own "southern" interests first. Arguments such as these were to crop up time and again as the years went by, often disturbing the unity of the "settlers' front" in the British Central African territories, and especially during the campaign for federation which was eventually crowned with a ten-year victory in 1953. But by then the rivalry of their southern neighbors had generally come to seem far less dangerous than a much more alarming alternative, the incredible but nonetheless real possibility of African enfranchisement. In the early years of Colonial Office rule, however, the settlers were well enough content with their lot. They had every reason to believe they were the heirs apparent.

IV

By 1924, when the Colonial Office took over, there were all told about 4,000 settlers; and it is from this time that a system that deserves to be called a system rather than a fragmentary political experience comes into being. The notion of imperial trusteeship of African communities is officially enshrined by the protectorate concept of colonial rule; and there are the beginnings of an effective local administration through British district commissioners with a hierarchy mounting to an all-powerful governor at Livingstone, and afterward at Lusaka.

From the outset this system was rigidly segregationist. Years later a hopeful young African waited on the district commissioner of Broken Hill with a small request. He recalls in his memoirs that when he got inside the DC's office, he said "Good morning" in English. "The DC turned to the head clerk and said: 'Tell this man in Bemba to say good morning, sir.' Throughout that interview the DC insisted on his head clerk interpreting everything he said into Bemba while I spoke in English."[28] The language of the master race—just, remote, and altogether of a different clay—was not for their inferiors.

Segregation and "trusteeship"—and therefore pluralism? Perhaps. The cultures of the Africans were recognized at an official level; it was vaguely understood that they were parts of the system. Yet recognition at the official level, one may repeat, had little more than theoretical impact on the realities of life. Pursuing their aim of self-rule in an atmosphere of "high imperialism" both here and in the mother country, the settlers found it easy to increase their weight and standing in the political affairs of the colony. If the members they elected to the Legislative Council

remained for long in a minority over against the official members nomi-
nated from the administration by the governor, the settlers almost invariably set the tone of debate. African affairs seldom or never appear in the
records of the Legislative Council except as distant and secondary matters pertaining to "natives" whose own voice remains entirely silent. Even
so, the settlers kept up their steady pressure for full control. In 1929 they
were granted seven seats to the governor's nine, and in 1939 they gained
equality with the official side. Yet at least from the copper boom of 1929,
their support for any crucial measure was in fact a practical necessity.

Until 1948, when four spokesmen for African interests were added (two
being Europeans and two Africans), the Legislative Council continued to
debate and consider African problems as though these belonged to a
subhuman species. The "natives" were "there" in a sense, but in a much
more important sense they were also "not there." "Their proper management, it was held, ought to be entrusted to individual European employers."[29] Leopold Moore put the point with his customary frankness when
he remarked in 1927 that "the natives do not come into contact with this
House. They are governed by the people of this country"—the *people* or
the *public* or the *nation* always being taken, one may note, to equal the
Europeans—"not governed in the sense that they are legislated for by the
people, but they are governed by the people who employ them."[30] It is
a somewhat sibylline utterance, but one gets the point: the "natives" were
not to be thought of as worthy of government in any constitutional or
organic meaning of the term. Persons of a more liberal trend of thought
often referred to them as "minors" or "children" or "wards," with the
implication that although Africans might eventually become members of
society, they had certainly not done so yet.[31]

And so far was this the prevailing attitude, as the records of what was
said and done by the Northern Rhodesian Legislative Council during the
first twenty years of its existence amply show, that one may, as I have
suggested, reasonably question whether the concepts of pluralism, even
when taken at the extremes of the conflict model, have any usefully
explanatory application here before the late 1940s. Yet what better
qualification can one meaningfully attach to it? I shall try to suggest a
term. Meanwhile, one may note that it was not a caste system, since that
implies the theoretical as well as the practical acceptance of some kind of
community between rulers and ruled, and here there was no such acceptance. It was not a slave society of masters and servants even in the early
capitalist sense, where both elements combined to a single if internally
differentiated cultural whole.

Here, on the contrary, there was in practice an utter domination and an unbounded subordination with no bonds or rights or obligations established between the two except those of the settlers' convenience. Nothing appears to have tied these two groupings together except a mutually hateful contiguity from which neither could escape. The Africans regretted that the Europeans were in the country—we have few samples of their opinion, but the statement risks little chance of being wrong—but could not possibly get rid of them. The Europeans longed for the Africans not to be there, physically not there, yet were unable to do without them. The Africans provided labor and in this they were horribly indispensable. If they had to be recognized, it was to the extent of their labor value (estimated at the lowest possible rate), and no further. The sentiment grew with time and habit. Discussing African opposition to settlers' amalgamation across the Zambezi, Moore remarked in 1939 that the "natives have got no grounds for liking it or disliking it; we are running the show."[32]

There were of course exceptions. Relations at the personal level might sometimes be cordial and even warm. But the exceptions only prove the rule, while personal relationships had no political effect. Nothing better illustrates what that rule was, perhaps, than a fairly routine statement by the secretary for native affairs, at that time J. M. Thompson, during a Legislative Council defense debate of March 1932. "Our knowledge of our native inhabitants leads us to believe," he reassured the settler members at a moment when unemployment was heavy on the Copperbelt and along the line of rail, and troubles were feared, "that we need have no anxiety about any internal disturbance on any large scale. There is no cohesion among the important tribes in this Territory, and there is no likelihood of it in the near future. In fact, the most important tribes cannot even speak each other's language or communicate with each other in any way, and it would be very difficult for them to discuss any matter of any importance at all."[33] Somewhere "out there" lay the dark sea of natives, silent and mysterious. Every now and then one sent out little expeditions of reconnaissance in the hope of finding out what was going on. Reassured by finding nothing, these returned; and that was all.

V

WE MAY BRIEFLY TRACE THE NATURE OF THIS SYSTEM IN THREE CRUCIAL fields apart from the machinery of legislation: agriculture, labor, and urbanization. Essentially, the pattern here was much the same as in other

African colonies of European settlement, and measures previously evolved in South Africa and Southern Rhodesia were duly imported as and when they promised to be convenient and useful. Malaria of a severe and epidemic type proved a major deterrent to European settlement in the early years, and it was not until after 1918 that Northern Rhodesia began to be looked upon as a "white man's country."[34] Yet as early as 1904 the few dozen farming settlers in the northeastern highlands, where the land was better than elsewhere, had been able to induce the company to set up a small "native reserve" for the defeated—and expropriated— Nguni who had themselves come there as conquerors some sixty years earlier; and in 1911 these and other settlers pressed for the generalization of reserves. They were to have their way. In 1913 the company in Southern Rhodesia had set aside 22 percent of the land of that country as "reserves" for some 45 percent of the African population; and what it had done south of the Zambezi it now proceeded to do in the north as well.[35]

This achieved three purposes. Land division enforced a measure of physical separation so that Africans in the nonreserved territory could be there only on sufferance, and thus in a servile status; they had to come as supplicants, in other words, or they could not come at all. Second, it opened the way for a more effective effort to "force labor out of the villages" and cause rural Africans, by hut or poll tax, to quit their subsistence economy for the cash economy of their new masters; the reserves being limited (though much less so here than elsewhere), they soon became relatively overcrowded. From this there flowed, as elsewhere, a steady deterioration in the fabric of village life, and, over a period of twenty or thirty years, an uninterrupted decline in rural standards of living.[36] Migrant labor now began to have a devastating effect, although this was for long ignored by administration and settlers alike. At the same time, it became steadily more available at very cheap rates, so that the "reserves" became an essential component in the whole system. Third (though this again was of less importance here than in other colonies of white settlement), the alienation of fertile land from Africans and the removal of established African populations made it possible to offer more land to would-be settlers.

By 1936 the land pattern had long since fallen into place. Three main divisions had come into existence. The Crown retained title over 11 million acres of forest and game reserve, as well as over 94 million acres which were unallotted; much of this was useless for settlement because of infertility or the tsetse fly. Africans retained title over a total of 71 million acres; of this, about 37 million were in the Barotseland Protectorate, while the remaining 34 million were the "reserves" in which the bulk of the population, now estimated at more than a million (although, in the light of better estimates made later on, it was probably much larger), were obliged to reside whenever they chose or could choose to remain at home.[37] For their part the Europeans had just under 9 million acres; 5.5 million of this block were held by two companies, mainly as *latifondi*, leaving a little more than 3 million acres for private farms. How few the latter were in 1936 may be guessed from the fact that they numbered only about 1,100 as late as 1950.[38]

Judged by the standards of South Africa, this division in favor of Europeans was far from severe for the Africans; the latter had lost a lot of good land, but much remained to them.[39] The Europeans multiplied, yet slowly; moreover, they continued to cluster along the line of rail from the Zambezi to Broken Hill and the Copperbelt in the north, and outside this corridor their presence was little felt except in a few rural centers such as Fort Jameson in the east and Abercorn in the far northeast. Inside the corridor, however, they increased their numbers steadily from 1925, when mining surveys led to major finds of sulphide ores with the relatively rich copper content of 3 to 5 percent. Soon the Copperbelt was booming. By 1929, Northern Rhodesia had become par excellence a copper colony, and from now onward it was to be the fortunes of the copper mines which would provide the final regulator in all large questions of policy. European immigration bounded upward. By 1931 the colony had 13,846 Europeans of whom only 1,291 had been born there, while 4,225 had come from the United Kingdom and 6,824 from South Africa.[40] On the eve of the 1931 Depression the mines were also employing no fewer than 29,000 Africans in unskilled or semiskilled laboring jobs.

This availability of African labor had the advantage of aiding low-cost production. Later in the 1930s, when the industry had recovered from the slump and was going ahead again, this copper could be delivered at Beira railhead on the East Coast at a cost per long ton that was about half that of United States and Mexican copper, and still considerably less than that of Chilean production. Not surprisingly, the industry prospered. By 1937, with the average London price of copper standing at more than £50 a ton, earnings on the ordinary shares of the copper companies were yielding about 80 percent; later they would go still higher.[41] As in other colonies, however, local taxation remained extremely low (much lower in Northern Rhodesia, for example, than in South Africa, where the white population could ensure that a higher proportion of earnings was kept in the country),[42] while income tax was paid in the United Kingdom. There was therefore a considerable economic expansion without a corresponding flow of wealth into the pockets of the European settlers (the actual miners excepted) or, of course, the local Africans.

High copper earnings could thus do little to ameliorate indigenous life. Administrative funds remained chronically in short supply, even while copper shareholders abroad won high rewards. And this occurred at a time when the use of African labor for industrial purposes had begun to pose a number of acute problems of urbanization. Here, as we shall see, the counterfactors making for pluralism soon came into play. One of them was trade-union agitation. Another was education. These were, of course, factors of acculturation; yet it needs to be remarked that they barely made themselves felt on any scale that could influence events until the early 1940s. In 1923, for example, administrative expenditure on African education was exactly nil (when about £7,800 was spent on European education),[43] while missionary education unsupported by government money was always a rare phenomenon. The Legislative Council did indeed debate "native education" now and then, although such debates reveal little but settlers' opinions on the unwisdom of any such dubious enterprise. In the fairly characteristic year of 1932, for instance, more pages of Legislative Council records are covered by anxieties over rabies caused by "native dogs" than by thoughts on the subject of "native education."

By 1938 the position had somewhat changed, with the government now spending about £44,000 on African education (and some £55,000 on European education).[44] Yet the advance was snail-slow and could not be otherwise, given the paucity of available funds, and it barely touched the secondary level. As late as 1958 there was only one secondary school in the whole territory capable of taking African pupils through the Cambridge Senior Certificate examination,[45] even though the African population by then was certainly more than 2 million. Of higher education for Africans there was, of course, none at all. To the settlers this appeared perfectly right and proper. "There is not one intelligent native in the country," a former Native Commissioner called Cholmely informed his fellow Legislative Council members in 1939; and they weightily gave him their assent.[46]

Throughout the period between the wars, then, this was a conjunction of communities that could be said to form a single society only in the extreme sense offered by Furnivall, one of utterly disparate sections among whom the highest common factor was economic, "and the only test that all apply in common is the test of cheapness: a process of natural selection by the survival of the cheapest."[47] Even this definition will not really serve, since the Africans were not expected to apply any kind of test or even, as J. M. Thompson had explained, "to discuss any matter of any importance at all." And if European spokesmen ever considered the human beings in Northern Rhodesia as constituting something like a single community, even for economic purposes, they did so only within the ideological framework of a crudely vulgarized Darwinism. "Are not biology, history, anthropology," queried Chad Norris of his Legislative Council colleagues in 1930, "all leading us to an appreciation of the supreme importance of heredity, the supreme value to civilization of superior race stocks?"[48]

If then one has to find a name for this curious system as it existed between 1924 and about 1948, one may perhaps best define it not as a pluralism, but as a despotism, though a despotism of a special kind. It was not a despotism of conquest, for there had been no conquest. It was not a despotism of caste, for the rulers were of different ethnocultural origins and were careful to remember the fact. Nor was it a despotism by an oligarchy, since this would have presumed membership of the ruled in the same community as the rulers, and no such membership was ever admitted. Least of all was it a despotism by an elite, because that would have supposed some training or preparation for the exercise of authority, and these settlers had known nothing of the kind. What then was it? Though a little modified by imperial hesitations in the 1930s,[49] it was a despotism by a haphazardly formed collection of men of whom only the merest handful seem ever to have had any conception of a common future with "their Africans," or of the social responsibilities which might have to accompany such a future; and whose absolute power was for a long time modified only marginally by the imperial factor of Colonial Office control or by the "metropolitan factor" of British public opinion. This was "differential incorporation" through the crudest regulation by force, supposing no consensus but only subjugation.

Even so, it was not a static system. It held within itself (and it is here that pluralist concepts may after all justify their application to Northern Rhodesia before about 1948) a number of internal factors of change, hard to perceive in the 1930s but steadily more visible in the 1940s, which worked for resolution of conflict and even for a measure of incorporation. In this the settlers were constantly surprised and disappointed. Their despotism supposed a world that stood still. "We came here and we are here to stay and dominate,"[50] as Moore pugnaciously explained in 1939. It turned out not to be so after all. But when the ground began slipping from beneath their feet, they did not revise their convictions. For a long time they preferred to ignore the evidence of their own senses.

V I

IN 1935 A NUMBER OF AFRICAN MINEWORKERS WITHDREW THEIR LABOR IN
protest against certain of their conditions of work. Any such African
action was completely illegal, and nothing like this had happened before.
A flurried police was called into action. Six African strikers were shot
dead, others wounded, many jailed.[51] Immediately, this achieved nothing
for the African mineworkers. Indeed, it set them back. Alarmed at possible
African encroachment on their "reserved skills," the European mineworkers (under advice from color-bar unions in South Africa) formed
themselves into a trade union two years later. and introduced a rigidly
formalized industrial color bar where only a customary one had previously existed. Yet the strike had other consequences, concealed at the
time, which were eventually to prove more important. For it really
marked the first small beginning of modern African politics, or the beginning, rather, of a mass participation in activities which acquired an increasingly political undertone.

This flowed from diverse sources. Not the least of these was the
influence of separatist Christianity with its rebellious implications for
colonial Africa. If Northern Rhodesia did not have its Chilembwe, as in
Nyasaland next door, to speak for the cause of Christians who happened
not to be Europeans, it had other men of lesser note who preached to the
same general effect. Their message was essentially the same as that of the
Mozambique pastor in Nyasaland, Charles Domingo, who asked rhetori-
cally in 1911 what the difference was between a white man and a black man,
and replied: "Are we not of the same blood and all from Adam? ... If we
had power to communicate ourselves to Europe we would advise them
not to call themselves 'Christendom' but 'Europeandom.' " Domingo
went on to rub in his point by observing that the life of "the three
combined bodies, Missionaries, Government and Companies ... is altogether too cheaty, too thefty, too mockery. Instead of 'Give' they say
'Take away from.' "[52]

Ethiopist ideas couched in similar vein were present in Northern
Rhodesia from the middle times of company rule, and were reinforced by
local variants of Watch Tower doctrine. It would be out of place to
discuss these here: I want only to make the point that dissident Christianity had taken an acutely, if indirectly, political form in Northern
Rhodesia by at least 1919, when ninety-nine adherents of Watch Tower
were charged with sedition and assault arising from refusal to pay tax or

admit colonial authority.[53] This current of dissent continued and expanded. By the middle 1930s, Watch Tower had become widespread in its propagation of anticolonial ideas, and may reasonably be seen as a parent of the Congress movement of the late forties and fifties.

Direct political action was long in making itself felt. Its incipient origins may be traced among urbanized Africans of the early thirties who had acquired some education. They came together and thought about themselves. Not averse to the emergence of a "middle class" that could eventually help to bridge the abyss between "the European nation" and "the natives," colonial authority even welcomed this development. "There is," remarked the Secretary for Native Affairs in 1931, "a growing tendency amongst natives of the educated classes to form Welfare Associations and Co-operative Societies, and to establish Reading Rooms and Libraries," and the government hoped that such organizations would "in time be a useful means of expression of native public opinion."[54] Later on, when these welfare societies flowered into the Congress movement, official benevolence toward "native public opinion" became rather less emphatic.

As it is, these little groups of literate men—there were as yet very few literate women—do offer some indication of African opinion in these otherwise silent days, though it generally came through European spokesmen.[55] One such indication, worth noticing here, was reported by the liberal-minded Sir Stewart Gore-Browne in May 1936 when telling his legislative colleagues about a meeting he had lately had at Lusaka with a group of "educated natives." They had questioned him intelligently, he said, on the subject of amalgamation of the two Rhodesias, then a matter much exercising settler opinion. At the end of the meeting, Gore-Browne recalled, "a native got up and said, 'Don't you think, sir, that a question like Amalgamation ought to be put before the native people, that they ought to be consulted?' I said, 'I certainly do and so do a great many other white people, but how should it be done?' He said, 'Our chiefs will speak for us.' At once about twenty natives in the room said, 'No, they cannot talk for us, they do not know what we are thinking, they do not know anything about it.' "[56] Here already, in 1936, one sees the essential cleavage between traditional loyalty and the new political opinions now being formed under the stress of breakdown of traditional life, and—another factor of increasing significance—under the pressure of example provided by settler politics.

Such political questionings as these, couched in a framework of modern political thought and action, even if still at an incipient phase of emergence, were joined to the mass influence of village protest through religious dissent as well as to the lesser but growing protest of semiurbanized Africans working in the mines. Once these elements fused together, however imperfectly, the politics of "national liberation" could begin. This process of fusion was slow and partial, and was further reduced by the circumstances of the Second World War; yet it went on quietly beneath the surface, exploding only now and then, so that when the Congress movement finally did appear, late in the forties, it surprised both the settlers and the colonial authorities by the strength of its appeal to natives not previously believed, as Mr. Thompson had said in 1932, to be capable of discussing together "any matter of any importance at all."

Formally grounded in 1948, the Congress movement had its organizational origins somewhat earlier in the Copperbelt townships. These origins took their rise not only out of sentiments of protest against job and wage discrimination, but also—and now it was that the politics of pluralism first began to play their part in the reality, as distinct from the theory, of colonial trusteeship—out of an attempt to borrow and reproduce settler methods of organization. We do not know just how much those little groups of clerks and other literate men of the late thirties and early forties were in the habit of reading the official reports of debates in the Legislative Council and drawing political conclusions for themselves. But the case of labor organization on the Copperbelt is highly instructive. In this respect the crucial year was 1940.

In 1935, as we have noted, there had been African disturbances on the Copperbelt arising from various causes; and two years later, prompted by their colleagues in South Africa, European mineworkers had formed themselves into a strictly color-bar trade union. This prospered. Well led, it secured concessions from the owners. Striking for still higher wages at the Nkana and Mufulira mines in March 1940, the European miners were again successful in securing most of their demands. But a day later something new occurred. About 15,000 African mineworkers also (though illegally) declared themselves on strike for higher pay. Not too surprisingly, perhaps: at this point the average European wage was above 800 shillings a month, while the average African wage at Nkana was 12½ shillings a month for surface work, and 22½ shillings for work beneath the surface,[57] a European-African differential of about forty to one. Faced with this large withdrawal of African labor, management attempted a compromise by offering an extra 2½ shillings a month which was rejected by the strike leaders, who challenged the management to allow the Africans to work a competitive shift underground with the Europeans in order to expose who were the real producers of copper. This was understandably refused; everyone knew already that most of the work was really done by the African crews while Europeans underground did little more than supervise. And management duly called for strikebreakers.

One has the impression that a few years earlier there would have been plenty of Africans to answer this call, and that strikers would have attempted nothing against them. But by 1940 things were different. On the sixth day of the strike at Nkana, a crowd of about 3,000 strikers tried to stop a line of about 150 strikebreakers from drawing their pay. Police and troops who were standing nearby moved to protect the strikebreakers and threw tear-gas bombs. This enraged the strikers, who thereupon assaulted the mining-compound office where all civilian Europeans in the vicinity had meanwhile taken refuge. The troops opened fire, killing seventeen strikers and wounding another sixty-five. This ended the affair, and the strikers went back to work.[58]

But it did not end the evolution of African opinion on the Copperbelt. If trade unions could be useful to Europeans, they could also be useful to Africans. And at this point there again intervened what may be called "the metropolitan factor," but it did so in a new way. If effective British metropolitan opinion during the twenties and thirties had been for the most part emphatically prosettler, there came a steady change with the outbreak of the Second World War and the formation of a Conservative-Labor coalition government in 1940. Pro-African views began to be heard at the official level in Britain. For several years the spokesmen of Labor opinion had developed a strongly liberal trend of thought in colonial affairs—one may see it in many directions, and most influentially, so far as the Parliamentary Labor Party was concerned, in pressures exercised by groups within the Fabian Society—but these spokesmen had wielded no power. Now the war gave them some. New things began to be said, argued, promised. Here, for example, is a fairly characteristic interchange on March 12, 1941, between a critical Labor member of Parliament (later to become secretary of state for the colonies) and a Labor minister in the Churchill coalition government:

Mr. Creech Jones: Will the Government throw the whole of its weight against the practice of the color bar in the [Northern Rhodesian] Copper Belt?

Mr. George Hall [under-secretary of state for the colonies]:   I think it necessary to make it quite clear that the Colonial Office and the Government do not stand for the color bar either in this country or in any of the Colonies.[59]

At least a new note had been struck; and it strengthened as the war went on. Labor ministers pressed for the right of Africans to form themselves into trade unions and carried their point. Nowhere did this have larger local consequences than in Northern Rhodesia. By 1958 there were as many as seven properly registered and organized African trade unions there with a total membership of between 30,000 and 35,000, most of whom were in the African Mineworkers' Union. A year later the unions formed a Trades Union Congress on the British model, while the African mineworkers, with the support of the British National Union of Mineworkers, successfully applied for affiliation to the Miners' International and thereby opened for themselves another useful window on the world. At home, meanwhile, the African miners' union formed in 1949 had pushed up the average level of African wages by 75 percent, and had won recognition as a responsible organization.[60] Viewed against the backdrop of all those Legislative Council debates when the natives had seemed no more than a lay audience of deaf-mutes standing somewhere in the wings, the change was enormous.

Politics followed: if the settlers could advance their interests by forming political parties, so also could the Africans. In 1948 the leaders of the Federation of African Welfare Societies (formed in 1946) decided to reconstitute their organization as the Northern Rhodesia Congress, and once again they were helped by "the metropolitan factor." In 1945 the British electorate had returned the Labor Party with an overwhelming majority, and the government arising from it began to put into effect some of the anticolonial ideas worked out during the 1930s. Contacts multiplied between budding African leaders and members or influential supporters of the government in London; at this point, indeed, the history of independence movements in English-speaking Africa becomes temporarily inseparable from their metropolitan connections.[61] In the wake of such developments, the Northern Rhodesian constitution was altered in 1948 (in line with a policy statement of 1944) to allow the indirect election of two Africans to the Legislative Council. Back in 1930 a member of the Legislative Council, Captain T. H. Murray, had spoken for settler expectations: "I cannot conceive the remotest possibility of Africans being able to sit in the Legislature in twenty, or even fifty years' time."[62] In fact, the event had come about in eighteen years.

VII

THERE WERE, OF COURSE, OTHER OUTSIDE FACTORS AT WORK. THESE WERE the years of early Indian independence. They were the years of African awakening in many lands: of the outset of anticolonial campaigning in most of the English and French territories, of the fruition in separate movements of the constituent elements in the old prewar National Congress of West Africa, of the foundation and onward growth of the multi-territory Rassemblement Démocratique Africain in the French West and Equatorial colonies, and of other such developments, all of which, indirectly or even directly, had their growing stimulus and influence on the nascent political elite of Northern Rhodesian Africans. Reflecting a new mood across the world, and taking advantage of it, a different Africa was taking shape.

As it did so, the central and enduring equivocation within British policy became increasingly clear. It had existed almost from the beginning, though obscurely, and must call for comment in any historical survey, however brief, of pluralism in the British tropical colonies. Were these colonies for emigration, for *Lebensraum* in the Hitlerite sense? Or were they brought into existence as a means of "advancing the natives to civilization"? It goes without saying, perhaps, that they were thought of as both, though not necessarily by the same people or at the same time or in the same degree. At the outset, of course, there was really no conflict between the two ideas: philanthropy toward the British laboring classes and philanthropy toward the poor savages of Africa could elevate the same comfortable bosom to a sense of charitable mission without any need for particular priorities. It thus inspired the excellent Mrs. Jellyby, for instance, in the heyday of Victorian paternalism. She was, wrote Dickens in 1852, "devoted to the subject of Africa; with a view to the general cultivation of the coffee berry—and the natives—and the happy settlement, on the banks of the African rivers, of our superabundant home population," and she hoped "by this time next year to have from a hundred and fifty to two hundred healthy families cultivating coffee and educating the natives of Borrioboola-Gha, on the left bank of the Niger."[63]

Later it became more difficult to reconcile these ideas. There were certain colonies in Africa, it appeared, which could well support far more than two hundred healthy British families, and really ought to do so. Kenya was one of them, and Kenya now raised problems. After 1918 the

Kenya settlers, well led and sometimes well connected with influential folk at home, entered the same demand, but far more forcefully, which Moore had bravely proclaimed in distant Livingstone more than a decade earlier. They pressed for an increasing share in the government of the colony. Matters came to a head in 1923. By now, however, there were also many Indians in Kenya; they "heavily outnumbered the Europeans and it was realized in Whitehall that any attempt to discriminate against them [on behalf of European self-rule] might have serious repercussions in India."[64] The duke of Devonshire, British colonial secretary in the Conservative government of the day, thereupon thought it well to discourage European hopes. He issued the famous declaration of 1923 which bore his name. It remains a capital document and is worth quoting in this context at some length because what it said was later applied to other settler colonies: "Primarily Kenya is an African country, and His Majesty's Government think it necessary definitely to record their considered opinion that the interests of the African natives must be paramount, and that if, and when, those interests and the interests of the immigrant races should conflict, the former should prevail. . . . His Majesty's Government regard themselves as exercising a trust on behalf of the African population, and they are unable to delegate or share this trust, the object of which may be defined as the protection and advancement of the native races."[65]

This caused angry protests among Kenya's Europeans, though it long remained without any practical effect. Elsewhere, and especially in the Rhodesias, British settlers tended to regard it as very much a Kenyan affair, and as no doubt unnecessarily provoked by the well-known arrogance of Kenya's political leaders. Southern Rhodesia, at all events, rapidly became after 1923 a standing denial of everything that the Devonshire Declaration might imply, while Moore and his friends, north of the Zambezi, generally assumed that what had happened with Southern Rhodesia would also in due course happen with them: free of "the Asiatic menace," or at any rate sufficiently so, they would steadily advance to settlers' independence.

Yet the equivocation was still there. The Devonshire Declaration remained on the books. It could be used by colonial governors who came under fire from recalcitrant settlers. It could also be repeated and enlarged. And in 1930, during a brief period of Labor rule in Britain, it was repeated and enlarged by the then colonial secretary, Lord Passfield (Sydney Webb), in a restatement of the doctrine of paramountcy which was now extended to other settler colonies.[66] This deeply shocked Moore and his colleagues. Not only did Lord Passfield gratuitously extend the doctrine of native paramountcy and go on to state that "immediate steps to ensure strict conformity" with it were to be taken, but—*O tempora, o mores!*—African development was to become a "first charge" on the territory's revenues. In the event, Lord Passfield ceased to be colonial secretary the following year, sharing in the general eclipse of Labor's fortunes which came with the great slump of 1931, and no steps, immediate or otherwise, were then taken to bring Northern Rhodesian policy into line with his directives.

Even so, the Devonshire-Passfield line of thought had its profound effect. It influenced settler communities to sink their differences and to press for self-rule more resolutely than before; at home in Britain, meanwhile, and on the other side of the equivocation, it gave the critics of colonialism and of settler politics their "charter" for increased political action. And when the Fabians and other Labor groups composed their anticolonial parliamentary questions and held their anticolonial gatherings and discussions during the 1930s and later, it was on the Passfield Declaration that they took their stand. By the late 1940s, in the wake of all that, the "metropolitan factor" had moved weightily to the "trusteeship" side of the old equivocation, and here it would remain right up until the day when British sanctions were declared against European rebels in Southern Rhodesia, and perhaps beyond. Arising from the very structure of British society, this equivocation lies at the heart of much that the British did and said in and about Africa through more than a century; and it makes repeated nonsense of any simplistic views on the nature of British imperialism in that continent.

VIII

By the late 1940s, accordingly, Northern Rhodesia was ceasing to be a system of extreme conflict. There were still two widely separated communities and, subjectively at least, one of them still held a posture of complete dominance over the other. But the objective relationship was changing. In many practical ways, some of which we have noted above, the official arbiter had come to recognize the existence not of one nation, but of two nations—of two nations, that is, which were members of a single society that had previously contained only one; and now, pushed on by the "metropolitan factor" under new management, the official arbiter had also begun to act on this recognition. From now on it becomes possible to speak of the evolution of a pluralist *society* in Northern

Rhodesia, as distinct from a pluralist *system* of extreme conflict, without doing violence to the term. With the steady growth of African representation at various levels, whether industrial, political, cultural, or even social, the internal dynamics of this two-nation society began moving, though slowly, out of a pluralist system of intense conflict toward a pluralist society of the equilibrium model "in which the units are bound together by crosscutting loyalties, and by common values or a competitive balance of power."[67]

It would be possible to relate this statement to a number of important developments which steadily revealed how conflict in one area of extreme tension after another could be and was resolved, at least partially, by the assertion of an organic balance of power between Africans and Europeans, and then, as events took their course, by the steady movement of that balance to the side of Africans who now outnumbered Europeans by perhaps forty to one. More democracy, in short, brought more internal peace. Regulation began to give way, if hesitantly and imperfectly, to integration; out of this, gradually, there emerged a structure capable of supporting a consensus.

Not easily, of course. There were times of acute strain and conflict. But the process visibly continued. In 1963 the Federation of Rhodesia and Nyasaland was broken up under African pressure in Nyasaland and Northern Rhodesia, and the two northern territories were allowed to move rapidly toward independence under majority rule. In January 1964 the United National Independence Party (UNIP), the militant and far more effective successor to the earlier Northern Rhodesian African National Congress,[68] won fifty-five out of seventy-five seats in a greatly expanded Legislative Council, and the party's shrewd and determined leader, Kenneth Kaunda, became prime minister in all but name. Independence followed less than a year later. Though all but a handful of the country's Europeans retained their white-supremacy convictions to the end, refusing to accept any of Mr. Kaunda's many appeals that they should give UNIP their support and voluntarily take part in building a new political system,[69] few of them left the country. Within a year it appeared—though in March 1966, perhaps, it is too early to be sure—that most of them had lost their worst fears of what must happen under "native rule," and were fairly content with their situation. They had accepted it with a bad grace, but they had accepted it.

This is not to say that the conflict pluralism of Northern Rhodesia's last fifteen years or so has as yet given way to a Zambian pluralism of equilibrium. Organic integration is still no more than partial. This applies not only between Africans and Europeans, but also among Africans themselves. There remain serious conflicts on the African side, conflicts essentially of the transition of a traditional society to a modern society, which range from the Lenshina separatist church with its painful sequel in violence and confusion, to a number of troubles between constituent peoples which are still imperfectly resolved. Cultural differences are so many and occasionally so acute that a more or less long period of organizational integration must be required before these can all be made to fit smoothly within a single society, or, one may perhaps say, within an effective modern restatement of the traditional pattern of checks and balances.

The leaders of UNIP were aware of this, and would argue that they conducted their political action and propaganda toward the building of a pluralist consensus even at moments when preindependence tension was at its height. Here are two examples—by no means exceptional, so far as I know the literature—from a provincial UNIP journal, *Zambia Patriot* of Abercorn far in the northeast, whose articles were printed in Bemba as well as in English. The first dates from April 1963 when UNIP was under fairly heavy repression by the authorities. A. J. Mulenga warns that determined enemies may suffer after independence but goes on to make an appeal for reconciliation: "It has been our sacrifice to suffer so great and liberate our Father Land Zambia. And if we would continue having our ill-feeling towards our supposed to be enemies because of the problems they laid ahead of our struggle we would be making a mistake. . . . Friends-come-we-unite. Enemies come and let us unite, but you stand as enemies if you wish to." Three months later, in June, the paper opens with an attack on Kenyan regionalism (then being conducted by the Kenya African Democratic Union under Ronald Ngala) which was called Majimboism from its Swahili translation: "UNIP stands for the creation of a sovereign Zambia Nation [hence National in UNIP] . . . It is thus important that all Majimboist tendencies be eliminated be they tribal, economic, racial or political. They must be eliminated voluntarily. If the people will it, let there be as many parties as they like. It is the people who must decide." In the event, as we know, UNIP was to remain the only African party of great significance, but again its protagonists would argue that this was so because only a single all-embracing party could at this stage satisfy the dynamics of consensus.

On a Zambian political view, then, things have come full circle. The traditional consensus of old is reproduced, or at least is on the way toward being reproduced, by a new consensus which reflects the needs and possibilities of modern nation-state existence, and has a wider democratic base. Before concluding this essay, and while rather keenly aware of the risks attendant on trying to isolate any constants in a pattern of events so persistently fluid, I should like to offer a few comments on this Zambian view. Though necessarily telescoped, they may serve to promote discussion.

Like many other African nationalists, Zambian politicians and writers have tended to draw a parallel between the "old consensus" of traditional times, precolonial times, and the all-embracing single party or movement of today. In this, no doubt, there is a degree of idealization—or of a necessary and saving belief, shall we say, in the possibility that good may overcome evil—which may be inseparable from all action-urging political doctrines. Very small or even medium-sized societies could indeed achieve a communal consensus in the old days, but wherever large systems emerged the apparent consensus was in fact more likely to "institutionalize elite or ethnic domination."[70] Many "one-party states" in Africa today manifestly do precisely that; and the inverted commas are needed here because this is also the case with states where many parties have been constitutionally free (as in Nigeria) to compete for governmental power. But others, it can be argued, are of a different type: they do not institutionalize elite or ethnic domination but really operate on broadening foundations of consent and participation, and therefore work for the maximizing of consensus rather than conflict.

Nobody has argued this particular view more tellingly, perhaps, than Julius Nyerere, president of Tanzania. Though by no means a materialist in philosophy, he has made it his central point that parties in Africa today can be of national value only insofar as they reflect clear social divisions of interest: "The European and American parties came into being as the result of existing social and economic divisions. . . . Our own parties had a different origin. They were not formed to challenge any ruling group of our own people; they were formed to challenge the foreigners who ruled over us . . . and from the outset they represented the interests and aspirations of the whole nation." To allow the operation of other parties could only be to give a voice to "a few irresponsible individuals who exploit the very privileges of democracy—freedom of the press, freedom of association, freedom to criticize—in order to deflect the government from its responsibilities to the people by creating problems of law and order."[71]

Where such parties have remained national in scope and democratic in structure, they are accordingly claimed by their exponents as being uniquely effective vehicles for a pluralism of equilibrium. In Tanzania, for example, there are many languages and acute contrasts of soil, climate, habitat, or cultural tradition; only a system of "diversity within unity" could hope to prosper. And this is the system of unified diversity which is argued as being inherent in the African one-party approach to pluralism—to a pluralism, that is, which contains within itself a dominant pressure toward the homogeneity postulated, ideally, by the ideology of nationalism, and, looking beyond that, by the ideology of Pan-Africanism.

How then do the ideologists of the "one-party state" meet the point that monopoly must mean corruption: repression and abuse, that is to say, of a kind making for conflict (as in the western and northern regions of Nigeria or in Ghana) and hence moving not toward but away from a pluralism of equilibrium? Some do not meet it at all; others brush it impatiently aside. Examples spring easily to mind. These examples, as it happens, do not include Zambia and Tanzania; or perhaps we should say, given the provisional nature of African political structures in the sixties, they do not include them as things stand at present.[72] It soon became clear to Mr. Nyerere and his colleagues in the national executive of the Tanganyika Africa National Union (TANU), Tanganyika's only legal party, that a one-party structure could easily degenerate into repression and abuse. In 1962 and 1963 they were called on to face several explosive cases of both. They accordingly cast around for new forms of "checks and balances," and called for advice from experts, both African and non-African. In the end, they evolved a system whereby candidates within TANU could stand for election against each other. Tanganyikan elections on this revised model brought several surprises in 1965, not the least of which was the fall of two members of the government.

Here then the traditional structure of checks and balances might be said to be coming into force in a new guise. It could be argued persuasively that TANU was not in fact institutionalizing elite or ethnic rule; on the contrary, it could be urged that the system within which it held a central place was institutionalizing a progressively wider measure of democratic participation, whereas a multiparty system would in fact have had the reverse effect, and have tended toward a pluralism limited to the effective presence of a "divided elite"[73]—in the circumstances, necessarily a pluralism of increasing conflict.

Necessarily? It would appear so. For this is exactly what happened with the federal Nigeria which became independent in 1960. Here the true situation was masked by the presence of many parties. Yet the parties in opposition had, in practice, no chance of assuming power except in the very limited sense of a handful of "elites" who were able to share the spoils of office. Increasingly, after the middle fifties, the effective corpus of Nigerian political life was limited to "a divided elite" with little or no opportunity for local candidates, unsupported by party caucuses, ever

achieving election. A small number of men in power (each belonging to
this or that regionally based party) was opposed in the federal Parliament
(and to a lesser degree in the regional parliaments) by a smaller number
of men who were not in power. Members of these two groups sometimes
acted with each other, and sometimes not, according to the pressures of
group or individual opportunism. There was a steady institutionalization
of elite rule which no proliferation of parties could in any way reduce;
and then, following logically upon this, there were the beginnings of the
institutionalization of ethnic rule—in this case of ethnic rule by the
emirate officeholders of the north acting through their parliamentary
delegates at the center.

This being so, the effective movement in Nigeria was not toward a
pluralism of consensus but toward a pluralism of conflict. Not surprisingly, the conflict came, and in no mere verbal form. The eviction from
power of the majority party in the Western Region, capped by its leader's
removal from political life in 1963, was brought about by the use of federal
power in conjunction with a small splinter party in the region itself, but
the federal power in question was federal in little more than name, being
more and more controlled in reality by the late Sir Ahmadu Bello,
premier of the Northern Region, and his built-in northern majority in the
central parliament. What resulted was extreme conflict: many hundreds
of people in the Western Region lost their lives in political strife during
the last months of 1965. Seen in this perspective, the destruction of
Nigeria's federal regime by army officers on January 15, 1966, could be
interpreted as a move to reverse the current, to dethrone the entrenched
elites, to prevent an institutionalized domination of all the regions by the
largest of them, and to initiate a pluralism of "diversity within unity."
Once again, it might be claimed, traditional approaches could receive a
new embodiment, but one that could hope to achieve an evolving democratic structure—a structure leading toward consensus—such as the
times both required and made possible.[74]

To argue my case beyond this might be merely polemical. Examination
of the precolonial Northern Rhodesian/Zambian structural series has
shown, perhaps, something of the breaks and linkages that lie between
several crucial phrases in the historical experience of these peoples over
the past century and more. The value of this demonstration will rest in
the degree to which it can illustrate and emphasize the underlying continuity of this experience—its changing content as well as its changing
form—from precolonial through colonial to postcolonial times. Further
reflection will also show, I think, that the problems of sociopolitical
transition posed by decolonization are essentially the same in all African

territories, whether or not, for example, they contain white settlers who have exercised local domination.

These problems are concerned above all with a striving for homogeneity, for the achievement of a society of common values by means of the winning of a normative consensus. Ideologically, this striving may be formulated in terms of a nationalism that is nostalgic for the unities, or imagined unities, of the precolonial past. Such formulations need not mislead us; sociologically, the colonial period was far more than an exotic interruption. Its effect was really irreversible. What is now in question, as so many recent tumults and upheavals prove, is the manner in which African authorities will organize, or fail to organize, the socially disruptive consequences of living in a cash economy, of earning wages, of accumulating capital, together with all the sociocultural phenomena associated with these activities. How will their striving for the homogeneity of common values deal with an increasingly acute stratification? Must they suffer this stratification? Can they find their own means of "unified incorporation"? These are questions that can find no answer here. But if the evidence of the 1960s is anything to go by, this striving toward homogeneity (however variously conceived, however differently clothed) is the one great influence that, above all else, will drive the wheels of change. And this, I suggest, is what the whole history of Zambia most clearly, if often contradictorily, demonstrates, and what gives the Zambian experience, in one guise or another, its close and organic linkage with the experience of every other decolonized territory in Africa, and perhaps elsewhere as well.

SYMPATHIES

THE THIRD QUARTER OF THE TWENTIETH CENTURY, SO FAR AS AFRICA was concerned, formed the arena of imperialist withdrawal and of the early efforts by a multitude of African peoples to recover their independence—in a large sense, to recover their self-confidence—after the suffocating consequences of dispossession. This proved to be a long process, in formal terms beginning with the independence of the kingdom of Libya (as it then was) in 1951, and continuing for forty years down to the independence of Namibia in 1990. Likewise, and unavoidably, this was a period of political and social upheaval as men and women came to terms with realities and problems not really understandable before. And then, of course, it was a period reached across a threshold of painful struggle, always difficult and testing of morale, as well as of counterviolence against the persistent violence of colonial powers.

Looking back on those years, as one observer who immersed himself in the hopes, fears, and perspectives of those who worked for anticolonial independence, I have not the slightest doubt that the project of regained African sovereignty was right and necessary not only in its own terms, but in any historical terms. Unless the humanity of this whole continent could restore to itself its own identity and self-respect, it was bound to perish in degradation. That was the inner sense of every genuine anticolonial movement, whatever the words on the banners it marched behind. The slogans might be nationalist, or something other than nationalist; they might be far-reaching in their implications, or merely humdrum in their pressure for a "better tomorrow"; they might be borne aloft by men and women of potent and selfless vision, or parroted by calculating careerists and other such poor creatures. In these lands of infinite variety and situation, everything was conceivable. Yet the inner sense of what was striven for, and striven for in one painful way or another by unforgettable multitudes of men and women, very young more often than very old, was never in serious doubt. It was for restoration of personal and historical identity, for recovery of self-respect, for reassertion of collective self-confidence. It was for the reversal and undoing of the dispossessions.

This seems often to have become forgotten, or written down in its sovereign importance, during the dim years of the 1990s. There were those now who spoke nostalgically of the beauties of subjection: hadn't colonialism, after all, offered a necessary prelude or preparation for Africa's entry into the "modern world"? Without that prelude, as we are reminded by Professor David Fieldhouse, who with great distinction holds the chair of imperial history at Cambridge University, "the alternative may have been increasing misery and disorganisation of indigenous societies as the outside world impinged on them."[1] Africa's structures of self-organization and self-defense, in this view, could never have resisted the pressures of the outside world, as the Japanese had resisted after their reforms of the Meiji period, and then marched into modernity on their own feet.

It is a view with a long heritage, and not only European. The need for a period of foreign rule, colonial rule, was accepted by the "morning stars" of African renaissance in the 1860s, Africanus Horton among them. Some such period was necessary, they believed, in order to give time and opportunity to introduce and carry through a modernizing revolution such as Africans on their own would not be able to introduce or carry through. But what the "morning stars" forgot or could not see was the driving essence of colonial dispossession, which was and is racism: the imposition, that is, of categories of systematic inferiority on colonized peoples. And when, in due course, they were obliged to recognize imperialism's driving essence, it was too late. They had lost their countries.[2]

Fieldhouse is far too good a historian to overlook this reality of the colonial condition. Unlike latter-day nostalgics, he sees it very clearly. "Colonialism," he writes, "offered one way of enabling these [African] societies to meet the challenge of the outside world, but it would have done so beneficially only if the imperial powers had set themselves to preserve the best of what they found"—of what they found at the time of their invasions and dispossessions—"and built on it, rather than reject the African past as 'primitive' and 'barbarian.' This they failed to do. Nor did they adopt the only morally acceptable alternative course of deliberately offering the African the opportunity to adopt Western democratic modes of thought and action. So Africa lost its past and was denied a future. That, at least, is indisputable."[3]

To this one must add, however, that the real and actual nature of colonialism—of imperialism in this particular guise—stood squarely against this morally acceptable alternative. Its nature was and had to be racist, as was thoroughly proved again and again in the years after the 1860s. Colonialism, whether British or any other, could never have applied the alternative that Fieldhouse indicates as being desirable, could never have stood back and allowed indigenous potentials to work themselves out to the indigenous good—any more, one should add, than any new sort of colonialism would do this. This "alternative" may have figured now and then on the personal agenda of this or that great colonial agent—as, in a limited sense, it figured on Frederick Lugard's in northern Nigeria a hundred years ago. But the agenda was never one that imperial power could have had it in mind to promote. The dispossessions were exactly what the word describes, and were intended to be so—culturally as much as economically, psychologically as much as materially. This too is indisputable.

The argument that colonialism was generally beneficial to the colonized, and could be so again in the world as we have it now—in a world distinct, for example, from the altogether different world that Britons knew when Rome withdrew her legions long ago—has to suppose that the leopard can and does change its spots: that imperialism-colonialism need not be racist in its policies and intentions. This is today an argument invariably made by those—unlike Professor Fieldhouse—who make this supposition. It is, therefore, an unreal argument; it is not worth pursuing. To divide imperialism from its driving motivations would be like removing an engine from an automobile and expecting the vehicle to move. Nobody among the anticolonial nationalists or activists, who were realistic persons, had any such intention. Then it was seen to be clear and undeniable that Africa's imposed inferiority could be successfully challenged only by the removal of colonial subjection: only by the undoing of the dispossessions. This was roundly stated by a galaxy of brilliant African intellectuals, historians or sociologists or men of action; or it could be stated by simple members of the public for whom freedom, however misty a term it might seem, was a true and graspable reality. The leopard did not change its spots because the leopard *could* not change its spots. The leopard must go.

Africa's anticolonial thinkers saw this with unflinching clarity and drew their conclusions. They and their successors, even in latter days of "neocolonial" misery, have little to apologize for. The notion now some-times heard that Africa's intellectuals have failed because the postcolonial politics of Africa have failed has little substance. Some proved overhope-ful, for which they may be forgiven. Others became discouraged (and who would not have been in the toils of this "neocolonial" period after the 1970s?). But no one at all significant among them was absent from the ranks of those who pressed for an end to subjection. If thieves and bandits arose to surge around them and against them, this was scarcely an exceptional case in our modern world. All this, I think, needs saying in the context of the anticolonial struggles. If Africa's thinkers seldom found the "right answers" to the problems that immersed them, who anywhere will care to cast the first stone? As it was, they sometimes *did* find the "right answers" and deserve the more credit for that.

Learning the realities of Africa's situation in those years had to be difficult. The extracts and commentaries that follow here bear witness to the difficulty. I do not offer them as containing any superior wisdom. But I hope they present useful insights into tremendous crises and controver-sies that governed those crucial years. Whatever wisdom they may con-tain, in relation to those crises and controversies, was mostly learned from African thinkers and activists not many of whom, to our sore loss, were able to survive the strains and murderous perils of those times. As with other essays in this volume, I have left them to stand without improve-ments by hindsight—like this they can, more bluntly, show how our history was lived and understood.

The direct and physical problems involved in observation of the decolonizing process were relatively few wherever, as in West Africa, there were few or no resident and permanent white settlers; but such problems were correspondingly harsh and many in all those colonies, whether in North or East or southern Africa, where permanent white settlement was comparatively large and long established. In those colo-nies the white minorities, although numerically small, had been encour-aged by their "motherlands"—France and Britain and Portugal—to regard themselves as the residuary legatees of imperial power: when that power withdrew itself (if ever this should come about), it was the white minorities who would "take over"—as indeed the white minority in South Africa had done in 1910. The racist categories of colonial rule would in this way be sustained and kept safe. The white settler minorities were entirely convinced of this, and said so on every possible occasion.

All this being so, it required no wisdom in the early 1950s to perceive that a prime subject of inquiry ought to be the condition of the black populations of these colonies. This inquiry was more difficult than it must now appear to have been. Archives were still closed or in any case sparsely useful on the subject of African conditions; books were few. Access for unofficial researchers such as myself was invariably hard to get, and soon became impossible. Each white-settler territory, at least within the British range, tended to copy the decisions, about who should be allowed in and who should not, from a then-dominant white-ruled South Africa. Being banned from South Africa after the 1952 publication of my admittedly critical survey, *Report on Southern Africa*, I found myself duly banned in 1954 from the newly formed Federation of Central Africa (the two Rhodesias and Nyasaland), and then worse still from my point of view as an apprentice in African studies, in 1956 also from the British East African territories (Kenya, Uganda, Tanganyika, Zanzibar). This last was a great and altogether unexpected blow to my plans for self-instruction, and came about because there was an agreement between the white-settler Central African Federation and the "common services commission" of the British East African territories, to the effect that each would ban the other's "prohibited immigrants." The long arm of apartheid South Africa, in other words, could reach far across the continent.

But misfortunes can have their unexpected benefits. So it proved in this case. Banned from vast territories, some of which I had never yet seen, where else could one usefully go? There was obviously the vast ex-colony of the Sudan; and there, to my great advantage, I was at once made welcome. Sudan had acceded to independence in 1956. A few months later I reached Khartoum, and applied to its Ministry of the Interior for permission to travel widely. No problem. "Yes," said Sayed Meccawi, then permanent under secretary, "we know that you've been banned from East Africa. But you are welcome here, for this is a free country now." And I traveled freely for many weeks, visiting Meroe and other memorable places.

Notably, as we saw in the second part of this book, there were also the Portuguese colonies, enormous "areas of silence"; and I began there with Angola. This again had consequences. One of these was easily foreseen once I had gathered the evidence on Angolan contract labor that was no different from old-style forced labor. My 1955 book on this subject, *The African Awakening*, had a powerful impact if only because the authorities in Salazarist Portugal (which we may reasonably term fascist Portugal) had yet to understand that they could no longer afford to admit the truth about forced labor; they had given me this truth without concealment and were correspondingly enraged when I published it in plain language. They slammed the door on me, but the horse (in a manner of speaking) had bolted—I was safely home again.

There was then a further consequence. The chapters in that book relating to forced labor in Angola were condensed in translation and reprinted in leaflet form, braving the political police (the infamous PIDE), by anticolonialists in the Angolan capital of Luanda. And when these brave men and women, or those that could escape, began to flee Angola a year or so later, mine was one of the names they knew in Europe. After 1952 my house in a London suburb became, for them, a port of call. One after another of the future leaders of anticolonial insurrection in these Portuguese colonies gave my wife and me the honor of accepting our hospitality. These often remarkable persons—Mario de Andrade and afterward Agostinho Neto from Angola, Marcelino dos Santos and then Eduardo Mondlane from Mozambique, Amílcar Cabral from "Portuguese Guinea" (Guiné-Bissau), and others who came in those years—gave us a vivid friendship but also, through their instruction, helped to open for us a whole new field of research.

This privileged access to information about life for Africans under Salazarist dictatorship carried with it an obvious obligation. One should go and see for oneself. And when the anticolonial insurrections were launched—essentially in 1961 in Angola, 1963 in Guiné, 1964 in Mozambique, these being led in each case by one or another of our "visitors to London"—the need to see for oneself became imperative. Long journeys in the bush, by way of guerrilla means of entry or exit and of guerrilla trails of communication, were now the only means of reliable self-instruction. Between 1967 and 1975, I traveled on foot, and for weeks at a time, in all these territories of insurrection. I was not alone in doing this.

But why, it may be asked, insist upon the liberating value of these insurrections in forgotten colonies of Portugal at a time, thirty years later, when Angola and Mozambique have become engulfed in the strife of various banditries? The answer, for me among many others, is that the moral and political value of those wars of anticolonial emancipation has not been overtaken or erased by subsequent disasters, appalling disasters for which the anticolonial movements in question—the PAIGC in Guiné and Cape Verde, the MPLA in Angola, FRELIMO in Mozambique—were in no way primarily responsible. As the records abundantly show, these disasters derived from apartheid South African imperialism and from those outside Africa who encouraged and promoted that imperialism. Blunders and mistaken policies on the part of the movements of independence were not few, but they were never more than of secondary importance, even of very secondary importance, in imposing the miseries we have had to watch since these movements won their wars of independence in 1974–75. History will remember these movements, and the men and women who made them, as having crucially changed the course of history throughout the vast regions of southern and central Africa. It will remember them for their persons, for their ideas, for their ardent belief in a different future, and, not least, for the savagely hostile circumstances in which they had to do their work and, all too often, sacrifice their lives.

It needs to be said that the world political background against which they had to build their fighting movements and survive—survive for years before they could have any immediate prospect of winning—was extremely unfavorable. Mozambique and Angola stood as flank guards, on east and west, to the racist powerhouse of South Africa; and South Africa in those years was designed to be the residuary legatee of British imperialism throughout the southern half of the continent. By 1970 it seemed that this was a design that would succeed. Governing circles in Washington and London certainly thought so, and framed their policies to confirm that the white-minority surrogates of apartheid South Africa were going to stay in place, whether in Rhodesia or in the Portuguese colonies of Mozambique and Angola.

But history decided otherwise. However improbably to the outside eye, the antiracist independence movements in Mozambique and Angola (just as in Guiné far to the west) were after all able to impose defeat—a shattering and unquestionable defeat—on the far larger and better-equipped forces of the Portuguese dictatorship, even though these forces were assured, to the end, of a more or less total support by major powers, not least the United States and Britain. This success in freeing great territories from foreign rule changed the balance of power and influence throughout the subcontinent to the immediate disadvantage of Pretoria's hegemonic plans. For the first time since about 1800 it became possible to foresee a time when the African populations of this huge subcontinent would be able to recapture control of their own territories. This prospect has not been reversed. Almost twenty years of reckless military and paramilitary aggression by the armies of Pretoria, again and again invading Angola or Mozambique or sending in their African mercenaries, have not availed to cancel the victories of 1975. Meanwhile, in South Africa itself, antiapartheid action of one kind or another has gone far to undermine the racist dictatorship.

How were these victories rendered possible? What was the living reality behind their courage and persistence? What was the sociology? Much will be written about all this in future years. Here are some contemporary reports and commentaries that may help toward providing answers. Read into them, please, an element in the success of these movements that was difficult to translate at the time—a certain bubbling sense of laughter as these young men and women savored the sheer improbability of their enterprise, just as David, I am sure, savored his challenge of Goliath. There was little that was solemn in the talk and posture of these unsung heroes. Theirs was a good companionship; but very difficult, mortally difficult. Laughter could be one of the few assets that they had.

Necessarily selective, these journalistic writings can do no more than suggest the wealth of experience produced and constantly extended in these insurrections by "militants who are not militarists." But they indicate, I hope, the profoundly original and democratic nature of that experience. This nature went wholly in the direction of *more participation,* and often it had to ask for much that human capacity could not in practice deliver. That too was "in the situation"; and again, a sense of humor was required. All the men and women who were outstanding in these movements, as it seemed to me, developed a sometimes dour but ever-ready sense of humor; and to fortify this they took from peasant wisdom whatever they could find to help them. Peasant sayings, for example. *E ka n'lidura di lagarto que na tudjibu canoa passa* was one, from Guiné Creole, that I heard being used in Guiné. The ocean creeks and waterways of Guiné are a home for crocodiles, and falling in among them is not advised, but it's worse to be afraid of them or, as this saying pithily explains, "It's not the dirty stare of the crocodile that'll stop your canoe going over [the creek or waterway]." What *will* stop your canoe would be your own want of care or courage.

These extracts are short on the Mozambican dimension, not because this was any less interesting or important than those of Angola or Guiné, but because, for various irrelevant reasons, chiefly lack of time available from other work, I made only one journey there during the insurrections. This was to attend the congress of FRELIMO that was held, in 1968, in the woodlands of Niassa Province in the north of the country—the congress which confirmed Eduardo Mondlane as the movement's chosen leader (until his assassination by Salazarist agents in 1969); which enshrined the movement's determination to fight on till victory was gained (as it was to be in 1975); and which brought to the fore the man who would carry on Mondlane's work and policy after Mondlane's assassination. This man was Samora Machel, another luminous personality to add to the long list of those whose lives would be taken.

By 1970 it had become clear that only men and women of outstanding courage and capacity could meet the obligations of leadership in these insurrections, and this is why these men and women, without exception, are memorable in the history of their times. It was my fortune to know many of them, and some of them very well, but the one I knew best, and with whom I formed close ties of friendship, was the founder of the independence movement in Guiné and Cape Verde, Amílcar Cabral (1924–73). In 1983, ten years after his assassination at enemy hands, the movement in Cape Verde Republic called together an international symposium on the legacy of Cabral; the essay which concludes this part was among the fruits of that initiative.

AFRICAN PEASANTS
AND REVOLUTION

T HE AFRICAN TERRITORIES OF ANGOLA, GUINÉ, AND MOZAMBIQUE[1] ARE today (1974) the scene of vast upheavals. These upheavals have arisen from the clash between an emergent African nationalism and an intransigent Portuguese effort to destroy this nationalism or, failing that, to reduce it to a tamed reformism. The colonial wars thus engendered began in Angola during February 1961, in Guiné during January 1963, and in Mozambique during September 1964, and they have since continued on a rising, if erratically realized, scale of effort on either side. Though probably not yet at their peak, they are already the largest wars ever to have occurred in African history, not excepting the Algerian war of independence.[2] On the African side they entirely overshadow anything in terms of "guerrilla warfare" witnessed in Latin America during these past ten years and more, and in those terms may be reasonably compared with the effort of the National Liberation Front of South Vietnam, although this comparison is in many other respects inapplicable.

These wars must therefore be of close interest to everyone concerned with the history of Portugal on one side and that of African nationalism on the other. But there are two persuasive reasons why they should also be of interest to everyone concerned with "peasant questions." Leaving aside their impact on the peasantry of Portugal, a desperately understudied subject, compared with which research into the African side is even abundant, the first of these reasons is that the vast majority of members of these African nationalist movements, and many of their best leaders,

This essay originally appeared in 1974 in the *Journal of Peasant Studies*. Reprinted with permission.

come directly from populations who are peasants in the sense defined by Teodor Shanin (1972, p. 28).[3] On any rational view of the matter, these struggles in "Portuguese Africa" are peasant struggles.

Second, they are peasant struggles of what may perhaps be called an especially "pure" type. For the most part, they are being supported and they are being fought by peoples whose economic system is certainly no longer one of "subsistence" in any complete sense of the term, but is just as surely nearer to one of subsistence than that of most other populations usually defined as being a peasantry. Here we find peoples whose economic and cultural self-sufficiency within sometimes very small geographical or kinship areas has quite often remained the central feature of their way of life and understanding of the world, whose literacy is nil or almost so, and whose use of modern technology, with everything that this implies, is much less advanced than what has long been generally found in Cuba, Vietnam, or Algeria. In the jargon of development studies, many of the populations who have fought off Portugal's armed forces with a continuous if uneven success, often a very costly success demanding a stubborn unity and will to suffer, are among the least "developed" peoples of any region of the Third World today.

Yet these peasants have received scanty or still inadequate attention from serious observers concerned to analyze their motivations and "mechanics," and in any case only a small fraction of the study directed to far smaller and less enduring peasant struggles in, for example, Latin America. Whatever the reasons for this neglect, the time has surely come to embark at least upon preliminary inquiries into the nature of these peasant struggles in "Portuguese Africa." In the hope of stimulating a wider interest and a more secure analysis, this essay will touch on several dominant themes. Necessarily selective in their scope, these themes are three. They concern the historical context of these struggles, their nature, and their ideas and aims.

I

THE PORTUGUESE HAVE LONG BEEN NOTABLE HISTORIANS OF THEMSELVES, at least until the general deterioration of scholarship under Salazar's regime had reached its midpoint around the 1940s, since when the scene has become ever more desolate and deserted; and there is accordingly a large if unequally valuable historiography devoted to the Portuguese in Africa. Recent work in English by a number of historians has widened it.[4]

In the Africans whom their governments have ruled and claimed to civilize, Portuguese historians may be said to have shown practically no interest at all, even to the extent of producing an Egerton or a Coupland. Save perhaps for the partial exception in the nineteenth century of Paiva Manso, who published the Kongo king Affonso's correspondence with Lisbon, the Africans have evidently remained for them a faceless mass of "natives," a cultural zero, a historical nothing; indeed the present prime minister of Portugal, when a professor at Coimbra, emphatically declared in tones that matched his master's voice that the Africans "have invented nothing useful, discovered no profitable technology, conducted no conquest of value to the evolution of mankind" (Caetano, 1954, p. 16). Again, others outside Portugal have lately begun to give serious thought to African history in "Portuguese Africa," and now it is becoming possible to understand the past of the indigenous populations of these territories as well as their overseas intruders.[5]

The Portuguese side of the story, providing much of the historical context of the great uprisings of the 1960s, falls into three principal phases. The first of these covers a long period, beginning after the middle of the fifteenth century, when the Portuguese made trading contact along the seaboard of western and then of eastern Africa, and conducted occasional armed forays into the interior, eastward from what later became the northern coast of Angola or westward up the course of the Zambezi. This "paleocolonial period" came to be chiefly concerned with the extraction of captives for use as slaves in Brazil; and its influence on the peoples of the interior was limited to the consequences of that enterprise, conducted mostly by African or part-African intermediaries working with Portuguese buyers along the seaboard, often to the accompaniment of Portuguese armed incursions.

A second phase opened with the Congress of Berlin (1884–85) and the effort to secure "effective occupation" of colonial territories defined by national frontiers on all the "inland boundaries." Military expeditions set forth from coastal or near-coastal bases, traversed the little known interior, clashed with armed resistance by various African peoples, established little forts at geographically useful places, and gradually advanced the claim that Portugal was "in occupation" of these territories. For a long time the claim had little substance in reality, and only in the 1920s, whether in Angola, Guiné, or Mozambique, was African sovereignty fully quenched.

There then opened a third phase of civilian administration (backed by the military whenever "secondary resistance" took the form of large rebellions), which also saw the beginnings of a *mise en valeur* on a low level of investment and the gradual establishment of an economic infrastructure, especially in the matter of road communications. The general principles of Portuguese colonial doctrine during this period were much the same as those of other colonial powers, though perhaps closer to Belgian principles than British or French. But Portuguese practice became in this respect increasingly eccentric after the installation of Salazar's Estado Novo, effectively in the 1920s, theoretically in the early 1930s. Reflecting Portugal's own situation, this eccentricity took the form of a systematic exaggeration of the practices of other powers. All of these supposed that African colonies should bring benefits to economic interests in the "motherland" and thus, indirectly, to the state;[6] but Salazar's regime made the maximization of such benefits into a cardinal aim of state policy for state advantage. And where at home the Salazar regime cut down social spending in the interests of a positive balance of payments, its governors in Africa were ordered to do the same in their fiefs. All the colonial powers did this, and the period between the wars was everywhere in colonial Africa one of social and cultural stagnation and also, if to varying extent, of stagnation in the *mise en valeur*. But this stagnation was probably far more complete in "Portuguese Africa."

It was nonetheless accompanied by erratic efforts at enlarging the extractive system. Again, the Portuguese regime carried to excess what other powers practiced more discreetly. All imposed forced labor in one form or another. But the more advanced powers increasingly imposed it, after the 1920s, by indirect means such as the imposition of poll taxes which had to be paid in cash, and accordingly earned by working for whites; direct forms of forced labor sensibly diminished. But not in the Portuguese colonies; there the old internal slavery, formally abolished before 1900, gave way to a massive use of forced labor by a so-called "contractual" system, the principle of the effective labor law being that Africans were not really "working" so long as they worked for themselves, but were really "working" only when they worked for wages and thus, overwhelmingly, for whites.[7] The rest of the system may be said to have closely reflected this crudity of exploitation, and was everywhere marked by the strictly authoritarian habits and approaches of the regime in Lisbon. Constitutionally, the populations were divided into two rigid categories, those of *assimilado* and *indígena*, the former being allowed the same civic rights and status, at least in theory, as metropolitan Portuguese, while the latter, being noncitizens, had no such rights and were subject to the full discrimination of the laws, notably those concerning labor and domicile. In any essential way the system was much the same in its effect, and often in its regulations, as that of Smutsian South

Africa. Its guidelines, interestingly enough in this context, were also pre-
Salazarist in origin, being laid down by the last "great" colonial governor
of the pre-Salazarist period, Norton de Matos.[8] What the Salazarist regime did, during the 1930s and 1940s, was to transform these discriminatory principles into a rigidly racist system,[9] rather as the South African
National Party, after 1948, systematized the discriminatory principles and
practices of Smutsian South Africa into apartheid.

Such were the formative circumstances of the great uprisings. Other
powers in Africa, after the Second World War, had adapted their essential
economic interests in their colonies to the policies of political withdrawal
and, at any rate after the early 1950s, had generally provided for the
opening of a more or less large number of "safety valves" in the "structural containers" of African discontent and demand for change. In 1959
even the Belgians were brought to see the advantages of this policy. But
Salazar and his spokesmen, including the present prime minister, Mar-
cello Caetano, would accept no such arguments and perceived in them,
as they often said, only the pathway to European disaster. How far they
really thought this remains arguable, yet much of what they said then and
since bears witness to a profound belief in their own mythology.[10] Behind
this intransigence, in any case, lay the painful fact of Portugal's own
economic weakness; whether they wished for it or not, the rulers of
Portugal were in no position to embark upon a "neocolonial period"
combining political withdrawal with continued economic hegemony. The
latter, from any reformist perspective, would then simply pass to the
United States, Britain, and the leaders of the international system of
which Portugal itself was economically little more than a satellite.[11]

This absence of any "reformist option," so formative elsewhere in the
development of African nationalism, has to be seen as a major factor in
the turn to armed resistance, for what remained was only a choice between war or continued surrender at a time when peripheral territories—
the Belgian Congo and Northern Rhodesia in the case of Angola, the
French colonies of Senegal and Guinea in the case of Guiné, Tanganyika
and Nyasaland in that of Mozambique—had gained or were about to gain
their political independence. The leaders of the nationalists, at that time
mostly townsmen and intellectuals, accepted the need for armed resistance with varying degrees of conviction and effectiveness. They were
followed by the peasants, but again with varying degrees of support or
participation: massively and explosively in a few cases such as the Kongo
of northern Angola, where colonial abuses had long been felt as severe
(and where, in the case of the Kongo, others of the same people had just

witnessed the withdrawal of Belgian rule); scarcely at all in many cases; elsewhere again, with doubt and hesitation.

Why and for what reasons did this initially hesitant support among the peasants grow into a widening involvement, and why has it continuously spread to new populations?[12] Here one may attempt at least the sketch of a historical reconstruction as a basis for discussing some of the answers; and I propose to do this not in relation to "highly colonized" peasant populations, whose reasons for resistance may be obvious enough, but mainly in relation to a peasant people who have been comparatively little touched, in the general course and structure of their daily lives, by the colonial occupation and its *mise en valeur*. Their case may be especially instructive, even if their strategic position is peripheral to the outcome of these wars, for their case can demonstrate in an unusually direct way the whole nexus of problems implied by transition from "traditional values" to struggles within a modernizing ideology and framework.

The example in question is that of the so-called Ganguela language-group[13] who live mainly in the remote plains of eastern Angola. Linguistically in close relation to Lunda and other Bantu-language peoples of central Africa, this "Ganguela" group has long occupied its present region; according to the official census of 1960, which I use here because it describes (approximately, at least) the situation on the eve of struggles which have greatly altered the population picture, they numbered 329,259 souls, making them the fifth-largest language group in Angola, although it is also true that their constituent languages differ considerably from each other.[14] More particularly, the example is that of the Mbunda,[15] whose exact number was not attempted by the 1960 census but may be of the order of 50,000. They may almost all be described as peasants, and live in the central-southern area of the great eastern district of Moxico, reaching from the Zambian frontier (here the territory of the Lozi, or what the British called Barotseland) for about 150 miles to the west. Their country is relatively poor savannah and sparse woodland of the soils that fringe upon the Kalahari sands, and their numbers, as one may see, match this ecology. After 1965 these people joined the Angolan resistance and became one of its effective pillars in the east.

Early descriptions of the Mbunda are few and hard to find, like their hamlets, and a later anthropology has had almost nothing to say about them. Silva Pôrto offers a few swift glimpses in his notebooks of the 1850s and after,[16] but Arnott and Serpa Pinto, who traversed their country in the 1880s, add almost nothing. Not until 1918, with Ferreira Diniz,[17] does one come upon any real attempt to describe the Mbunda and their neighbors.

This leaves much to be desired. The "Ganguela" as a whole, he says, have "federations" consisting of small nuclei "linked by family ties, but more or less independent of one another." Each nucleus has its chief assisted by a council of elders who take decisions by majority rule. "These small states, if one may call them such, are subordinate to the chief of the tribe, to whom major questions are taken for hearing and judgment by the councillors, upon which occasions, these being important moments of great interest to the tribe (such as declarations of war and succession questions), there assemble all the chiefs of the *libatas* [nuclei] and their kin, the decisions again being taken by majority. . . ."

The chief of the Mbunda, Diniz continues, is Mwene (Chief) Bando, "who has exercised this function for about twenty years"—since, that is, some years before 1900—"and is one of the few tribal authorities to have conserved power and prestige among his subordinates. His residence is along the banks of the Luati. . . ."[18] In that period, then, before any effective Portuguese occupation of this region save for a handful of forts established by João de Almeida in 1909 and garrisoned by a few soldiers, black as well as white, the Mbunda were organized politically in a manner familiar to many regions of Africa. Sparse occupants of a large if little-fruitful land, their "nationalism" was that of a cultural identity and a minimal political loyalty to chiefs whose secular power, insofar as they had any, derived from the "charters" of ancestral tradition.[19] In other words, they lived in the general pattern which had enabled the peopling of these solitudes during an Iron Age which began, here in eastern Angola, around the middle of the first millennium A.D. Based on a system of beliefs about humankind and its environment, itself the product of this people's survival and development, the "charter" of the Mbunda had evolved to give them the "community cement" they needed, and to provide both for explanation of the world they knew and prescription of the way that they should live in it.

Mwene Bando was their last independent king or paramount. Exactly when he was overthrown, and in what manner, and to what extent the Mbunda were then "colonized," is anything but clear in the secondary sources, while the primary sources in Lisbon and colonial archives have yet to be explored or, indeed, opened for exploration. Yet one may note that Henrique Galvão, writing much later, in 1930, notes of this area that "our influence, Portuguese occupation and territorial organization, are incomparably less intense and perfected than they were after the action of Almeida" in establishing forts as far as Mucusso, in 1909.[20] Clearly, the Mbunda and their neighbors were anything but completely "pacified" even at the outset of the 1930s. But the 1920s appear to have brought the small beginnings of colonization in Moxico, as in Cuando Cubango to the south and Lunda to the north, and it would seem that the 1930s carried the process further by establishing a direct political control through Portuguese administrators and such coercive force as they could bring to bear. The means were small, but were used with a determination characteristic of the Portuguese.

If "pacification" was more or less achieved by the mid-thirties, it was little exploited. These eastern lands were poor. They offered little in the way of exportable produce, and few Portuguese cared to come and settle here if they could possibly live somewhere else. Administrative centers were "towns" of the "third class" or the "fourth class," handfuls of huts and sheds, remote, forgotten, abandoned to their isolation. The Mbunda and their neighbors appear to have felt the "colonizing process" in little more than demands for free labor and in whatever taxes could be raised from any of their economic activities. The 1960 census says much about their situation when it speaks of religious affiliation. For the whole Angolan population, put at 4,830,449, Catholics were numbered at 2,454,401 and Protestants at 800,091, so that far more than half the population was claimed as Christian. But for the Circumscriçao dos Bundas (Mbunda), only 2,096 Catholics and 3,521 Protestants were claimed in a total population of 49,805, or little more than a tenth for both Christian denominations. The number of whites was exactly 63. Thus the Mbunda adhered to the appeal of militant nationalism while standing in the "colonial spectrum" at a far extreme from other peoples, such as the Kimbundu and Kongo, whose experience of the "colonizing process" had long been intense in every aspect of their lives.

Living briefly among the Mbunda in 1970, one had the impression that much had changed because of the war, but little in the basic characteristics of their organization. Hostilities had driven many of them into refuge in Zambia. Others had abandoned their riverside hamlets, placed traditionally along the woodland edge of wide channels of grassland through which their rivers flow in all seasons, chill and clear and rich in fish. These others had retreated into the woods where they had built new villages in areas where their guerrilla fighters could protect them from Portuguese raids, or else, when such protection was difficult or uncertain, they were now living in flimsy camps of brief duration, cultivating fields of millet or other crops in woodland clearings and returning whenever they could to fish their rivers. Colonial rule had long since dismantled their "federalist" structure, and their ethnic authority—as distinct from the new modernizing authority that springs from the nationalist movement—was evidently limited to "nucleus elders." Otherwise, discounting for a moment the profoundly dislocating consequences of the war upon daily habits and food supplies, their pattern of life looked very much the same as Diniz described half a century earlier when Mwene Bando ruled. And this impression was deepened by the presence of shrines and other objects of divination or appeal to spiritual powers, it being generally held, by all those whom I was able to consult on such a point (in the circumstances, admittedly, an often interrupted effort at research), that all this was much the same "as it used to be."

All this remains unsatisfactorily vague. There is simply no way, for example, of knowing how many Mbunda are still living in eastern Angola, and how many have fled to Zambia, since by no means all of the latter are prepared to register as refugees and thereby find themselves in refugee camps; many Mbunda near the border, on the contrary, move back and forth according to the fortunes of the war in these parts. Nor is there any reliable way of knowing how many Mbunda have been rounded up by the Portuguese army and driven into *senzalas de paz* (peace villages) or other wire-encircled and garrisoned encampments of that kind; or how many remain under guerrilla protection in the woodlands round the Shekului, Luati, and other rivers. What may be stated with confidence is that the Mbunda adhered to the nationalist movement and resistance, after 1965, in a number that was sufficient to enable this movement to count on their region as one of its chief bases in the east. This is not the place to discuss the effectiveness of this adherence in terms of advancing the nationalist cause, a quality which depends on many contingent factors such as porterage, food supply, and the intensity of Portuguese ground raids and aerial bombing or defoliation, as well as the general pattern of nationalist plans and effectiveness. (See my book, *In the Eye of the Storm: Angola's People,* for an extended discussion.) Effectiveness is not the point here: what signifies in this context is that these people, or a large part of them, wished to join the nationalist movement, and did so.

In the historical context, then, the revolt of the Mbunda beginning in the second half of the 1960s may be interpreted in several different ways. It may be considered as another, if major, act of resistance within the traditional framework of anticolonial peasant struggle: as one more attempt, like others before it, to restore the "right and proper way of life" by restoring the rule of the ancestors and their spokesmen here on earth, as well as to free the Mbunda from colonial exactions of one kind or another. For many Mbunda—supporters of the nationalist movement as distinct from participants—this is probably a correct interpretation; for them, after all, the concepts of nationalism, let alone the whole range of ideas concerned with far-reaching social change, must remain extremely remote. Their precolonial development had enabled them to populate an unusually difficult country, and, by the use of crop cultivation, canoe building, iron working, and hunting, to secure an adequate standard of living for a total population of very slow growth while achieving that tolerant kind of relationship with their world and their neighbors that Silva Pôrto sketches in his notebooks of a century ago, a relationship which the visitor of today can still trace, or believe that he can trace, even under the ferociously disturbing conditions of colonial war. What is needed for a good life, by Mbunda concepts, may be little more than a revival of a vividly remembered past before the arrival of Portuguese troops and tax collectors. Let us call this "the traditionalist aim." It has certainly played its part.

Yet Mbunda involvement and participation can be viewed, and to a quite a large extent even must be viewed, in other ways as well. These appear from a consideration of the nature of the struggle.

II

THE ANGOLAN UPRISING BEGAN IN 1961 IN THE FAR WEST AND FAR NORTH of the country, and in complex circumstances. It spread, or could be spread, to the eastern districts only in 1965—only, that is, after its heralds were able to count on the friendship of Zambia, which ceased to be the colony and protectorate of Northern Rhodesia in October 1964. The Mbunda, by all the evidence, began in the latter part of 1965 to hear at firsthand about what they must have long heard by rumor, and their early attacks on Portuguese objectives began soon after that. These were conducted very much within the "traditionalist framework" of ideas and values, with arrows rather than with bullets, and with charms for protection against the white man's rifle fire; insofar as there was any nationalist leadership, it appears to have been merely adventurist, and its influence on the Mbunda failed when promised rifles were not delivered. In all these respects this early Mbunda uprising in 1966 was much of the same type as that with which the Pende of the Congo had responded to Pierre Mulele's call a year or two earlier (see Verhaegen, 1967), or, at least in essence, as that with which the Kongo peasants had responded to the agents of Roberto Holden in 1961. It was, in short, a response which had in its elements both modernizing and traditional, but the latter heavily prevailed. Perfectly unshaken by these early attacks, which they easily dispersed, the Portuguese could now have ceased to worry about the

Mbunda had not another factor intervened. This was the arrival on the scene of the spokesmen of a nationalist movement, the MPLA (Movimento Popular de Libertaçao de Angola),[21] which proved to have the capacity to reverse the balance, and to embrace the Mbunda in a movement of resistance that was still both modernizing and traditional, but in which the modernizing elements were increasingly to have the upper hand. Under this new leadership, whether of rural or urban formation and equipped now with at least some supply of MPLA small arms, the Mbunda rallied and began again. With varying fortunes they have since continued against a stiffening Portuguese military effort to destroy them. By 1970, at least, they had gone far toward transforming their resistance from the old type to a new type, abandoning much of their faith in charms and spells (at least in the matter of bulletproofing), and gradually, if with many false starts and setbacks, to see themselves as component parts in the realization of a program of *national* unity and change such as they had not conceived before.

Here we reach, undoubtedly, the central achievement of the MPLA and its companion movements in Guiné and Mozambique. Rejecting any mere reform of existing structures and institutions—at first because they were offered no opportunity for their taking part in such reforms, afterward because they became convinced that no such reforms could yield national unity and change—these leaders have led their supporters and participants in a major effort toward the building of new structures and institutions. Politically, this has meant the promotion of representative committees for single communities or groups of adjacent communities; socially, the widening and intensification of participation in activities and decisions concerned with local self-rule and elementary social services and with the production of food, as well as with other activities concerned with the support of their fighting units; and culturally, the provision for at least the beginnings of a modernizing education, starting out with a campaign against illiteracy. Little by little, as the wars continue, at least the outline of a new society begins to take shape.

How far has this modernizing process gone? Here, admittedly, one stands on difficult ground, for these are struggles that are still in mid-course of their development, and objective judgments on their meaning and effectiveness, on their maturity, are necessarily hard to make. Yet the evidence for an objective answer is now of many kinds, and at least a start can be made toward the conclusions that history will reveal. These struggles in the Portuguese colonies are successful guerrilla-type wars. To begin with, therefore, one needs to arrive at a general understanding of what success means in this context, and all the more because so much misconception and even nonsense has been wafted around the scene by amateur enthusiasts or would-be "Guevaristas." It must probably be emphasized, even at this late point in time, that a successful guerrilla-type resistance can never stem from military adventure, however motivated, but only from the political exploitation of a general situation which is felt by a mass of people to be hatefully and obviously unjust to them. "Big words" about freedom and independence can achieve nothing if the "little words" about local oppression are not persuasive. Second, this political exploitation will still fail unless it can pass from the mobilization of mass support to the mobilization of mass participation. It is one thing to want change and quite another to fight for it, but sympathy is not enough. Without a steady stream of new volunteers, the most courageous band of "initiators" will soon find themselves in isolation and defeat.

Third, this move from support to participation will not take place unless the right arguments are found, while the finding of these depends not on any general understanding of the situation or "analysis of history," but on the most intimate knowledge of local habits, languages, hopes, and fears. There can be no question, à la Regis Debray or Frantz Fanon, of "carrying the revolt from the towns to the countryside" by mere optimism or exhortation. Peasants are not optimistic people, and they will not be persuaded by those who do not closely understand them and share their lives—in the beginning, at any rate, by those who do not come from their own ranks. Fourth, and in step with the development of the *resultant* political and military struggle (the two becoming inseparable), the organization of this type of modernizing peasant movement must be such that the fact and influence of mass participation becomes, and remains, a dominant and manifest factor in the whole process. The peasants want to be sure they are fighting for themselves; only then will they become willing to fight for their neighbors as well. Fifth, and following from this, the growth of mass participation must never be allowed to rob the new vanguard of its leading role; otherwise their leaders will move in one direction while the peasants go off in another.

It would be possible on the evidence available to draw other conclusions from the record of these movements (PAIGC in Guiné; FRELIMO in Mozambique; MPLA in Angola), and to test all these conclusions against their relative success, or against the relative failure of other movements conducted in another way. Even the limited record of the Mbunda and the MPLA shows how sharply the conflict between the traditionalist and the modernizing elements in their movement can strike and chafe against each other, while the comparable movements in other territories have often shown the same tension or open strife. One important implication of these rules, for example, is that the pace and progress of military operations, whether in intensity, weaponry, or type of objective, must not outstrip the capacity of mass participation to absorb and understand them, for, if it does, this will lead to "overheating" just as surely as military *attentisme* will lead to disbandment. Another implication is that the structure of the movement must be constantly reviewed and overhauled so that the inner mediation of power remains an interplay between leaders and led. One could add other rules, but these five and their implications are of an iron necessity. They must be met substantially, or the end will be disaster.

But if they are met, as all three major movements in Portuguese Africa have each met them in the measure of their political and military success, then the struggle can acquire a meaning and momentum of its own, and can lead continually and consciously toward original solutions capable of solving what existing attitudes and structures, whether colonial or traditional, cannot solve. There takes place what Amílcar Cabral, in one of his memorable passages has called "a forced march on the road to cultural progress" (1969a),[22] and here he is using "cultural" in the widest sense, and above all in the sense of a developing sociopolitical consciousness on the part of individuals who, developing together in this way, come to form a new community, begin to shape a new society. Thus

the leaders of the liberation movement, drawn generally from the "petty-bourgeoisie" (intellectuals, clerks) or the urban working classes (workers, chauffeurs, wage-earners in general) have to live day by day with the various peasant groups in the heart of rural populations, and they come to know the people better. They discover at the grass-roots the richness of these peasant cultural values (philosophical, political, artistic, social, moral). They acquire a closer understanding of economic realities. . . .

Not without a certain astonishment, the leaders realise the richness of spirit, the capacity for reasoned discussion and clear exposition of ideas, the facility for understanding and assimilating concepts, by population groups who yesterday were forgotten, if not despised, and who were considered helpless by the colonisers and even by some nationalists. The leaders thus enrich their culture. They develop personally. They free themselves from complexes. They reinforce their capacity to serve the movement in the service of the people.

On their side, the working masses and in particular the peasants, who are usually illiterate and have never moved beyond the boundaries of their village or their region, come into contact with other groups and lose those complexes of their own that constricted them in their relationships with other ethnic and social groups. They realise their crucial rôle in the struggle. They break the bonds of the village universe. They integrate progressively into their country and the world. They acquire an infinite amount of new knowledge that is useful for their immediate and future activity within the framework of the struggle. They strengthen their political understanding by assimilating the principles of national and social revolution postulated by the struggle. They thereby become more able to play the decisive rôle of providing the principal force behind the liberation movement. . . .

The struggle brings other profound modifications in the life of the population. The armed liberation struggle implies, therefore, a veritable forced march along the road to cultural progress.

The evidence so far to hand suggests that the most successful of these movements have by this time advanced far along this line of march. None of them has done so without serious setbacks, internal failures, grave betrayals, numerous mistakes, not so numerous but still serious blunders, and several severe defeats.[23] Yet the march has everywhere continued, partly by the spur of its own momentum and success, a great deal because of effective leadership, and to no small extent because of the sheer intransigence of the colonial power. A full review of these wars would show that the Portuguese commanders have at last begun to understand the force of at least this third element, so that the recent period has produced the strange spectacle of a most orthodox and authoritarian commander, General António Spínola in his embattled colonial capital of Bissau (Guiné), advancing the claims of a Portuguese "social counter-revolution" which in his view is to cut the ground from under the feet of the nationalists.[24] For some time now there has been much talk of Portuguese concessions and the reform of "what exists"; but the situation that has now evolved in nationalist-held areas is such that no conceivable reform of "what exists," when compared with the new structures and institutions of self-rule taking shape there, could be more than a return to the colonial past.

This is true in obviously varying degrees of maturity and effectiveness. New structures and institutions come to life with great difficulty, and can be kept alive only by the most devoted effort in nationalist areas subject to frequent Portuguese raids and counteraction. This has been the case with the homeland of the Mbunda, repeatedly swept by Portuguese incursions of helicoptered troops combined with large units sent from strong garrisons to the west. Elsewhere, in areas which the Portuguese army has long found it hard or impossible to overrun, or even to reach except at rare intervals, the outlines of a new society are already very clear. Another illustration from my own observation, that of the Balante and their neighbors of southern Guiné, offers a case in point. These peasants are much more numerous than the Mbunda and may total about 250,000. Traditionally, they are in most respects a characteristic "stateless society" of West Africa, being organized in a segmentary structure whose details have yet to be scientifically assessed but whose general pattern is not in doubt. Their situation at the outset of the war was somewhat the same as that of the Mbunda in that they were subject to "minimal administration" or, from another, if subjective, angle, a more or less total "colonial neglect." Direct Portuguese rule had been installed in the 1920s, though not easily, since when the tasks of administration were concentrated in collecting taxes and protecting the commercial monopoly of local Portuguese traders. Portuguese-nominated "chiefs" were appointed and seem generally to have had the same ineffectual status as British-appointed "warrant chiefs" among the "stateless peoples" of, for example, eastern Nigeria. These men played the role of colonial agents or messengers, while the traditional structure of the Balante carried on much as before.

The Balante embraced the cause of anticolonial struggle from the first, and have provided the national movement (African Party for the Independence of Guiné and Cape Verde, PAIGC) with its principal ethnic support. Like the Mbunda, they began by responding to "small words" about local injustice, and have gone on to embrace the ideas behind "big words" about liberation and independence. They responded, in other words, to the prospect of relatively minor gains of a generally reformist nature, but, with the development of their participation in the nationalist movement, they have since embraced the institutions of a new society. This is what they claim, and their claim reflects a patent truth. Consider, for example, the situation that one could examine during 1972 in one of the areas of southern Guiné that have long been freed from Portuguese control. This particular area consists of the sector of Como, a small group of "islands" divided from the mainland by narrow creeks and waterways. The Portuguese had garrisoned these islands until 1964 but were then driven out; the whole sector was cleared of Portuguese troops in 1965, and these had not been able to return. By the end of 1972, in other words, the people here (Balante and neighboring groups) had ruled themselves without Portuguese intervention for rather more than seven years.

Like others, the peasants of the Como sector are protected from Portuguese raids by local units of the full-time army of the PAIGC,[25] and partly by a militia of local men under PAIGC command; the latter also provide, insofar as it is needed, a local police force. Nearly all of the men of both forces are peasants, with many of local origin, and so are most of their commanders, the exceptions being a few of those "petty-bourgeois" elements from Guiné towns to whom Cabral referred in the passage quoted above. Their tasks and their behavior are the subject of consultation between the senior local PAIGC command (consisting of a full-time military commander and a full-time political commissar, both of peasant origin) and the elected sector committee. This committee, also all of local origin, derives its representative character from fifteen elected village committees, some representing a single village, others a group of adjacent hamlets. These committees have a range of responsibilities which has continuously widened with the improvement of their representative character and the development of the struggle as a whole. They have become responsible for the supply and supervision of local schools, clinics, and other welfare institutions, none of which had existed before the coming of the national movement; and they carry out these responsibilities in what is evidently a close cooperation with the full-time workers of the movement, most of whom, of course, are also of peasant origin. During 1972 they added to these responsibilities with the creation (as elsewhere in liberated Guiné) of village tribunals composed of selected committee members within an overall framework controlled by the PAIGC.

So it appeared to a visitor, in Como in 1972, that nothing happened or could happen, save for accidents or defaults of duty, without the active participation of its local people, and this was true even down to the organization of canoe transport for crossing creeks or to the handing out of permits to visit relatives in towns on the mainland that are still garrisoned by the Portuguese; the largest of these, Catio, is only a "tide's distance" away by double-paddled canoe. Here one sees in vivid everyday detail the difference between support and participation, and the many ways in which these peasants, through active involvement, have begun to change not only their social structure but also, and much more, their ideas about the present and the future. They are a remote population, utterly "forgotten, if not despised" in colonial times, and they have lived very much to themselves. Yet it seemed very obvious, in 1972, that they were well aware of being a part of a wider struggle as well as of a battle for themselves.

In 1972, moreover, these peasants took part in a general election for a

National Assembly of Guiné and, after direct and secret ballot in their villages, sent elected members to a regional assembly for Como and two neighboring sectors (Cubucaré and Tombali), which, with fourteen other regional assemblies, in turn chose national representatives. Promoted in all the liberated areas, this general election was seen by the PAIGC as providing a democratic basis for an assembly which would declare the country's independence, and as initiating a constitutional separation of powers between state and party; but it was also seen, undoubtedly, as another means of widening and intensifying mass participation, and it was so discussed, repeatedly, together with its other aims, at electoral meetings. One of the PAIGC leaders who spoke at these meetings used an explanatory phrase in Guiné Creole, more or less a lingua franca there, which seemed to me to strike an always dominant note: *Que povo na manda na su cabeça* ("People have to do it for themselves"). As support moves into participation, and participation into deeper understanding and involvement, so does the content of the struggle acquire its profoundly educational and liberating role.

So too does the ground for reformism narrow and disappear, and the realities of structural change then begin to crystallize, whether in relation to "traditionalist" or imposed ideas and beliefs and institutions. That is why these peasant movements have to be seen, along the spectrum of nationalist development, as movements of a new type, of a postreformist type, of a revolutionary type that is very distinct from the nationalism of the 1950s and early 1960s elsewhere in Africa. That is why Cabral, in the perspective of these struggles, defined "the phenomenon of national liberation" as being "necessarily one of revolution."[26]

III

MOST OF THE LEADERS OF THESE MOVEMENTS WOULD DESCRIBE THEM, I think, as vanguards of a national unification still to be made complete within national frontiers. The primary task is to promote this unity to a point where colonial rule can be destroyed. But this involves another task which is integral with the first: the promotion of a necessary unity by means that go necessarily toward the building of a social system which is politically and culturally new, and can derive in no essential sense from the mere reform of "what exists." This second task is integral with the first because the first, the mere removal of colonial rule, proves impossible without the second, and the second imposes its own dynamic in ways which the initiative of the Balante, for example, dramatically show. Hence these vanguards can be defined as movements of *revolutionary nationalism.* They accept the nationalist framework because it is as much a given condition as the fact of colonial rule. But they reject its colonial content, and this, by logical extension, means that they also reject its reformist potential. They look to a future when self-identity will be able, within postcapitalist structures, to pass beyond the limits of reformist nationalism.

Their leaders have offered definitions at various times. "We are trying," observed the MPLA leader, Agostinho Neto, in 1970, "to free and modernise our people by a dual revolution—against their traditional structures which can no longer serve them, and against colonial rule" (quoted in Davidson, 1972, p. 279). Or Cabral, in 1966 (in his Havana address), expressing the same developmental (hence, in these circumstances, revolutionary) theme: "For us, the basis of national liberation, whatever the formulas adopted on the level of international law, is the inalienable right of every people to have its own history, and the objective of national liberation is to regain this right usurped by imperialism: that is to say, to free the process of development of the national productive forces." Expressed in other statements and often in conversation, Cabral's view was that the precolonial development of Africans, stopped or distorted by colonial conquest and control, must now be made to begin again; that this involves the kind of "dual revolution" defined by Neto; and that, this being so, "the principal aspect of national liberation struggle is the struggle against neo-colonialism": against, that is, the reformism which would prolong or merely modify existing structures of stagnation or, at best, of "growth without development." He further held that if this struggle could be won, then conflicts of international rivalry or strife within Africa could be resolved as surely as revolutionary nationalism could also resolve, even was already resolving, intranational conflicts of "tribal" or other sectoral rivalries.[27]

If one goes on to ask how far such ideas and aims may be shared by the peasants who form the vast majority of the membership of these vanguard movements, or may even be understood by them, one is returned directly to the consequences of participation as distinct from sympathy or support. So long as one avoids any "voluntarist" implication,[28] there is a sense here in which it appears true, as Jean-Paul Sartre has remarked in quite another context, that "the real locus of revolutionary consciousness is neither in the immediate class, nor in the party, but in the struggle."[29] For the peasants in Africa were slow to move and possessed at the beginning nothing that remotely resembled a "revolutionary consciousness," while

"the party," on the other hand, likewise began with aims that were often
confused, sometimes merely reformist, or else distant from those practical
realities of the "here and now" in which a revolutionary consciousness
can take effective shape. But that was ten years ago and more; and in the
interval the dialectics of political participation, constantly opposing new
ideas to old ideas, new aims to old aims, and repeatedly pushing past the
mental barriers of the past, have had their full effect. The handfuls of
"petty bourgeois" who launched these struggles have long since found the
company of countless peasant participants who have also long become, at
one level or another, in one capacity or another, leaders of their movements. Some have fallen by the wayside, others have pulled back into
neutrality or gone over into hostility, and many have been killed in
warfare with the Portuguese. Yet the balance of the evidence suggests that
these movements have continued to grow in their internal solidarity as
well as in their strength of numbers, and nothing in the evidence suggests
this more clearly than the nature of the defections they have suffered, or
the action taken to overcome these defections.[30]

One can approach the question of "understanding" from another useful
angle: from that of the ways in which the problem of the mediation of
internal power has been handled. Few problems have been harder for
these leaderships to solve; even today few remain as hard, especially in
countries as vast as Angola or Mozambique, where the facts of geography
and intercommunication pile huge difficulties on top of the frailties of
human nature. Initially substitutionist because they could be nothing else,
"nationalists without a nation," the leaderships proclaimed the nation and
set about realizing it. Their records show how arduous and difficult they
found it, and how large the difficulty still remains; they also show how
seriously it has been tackled.

The central task, as they have seen it, or at least as their clearest heads
have seen it, was to displace "substitution" by "participation." Given the
complexity of the problem, greatly increased by an illiteracy rate of 90 to
100 percent and the consequent absence of any reading habits, as well as
by the subtle and continuous interplay or conflict of individual motivations with collective aims, the task is obviously still there and, indeed, can
never be fulfilled in a final sense. But the general measure of their present
success in solving this problem of the mediation of power, in making this
necessary displacement, is given by these movements' survival and expansion. Only an increasing participation in thought and action can
explain such survival and expansion, for it is the evidence of every known
case in modern times[31]—in those cases, that is, for which good evidence
is available—that an armed struggle of this kind will otherwise dwindle

and fail. So true is this, by all the evidence, that one may even take from it a general rule.

It thus appears that a struggle of this kind (and perhaps *any* revolutionary struggle) will succeed so long as mass participation gains progressively on the substitution that is practiced, necessarily, by an initiating vanguard—by a vanguard, that is, which has the political skill, courage, and readiness for self-sacrifice required to launch the processes of mass participation in the making of systemic change. It fails in the contrary case: wherever, that is, substitution gains progressively on participation. If participation gains, the revolution is made; if participation thereafter continues to gain—but only if—then the revolution is made good. This, in any case, is what the African evidence combines to show, and does so as the only tenable explication of the aims and ideas of these movements, of the content of their policies and methods, and of their failures and successes. If these are peasant movements of a new type along the "continuum" of African nationalist development, then they are centrally so because they have tackled and at least partially solved the problem of peasant participation in the thinking and the action, cultural and political far more than military, that enable a new society to liberate the future from the past. If so, they are movements which can claim a place in world history as well as the assured place they already have in African history, for in that case they demonstrate, along with their own particularities, the initiation of Africans into large movements of modernizing change whose comparability with other such movements up and down the world is evidently beyond question.[32]

VOICES FROM
THE FRONT

I T IS 1967, AND I AM WALKING, OR RATHER STUMBLING, AMID THE SWAMPS
and woodlands of coastal Guiné, in the company of peasant fighters of
the PAIGC (African Party for the Independence of Guiné and Cape
Verde), so as to see what is going forward here. This is the fourth year
of their insurrection, and their routines are well established. This is just
as well for visitors.

I

T HE SMALL JET BOMBER DIVES FROM AROUND FIVE THOUSAND FEET, ITS
engine drilling like a monstrous fly. Two others follow: Fiats, I think, of
the type they make in West Germany. About five miles away.

We stand near the edge of the clump of trees that conceals our base,
a dozen huts, a small dump of 75-mm shells—watching. It is otherwise a
quiet Monday morning. October 9, 1967.

A great wedge of black smoke fans out above the skyline fringe of
coconut palms.

"Napalm," says the man from the Vietcong who is standing beside me,

This essay is composed of four extracts: the first from my book of 1969, *The Liberation of Guiné*; the second and third from my 1973 *A Report on the Further Liberation of Guiné*; and the fourth from *The People's Cause: A History of Guerrillas in Africa*, published in 1981.

a visitor like myself. His tone is of the bitter weariness that a doctor in a plague might use when identifying yet another onset. Tran Hoai-nam, veteran member of the central committee of the National Liberation Front of South Vietnam, has seen it all before, has seen it many times.

I myself have seen no warfare since 1945; and then at least there was no napalm. Besides, this isn't Vietnam. This is West Africa. Would the Portuguese—even these Portuguese of Dr. Salazar's most imperial Portugal—really drop napalm on villages and rice fields in rural Africa? Somehow I still have a hope that it isn't true.

We move that afternoon. *Nô pintcha*, as Pascoal is always saying: "Forward, on our way, let's go." An appeal as well as a command. It takes me back to Yugoslavia in 1943, to the hills of Bosnia and the plains of Srem: *pokret*, a word to galvanize the limbs even of the weariest partisan alive, a flag of victory or a flail of fear, take it as you can.

Nô pintcha. We get into line and move out across the rice fields, walking easily. This time it is neither victory nor fear, but routine. We are on a tour of inspection, and Amílcar Cabral is in a hurry. Guerrilla warfare is nothing if not movement, constant movement, merciless movement, movement in the mind even when you are sitting still, sitting still and calculating what has happened, what is going to happen. Here inside this country which is called a Portuguese "overseas province," a country of strange wilderness and beauty about the size of Switzerland or Holland, we have moved and we shall move for days and nights.

We slop across rice fields yellow with the weak sunlight of the last of the rains. We splash through miles of ankle-deep water, our rubber soles clopping and clucking to each other. Three villages, one after another on our route, are each encircled by a clump of trees in this thin near-coastal forestland. More rice fields. After that a big waterway, a mile width of bottle-green sea that penetrates upcountry from the Atlantic and looks like a river but isn't one. A majestic landscape, superb, defiant.

Canoes. We can stop walking. We load into these long dugouts until their freeboard laps an inch or two above the waterline, and crouch with a relief that doesn't last. There is nothing less comfortable than a crowd of men in a canoe, for you can neither sit nor stand. Balante paddlers take us out into the current. Someone's rifle is sticking into my back. Someone's boots are cradled in my stomach. Never mind. *Nô pintcha*.

I think of the last time I was waterborne on a guerrilla expedition, crossing the moonlit Danube in the summer of 1944. Now it is daylight, sleepy tropical afternoon time, but otherwise the mood is pretty much the same. It is so uncomfortable, in a sense so unreasonable, that we have to laugh. The laughter echoes back and forth between the walls of mangrove forest. You might think the Portuguese were a hundred miles away. Actually, they are eight or nine: but hard watched, well contained. This is a liberated zone, the coastal zone of Quitáfine. Here is how the kids were singing in a guerrilla school the other day:

> *The guerrilla walks proudly on the land*
> *While the little Portuguese commands the clouds . . .*

Those Balante paddlers, their rifles slung, swing their blades as though they will go on forever. There are moments when I think this is what they are going to do. But all things come to an end, even journeys by canoe. We climb up a bank of mud and walk into the forest as twilight falls. Now it is only the ants, the marching ants, that bother us. Linger in one of their trails for an instant and their black little teeth will be stinging into your ankles, your legs, your thighs. Whenever this happens, we break into a trot, slapping at our trousers, stamping our feet. As for snakes, nobody worries anymore. Pascoal said the other day, "We have learned to live with the snakes."

Late at night we stumble through trees into another base, at this time the main military base for Quitáfine, a regular camp well sentried and composed. Here is Mateus, commander in Quitáfine along with Pascoal who is regional commissar. A tall grave figure in the night, Mateus is a veteran of three years' fighting just like Pascoal. Limping from an old wound, Mateus makes us welcome, inquires for news, offers his own.

We stand about, relaxed and even happy. Really, there is nothing happy about guerrilla warfare. There are only moments of good effort made successfully, of tasks accomplished, that one afterward remembers with a certain joy. There are others, of a different kind, that one remembers with horror—or tries not to remember. This is one of the good moments.

The guard section who have come with us go off to feed and rest. We sit in a hut and wash our feet, gently comfortable. The paraffin lamp makes a shadow play. We see each other as fleeting shadows, but as solid ones: Cabral, who is the founder of this movement, its inspirer, its leader, its relentless critic, a man of unforgettable moral resonance and strength of purpose whom I first met in 1960 when he came to my house in London, then as "Abel Djassi," and whom I have stayed in touch with ever since. Tran Hoai-nam and Pham Van Tan of the Vietcong, who are as tired as I am but, unlike me, would never think of saying so. Another old friend, Mario de Andrade from Angola, a poet with the history of his people in luminous eyes and dancing hands, a fine intelligence who has not allowed his Latin and Greek, seminary learned, to cloud a shrewd appreciation of the world.

Amílcar looks across at me. "What would you say to a glass of Scotch?"

"Ah, don't be silly."

"You never know," says Mario, whose talent is for not being surprised.

And after all Amílcar has brought a bottle of Scotch. "First appearance on this scene," he chuckles—"just like you. You see, we think of everything."

We sit with our feet in warm water and pass the bottle around.

Next morning we learn that yesterday's bombing was lucky for the Portuguese. After weeks of trying they struck an antiaircraft gun served by two guerrilla soldiers. One of these was burned to death. The other managed to fling himself clear of the gun pit, but with major burns.

Cabral goes off on business of his own, visiting military units and schools and village committees. Pascoal Alves takes us four visitors to see the wounded man.

On the way we pass another antiaircraft post, consisting of one four-barreled gun and with two single barrels, all three from Czechoslovakia and served by eight or ten young guerrillas. These guns are well placed in good pits with an open field of fire all around. The gunners explained their weapons. But will they use them when it comes to the point? After all, these gunners are out there in the open and they know about yesterday's bombing. I don't ask this question. But I think it.

A few minutes later, when we're half a mile along the path, today's bombing begins. The Portuguese seem to come every day at about eleven in the morning, and sometimes after lunch—after their lunch, I mean—with two or three planes from the air base at Bissau, the country's capital. This time they come with two planes: Fiats again. They go back and forth over us at about four thousand feet and drop high explosive on a fancied target some six miles away. But my question is answered: down the path our gunners open up on them at once, and with calm, short bursts which continue till the planes go away again.

The hospital is in a forest clearing. A few beds for casualties and serious civilian cases, but mainly a clinic and dispensary for the neighboring population. Daily clinics. One doctor, a quietly confident young man who has lately returned from six years of medical training in Moscow; and three nurses (normally, he explains, there should be five) who have each had one year's nursing training in the Soviet Union. I chat with the nurses in the little Russian that I have. It seems odd to find these young women speaking Russian, but why any odder, after all, than if they'd spoken French or English? Like the doctor, they are absolutely indigenous, absolutely *of the country:* young women who have gone from their Balante villages and learned a useful trade and now come home again to exercise it.

In a darkened hut there is Tengbatu, a Balante soldier. A long figure made huge with bandages that cover almost his whole body. About twenty-three. A nurse hovers. The doctor reassures her. He says to us: "Tertiary burns only on the extremities. We shall save him." A few days later the army takes Tengbatu to a base hospital near Boké in the republic of Guinea. He went on the same boat as myself.

Next morning, back at base camp in Quitáfine, I walk across the parade ground and find, in the shadow of a hut, a large fragment of an unexploded napalm canister dropped at the same time as the one that scorched Tengbatu. It is neatly printed with its identity: FCM-1-55 NAPALM 300 KG-350L M/61. It is part of the military matériel which the North Atlantic Treaty Organization supplies to Portugal. For the defense of the Free World. A strange region, this Free World.

Napalm, like high explosive, has been used by the Portuguese in Africa since the early months of the Angolan revolt in 1961. They use napalm a great deal, although they do not make it themselves, any more than they make jet bombers. The little hospitals and clinics of guerrilla-held Guiné are filled with its victims, not only men, but women and children as well. Some die from it. Others are mutilated by it.

II

"SHARP AND FINE EVENING LIGHT; GOOD GOING SINCE ABOUT 2 P.M. AT USUAL 4 mph or so. High tide, so not much mud." Afterward, with luck, such notes can shift the tenses of recalled experience. A single word can do that—in this case, for example, *mud.* To move about the seaboard zones of these great forests, forked by estuaries and ocean creeks or farmed in plains of rice that push away one woodland border from another with miles of dike and paddy, you must endure a wilderness of mud. And at low tide, of course, you must wade still farther so as to reach canoes or leave them. This the peasants do not mind. Whether or not they carry burdens on their heads or weapons on their shoulders, the peasants float across these shores with a barefoot elegance of levitation. The booted foreigner plods and then, shin deep, gets stuck. Made presently aware, the peasants come floating back again and haul him out.

Today we have taken canoes across a couple of minor rivers, and walked and talked, and come before sundown to the ocean creek which divides these islands of the southern coast from the mainland. These sectors are part of the southern liberated regions. By virtue of their location and relatively dense population, they and other sectors on this tour can be counted among the most important in the country. They reach over on the west to the borders of the Rio Grande, the great ocean estuary of Bissau, and on the north to the savannah, lands beyond the Corubal River; and they can certainly be taken, allowing for local differences elsewhere, as representing the general situation in all the liberated regions.

On this November day, the seventeenth since I crossed the frontier from the Republic of Guinea, we have marched hard from the central villages of Como and reached the brink of this wide ocean creek with a little time to spare before the canoes will be assembled. A long sleeve of darkness, nearly a kilometer wide, separates us from the mainland and the rest of the way we shall march tonight. The sky is clear above this ocean creek, for the rains of 1972 are almost over, and beyond the creek, as they glow like luminous mushrooms in the night, we can see where the lights of the Portuguese garrisons at Catio and Bedanda to one side, and at Cabdue and Cassine to the other, make small circles on the skyline.

Hard beset by PAIGC ambush, these garrisons have long since ceased to possess any communication with each other, save by naval convoys from Bissau once a month or occasional helicopter sorties. Tonight we shall cross the water and approach two of them. Tomorrow we shall continue by day, skirting these garrisons within three or four kilometers while we march along the regular lines of communication of the PAIGC. But now there is an hour to rest and eat.

We sit around the verandah of a large village house—a company of a couple of dozen soldiers of the PAIGC, two or three political workers, a PAIGC leader who is Vasco Cabral, head of the movement's economic planning department, and a foreigner who is myself. The sun falls into the western ocean, and almost from one moment to the next it is cool again, even cold with the breath of the long night ahead. We lean against each other, for everyone is tired; and we are glad when three women of the house bring bowls of rice and roasted chicken legs. There are incidents of clear simplicity and calm in this forest war, and this is one of them.

Not far away, perhaps fifteen kilometers, an artillery battle is in full swing. Arafane Mane, who is in charge of our party, explains it to me. The Portuguese commanding general, António Spínola, has his main garrison in these parts at Catio, on the estuary of the Cumbije River that flows into the ocean creek which we shall cross. Just now, it seems, he is planning

a big offensive raid with troops from Bissau. To that end he is trying to
tar the eight kilometers of dirt road which separate Catio from his only
available jet-bomber airstrip at Cufar, where he also has a garrison. With
a tarred road he can probably guarantee a land communication between
Cufar and Catio, at least for a while. If so, he can use the airstrip to supply
Catio, and vice versa; and this will help his raid. Well aware of all that,
the army of the PAIGC has set itself to stop him from tarring the road.

   This particular contest will go on for most of the rest of the time that
I am in the region. Day after day, it follows a familiar course. Late in the
afternoon two or three small bombers of Fiat-91 type (manufactured for
NATO, and sold to the Portuguese by the West German Defense Ministry) appear from Bissau. They drop their bombs into the forest around the
Cufar–Catio road, and then shoot off their cannon in the same blind way.
I have watched them doing it several times. Not knowing the precise
location of PAIGC units, Spínola's aircraft are reduced to hitting at
random. As soon as they have done that, toward sundown, these PAIGC
units move in and bombard the garrisons, as well as the road between
them, using bazookas, mortars, and, occasionally, 122-mm ground-to-
ground rockets. The latter can be distinguished, even from a distance, by
the sharp roar of their explosion. This evening we hear several such
explosions.

   When we have eaten and rested, it is time to go across. Our village host
is in charge of all boat movements in this locality, for the PAIGC leave
no such matters to chance, and comes now to say that the canoes are
ready. He is a powerful rice farmer with a lively smile, manifestly proud
of his responsibilities. "Years ago," says Arafane, "when the Portuguese
tried to push us out of Como Island, back in 1964, it was this man who
always managed to paddle across with supplies of ammunition from the
mainland." Since then the Portuguese have not set foot on Como Island,
nor in any part of the Como sector, since 1965. These are liberated areas
with nearly eight years of complete self-rule behind them. I am the first
European to come here since the visit of a distinguished French cineaste
in 1964.

   The boats are at the brink of a high tide. We embark silently and
paddle out across mirrors of gray water lit only by a failing moon and the
distant glow of Portuguese garrisons. It is a routine journey, and has
nothing in the least of the "romance" which has somehow got itself
attached, by a terrible misunderstanding, to the nature of guerrilla operations. Disembarking on the other side, we shall plunge at once into the
grim reality of knee-high mud and numbing weariness. Neither is romantic by any stretch of the imagination.

III

ASKED AGAIN WHY THEY HAVE FAILED TO WIN THIS WAR IN GUINEA-BISSAU, to which (on a per capita comparison of the populations of Portugal and the USA) they have long committed an army larger than the largest U.S. Army in South Vietnam, the Portuguese regime falls back on a convenient explanation. Yes, they will agree upon being pressed, it is true that the rural people support the PAIGC, but they do this only because the PAIGC have terrorized them.

One cannot help thinking it the argument of men who refuse to face the reality of their own defeat. For it is an explanation which entirely ignores the fact that a guerrilla resistance which is not an *increasingly* popular resistance is one that irrevocably fails. Every historical example one can bring to mind, above all within the last thirty years, bears out the truth of this. If the cause of the PAIGC has prevailed, it can only be because an ever-growing number of people have willingly embraced it.

Traveling in areas under PAIGC government, the visitor finds the evidence of this on every hand. But in this respect, perhaps, there is nothing more convincing than the ideas and attitudes of those pioneers of the PAIGC—Amílcar Cabral and his brother Luiz, Arístides Pereira, Bernardo Vieira, Osvaldo Vieira, Chico Mendes, and others like them— who have led the PAIGC since the 1950s. These ideas and attitudes, as one quickly discovers, are concerned above all with the problems of broadening and intensifying even the large degree of popular participation which they have so far achieved. No doubt they may be strong enough now to impose their will; yet they remain resolutely attached to the methods of political persuasion with which they began.

"We are armed militants, not militarists," Cabral has said in a characteristically neat turn of phrase, and it seems to be the basic lesson that they teach to everyone. For liberation, as one may hear it repeated in dozens of "forest conversations" and meetings, can be of no value unless it means the liberation of the mind, the widening capacity of everyone to think and act for themselves. They would betray their whole purpose as well as invite defeat, they will tell you time and again, if they were to fall back on "orders from above." Such orders might be obeyed in these liberated areas, for the PAIGC has great prestige as well as commanding armed force; but orders from above cannot educate. Only the experience of voluntary participation, of "educated participation," can do that. And it is this kind of participation which can alone make liberation more than a change of masters.

For those with a taste for revolutionary theory and its embodiment in praxis, the implications of these ideas and attitudes are of more than passing interest. When they began, like every other minority of their type, the pioneers of the PAIGC were obliged to substitute themselves for "the will of the nation." They had to do this all the more because then, and for a long time afterward, they were (as they also say, recalling those days) "nationalists without a nation." Making this "substitition," they did not forget their own weakness. When Frantz Fanon and other well-wishers urged them in 1960–61 "simply to begin," they stuck in their toes and refused, even at the cost of losing useful support. Others might think that the village farmer in Guinea-Bissau would "rally to the sound of a guerrilla rifle": they thought it far more likely that he would run away from it as fast as he could. They would accordingly begin, Cabral replied to such urgings, only when they were sure that they had persuaded a substantial number of rural people into active participation. Otherwise their act of revolutionary "substitution," no matter how well phrased or fought for, could degenerate only into an irresponsible adventure.

The task was therefore to set going a process whereby mass participation would gain steadily over minority substitution. They found this very hard in 1960–61, but they persevered. Even in 1963, after they had shown what they could do in the southern regions, where they first began armed resistance, peasant skepticism remained hard to overcome. I lived for ten days of last November in a forest camp, far inside the country, commanded by Osvaldo Vieira, inspector-general of the armed forces of the PAIGC; it was he who began resistance in the north. His group then, in 1963, consisted of ten men with three rifles. "The peasants didn't believe that we could hit the Portuguese, or even that we would try. 'You've scarcely any arms,' they said, 'you're nothing.' So we had to show them." He laid an ambush, smashed three army vehicles, killed seven Portuguese, and captured eight weapons. "After that, it began to be different."

Today the process of making participation gain over substitution, but without the vanguard's in any way abdicating from its task of leadership, has gone very far. Five years ago I heard an old man in the Kitafiné sector describing that process. He began by talking about life under Portuguese rule. He said it was "like living in a cave." But "we didn't think it could be different. Party work and Party talk, it's like a big lie at the beginning. But in the end it's the real truth." It is an explanation that Cabral liked to remember. That old man, he would tell you, had got to the heart of the matter with a minimum of words.

The secret of its success has lain in clearing liberated areas and then, inside them, building new structures of everyday life. Politically, these structures have consisted at the base—and the base is everything in this context—of a dense network of village committees which, as they became increasingly elective and representative in nature, have repeatedly taken over fresh responsibilities. On the Como group of islands, for example, there is a total of fifteen committees; at various meetings I was able to identify members of thirteen of them. In another sector I was present at a meeting of representatives of seventeen of the sector's committees.

At one level or another, these committees are concerned with every aspect of public life in their localities. They look to the full-time workers of the PAIGC for leadership, but are encouraged to take over as much responsibility as they are able. New activities are continually being added to their work. The latest in importance, initiated since 1970, is the formation of a network of village courts; each of these tribunals consists of a judge (or, as we should say in England, a justice or magistrate) and two assessors appointed by their respective village committee. They hear all cases, but send difficult ones to a sector court, and this in turn sends the most serious cases, those consisting of assault or other violence, to a supreme military court. Minor offenses, such as trading with the enemy, are punished by fines in kind (usually rice) or assignment to porterage services. Serious cases can be punished by imprisonment, but there is no capital punishment. A legal code, based on the transformation of customary law, is now in course of completion.

So it is that the force which promotes the enlargement of the powers and functions of these village committees is not only the administrative hand of the PAIGC but also, and probably even more, the new opportunities which the PAIGC have opened for them. One sees this especially in education and public health. The PAIGC began to found primary schools inside the country in 1964. Today they have 156 such schools, functioning where no schools have ever existed before, with about 250 teachers, as well as one secondary school and a nursery school in the Republic of Guinea. For October 1972 the breakdown of attendances showed the following results:

First year	6,988 pupils	
Second year	849	
Third year	506	
Fourth year	172	
Fifth year	31	} Both in Republic of Guinea
Nursery	28	

Of this total of 8,574 pupils, 2,155 were girls: not a just proportion, according to Carmen Pereira, who is in charge of education in the south, but at least a start toward a greatly improved status for women among people who have often grossly abused the status of women in the past, and often continue to do so today. To this total of 8,574 in regular full-time schools, another 7,000 or so must be added who are men and women attending part-time adult classes of one kind or another, concerned chiefly with literacy and elementary arithmetic, in fighting units or hospitals, clinics or other institutions inside the country where they live and work.

IV

NATIONALISM, BECOMING SUCCESSFUL, COULD MEAN ONE THING FOR ONE group or class of persons and a different thing for other groups or classes. It could be destructive and disintegrating as well as constructive and unifying. Some gained, but others lost; and those who lost could become many more in number than those who gained, or feel themselves to be so. New forms of intranationalist conflict accordingly appeared, and there were also forms of class conflict, more acute than any known before.

So the question of ideological development, of the meaning of an ideology of liberation, then became a new one. How could the ideology of anticolonial nationalism be moved forward, further developed, into an ideology of postcolonial progress? To this a new reply began to emerge: an ideology of postcolonial progress must go beyond the removal of colonial controls and the writing in of "black" where "white" had previously been stated. Beyond all that it must resolve the resultant class conflict within the new nation-state, and resolve it in favor of the many, not the few. This was why all the major insurrections of the late colonial or neocolonial period took a dual form. They combined a struggle against colonial or paracolonial rule with a class struggle of the "many dispossessed" against the "privileged few."

This seems to have been the case everywhere, and explains why all the major successes of this period were both the product and the producer of new perspectives within a new consciousness. The unity that brought success was the unity which could achieve participation. Men might embark on armed struggle with divided minds and allegiances, suspicion of neighbors, doubts about the value of combined effort. But the joining together in action against a common enemy could overcome this divided consciousness. It did not work easily and sometimes it did not work at all. Generally, though, the evidence seems to show that the practice of participation could evolve a new unity of consciousness, a new morality of common purpose in the service of a new society. Even while besieged by the squalors of war, men and women could feel themselves changed and enlarged: dragged from personal concerns, fortified in companionship, capable of confronting what before had seemed impossible. Or else, falling short, the failures could end only in disaster, and the move into a new consciousness was then reversed into a destructive caricature of the consciousness of the past.

The process was all the more striking in regions where armed struggle was developed by peoples enclosed within small-scale societies, remote clans, ethnic groups with little or no experience of the world outside their boundaries. Their problems of ideological development could be extremely severe. They lacked the kind of "transcultural cement" or "worldview" long provided, for example, by Islam in various regions, or by the memory of having belonged to prestigious unities in the past. Their leaders had to find a way, in practice, of transforming local objectives into wider ones, of building a multiethnic consciousness of common aim and interest. This was always difficult. . . .

No less difficult, leaders had to find a way of carrying insurrectionary peoples out of old interpretations of reality, such as the notion that charms can render bullets harmless. The movements that were to succeed had to insist on tactics before divination, on weapons training before amulets, on military analysis before magic. They had to persuade the spokesmen of ancestral shrines to see beyond local priorities and speak in broader terms, even in national terms.

And all this they had to do while fighting the colonial enemy in unrelenting danger, deprivation, loneliness, and at times the fearful onset of despair. These realities have been touched on earlier; it may be well to touch on them again. For any condensed history of these extraordinary confrontations risks overlooking the conditions under which they had to be accepted on the insurgent side. They were realities where strain and weariness, hunger and uncertainty, became a living presence, a drag upon the limbs, a weight upon the mind, a potent enemy among so many other enemies and one, besides, that was almost never absent. For months and even years men and women had to live as the hunters and the hunted, moving as the wild animals they grew to understand so well, sympathizing even with the snakes, enduring every manner of physical and moral test, braving old beliefs and taboos, fending off the rumors and the intrigues that grow and burgeon under such conditions, often in small groups or even quite alone, sometimes battling for sanity as much as for bodily survival, and always with a host of daily troubles and distractions crowding across their vision of the wider problem, of the contest as a whole.

THE LEGACY OF
AMÍLCAR CABRAL

I

THE LEGACY OF AMÍLCAR CABRAL LIVES IN SEVERAL HISTORICAL achievements, each of which has marked the trend and temper of our times. Most obviously and directly, those achievements are to be found in the consequences of anticolonial liberation in Portuguese Guiné and Cape Verde that flowed, and in more or less large measure continue to flow, from a practice and theory associated inseparably with Cabral's action and thought. Other achievements, less direct but no less real, may be seen in Cabral's contribution to the development of national-liberation strategy in a wider and possibly an all-African context. And others again, politically less operative but still with a living significance, have taken shape in Cabral's influence on the thinking of non-Africans concerned with general or specific issues of sociocultural change—revolutionary change—in the world we have now.

What kind of a person could do all that? Cabral was a man of complexity and breadth of temperament, but whose cast of mind and character could and often did project an almost bare simplicity of purpose. This could be superficially misleading: Cabral's road to simplicity of purpose had passed in fact through an arduous struggle of mind and emotion; and the strength of character and conviction that he had won lay also in his

This essay was originally delivered in somewhat different form in 1983 at a memorial symposium held in Praia, Cape Verde. It was published under the title "On Revolutionary Nationalism: The Legacy of Cabral," by *Latin American Perspectives* (Spring 1984). Reprinted with permission.

capacity to understand the inner struggles of others, however different in mettle they might be from himself. Yet the impression of simplicity of purpose was never misleading in its essence. Here was an intellectual—one, indeed, of rare and shining talent—who believed that the reaching of conclusions *without* the taking of appropriate action was self-frustration or betrayal. At the same time, Cabral believed that while theorizing without action must be vain or irresponsible, action unshaped by theory was bound to fail, or, more exactly, that action leading to no embodiment in effective theory—in *appropriate* theory—was only the road to delusion and therefore to defeat.

Such beliefs, together with their extraordinarily resolute practice in his own life, gave him a power of leadership that was most unusual in the societies of late-colonial Africa, and probably in any of the societies of our time. What made him still more unusual was that the action he proposed and took and the theory that he drew from it (which afterward constantly nourished his actions) were able to succeed in the most hostile and forbidding of circumstances—the circumstances, precisely, that he had chosen to face.

This essay is little concerned with the record of events. They are well known, or may be learned from documentation. In that respect, besides, there was Cabral's additional achievement of being able to explain himself. Combining rigor with notable expository skills, Cabral explained himself at every important step and to every audience he considered useful or deserving: first and foremost, in Guiné Creole to those who gave him leadership, young or old, peasant or petty bourgeois; then in Portuguese to any who spoke that language; and afterward in French or English to audiences in Europe or America and to visitors from overseas. He wrote all the time, from the poetry of his youth to the lectures and addresses that brought him countless readers throughout the world, as well as the regular "reports on the progress of the struggle" in which he marked the onward movement of events and a great deal more besides. His published writings give the substance of his action and thought. They are relatively copious but still form only a small part of all that he discussed and that remains available on paper. They are all marked by two characteristics. One of these is their consistency: what he wrote for "external" use and consumption was exactly what he wrote, however different in style and form, for the militants who followed him. The other is their severe and practical rigor: nothing will be found of empty rhetoric, of "revolutionary" verbalism, of bombast or pretense.

The issues considered here can therefore take the record for granted, but the merest outline may be useful. In 1956 Cabral clandestinely formed the Partido Africano de Independência de Guiné e Cabo Verde (PAIGC) with five other men. There followed six years of political trial and error, experience and effort, and then, after January 1963, eleven years of anti-colonial warfare linked to further political development, always against extremely heavy odds until very near the end. In 1974 the PAIGC won complete and unconditional freedom for Guiné, wresting independence from a colonial power defeated both militarily and politically, and then, twelve months later, for Cape Verde as well. This remarkable success was crowned, moreover, by another in some ways still more remarkable. The ideas, methods, and morals of the PAIGC had their instrumental effect on the colonial enemy and, in significant degree, lay at the base of the Armed Forces Movement which overthrew the dictatorship in Portugal and enabled the colonial wars to be brought to an end. When had revolution-ary change in Africa ever helped to promote revolutionary change in Europe? Hadn't "all the books" declared that such a thing was impossible, even unthinkable? Yet it happened; and this was another part of the legacy of Cabral.

Cabral was murdered by agents of the Portuguese dictatorship in January 1973, one of the last and most baleful acts of horror of that already agonizing regime. He was only forty-nine, and at the height of his energy and intellectual power. One can only speculate, fruitlessly, on what he would have done with the rest of his life. It is clear that the full dimen-sions of his legacy have still to be revealed. Yet there may still be some use in attempting an estimate, even tentatively, of the value of his leading ideas, proposals, and conceptions in the context of his period—that is, the late-colonial and neocolonial period (or, if you prefer, the period of transnational capitalism), which is by no means at an end.

II

JUDGED BY A GROWING VOLUME OF COMMENT, SEVERAL OF CABRAL'S concepts have captured the attention of a wide audience. One of these is his concept of a colonial petty-bourgeois leadership that must "commit suicide" in its class consciousness (and class interests) if it is to be able to lead beyond a merely reformist (that is, neocolonialist or collaborationist) nationalism. Another is his concept of national liberation as involving, necessarily, precisely this "leadership beyond reformism" which "born again" petty-bourgeois revolutionaries must make their own, or, as he put it succinctly, any real liberation has to be a process of revolution. Some consideration of these concepts in their practical integument will then perhaps reveal a further and still deeper dimension of his legacy to Africans and, as seems likely, to other peoples as well.

Historians can sometimes feel that the old reductionism of the social anthropologists, denying the relevance of process, has repeated itself among the political analysts of more recent years. The anthropologists, as it happens, said their *nostra culpa* for turning their backs on history a long time ago—in fact, as long ago as Evans-Pritchard's famous lecture of 1950 (see Evans-Pritchard, 1962)—but it scarcely appears that their sociological successors, whether or not they claim the laurels of political science, have pondered the implications of that notable turnabout. The vocabulary may have changed, as well as the symbols of debate (or is it just the jargon?): one or other functionalism is out, one or other structuralism is in. But *process,* as a dynamic factor in *situation,* still often seems imperceptible.

The modern version of a naturalistic study of society, wrote Evans-Pritchard (1962, p. 19) in his Marett Lecture,

> claims that for an understanding of the functioning of a society there is no need for the students of it to know anything about its history, any more than there is need for a physiologist to know the history of an organism to understand it. Both are natural systems and can be described in terms of natural law without recourse to history.

But is the claim greatly different among many analysts today, including some of those who seek to use a Marxist tool kit? The latter, of course, make no reference to "natural law" in the sense of Evans-Pritchard more than thirty years ago, but in place of this "natural law" there seems often to be smuggled in another kind of "law" that is no less mandatory (or mysterious) in its workings. This new "natural law" refers, usually, to class attitudes, class crystallizations or tendencies toward such, and class potentials according to received schemes; and it does all this, one can't but observe, without caring to plunge its pristine beauty into the bathtub of real life—that is, into the realities of process as recorded and revealed by the history of ideas, developments, and events. So the "theory of petty-bourgeois suicide" attributed to Cabral is taken up and used as a "given symbol" in a generalized debate, rather than as what it actually was or is—a strictly limited option in a strictly defined situation. Old Marx, one may fear, will be turning in his grave once more.

A sociologist with experience of Tanzania recently wrote a perceptive book called *Beyond Ujamaa in Tanzania,* and was rightly thanked for a freshness of approach to that concept and debate. Was the legacy of

Cabral of any value here? Evidently not. Göran Hydén (1980, p. 228) found that "the notion that the African petty bourgeoisie should be capable of committing 'class suicide,' as Amílcar Cabral once put it, is hardly compatible with the development realities of contemporary Africa." And this was all that Hydén found useful to say upon the subject. If he was right about this, then clearly it would be of little worth to discuss Cabral and his ideas further. Anyone with relevant experience who could suggest that the African petty bourgeoisie en masse was ever going to commit class suicide, when presented with or grasping the reins of state power, must indeed be a fruitless optimist, if not entirely soft in the head. Cabral was not that kind of person, however, and proposed no such fatuous dénouement. It can only be, I suppose, that this writer on Tanzania had simply not bothered to find out what Cabral did propose, but preferred to treat a subtle and precise discourse as though it were another given symbol, a sort of convenient straw man to be overturned by some handy missile of superior analysis.

The fact is that Cabral, whatever his faults of analysis (and of course he committed some of those) never made the mistake of arguing from ignorance—of attempting, that is, to make good his case outside the limits of its own historical process. If he gave way now and then (but remarkably seldom) to the temptations of intellectual generalism, he was always careful to argue by extension, saying, effectively, that "if your situation is comparable with ours, within *this* situation in Guiné or Cape Verde, then you may expect this or that to follow." So let us recall what he really said about the petty bourgeoisie and its so improbable suicide as a class. The essential references were not singular, as Hydén thinks, but occurred on at least two public occasions: once during his lecture on social structure—strictly of Guiné, please note—given at Milan in 1964; and the second time during his address at Havana in 1966, well known by its title, "The Weapon of Theory."

His central point here was that Guiné possessed no "national bourgeoisie," nor working class in any way conscious of its nature and potentials. As a possible instrument for initiating change, there was only the beginnings of a petty bourgeoisie—or in class terms, of its embryo—that had learned how to manipulate the state through its urban, literate, and semiprivileged position in colonial society:

> This is the only stratum capable of controlling or even utilizing the instruments which the colonial state used against our people. So we come to the conclusion that in colonial conditions it is the petty bourgeoisie which is the inheritor of state power (though I wish we

could be wrong). The moment national liberation comes and the petty bourgeoisie takes power, we enter, or rather return, to history, and thus the internal contradictions break out again [Cabral, 1969a, p. 69].

No question, as you see, of supposing that the petty bourgeoisie, *telle quelle*, will ever commit suicide in order to lead a revolution. On the contrary, at this stage in his thinking (1963–64), faced with the manifest realities of what was then happening to Africa (especially to West Africa), he was even inclined to argue that the whole process of colonial "liberation" within the situations then at hand might be reasonably seen as "an initiative of the enemy":

> The objective of the imperialist countries was to prevent the enlargement of the socialist camp, to liberate the reactionary forces in our countries which were being stifled by colonialism, and to enable these forces to ally themselves with the international bourgeoisie. The fundamental objective was to create a bourgeoisie where one did not exist, in order specifically to strengthen the imperialist and the capitalist camp [Cabral, 1969a, p. 71].

What then should be done? Go with the current and let it carry history wherever it would? Bow to the overweening might of the Portuguese dictatorship and wait for better times? Many thought so. But Cabral's choice, and the choice of the few who followed him, was to form a "party of struggle," and to use that party as a weapon of real change. They looked for the working class that alone was capable (as many outside Guiné told them) of leading that kind of struggle, and they did not find it. They searched for revolutionary intellectuals ready for "class suicide," and scarcely found them either: in all the history of Guiné, fewer than a dozen Africans (or *mestiços, assimilados*) had achieved a university degree, and most of those were dead or in close service of the colonial dictatorship. There remained some available individuals of the petty bourgeoisie: not many, as it proved—a very little group.

This is where we have the nub of the process. For what was done by this handful, tentatively at first and then resolutely after August 1959, was to turn its back on the bulk of the petty bourgeoisie and to set themselves to act as the revolutionary segment of a working class that did not, in fact, exist. They defined themselves as such, and acted as such, rallying wage-workers in Bissau as best they could until with more effort—having prepared about a thousand militants (or cadres in their usage) by the end of 1962—they could begin to win support and then participation among the village masses, not for a petty-bourgeois reformism, but for a movement capable of developing into a revolution.

How original was this? To be sure, it occurred elsewhere in Africa, notably in Mozambique and in Angola. But I think its originality, in each of these cases, was perfectly genuine—it came, that is, out of the given situation for men and women whose political formation had no international background, or, at best, rather little of one. It was taught by the brute facts, but the gift, of course, was to be able to learn. It had happened before, after all, and to other peoples striving for the road ahead in times of darkness. In colonial Vietnam, for example, we find the journal of Thanh Nien (forerunner of the Viet Minh) discussing the role of the revolutionary petty bourgeoisie as early as 1929:

> The history of the world revolution teaches us that the intellectuals are the very first elements which sacrifice themselves for the revolutionary cause . . . [but] unfortunately these intellectuals are also in general opportunists. . . .
>
> To put an end to the lack of discipline . . . the party must adopt a purely revolutionary method of education. In effect, it is indispensable that all the comrades "proletarianise" themselves, "revolutionise" themselves, in order to have the same thoughts, behavior, language, etc. . . . [They must] abandon their rich clothes and don the rags of the proletarians, become workers, peasants, men of the people, etc. [Hodgkin, 1981, pp. 228–29].

The petty-bourgeois clerks, mechanics, chauffeurs, hospital servants, and the rest scarcely had any rich clothes to abandon in the Guiné of 1956. A regular wage, a seat at a café table, and a choice of shirts and shoes was about all they aspired to. Yet the parallel is otherwise exact. The project of Thanh Nien was precisely the project of Cabral thirty years later and far away; but the one proved as compatible with the "development realities" of Vietnam as the other with those of Guinea-Bissau.

In the case of Guinea-Bissau this project was fairly well established by the time of Cabral's Milan lecture of 1964, a fact that emphasizes that the early years, 1956–64, were the really crucial ones. By the end of 1963 the fighting movement had won firm hold on small but decisive areas of liberated territory, while the political movement (insofar as the political can be said to have been separated from the military, which was not very far) had survived some almost mortal tests and trials. In February 1964 the party's first congress was able to secure strong internal discipline, lay out the program that would liberate the country ten years later, launch the beginnings of mobile warfare with a regular guerrilla fighting force, and reaffirm the revolutionary perspectives of its leadership. Speaking at Milan, Cabral could now affirm with confidence that

> the revolutionary petty bourgeoisie is honest: that is to say, it remains identified, in spite of all the hostile conditions, with the fundamental interests of the popular masses. To do this it may have to commit suicide; but it will not lose. By sacrificing itself it can reincarnate itself, but in the condition of workers or peasants [Cabral, 1969a, p. 72].

Two years later, in Havana, he returned to the same theme, and further clarified his meaning. And here, one may recall, he was speaking in a Cuba that could well take his point: For what would have happened there had a revolutionary segment of the petty bourgeoisie failed to appear and act?

A reformist petty bourgeoisie, he repeated, must lead simply to a neocolonial outcome. The result was all the more assured because

> events have shown that the only social sector capable of being aware of the reality of imperialist domination, and of directing the state apparatus inherited from this domination, is the native petty bourgeoisie . . . [and] this specific inevitability in our situation constitutes one of the weaknesses of the national liberation movement [Cabral, 1969a, p. 108].

By virtue of their position, members of that sector or stratum were those who first became aware of the nature of foreign domination and thus of the need to act in order to remove it; and

> this historical responsibility is assumed by the sector of the petty bourgeoisie which, in the colonial context, can be called *revolutionary*, while other sectors retain the doubts characteristic of these classes or ally themselves to colonialism so as to defend, albeit illusorily, their social position [Cabral, 1969a, pp. 108–9; emphasis in original].

But would this revolutionary segment necessarily remain true to its responsibility? Would its class suicide prove irreversible? Cabral neither thought so nor said so; and leaving the question open would influence first the whole further process of struggle for anticolonial liberation, and then, as was seen so clearly in Bissau before and during November 1980, the postcolonial effort. Meanwhile, and very patently by 1966, there was no doubt that the revolutionary segment's "suicide" was not only far advanced, but was proving fruitful in its reincarnation. Former clerks and their kind, and even a handful of highly trained intellectuals (for example, José Araújo, Vasco Cabral, Dulce Amada Duarte, to mention only three) had come into the movement and sunk their social and moral identity into the embrace of the village masses, living as peasants, fighting or working in forests and swamplands, learning local languages, eschewing privileges. This was the actual process and experience from which, at Havana, Cabral could elaborate his argument that the revolutionary petty bourgeoisie had only one road if it were not to betray itself; and that was

> to strengthen its revolutionary consciousness; to reject the temptations of becoming more bourgeois and the natural concerns of its class mentality; and to identify itself with the working classes [Cabral, 1969a, p. 110].

Then came the well-known formulation:

> This means that in order to truly fulfill its role in the national liberation struggle, the revolutionary petty bourgeoisie must be capable of committing suicide as a class, in order to be reborn as revolutionary workers, completely identified with the deepest aspirations of the people to which they belong.
> This alternative—to betray the revolution or to commit suicide as a class—constitutes the dilemma of the petty bourgeoisie in the general framework of the national liberation struggle. The positive solution, in favour of the revolution, depends on what Fidel Castro recently correctly called the development of revolutionary consciousness [Cabral, 1969a, p. 110].

Again it was this development, inside Portuguese Guiné, that precisely formed the process on which Cabral could stand and know that he stood, by this time, on good ground. The little group of 1956 had greatly grown in numbers; more important still, it had gone far to change its sociocultural nature. Having thus changed, it had led to a situation by 1966 in which it was already clear that the colonial dictatorship no longer held the initiative, while the PAIGC had become a "vanguard party" with increasing mass participation. The politics of liberation were now at large among this people, and it was the revolutionary segment of its petty bourgeoisie that had forced open the gate.

A segment, of course; even, still, a small one. Most of the petty bourgeoisie had fled into exile or remained in the service of the colonial regime. Some of the latter, later still, would accept a "junior partnership" in the dictatorship's fruitless program for a "better Guiné" (*Guiné melhor*) and would connive not only in the murder of Cabral but also in efforts to set up a rival "movement" under Portuguese guidance (Frente Unida de Libertação, FUL). The bulk of the Guiné petty bourgeoisie, even at the end of the war, was still openly or covertly on the side of the colonial regime.

III

AGAINST THIS RECORD, IT SEEMS RATHER MORE THAN A PITY THAT OTHER-wise thoughtful observers should blandly affirm that Cabral's ideas were incompatible with reality. But leaving this aside, as another, if incidental, warning of the dangers of hasty judgment, one may still ask why Cabral should have cared so greatly to elaborate and argue formulations open to controversy even among those whose sympathy and support the PAIGC greatly wished to secure and hold? It is a useful question because it takes one directly into the workings of his mind and the ways in which he conceived the realities of his time and place.

There were, it has seemed, two cultural constructs of pressing relevance. One was (or still is?) concerned with the overhang of colonial racism and its effects not only on colonized Africans but also on noncolonized peoples, especially in the imperialist countries. The other—which we will come to in a moment—was (or still is) concerned with the nature of Marxist or *Marxisant* thinking about the roles to be played by revolutionary groups or "protoclasses." So far as both were important, Cabral and his comrades in the lusophone liberation movements suffered a special disadvantage. They carried a heavier handicap than others; they came from colonized peoples of whom little was known outside their frontiers, sometimes nothing at all, but whose capacities were regarded as being still smaller (if that were possible) than those of British- or French-colonized peoples. They had to make good their right to be heard, and respected, from the shadows of a double and extremely deep provincialism: the provincialism of Portuguese culture but also, beyond that, the provincialism of peoples despised even by Portuguese culture. Most of the reformist or quiescent petty bourgeoisie in these colonies never succeeded in emerging from that isolation and sense of inferiority. Even to this day one can find clusters of them (in Bissau, Luanda, Maputo, and elsewhere) capable of falling into the grossest illusions and superstitions about the nature of the world in which, often to their persistent and astonished skepticism, they are now called to live and work.

Like others in his pioneering group, from the middle 1950s on, Cabral saw it as imperative to break through "the wall of silence built around our peoples by Portuguese colonialism." Only thus could they attract understanding and help from the outside world. Only thus—still more important—could they or those who sought to lead them become capable of reducing their provincialism, ending their isolation, and so, little by little, mastering their condition. It may be said that all of Cabral's early efforts were aimed at piercing "the wall of silence" and ensuring a two-way communication—a traffic of facts, new ideas, fresh confidence.

These pioneers set about to learn, but also to explain. They found this difficult at home because of a repression that was greatly intensified after about 1955. As to explaining, they found this still more difficult abroad because of the myths that the repression had used in defense of itself, and, as Cabral recalled in 1967, used

> not without success, as shown by an incident during the second All-African People's Conference in Tunis during 1961, where we had some difficulty in being heard. One African delegate to whom we tried to explain our situation replied in all sympathy: "Oh, it's different for you. No problem there—you're doing all right with the Portuguese" [1969, pp. 9–10].

Even a politically minded African in 1961, after repeated massacres of anticolonial protesters in Angola, Guiné, and Mozambique (not to speak of mass shootings on São Tomé in 1953), could still say that. So a great deal of patient explanation was required as to the real condition of the peoples in the Portuguese colonies, and then, as things developed, as to the real ability of the leaders of those peoples to find effective strategies of anticolonial action, and deploy them. This was all the more difficult in years when ignorance of the "Portuguese position" went hand in hand with an equally general assumption that merely constitutional or political pressures—of course, with a little carefully fostered "trouble" now and then—would be enough to bring decolonizing change. Wasn't this, after all, the comforting reformist lesson taught by so much of British and French African experience?

Along the way, explanation also had to deal with attitudes of a different sort; and it was these, more than anything else, that may most probably be seen as holding the key to the motives behind Cabral's lectures abroad, and behind other such lectures by his comrades from Angola and Mozambique. These attitudes derived from one or the other of two chief assumptions, or from both at the same time. Foreign sympathy and support might accept the need for revolutionary action in the Portuguese colonies. But such acceptance tended to have its own strong preconceptions about how, when, and by what means this action should be opened and advanced.

One of these assumptions was that applicants for aid from the Portuguese colonies could not be expected to know the necessary answers, and must be provided with them. Thus it came about, in 1960, that the relevant delegate of the Algerian Front of National Liberation, who happened to be Frantz Fanon, urged both the MPLA in Angola and the PAIGC in Guiné (the Frente de Libertação de Moçambique, FRELIMO, in Mozambique, had yet to emerge) simply "to begin" their armed struggle. If they would only set aside all further delay and begin, the peasants would rally and insurrection would irresistibly widen almost of itself. The MPLA in that moment was unable to "begin," at least with any hope of consistent success, whereupon Fanon, finding that Holden and his União das Populações de Angola (UPA; later, Frente Nacional de Libertação de Angola, FNLA) were ready to start an insurrection without having prepared it inside the country, threw Algerian military and political aid behind that fruitless "movement." Disasters accordingly followed. Cabral and the PAIGC, for their part, were well advanced with their plans but were still not ready for insurrection. They flatly refused "to begin," and were roundly insulted for thus having minds of their own.

Making their analysis of what could be done in Guiné and Cape Verde and by what means, they ran into a second assumption then common on the left (the right, of course, either ignored or persecuted them). This was that the colonial revolution must take its line and measure from the revolution in Europe. That particular ethnocentrism followed from the doctrinal conviction that nothing useful could be done, in any seriously revolutionary way, without working-class leadership. As there was none to be found in Africa (or, at least, in tropical Africa), such leadership must be provided in Europe, or, in the case of Portugal's colonies, in Portugal. Any such prescription must seem perfectly unreal to latter-day eyes, but in those years it had its power. The crucial date in this context seems to have been 1957, and applied necessarily to the Communist movement— necessarily, of course, because there was no other movement or party in Portugal committed to decolonization. The Portuguese party agreed at its clandestine congress of that year to cease trying to launch African territorial branches (it seems that only one, in Angola, had in fact been tentatively formed), and to accept that Portuguese Communists would throw their support behind new movements or parties of national liberation (two of which—PAIGC and MPLA—having been founded some months earlier).[1] One may note in passing that this is what Portuguese Communists in the colonies, often with outstanding courage, then did; few of them escaped long imprisonment, torture, or death at the hands of the dictatorship.

It still remained to argue the analysis, reached by these nascent liberation movements, on the broad terrain of the left. There were those in Europe or America, for example, who wished to believe that the peasants were to be regarded as the chief initiating force for revolutionary change, when, according to all the evidence, the peasants would act as no such thing. There were those who added that the necessary vanguard party, even if it were to be autonomous in its choice of policy and timing, must somehow still be "proletarian" in its composition. Alas, the facts showed that no such basis could be reached; or, if reached by various stretchings of the term "proletarian," could become capable of coherent action. There were even those—and this persisted almost to the end, notwithstanding every effort at explanation—who made a touchstone of revolutionary authenticity by setting up other "conditions of reliability" drawn from a completely non-African experience, such as land nationalization, the rapid incorporation of individual peasants in rapidly expanding cooperatives, and so on. Both the Milan and Havana lectures have to be read against this often difficult background.

Each form of provincialism—that of the colonialist overhang or that of ethnocentrism—led in fact to the need for a sharp clarity of analysis; and no doubt the challenge was useful. One may think that Cabral would have deepened and refined his analysis in any case; it was the man's nature to wrestle with the "here and now" and make it yield positive solutions. But the dual challenge from skeptics and supporters was still a valuable incentive. In the early years, although much less later, he had time to respond to it. Most of his well-known formulations and proposals date from the time before 1970 when the slow takeoff of a protracted guerrilla war gave him opportunities for standing aside from immediate tasks. Those were the years in which he struck out a solid claim to African originality of revolutionary action, and to African originality of thought in theorizing that action and impelling it further.

By 1965 he had similarly composed his *Palávras Geráis* (Cabral, 1979, pp. 224–50), his directives for the continued advance of the PAIGC on the

mainland and in the islands; and in this context there was really nothing
further to say until liberation came. I recall having asked him in 1967
(when I had not yet seen a copy of the *Palávras*) why he did not write a
full account of PAIGC strategy and principles. His reply was that he had
nothing to add to the *Palávras*. Having got so far, in other words, the
experience of the PAIGC had become, in itself, sufficient to explain its
nature, aims, and potentials; anyone who wished to know what these were
could now come and see for himself or herself. By now too this experience
confirmed Cabral's dislike of doctrinal labels. Apart from tactics on the
international scene of politics, he considered that labels were a probable
source of error. He was patient with those in distant lands who wanted
him to proclaim a "Marxist revolution," a "battle for socialism," or the
like, but he seldom refrained from repeating, on such occasions, his
reference to reality:

> Every theory of armed struggle has to arise as the consequence of
> an actual armed struggle. In every case, practice comes first and
> theory after.... If you really want to advance the struggle, you must
> make a critical assessment of the experience of others before apply-
> ing their theories, but the basic theory of armed struggle has to come
> from the reality of the fight [Cabral, 1971, p. 20].

As to his own ideology and that of the PAIGC, an answer must be drawn
from their practice:

> If you decide it's Marxism, tell everyone that it is Marxism. If you
> decide that it's not Marxism, tell everyone that it's not Marxism. But
> the labels are your affair.... People here [in London, as it happened]
> are very preoccupied with the question: are you Marxist or not
> Marxist? Are you Marxist-Leninist? Just ask me; please, what we are
> doing in the field. Are we really liberating our people, the human
> beings in our country, from all forms of oppression? Simply ask me
> this, and draw your own conclusions [Cabral, 1971, p. 20].

Offered to questioners of undoubted goodwill, this may sound somewhat impatient. In other circumstances he might have phrased it differently and embarked on a restatement of his chief theses. But perhaps there
was some reasonable ground for impatience on that occasion. Although
political scientists for the most part, his questioners turned out not to have
read his chief theses, although these had been handily available in English
since the end of 1969. On top of that, three or four exponents of the

Provisional Irish Republican Army had just sought to destroy the meeting (held in a lecture room at the University of London) on the grounds that Cabral was talking about Guiné and not about Ulster. Third, he was speaking in English, and his grasp of that language was still inadequate. Cabral believed most firmly by 1971—when this particular meeting was held—that the development of the PAIGC was sufficient to speak for itself, whether in demonstrating the point of process then reached or the meaning and direction that it marked.

I V

THERE WERE MANY DIFFERENCES OF APPLICATION OF STRATEGY BETWEEN that of the PAIGC and those of FRELIMO and MPLA, but the strategy itself was strikingly the same in all three cases. The reasons why this was so lie outside the concerns of this essay, although the clarity and force of Cabral's thought were certainly high on the list of them. One could pass from the liberated zones of one of these three movements to those of the other two, and find in each of them—if often under a different guise or stated in somewhat different terms—precisely the same policies at work and with much the same results. The underlying unity of action and thought was invariably impressive, even if the "point of process" at any one time varied from one movement to the other. Considering that the same has been true of postcolonial development, one may well ask what will be the further impact, generally in Africa or elsewhere, of the practice and theory of these lusophone liberation movements. Can they be seen to have introduced a new trend toward effective self-development? Do they indicate a qualitative advance on the road to progressive change? Will they appear, in twenty years' time or so, to lie at the start of new African modalities of struggle, organization, understanding of socio-cultural and economic needs and possibilities? Even by 1981, there seemed to be reasons for thinking so.[2] Whether or not that is agreed upon, the crucial legacy of these movements in their years of warfare—the particular legacy, in our context here, of Amílcar Cabral—will in any case be found to originate in the practice of their liberated zones.

This practice developed from two principles. One of these was that no worthwhile success could be gained without a growing and ever more effective weight of rural (if you wish, of peasant) initiative in fighting and organizing for anticolonial change. The other was that this initiative could be evoked usefully—that is, purposively, on behalf of a program for such change—only by a steady and continued converting of rural support or sympathy into rural participation. *Que povo na manda na su cabeça*—"Let people do it for themselves," as the Guiné Creole slogan has it otherwise "it" would be done to them and could possess no culture-changing value. Further, as one of Cabral's deepest moral and political convictions was that culture-changing value was what really counted, its promotion had to be a central test of good leadership.

In this respect the Portuguese colonial system and ethos had possessed their own legitimacy within the dynamics of imperialism. They had stopped the process of indigenous cultural development and had interjected the culture of imperialism. For that they had used the weapon of *assimilação* (essentially, of racism) to produce a stratum of "African Portuguese," as well as their corresponding weapon of the *indígenato* (essentially, of domination) to depersonalize the mass of their colonial victims. Hence these colonial populations consisted of a very small minority of persons who were recognized as such, even with many reservations, because they had ceased to be Africans and had become Portuguese, and a very large majority of "natives" who were in all important ways (whether by law or colonial usage) the mere objects of exploitation. No doubt the essence of this disembodiment belongs to every form of systematic dictatorship; but here in the Portuguese system and ethos it reached an often remarkable extreme of alienation. Anyone who cares to wade through the colonial literature will see as much. In a thousand ways, abrasively or sentimentally (or both), alienation was preached and practiced by generations of governors, theorists, priests, poets, and others as a necessary "colonial mission." Every kind of coercion was found to be legitimate, not least by a Portuguese religious hierarchy whose general contempt for African humanity would be hard to overstate.

How far this culture of domination really destroyed the culture of the colonized peoples naturally depended on the circumstances, including the geographical location, of this or that people. For a few widely scattered communities, living outside the confines of intensive colonization (usually identical with regions earmarked for white settlement), the colonial system and ethos seem never to have been much more than a spasmodic influence to be suffered or evaded as a calamity coming entirely from "outside," and, as such, always rejected. That, largely, was the position and attitude of Mbunda-speaking communities and their neighbors in eastern Angola. They continued to worship at their woodland shrines even as late as the 1970s, and seldom knew a word of Portuguese. They had long since lost their traditional chiefs (in fact, by the middle 1920s) but retained a strong sense of their own identity. They were persecuted, but not alienated. They still stood, if painfully, on their own ground.

There were other such cases. Yet for most of these peoples, living under the heel of the system, mere endurance without acceptance was much more difficult, and sometimes it was impossible. More than others, these peoples went far toward losing their own history. As rural multitudes sought relief from rural starvation in ever greater numbers after the 1940s, the towns became the home of populations for whom the old values had lost their power to save, but for whom the new values meant *assimilação* (or its simulacrum) and imposed a further alienation. In between these "categories"—never, in any case, clearly defined or cut-and-dried in their limits—there were of course many diversities of level and stability. We do not know enough about that yet. Much more study will be required before we can approach the inner thinking of most of these colonized communities. Yet we know enough to be sure that one or another form of imposed alienation had spread confusion, decay, and loss of self-confidence.

How to make this good, how to reverse the trend of despair? How to give back to these communities the conviction of being able to master their own destiny? They had possessed that conviction in the past, but it was no good trying to return to the past. For national liberation to have a meaning that went beyond a mere change of masters, Cabral held that its mode of action must introduce a culture-changing process capable of stemming from precolonial development but, at the same time, of assuming entirely new dimensions of independent self-realization. A valid system to replace and overcome colonial values could never be a reversion to those of the past, even if any such reversion were in any case practicable. On the contrary:

> Our cultural resistance [to colonialism] consists in the following: while we scrap colonial culture and the negative aspects of our own culture, whether in our character or in our environment, we have to create a new culture, also based on our traditions but respecting everything that the world today has conquered for the service of mankind [Cabral, 1969c].

The full development of a new cultural hegemony, through the action of liberated peoples, would have to come after the smashing of the colonial system and years of independent effort in the building of a new community. But the launching of this new culture, at least in its essentials and foundations, was the central aim of the liberated zones, and of their democratic self-organization. That was what had to be done, no matter how hostile the circumstances; without it, nothing else would count for much.

This was the synthesis, highly original in its forms and methods, that combined the short-term need with the long-term need. Short-term, because the means of participation arising from those types of self-organization were vital to the "mobilization" (PAIGC parlance, meaning "participation") of ever larger numbers of rural people, and thus to the winning of the war. But also long-term, because that same participation was vital in a deeper sense. It was vital to the opening of minds and the uniting of wills out of which, in due course, a new culture could steadily take shape and grow into command of the future. Hence the "war aim" marched together with the "peace aim," and perhaps it is in this synthesis that one may best measure the power of Cabral's conception of progress. Few outside observers perceived this at the time, and even fewer outside commentators. At one extreme there were colonial apologists or propagandists who saw the process as being one of coercion. Armed militants "conscripted" rural people and "punished" any who held back. No such thing would have been in any case possible, but the impossibility never prevented it from being alleged. At another extreme there were those who wished to sympathize with the anticolonial struggle, but could never understand the difference between the fake movements (such as the União Nacional para a Independência Total de Angola, UNITA, in Angola) and those (such as MPLA in Angola) whose strength came from the processes of expanding participation.

The truth of the liberated zones, by contrast, was one of partial, painful, but always stubborn effort toward a liberation of minds that was mental and moral, in that it was essentially political, even more than it was a physical liberation from colonial oppression. This was also why the anti-colonial wars had to be conceived and fought as "struggles of long duration." Given Portuguese military superiority in arms and numbers of troops, these wars could not be won quickly. Just as surely, however, they would be lost if they were won quickly, for in that case they would be won before the culture-changing process had time to reach its stride and make significant gains.

Cabral argued the absolute priority of this culture-changing process in many lectures and addresses, as well as in countless conversations "internally" or "externally"; and it would be out of place to repeat him at length. All that he said and thought on the subject was drawn together well enough in his Syracuse lecture of 1970. How could it come about that this armed struggle did in fact put down the foundations of a new culture?

"Consider," he said in one of his most important passages, "these features inherent in an armed liberation struggle" conducted on the principles of the PAIGC:

> the practice of democracy, of criticism and self-criticism, the grow-ing responsibility of populations for the management of their life, literacy teaching, the creation of schools and health care, the train-ing of cadres from peasant and labourer backgrounds—and other achievements. We should thus find that the armed liberation strug-gle is not only a product of culture but also a . . . *determinant* of culture. This is without doubt for the people the prime recompense for the efforts and sacrifices which are the price of war [Cabral, 1979, pp. 152–53; emphasis in original].

It may be important to insist that these features were not identified a priori or by any preliminary blueprint. Going by early conversations with him (in London, 1960; in Conakry, 1961), I do not think that Cabral (with his leading colleagues, most notably Arístides Pereira) had any detailed plan for what was to be done in eventually liberated zones. They had ideas on the subject, of course, but were well convinced that actual practice must be their guide. Given their principles, they believed that life in its richness and variety would teach the necessary lessons, and so it proved. For the real attributes of the liberated zones emerged in the course of winning them and working in them, especially at and after the critical party congress of February 1964 which, in the nick of time as it also proved, was able to make good the blunders and indiscipline that had begun to ruin the fighting movement, and then, having done that, to identify the new initiatives that needed to be made. Hence Cabral's characteristic insistence (parallel, one may note, to Samora Machel's in Mozambique and Agostinho Neto's in Angola) that "practice comes before theory." The "features" listed in his Syracuse lecture—whether in the fragment I have just quoted or in other passages—were precisely those that practice had proved to be fruitful. Their *determination* of a new culture—of its foundations, of its early outlines—was no kind of theoreti-cal claim, much less a theoretical abstraction; most exactly, it was the *achieved* product of a particular practice and experience.

That the further development of "full maturity" of this new culture, direct product of mass participation in liberated zones, was not and could not be guaranteed—any more than the class suicide of a widening num-ber of the petty bourgeoisie and their reincarnation as revolutionaries— was and is beside the point. I am very clear in my mind that Cabral never thought that any such process could be guaranteed; his optimism was not of the utopian kind. The affirmation that he made was a different one. He affirmed that only this process, and no other, could open the way to a true development—initially, of a liberation movement fighting for power and winning it, and then, later, of a liberation movement in power that would be capable of maintaining and enlarging the requirements of this new progressive culture. He would have greatly condemned the resort to a coup d'état in the Guinea-Bissau of November 1980. He would not, I think, have been as greatly surprised by it in any essential way. The dialectics of process were what, among many other things, he thoroughly understood.

The facts showed, meanwhile, that the determinant was fruitfully at work, as each of a number of foreign observers (e.g., Chaliand, 1969; Davidson, 1969 and 1981; Rudebeck, 1974; and Urdang, 1979) in the liberated zones of the PAIGC had noted or continued to note in his or her own way. Thanks to a common effort for united aims, the thought and behavior of leaders converged on those of the peasant mass, shedding their petty-bourgeois prejudices of superiority, learning a new respect for village people, and enriching their grip on reality.

> [While] on their side, the mass of workers and, in particular, the peasants, who are generally illiterate and have never moved beyond the confines of the village or region, in contact with other categories shed the complexes which constrained them . . . understand their situation as determining elements of the struggle . . . break the fetters of the village universe to integrate gradually into the country and the world . . . [and] become fitter to play the decisive role as the principal force of the liberation movement [Cabral, 1979, p. 152].

Encapsulated in what Cabral said to his Syracuse audience, all this was going on in Cubucaré, Quitáfine, Como, Tombali, Kinara, and other districts. It was because it was going on that the movement could win a strategic initiative by 1968, drive the colonial armed forces and administration from more than half the country by 1972, and go on to drive them from the rest of it in 1974. It was because all this was going on, and in countless ways, that Cabral, if then posthumously, was to be awarded his unique title, Fundador da Nacionalidade, Founder of the Nationality. Not, please note, Founder of the Nation, because the nation was and is a collectivity and necessarily founds itself, but founder of the process whereby this collectivity could (and does) identify itself and continue to build its postcolonial culture.

This then is the process through which one must seek for the subtle truths of development within the system and potentials of the national-liberation struggle of the PAIGC. Outside Africa, and sometimes inside—all too understandably in view of the Stalinist outcome—many have argued that Lenin's concept of the vanguard party must inevitably lead to a party dictatorship within ever-narrowing limits. Given that the PAIGC was a vanguard party and that its leadership was both self-appointed and, at least in those years, self-perpetuating, how could the peasantry or other "proletarian" strata (insofar as these existed) then play a decisive role? How could there be an increasing democratization of state power, or, at least, of power to control the state? The Lenin of the middle of 1917 might look toward a time, after revolution, when the soviets—the mass-elected committees of local and then national power—should effectively rule. What came after outside intervention, civil war, and great disasters was something very different, as everyone knows. All power to the soviets became all power to the central committee, and then, soon enough, to the controller of that committee.

Cabral never formulated or, as I believe, felt the need to formulate any specific reply to this large question; but just as certainly he thought about it. I have the best of reasons for knowing that he was thinking about it in the very weeks before his murder, because he told me so. At that point he was thinking in institutional terms: how best to organize a separation of powers and functions between state and party, how best to endow the "soviets" of Guinea-Bissau—the elected committees of self-government in the liberated zones—with a political identity that should not become, in any restrictive sense, a party identity. (It went without saying that all these committees saw themselves as part and parcel of the PAIGC—"our party"—but this affiliation needed to be something different from being branches of the PAIGC.) Immediate answers were provided by developments then in motion. The previous year had seen a general election by secret ballot and adult suffrage, throughout the liberated zones, for regional committees. These in turn, during November, had elected their representatives to a People's National Assembly (PNA). This PNA, it was decided by December, would have its first session sometime after the middle of 1973. It would have the supreme legislative power, and would proclaim the independence of a republic of Guinea-Bissau, even if the colonial armies still held part of the country. (This first session actually took place in September 1973, eight months after Cabral's murder, and the planned decisions were taken.)

At a deeper level, however, I believe that Cabral was thinking of the crucial cultural determinant. The vanguard party must continue to lead,

reinforced by continuing new intakes from the product of the determinant—the product, that is, in terms of men and women formed and
prepared by the struggle. Yet the dialectics of the process would ensure
a synthesis, as between vanguard and masses, whereby democratic control
would increasingly emerge. There had been no such control in 1963, when
the armed struggle had begun; there had only been colonial dictatorship.
Now there was some, and certainly far more than a few years earlier.
Progressively, as the democracy of the liberated zones grew stronger,
there would be more. This initiation and extension of democratic control,
after all, was what the process had proved it could achieve. Politically
speaking, that indeed was the essence of the process.

This synthesis, in turn, would produce its antithesis. Naturally, an
antithesis between a politically *lumpen* petty bourgeoisie (concentrated,
largely, in the colonial capital, Bissau) and a politically developed liberation movement would surely be among them. For *a luta continua*—the
struggle for liberation continues—and the notion that history is a series
of disconnected situations rather than a dialectical interplay capable of
retrogressions as well as progress belongs, in any case, to a philosophy in
which Cabral had no part.

To the degree that the crucial determinant, the builder of a new
culture, could hold its ground and maintain its creative influence, to that
same degree would the peoples of Guinea Bissau and Cape Verde truly
come to govern themselves and make their own history. Fine words and
promises could have little value, or none. The deciding factor always
remained the degree to which the determinant was really at work. New
laws and structures would help, shaping a system that would be antiracist,
antichauvinist, targeted against every form of systemic exploitation and
therefore anticapitalist; but these would constitute only an empty shell
unless they were applied with the strength, resilience, and potential of an
ever-extending democratic control. By the end of 1972, Cabral knew that
the concept of an ever-extending democratic control, as well as the means
of realizing it, were rooted deeply in the liberated zones. He had worked
for that, ever since the congress of February 1964, with unbending purpose. Behind the scenes of military success, it was perhaps his greatest
achievement.

V

WHAT WOULD HE HAVE DONE AND SAID ABOUT MANY ISSUES, GREAT OR small, if only the assassins had failed and he had lived into the time of complete territorial liberation? It remains tempting to wonder. The legacy of his work ensured many new gains: a final territorial liberation of examplary lack of violence (both in Guinea-Bissau and Cape Verde), fruit of the skill and courage of men and women who had undergone the necessary process; the all-decisive influence of the determinant—all results of the teaching and leadership that he had given. His own continued presence, one may think, would have enlarged those gains and better defended them on the mainland against the petty-bourgeois antithesis. No people, after all, loses an outstanding leader without paying a price, and the price, usually, is high. Already there were signs by 1977 that the price being paid for the loss of Cabral was becoming higher on the mainland than was clearly recognized or, at least, provided for. Some fairly acrid discussion at the third party congress (Bissau, November 1977) showed that a gap in trust and solidarity was already opening in Guinea-Bissau between countryside and capital, and the next two years seemed to achieve dangerously little in closing it. By November 1980, in any case, the petty-bourgeois antithesis had taken command to a point where a coup d'état of that month could even appear, in its early days, to have overthrown all that the PAIGC had stood for and striven for.[3]

In fact, it soon became evident that the PAIGC could not be canceled out so easily. The "other side" of the antithesis was also there, and was clearly reinforced within several weeks of the day of the coup by the presence and action of militants, at many levels, who stood solidly by PAIGC practice and principle. A political struggle developed. Much about that struggle remained obscure a year later when this was written. Yet there could be no doubt that the legacy of Cabral, the cultural determinant at work in the will and attitudes of thousands of party militants, remained a living force in Guinea-Bissau. That force in Cape Verde, meanwhile, continued to make fresh gains. This same year of 1980 was the one in which a large extension of democratic control in all the islands acquired fresh dimensions. These came with the launching of assemblies and committees of local government, *commissões de moradores*, such as had never existed in any form before.

In conclusion, I wish only to raise a single large issue for Africa today in the light of Cabral's thinking and of the implications of the process

whereby the PAIGC destroyed colonial systems in Guinea-Bissau and
Cape Verde. This issue concerns the limits of nationalism. Cabral had
long foreseen (as noted earlier in this essay) that decolonization on the
British or French pattern, adapting the "Western model" of the nation-
state within frontiers traced by imperialism for the use of imperialism,
could well lead to little more than an "updating" of the old relationships
of domination. He had also seen, however, that African use of nationalism,
as a weapon to get decolonization, was not an optional alternative to the
use of some other weapon. There was no other weapon, or one that could
have the least prospect of becoming effective. He was not insincere in the
least in paying homage to Kwame Nkrumah as "the strategist of genius
in the struggle against classic colonialism" (Cabral, 1979, p. 115).[4] There
was no other way ahead, after 1945, than the road opened to and by
nationalism; and the petty bourgeoisie, however blinkered in its majority,
was the stratum that must lead along it.

What force could then be set against the neocolonial antithesis, the
petty-bourgeois antithesis? The PAIGC, and other parties or movements
like it, could answer this question from their long and varied experience.
Beyond that answer, however, what could nationalism then promise to an
Africa divided by the frontiers of the colonial "share out," chopped into
pieces that often made no economic or political sense for postcolonial
development and still subject to a "world order" within which Africa
remained in many ways a victim? I believe that Cabral had no illusions
about the incapacity of nationalism, as such, to solve the basic problems
of postcolonial development. If he was Fundador da Nacionalidade, insistent always that the PAIGC was concerned with *national* liberation, this
was because the nationalism he believed in and fought for was always
revolutionary. Yes, a liberated Africa must begin by becoming an Africa
of separately independent nations. That was what the heritage of colonialism had dictated; only an empty verbalism could find a way to reject this
destiny. Reality enforced its acceptance. But reality, fully understood, was
dialectical in its own development. The acceptance of an Africa of separately independent nations must lead, if development were to continue,
to a progressive rejection of that outcome. The true vocation of these new
nations—true in the sense of a capacity to yield a further process of
development—was to overcome the colonial heritage by moving
"beyond nationalism." Otherwise the tides of liberation would turn back
upon themselves, as they had so manifestly turned in all those countries
where the petty-bourgeois antithesis was in command, and consign those
countries to a new colonialism.

How was a revolutionary nationalism to get itself beyond the limits of the nation-state—and this, of course, without in the least denying the rights and needs of as many autonomous national identities as Africa's diversity might require? I think that Cabral would have had much to say upon the subject, and that this, perhaps, remains the arena in which his thought and action are most sorely missed. As it is, some of his answers were available before he died. They were embodied in his concepts of "unity and struggle." A revolutionary struggle, fighting and working for social gains as its primary and essential target, had already gone far to unite the diverse peoples and cultures of Guiné. Further action along the same lines would deepen and strengthen this unity. Balante had left their forests and gone to fight in the grasslands. Pepel, Mandjak, and Mandinka had done the same or the territorial reverse. Guiné Creole had become, increasingly, a lingua franca where none (and certainly not Portuguese) had existed before. These hitherto divided and often mutually hostile communities now stood on the same political ground. They strove for the same objectives. More and more clearly, they saw these objectives in terms of their unity as a nation of peoples.

Yet if Balante and Mandinka, Nalu and Mandjak, Pepel and Fula (the last, as it happened, developing the latest) could achieve this sense and fact of unity on the ground of common interests and objectives—in removing the colonial system and its coercions, in beginning to govern themselves in their own communities and then, after 1973, as a union of communities—what objective reason could exist for sealing off this process at the frontiers so arbitrarily drawn by intercolonial agreement in the nineteenth century? Why should a revolutionary nationalism not grow in time, organically, regionally, into an internationalism? What other destiny could now lie ahead of liberation movements in power except frustration and defeat?

Such questions were never posed in those years, and perhaps it is needless to say that they were vastly premature. If they remain premature today, however, this is only because the neocolonial antithesis holds firm in the anglophone and francophone countries or in most of them, and is opposed, so far, only by a deepening crisis. There, the petty-bourgeois inheritors reign in their own interests and try to wrest what gains they can from "imperial partners"; as the gap between the few with wealth and the many without widens, so too does the gap between countryside and town. Even intelligently remedial steps toward reorganization such as began to appear toward the end of the 1970s (as with the Economic Community of West African States) are only steps taken "from the top down": agreements between governments and not between peoples, and, as such, capable of yielding no radical advance. Reformist nationalism continues to dig its own grave; and as the grave deepens, fewer and fewer persons in command are able to get their heads above the edge of it. To the tune of requiems sung in solemn chorus by hosts of foreign experts or would-be *fundi* (specialists) of one profession or another, often on very comfortable (and comforting) salaries, the funeral proceeds. The frontiers are there, the frontiers are sacred. What else, after all, could guarantee privilege and power to ruling elites?

Yet the peoples, it would seem, see matters differently. They have their own solutions to this carapace accepted from the colonial period. For them, the frontiers remain a foreign and unwanted imposition. What the peoples think upon this subject is shown by their incessant emigration and immigration across these lines on the map as well as by their smuggling enterprises. Even while a "bourgeois Africa" hardens its frontiers, multiplies its frontier controls, and thunders against the smuggling of persons and goods, a "peoples' Africa" works in quite another way. For if the smuggling of goods and persons appears perverse and wicked when seen by governments in place, peoples in place can evidently find it right enough, and even natural.

Even so, smuggling is not a program for a people's development. Today, it appears, a people's development can only be the task and product of a revolutionary nationalism of the nature conceived by Cabral and by those who have thought and acted, elsewhere, in the same direction. Exactly how this revolutionary nationalism will now take further shape and movement will remain, of course, as much a problem of practice as has every other forward step in the strategy of liberation. Whatever Cabral might now have said in this arena, he would surely not have prophesied. He would have looked for the practical route—for the immediate steps that could lead on to others.

The unity of Guinea-Bissau and Cape Verde was one of those steps. He saw this unity as being able to give a historical culmination to all those ties and trends that have existed between the two countries—between the mainland and the islands—since, at any rate, the end of the sixteenth century. He saw it during the 1950s as a political necessity, because a struggle for liberation in the one would not avail without a corresponding struggle in the other; and this, indeed, is what was repeatedly demonstrated through the years of armed conflict. He saw it, furthermore, as a guarantee that the most could be gotten for each country from the gains of anticolonial liberation. Then, looking ahead again, he also saw this unity as a logical development of the anticolonial struggle. If peoples in many ways so different from one another as those of Guinea-Bissau and Cape Verde could thus find common ground and use it to good mutual purpose, then the nature of their anticolonial liberation would reveal its fuller potential for Africa's postcolonial liberation: for moving "beyond nationalism," for climbing out of the neocolonial grave, for broadening the route to radical renewal.[5]

DEBATES

THE SEARCH FOR AFRICA ACROSS THE YEARS, FOR ITS HUMAN TRUTHS and a route to understand these truths, has passed through various stages. It was never an easy search, and nowadays, with the advance of Africanist scholarship growing stronger in many lands from many hands, so too, and happily, has the density and vigor of debate grown stronger. The search for Africa, in the sense I am intending here, has become more intensive even than before. And while our century is drawing to a close, and our search encounters new and jagged landscapes of social conflict, voices of a passionate urgency are added to questions about the present and the future.

Such questions are now, all too painfully, questions about survival. Thirty or so years earlier there had seemed, for Africans, to be time and opportunity for everything while the beckoning threshold of anticolonial independence opened out, as it appeared, upon endless possibilities of progress. By the outset of the 1990s, in one of history's reversals, these possibilities could appear all too completely to have vanished from the scene.

That was one scenario. Many saw it. Many shared its gloom-laden prospect. There was more than one dimension in which the decades since decolonization had come to seem a tale of wasted years, with one enterprise after another leading out of hope into frustration. A great continent whose people—a good half of whom were under the age of fifteen, with all of life before them—could expect, it now appeared, little but deepening poverty and the denial of employment. As was remarked in another situation of disaster, that time in Europe, those who remained cheerful were those who had still to hear the news.

There were, all the same, others who refused to accept this relegation to disaster. Whether young or even not so young, they argued for resistance. Historians among them, for example, pointed out that African peoples before the colonial dispossessions had known periods, even long periods, of fruitful expansion of society: in those times, successful communities had been neither confused nor victimized by corruptions of executive power. Without for a moment supposing that this modern Africa of the 1990s could in some way return to the culture of the past, there had to be a case for learning from its lessons. If ancestral communities had invented efficient methods of facing and averting the abuse of executive power—whether in small-scale states or in some that had not been small in scale or in reach—surely the successes of the past could be repeated by whatever new and better ways the twenty-first century could afford.

In one form or another this question was put insistently. Answers were heard. A debate began. What exactly was it, inside the institutions of self-government since the beginnings of postcolonial independence, that had failed to safeguard civil society? What hindered reconciliation? What prevented the broadening out of an acceptable, and accepted, law and order?

Early answers were relayed into further debate. In this respect the brief period of 1989–90 can seem, even at this short time in retrospect, to have produced a tremendous surge of liberating discourse; and such was its power and pressure that the worst of the dictators then in power—Sese Seku Mobutu in Zaire, Gnassingbé Eyadéma in Togo, others of their kind—stumbled to the verge of overthrow. The moment passed, and yet the discourse remained. If countries fell into sterile chaos or worse, while men and women walked in peril of their lives and with dismay at the fate of their children, this was not, essentially, because Africa's humanity had failed in its potentials. It was because of hard circumstances possible to identify. Above all, here in Africa, it was because their structures of government and administration, their networks of executive power, had lost or thrown away the legitimacy that comes from people's recognition and acceptance. Africa's new nation-states—or, as Professor John Lonsdale has rightly preferred, state-nations—had arrived at a void of mass rejection.[1]

In one guise or another, it was now argued, the culprit in this situation stood out and was perceived. This, above all, was the autocratic centralism which had characterized the colonial state—necessarily characterized it, since in that state all real power of policy and decision was gathered at the executive summit, embodied in a supreme governor appointed in

London or Paris or some other remote foreign capital, and kept safe at the summit by all the abrasive and coercive practices of imperial racism. From this autocracy, in colonial times, there had derived a more or less total alienation of governors from governed, intellectually and morally, and in all the customary attachments of everyday life.

Decolonization then undertook to remove these extremes of alienation dividing the many without power from the few with power. But for whatever reasons (and it was seen that there were many reasons), decolonization failed in this undertaking. More often than has proved easily bearable, the interests of bureaucratic autocracy, of an abusive "top-down" attitude and practice of governance, were able to resume. This being so, and being ever more clearly seen to be so, and all too likely to remain so, citizens came to feel themselves excluded from the practical affairs of the states to which they formally belonged. Alienation ensured a new dispossession.

I have called this new alienation "the curse of the nation-state," meaning by this the curse of the nation-state which was formed from, and has derived out of, the colonial state in Africa.[2] It is to that degree a restricted meaning. I do not mean to suggest that Africa's fifty or so states formed from the consequences of the colonial partition will, therefore, disappear as these consequences lose their mandatory force, or even that these states *can* disappear. I agree that "thirty years of statehood may in some African countries"—perhaps in most of them, conceivably in all of them—"have created what even nineteenth-century Europeans would recognise as a 'nationality principle.' "[3] For the nation-states are there, and they have their uses and conveniences along with their obstructive miseries. Without them, it might even be necessary to invent them afresh. At the very least, they are valued labels of self-identification, even if, within them, bottled-up ethnicities dispute the value. Their survival seems guaranteed by popular usage, and not only by soccer fans and enthusiasts of athletic rivalry.

This much appears as sure as that some of the rhetoric and no doubt a part of the force of statist nationalism will likewise remain. What I am insisting on here is that the postcolonial nation-state in Africa has been derived from consequences of the English and French revolutions of two centuries ago, even if the derivation was sometimes indirect and only potentially specific. Thus arose the model or pattern that has steered all our constitutional histories: with overwhelming success, or else with mean disaster. But this "all-purpose" model, latterly and now, seems to have reached the end of its useful life; and the evidence for this, contradictory though it may sometimes appear, lies on every side. This is not at all the same as saying that nationalism has reached the end of its useful life and will vanish from the scene. On the contrary, we may be sure that nationalism—the phenomenon of national consciousness, the sentiment of national community, the fact of national culture—will remain, and even must remain, vividly alive.[4]

Yet these nation-states formed from the legacy of the colonial states, and bearing within themselves the assumptions and structures of the imperialist era, have lost the virtue they have claimed to possess. They have fastened a deadweight of discouragement to every real chance of civility; all the evidence of the 1980s, and much of the evidence of the 1970s, is there to show this. No doubt these nation-states will survive; but if they are to survive to good purpose, they will have to be reformed, changed within themselves, even to the point of constitutional dismantlement and reassembly.

This kind of thing was now being said. One talented and authoritative African voice after another was heard to assert the same conclusion: He or she said that the "neocolonial" nation-state must be deprived of its autocratic centralism in the exercise of executive power, to the benefit of structures of democratic participation. Only in this way would state legitimacy be restored and the laws obeyed, because the laws would then be the decision of democratic assemblies and of those who would elect those assemblies. And the way to achieve this restoration, it was added, must be to devise modern, and therefore effective, equivalents of those precolonial mechanisms and modes of self-organization which had brought success to precolonial states.

To some, mostly distant from Africa, this kind of advice came as unrealistic, sentimental, even crassly utopian. Knowing little about precolonial history, or at times nothing at all, there were critics who remained within the cliché-grip of all those stereotypical accounts which have harped for so long about the "vacuous barbarism" of Africa before colonial dispossession. If the new nation-states had become derailed, then on this view they must be told what had gone wrong with them, so as to become corralled again into the structural pattern laid down by departing imperial powers in and after 1960. If the pattern had been tried and had failed, it must simply be tried again.

Yet there were African voices now beginning to be heard who did not sound convinced. They wanted an end to tyrants and dictators of every sort, no doubt of that; but the way to replace the tyrants would not be to try repeating the failed policies of European decolonization. There could be a better way.

Looking back on all this debate in 1992, the leading Nigerian economist and reformer Adebayo Adedeji had interesting reflections to add. "So great and pervasive has been the down-thrusting of colonial rule that many Africans and most non-Africans have persistently denigrated the precolonial historical achievements of the continent—its arts, customs, beliefs, system of government and the art of governance. Indeed, the tragedy has been that when the opportunity came to cast aside the yoke of colonialism, no effort was made to reassert Africa's self-determination by replacing the inherited foreign institutions and system of government, and the flawed European models of nation-states, with rejuvenated and modernised indigenous African systems that the people would easily relate to and would therefore be credible." And Adedeji concluded: "There can be no doubt that Africa needs a new political order which breaks the umbilical cord from its unenviable colonial inheritance."[5]

I do not believe that this Nigerian initiator was for a moment thinking of any kind of sentimental "return to the past." The drift of his argument, on the contrary, lay in pressing the need for "rejuvenated and moder-nised" systems such as could draw strength from civic traditions evolved before the colonial dispossessions, these traditions being regarded not as barbaric oddities or quaint survivals but as "a fountain of inspiration, a source of civility, a power of self-correction." The answer could not be to try to revive precolonial forms of power control such as the Ogboni in Yorubaland or the Asantemanhyiamu among the Akan, but to develop appropriately modern forms of participation. For "no-one now disputes the centrality of popular participation and the human factor as the only viable development paradigm for Africa."[6]

The debate, of course, continues. And this debate may already be seen as the catalyst of new African thought in response to the crisis of the 1980s. How this debate took shape and evolved has acquired a historical value, to the point, even, that its intellectual thrust is destined to become a central theme of inquiry and debate as the future now unfolds.

Three essays that follow here—of 1976, of 1987, and of 1992—are offered as contributions to this debate. They were evolved in what has seemed to me a logical succession from concerns with studying history, and they should be read within this "historical dimension"; but of course they are mere fragments from a vast and various debate, the very reverse of all-inclusive. Others have spoken on the needs and purposes of participatory structures with far more authority and wisdom than I can; but within the range of my work and preoccupations, these essays can claim to link back to many of the enterprises of the 1960s and later, and to the relevant striving and experience of a wide panoply of African thinkers and activists in many lands.[7] It is within the arena of these ideas that the whole question of Africa—the whole search for Africa in the world as it now exists—is to be found.

NATIONALISM AND ITS AMBIGUITIES

THE ELUCIDATION OF AFRICA'S HISTORY HAD REACHED A LEVEL OF understanding, by the decade of the 1970s, where a socioeconomic and therefore cultural process of indigenous development was clearly perceptible for at least six centuries into the past, less clearly though still insistently for as many centuries before that again, and even, in certain cases of exceptional achievement, back into a remote time before the beginning of the African Iron Age around 400 B.C. The resultant synthesis is admittedly weak in many places, even in most places, while intuition has often had to serve for certainty in leaping over cliffs of ignorance and rivers of doubt. One may expect the next two or three decades of research to improve upon this situation, even though it may still appear unlikely, at least as matters stand today, that anyone will ever know many more precise facts about the Africa of A.D. 1400, not to speak of the Africa of 1400 B.C., than those that can be known today. Perhaps the most useful advances will come in the field of improved interpretation of ambiguous evidence, and in securing a historically more accurate balance of significance among such precise facts as are thought to be securely known.

Even so, the achievement is a large one. Perhaps it may even claim a place in history for itself. For we undoubtedly stand today at a point of understanding Africa's past that is almost infinitely superior to any attainable by previous generations. The African historiography of the past thirty years has forged a tool of eminent value for inspecting the origins

This essay was originally presented in 1976 at a symposium held by UNESCO in Maputo, Mozambique. It was published under the title "Questions About Nationalism," by *African Affairs* (January 1977). Reprinted with permission.

of contemporary cultures and therefore, through the enlargement of consciousness and inspiration that must come from this inspection, for the further development of these cultures. And this tool may well have done good service to non-African cultures by cutting through and exposing the superficiality and even malice of many of their "traditional" attitudes to African modes of self-expression. However that may be, and perhaps one should not be overoptimistic on that score, the advantage that we have in possessing this tool should at least enable a meaningful approach to the largest cultural phenomenon of twentieth-century Africa—the advent and advance, one may even say the overwhelming victory, of nationalism and all its implications.

It is now possible, and perhaps it may be very useful and even urgently desirable, to ask a number of questions about this phenomenon of nationalism in Africa, so surely, as it is, the ambiguous fruit of an opposition or a counterpoint between the themes of the African past and those of the cultures of the imperialist nations which colonized the continent. Is this nationalism to be understood and accepted (in line with the ideas of its early African promoters) as a mere version of the European nationalism which provided both its model and the spur to its emergence, and, as such, culturally a liberation but also a reduction, and self-defeating in the end because vowed, as in Europe, to a history of international conflict, rivalry, and mutual destruction? Is it another scaffolding for a house of freedom whose walls are then found incapable of standing free? Or does this nationalism possibly contain within itself the seeds of a different development, a development toward regional and even subcontinental systems of organic union, and therefore toward new modes of cultural emancipation?

Difficult questions in the Africa of today, sown with conflicts and complexes which suggest all too easily that the gains of nationalism may be already more than canceled by its losses. Pretentious questions too, perhaps, for who can claim to know the minds of men in matters so elusive and involved? All the same, the questions are stubbornly there, and they demand an answer. Here in this small contribution I want only to try to place these questions, however sketchily, within their historical framework.

I

THE FIRST POINT TO INSIST UPON APPEARS VERY CLEAR. IT IS THE CONTINU-ity of African *development*—or, if you prefer, of African history, in this context of African culture—over an immensely long period. Taking their rise "in the time before the ancestors," the cultures of the Africans in the moment of their subjection to colonial systems were not the simple fruits of long stagnation any more than they were the features of "primeval innocence." They were the most recent stages in a complex evolution of beliefs, arts, technologies, and explanations of the world in which they had acquired being and form. As V. L. Grottanelli remarked very well of African sculptures discovered by Europeans late in the nineteenth century and labeled then as "primitive," these cultures were not "points of departure" but "points of arrival," the product of a long and meditated experience and by no means the raw material of an uninstructed imagination.[1] Insofar as the term has developmental meaning, these cultures were mature.

The point may be worth emphasizing even today. Only a few years ago, for example, an otherwise thoughtful historian of African nationalism in South Africa could aver that "the origins of African political consciousness in southern Africa can be traced back to the first half of the nineteenth century, to the impact of Christian missions, and to the development of a non-racial constitution in the Cape."[2] Now in the context of nationalism this is tantamount to saying that the origins of English political consciousness began in 1688 or of French political consciousness in 1789. Or, in African terms, it is much the same as saying that the polities of the southern Africans before the nineteenth century were not polities; that their self-organization had not involved a political culture; and that these groups, or however one should describe "nonpolitical communities" (if any such can be imagined), had known no sense of distinctive community, had elaborated no rules for community behavior, but had managed their affairs like the birds of the air or the lions in the bush. The proposition is nonsensical; and yet it could be seriously made.

We need not follow that argument further. The cultures of precolonial Africa became "mature" (insofar, that is, as any cultures are ever that), and it would be possible to discuss this maturity under many headings, whether political or not. Here I want to draw attention only to one of these. It relates to the self-organization of African communities in the days before nationalism.

By 1850 the peoples of Africa, then about to be colonized, had organized themselves into a number of communities. These many hundreds of communities were of differing size and power, and they stood at differing levels of socioeconomic development. Some of them, such as the community of the Asante in (modern) Ghana, appeared to voyaging Europeans to have become nations, and were often reported to be such. Others, such as the Tallensi of the same country, were allocated to a far less prestigious category in European thought; these were labeled tribes. The European decision as to whether a people composed a nation or a tribe appears to have turned, more than on anything else, on whether or not they possessed a kingship. At least for the British of those times, it was perhaps natural to suppose that peoples who had kings were somehow superior to peoples who had not.

Thinking otherwise today, we can scarcely be content with such rough-and-ready awards of relative merit. Yet defining these African communities in terms of general usage remains difficult. If they were not nations in the sense we apply the term today, what then were they? Nationalities, *narodnosti*? But that, however appropriate, gets us little further. Perhaps we need an altogether new word? What is evident about these communities, in any case, is that they each possessed a community consciousness, a sense of belonging, and it may be in attempting to understand this consciousness that we shall make progress.

This community consciousness, this sense of belonging, certainly took shape in a very wide range of forms and images. Yet the range was nonetheless specific. Culturally, all these communities of precolonial Africa drew their potency from beliefs and intuitions—themselves the fruit of an experience which had solved the problems of survival, growth, and development—which, when considered together in their often astonishing comparability, may be said to have embodied Africa's distinctive and original form of civilization—civilization which, in Matthew Arnold's memorable phrase, promotes "the humanisation of man in society."

Most characteristically and pervasively, this range of ideas (and their cultural integument) was founded in the relationship between living people and their ancestors who, interpreting for the force of nature—for the spiritual force of good which was also in ultimate command of the spiritual force of evil—both guarded and guaranteed the life that any community could lead. What we reductively call religion, in other words, was for these communities the necessary regulator of all political and social action, just as it was unavoidably the mode in which every individual explained his world, and in which his culture acquired its meaning and its value.[3]

No doubt the guiding principles of community consciousness were as diverse as the separate "ancestral charters" which steered the life of each community. It remains, however, that in this fundamental aspect of adherence to a "founding charter" of validity and possibility, received by advice from ancestral shrines (or from cultural equivalents), and modified by reference to the same source, all these communities derived from the same model or group of models. Earlier anthropological attempts to categorize these communities into "states" and "stateless societies" could have no more than limping value. All of them stood, in fact, along the same continuum of consciousness, whether with kingships or not, whether with central authorities or without them. The Asante were very good at long-distance trade and developed a kingship of great power. The Igbo were no less good at long-distance trade but had little or no use for kings. The reasons for the difference are to be sought in local circumstances.

However one may care to label it, this African model of community has been undoubtedly one of the begetters of African nationalism. It is possible to argue that this would have emerged very clearly if there had been no colonial intrusion. There is much to suggest that the modes of self-organization of a significant number of African peoples in the nineteenth century had reached a point of growth where forms of large organizational change were in course, or at least in prospect. Kings in some polities acquired more power than before. Peoples without kings developed new forms of central authority. Groups of neighboring communities were perhaps on the verge of forming new constellations of multiethnic composition. As it was, there came instead the colonial intrusion; and the history of the Africans became, for a while, much more the history of the Europeans than the history of themselves.

II

THERE IS NO NEED HERE TO DWELL ON THE DESTRUCTIVE ASPECTS OF THE colonial enclosure. Catching Africa in midpoint of adjustment to the outside world—one sees this adjustment most easily, perhaps, in the huge rise of raw-material exports after the decline in the export of captives for enslavement—the colonial enclosure sharply forced the pace. This meant pain and suffering from acutely violent forms of exploitation, notably in the use of labor. But in the context of our discussion here, it also meant the introduction of a new concept of community modeled on the European nation; and it is with this new concept that the historical cultures of Africa have wrestled ever since, and, as we now see on every side, are wrestling still. For the colonial enclosure did not destroy the African model. It often hit it very hard, and yet it barely touched the inward convictions of that vast majority of Africans who continued to live outside colonial towns and administrative centers. What the colonial enclosure did for the African model was something different, and in certain ways something more painful than outright destruction. This was to prove and demonstrate, in a myriad incidents, that the ancestral model could no longer work, while suggesting, at the same time, that the European model was the substitute which could meet those very problems of the "modern world" against which the ancestral charters struggled in vain.

One could emphasize here, perhaps, that this European model was also a most specific one. It was not by any means the mere and already old idea of a "nation," however one defines that entity (and a host of possible definitions are to hand). This particular concept of community was the European nation-state such as it had emerged from the economic revolution of Britain and the political revolution of France in the late eighteenth and early nineteenth centuries. It was, in short, the model of the bourgeois nation-state, the capitalist nation-state. So the real question then became one of asking how far this highly specific European model could be made to act as the adequate and "naturalized" successor of an entirely different African model. This was not a question, very evidently, which was asked or even could be asked for a long while after the "morning stars" of African nationalism, the pioneers of the 1880s and their like, had made their calls for a *nationalist* liberation from colonial woes. Culturally, there came a divide. On one side were those who sought, often desperately, to make the African model answer to the problems of colonial enclosure and of European behavior in a world which seemed, as often, to have gone mad. On the other side were those, very few at first, who believed increasingly that nothing could save the situation but full acceptance of the nationalism proffered by Europe.

This is not the place to attempt to show the drama of that divide or its many episodes and adventures. To the Western-educated few, nationalism on the European model acquired the status of a manifest destiny. Only by turning themselves into nations on the European model—on this model and no other—could Africans, they held, win free from tutelage and build a new independence. The Western-educated few strove hard and labored long, beginning with adulation of the British model or assimilation to the French model (the other empires produced variants on these two themes), but gradually, through disillusionment and the rise of new generations, turning to less obedient attitudes. Up to 1945, at any rate, the politics of the educated few (and their cultural assumptions) have been aptly described by Ade Ajayi as the "politics of survival."[4] Then came the climactic years of the Second World War, and this "politics of protest" merged into the period when the masses at last joined the game, and nationalism could win its early victories and make its breakthrough into a partial independence.

On the other side of the divide, through the 1930s and 1940s and later still, the masses continued with their efforts to use their own model as the means both of resistance to the cultural suffocation of the colonial enclosure and of reaching toward a regained freedom. The long ideological process of their movements of cultural resistance, whether inspired by purely indigenous beliefs or by the assimilation of Christian beliefs (as, for example, in the case of the many Ethiopianist churches), or by the imbrication of the one with the other in a host of messianic gestures and uprisings, throwing up new prophets, new doctrines, new songs, new dances, new modes of self-organization—this long process holds a central place in the African history of our century. And just because this is so, there can be no sense in considering the phenomenon of nationalism as being somehow apart from the responses of indigenous culture. Insofar as nationalism has acquired real substance, this is because the masses have breathed life into it.

All this being so, the question has remained: how far, and with what modifications of content, can the European model of the nation-state, now so widely assumed and even taken for granted, be made to act as the adequate and legitimized successor of the African model it has claimed to displace? Without following this question into its more obviously structural aspects—and it can be no accident that all the valid national-liberation movements have rejected the bourgois-capitalist content of the European model—one may at least point to one overriding cultural consideration.

This is that the viability of nationalism in Africa now can be manifestly gauged by the degree in which the gap is closed between the educated few—the culturally alienated "elites" of the European model—and the rural and now increasingly urban masses for whom the new nation-state, so long as this gap exists, can only be an enemy. Why necessarily an enemy? Because the African model rested on the assertion of an all-embracing community (whatever inequalities may have existed inside it, and many certainly existed), whereas the European model rests, and necessarily rests, on the advancement of the few at the expense of the many as a basic and unavoidable *principle* of capitalist formation.

The problem has been widely recognized. The European model is there all right, but it has not worked, and not even its warmest admirers can now be heard to claim the contrary. Wherever it persists, the gap widens, the strains multiply, the coups erupt. On the other hand, the

African model is also there, however much decayed by circumstance and driven to despair; and yet it too does not work. The young men leave their villages and do not come back; increasingly, the young women follow them, no matter what dire warnings the ancestors may proffer on the subject. And then nearly half the whole continental population has still to reach the age of fifteen, yet to them the ancestors say little, or say it only in voices which seem strange and faraway.

Very plainly, a new synthesis is needed. Yet this cannot be a mere patching together of old and new: the addition of a few African dance teams, as it were, to urban entertainment, or the dispensing of picturesque garlands of sentimentalized folklore. It has to be a vivid and robust reality which derives firmly from the African past yet fully accepts the challenge of the African present. Where shall it be found?

III

IN THIS SEARCH FOR UNDERSTANDING, IT IS NATURAL TO TURN TO THE experience of the movements of national liberation in what so recently were the colonies of Portugal, and all the more, in the context of this meeting in Maputo, because the liberation of the Portuguese colonies has decisively changed the balance of power in the southern half of Africa. It is natural because it is above all in these movements, as an abundance of evidence is there to show, that the rural masses and the educated few have closed the gap between them and, in thus closing it, have opened the way to a new synthesis. And it is natural because it is they, above all, who have made what Amílcar Cabral so suggestively defined as "a forced march on the road to cultural progress," the road to a new community conscious-ness, fruit of the past as well as of the present, or, as they might prefer to express it, to a "national unity of work and struggle."

This again is not the place to discuss why these particular national movements should have been able to succeed in building and maintaining mass participation where so many older movements have as yet to admit a partial or even total failure in that respect. One may merely note here that their politics of armed struggle could be effective only by ensuring an ever-widened involvement of the masses, an involvement going far beyond mere support to the acceptance of a conscious and voluntary commitment to the community of the national liberation struggle, and therefore to every aspect of the organizations concerned (MPLA, PAIGC, FRELIMO).[5]

Participation of that kind has implied a mental and moral commitment as much as a physical one. In so doing, it could open the way for a critique not only of the European model, the manifest enemy, but also of the African model in its various situations of inadequacy and restrictive anachronism. That is evidently why President Agostinho Neto could remark in 1970 that the MPLA was engaged in an effort "to free and modernize our people by a dual revolution—against their traditional structures which can no longer serve them, and against colonial rule,"[6] and why many statements by President Samora Machel have enlarged on the same theme.

And it is for the same reason, no doubt, that all the qualified spokesmen of these movements have repeatedly insisted on the primacy of *cultural* change, whether as an indispensable instrument for achieving political and economic renewal or as a necessary consequence of having begun to achieve that. Amílcar Cabral's contribution to a UNESCO meeting of July 1972 is especially rich in its elucidation of this insistence.[7] "Oppressed, persecuted, humiliated, betrayed by groups that have succumbed to foreign pressure, African culture has taken refuge in its villages, in its forests, and in the souls of the victims of oppression. It has survived all these trials and, thanks to the struggles for liberation, it has regained its capacity for new life. . . . [Thus] the struggle for liberation is not simply a consequence of culture, it also *determines culture.*"[8] Thus the struggle for national liberation in these circumstances, closing the gap between the few and the many, building a new consciousness of united community, becomes a *determinant of culture* as well as a liberating force.

These movements would claim, I think, no exclusive wisdom. And indeed there would be no difficulty in showing the same essential process in other countries where mass participation in the closing of the gap between the many and the few, in dissection and constructive criticism of the past as well as of the present, and thus in the installing of a truly indigenous content within the framework of the exotic model, has been at work. One thinks of Tanzania, launched in the same direction; or of Somalia and her nomads who are learning to read and write and direct their own affairs in entirely new ways which they can nonetheless recognize as belonging to themselves[9]; and of other examples. All these, it seems to me, are concerned with the restarting of the processes of African history after the long episode of colonial alienation. All these are involved in the further development of systems adequate to indigenous reality as well as to the world in which this reality must operate. All these are occupied with the elaboration of a culture capable of

drawing the civilization of the Africans out of the fetters into which it
has fallen, and of giving that civilization, in its multitudinous aspects
and varieties, a life and meaning appropriate to its present tasks and
destiny

NATIONALISM AND AFRICA'S SELF-TRANSFORMATION

L ET ME BEGIN BY THANKING YOU FOR GIVING ME THE HONOR OF delivering this first Founders Day Lecture of your distinguished institute, today upon the eve of its twenty-fifth anniversary. It is an honor which I greatly appreciate, and not least because I know that here, tonight, there are present some of those Nigerian friends who guided my first faltering footsteps in the study of your continent some thirty-five years ago.

That was back in the days of WASU [West African Students Union, London], long ago when we were all young and when we found each other across a wide gulf of mutual ignorance of the world in which we were placed: you knowing little of Europe, we knowing even less of Africa. So far as Britain was concerned, I think it would be difficult to exaggerate the depths of our ignorance of the realities of this great continent. Today, by contrast, these realities are often well understood. Thanks to Africa's throwing off of the colonial systems, Africa has become fully alive in the consciousness of the world. More is known and understood about Africa than by any previous generation—not only in my own country, indeed, but throughout the world. The breadth of this knowledge, compared with the general ignorance about Africa that prevailed thirty-five years ago, is at least one good measure of the distance traveled since independence came.

There are other measures of that distance.

In my own discipline, for instance, that of history, the contrast is

This essay was originally delivered as an address in 1987 to the Nigerian Institute of International Affairs in Lagos, Nigeria.

extraordinary. When I was young, the general orthodoxy of the "developed world"—whatever that term may really mean—was that Africa's history could not be studied because, in truth, there was none to study. As our principal colonial historian, Sir Reginald Coupland, had carefully explained, "the heart of Africa was scarcely beating" before the arrival of the nineteenth-century Europeans. All that, today, is happily changed. The study of Africa's history has become a respected discipline in a host of universities across the world, and African historiographical scholarship stands centrally in that arena.

Yet it is still sometimes forgotten just how deeply this European belief in Africa's historical nonexistence had penetrated into minds and beliefs. Whenever any historical site or achievement in old Africa was found to be large and impressive, it was at once put down to the work or influence of peoples who had come from somewhere else. You will recall that it took modern archaeologists and historians more than seventy years to overcome the European belief about the monumental stone ruins of Great Zimbabwe in the country which, happily, is no longer Rhodesia. These proud walls, it was said, could never have been built by Africans but must have been built by some altogether foreign and immigrant people who had come from across the seas: the Hittites, or the Phoenicians, or others yet more remote. It is in fact eighty-one years since the Scottish archaeologist, David Randall-MacIver, demonstrated that the walls of Zimbabwe were built by Africans, and their date was medieval. But only the other day, when I was revisiting those ruins and standing there and looking up at them, I was accosted by an elderly tourist from Europe—but I think, in truth, from South Africa—who said to me, "Young man"—she was, you see, rather an old South African lady!— "Young man, who built those walls out here in the bush?" And I replied, "Madam, Africans built them, Zimbabweans built them." "Oh, no," she said, "*that* can't possibly be true." All the same, the truths of Great Zimbabwe are well established and accepted.

The greatest measure of the distance traveled since my WASU friends and I first met, back in about 1951, lies precisely in the title of the theme which you have proposed as my subject tonight: the process of nationalism and of nation building. No other brief period in Africa's long history has known or could have known such a time of change and challenge, such years of stress and tension, advance and retreat, success and failure, and stubborn effort at renewal. When the youngest historian here present, or now working for his or her first degree, sets out at last to write, in the fullness of time, the history of these years since independence, that young historian will be filled with pride but also with astonishment that so much could have been attempted and so much achieved. Truly, it can be said that the history of our times has been the drama of our lives. Truly, the gains of national liberation, of anticolonial liberation, have proved many and irreversible.

None of this is said to please, much less to flatter, but simply to insist upon the grand historical significance of the last few decades, upon the sheer importance of the issues faced and the confrontations met with. History in this Pan-African dimension has been like nothing else the world has seen before.

In any case, the subject you have given me points not at answers but at questions—above all, at the central question of these years: how best should the peoples of Africa carry through a self-transformation capable of enabling them to meet the modern world on equal terms—on equal terms of self-organization, of self-confidence, of opportunity?

And it seems evident, looking around today, that the answer to this central question has not been found.

For whatever reasons, most of Africa today is in the midst of an institutional crisis—political, cultural, economic—from which, as yet, there is no clear route of escape.

The new nations—as distinct from the venerable and very different old nations which existed here before colonial times, before the onset of institutional crisis, before the coming of this need for self-transformation—these new nations, more often than not, have not been built. The new states, called into being at independence so as to build the new nations, themselves totter in fragility, all too often at the mercy of persons and powers of whom the wisdom of the ancestors could not possibly approve.

Should we have foreseen this crisis of institutions? Could we have foreseen it? I think that some of us did indeed foresee it, at least in the sense that we understood that full acceptance of the colonial legacy could only reproduce and exacerbate the problems inherent in that legacy. The history of modern nationalism in Europe—of the bourgeois nationalism of the new capitalist states of Europe—had taught us that this hugely explosive force, nationalism, was a political god that looked both ways—a Janus-headed god looking to good, but looking also to evil.

Nationalism in nineteenth-century Europe had been a route to freedom for oppressed or marginalized peoples: for the Italians in the 1850s, for the Balkan peoples later on, in their struggle to free themselves from the suffocation of various empires, whether Austrian or French or Ottoman. But nationalism in twentieth-century Europe has displayed a very different and terribly destructive face, opening eventually to the horrors of the Second World War. And even now the nations of Europe continue to find great difficulty in overcoming the divisive legacy of that very nationalism which brought them into being.

So it was possible, and even easy, back in the 1950s, to foresee that an escape from colonialism by the nationalist route could lead to a load of trouble, and that nationalist acceptance of the frontiers of the colonial partition—to mention only this one aspect of the legacy—might exact a hard and heavy price from independence.

It stands, moreover, on the record—what is sometimes also forgotten— that the most clairvoyant nationalists of those years, of the 1950s, very well understood that they were asked to accept *both* faces of the Janus head of nationalism, and that the negative face of this acceptance must work sorely against a rational reorganization—a reorganization of the continental pattern—on lines which could reinforce the underlying unities of Africa rather than its obvious disunities. With this acceptance, nationalism could easily become the reductive "tribalism" of the colonial period; and this "tribalism" could quickly spread confusion.

It further stands on the record that serious efforts were made to limit this danger, to write into the early independence constitutions the notion that the colonial frontiers, now reborn as national frontiers, need not be immutable, unchangeable, traced as it were by the hand of God. There were real projects of postindependence federalism or confederalism. There was, as I recall it, a clarity of mind upon this subject. The territorial reorganization of the continental pattern seemed not only possible, but entirely desirable. This was particularly true among the nationalists of West Africa, but to some extent also among those of East and even of North Africa.

Alas! Except in one saving case—your own—all these projects of postindependence federalism came to nothing. Nigeria held out against intrigue and subversion, rebellion and civil war, and when our grandchildren reflect in their maturity upon these years through which we have lived, they will surely see this preservation of Nigeria, of the federation of Nigeria, of its progressive and internal reshaping—no doubt not yet ended—as a decisive victory for the future as well as for the past.

Otherwise all the projects of unity came to naught: even while the aims and ideas of the OAU [Organization of African Unity, launched in 1963] may have nonetheless survived.

They came to naught because the nationalists, like Faust in the fable, could not master the force they had called to their aid: "*die ich rief, die Geister, werd'ich nun nicht los!*" Once out and about, the divisive spirit of nationalism proved too strong for those whom it had been called upon to serve. Yet the federal or federating projects also came to naught for another reason, and this other reason was that the imperial powers, still in control, did not wish these projects to succeed. The French, for their part, were sufficiently convinced that they could continue to control their former colonies upon condition that these former colonies remained distinct and separate from one another. Against the majority of African nationalists in the French territories, organized as these were after 1946 in the multiterritorial movement known as the Rassemblement Démocratique Africain, and vowed as these were to building two independent confederations—one in Equatorial and the other in West Africa—the French worked to build a multitude of separate ministates; and, as we know, the French succeeded in doing this.

The British, on their side, used a different language but meant the same thing—always, again, with the exception of Nigeria. Their claim in the 1950s was that they had clearly traced the proper route ahead, and that the Africans in British colonies need simply follow it for all to be well, and for every problem to be solved. Consider, for example, the certainly authoritative view of this subject provided by Sir Hilton Poynton, for long during that crucial period the permanent under secretary of state at the Colonial Office. The objectives of British colonial policy, he insisted only a few years ago, could be variously defined, but—and I quote—"the shortest and simplest formula of definition is 'nation-building,' or, as Edmund Burke had said of British policy in India as early as 1783, 'trusteeship.'"

What the British were doing, in this view, was to create new nations out of the matrix of peoples within the colonial frontiers they had imposed. As soon as these nations were "ripe and ready," there would be what became universally known as "the transfer of power"; or, as Sir Hilton put it, "the culmination of an evolutionary process traceable to the end of the eighteenth century, consistently and on the whole logically carried out."

I must say that for myself, thinking back to those years before this so-called "transfer"—the years when I myself began first to study Africa and its circumstances—Sir Hilton's picture of what happened is not in the least the picture which I remember. On the contrary, what I seem to remember, rather, is the consistent frustration and repression of consistent and logical efforts by Africa's leaders to assume their responsibilities and take command of their destinies. And it seems more than difficult to discover a factual basis for the British claim to have prepared a grand imperial plan for the decolonization of British Africa.

Not long ago, in 1983, a number of historians of many nationalities came together at Harare, Zimbabwe, to reflect upon this mysterious "transfer of power" which arrived as soon as the magic wand of supposed maturity had been waved across the grand imperial plan. None of us was able to find the evidence which could support Sir Hilton's claim. Our general conclusion, I think, was epitomized by Professor Ajayi and Dr. Ekoko when, speaking to the Nigerian evidence, they concluded that there had been apparent "no conscious British initiative to liquidate the empire." The consensus among us, furthermore, was that independence came, when and how it did, not because the imperial powers were ready to set Africans free, but because Africans were determined to be free.*

What the record tells us is that the British and the French imperialists stumbled out of Africa as best they could, while trying to save for themselves whatever could be saved. There was no planned and prepared "transfer of power" except of course in the terminal years; the colonial legacy was simply handed on intact, no matter what might be the condition of that legacy. As for the Belgians, they merely abandoned power, while the Portuguese had power taken from them by force of arms.

All the same, so much has been said on the other side of this debate that one is inclined a little to insist upon the evidence. One small illustration may be permissible here. It recalls an anecdote from another conference on the transfer of power, a conference held at Oxford in 1978. One of those who spoke there was a former deputy governor of Tanganyika, Sir John Fletcher-Cooke. A trifle naughtily, no doubt, he recalled having traveled through Tanganyika, in 1957, with its then governor, Sir Edward Twining. "During our travels, Twining mentioned in passing a certain Julius Nyerere: 'a bit of a troublemaker, I think,' he added. He told me that he had let it be known among all his senior officers that he thought it would be best if they avoided contact with him [Nyerere] as far as possible, and did not receive him in their offices." Now that, ladies and gentlemen, was in 1957: just four years before Julius Nyerere became the unquestioned and immensely popular prime minister of an independent Tanganyika. Hard indeed to perceive the grand imperial plan!

But if no grand imperial plan for independent progress was transferred, what exactly was it that *was* transferred?

Subsequent replies to this question have greatly differed.

Some have held, in hindsight, that nothing of essential importance was transferred; and this certainly does seem to be true of most of the former French territories. Others have affirmed, on the contrary, that decisively

*Conference papers published by Prosser Gifford and William Roger Louis, eds., *Decolonization and African Independence* (New Haven: Yale, 1988).

important rights and freedoms were indeed transferred to Africans—above all in what was then British West Africa—and this again must be hard to deny.

What may be agreed, on either side, is that it took several years for the newly empowered nationalists—of the late 1950s and early 1960s—to measure the weight of whatever was transferred. And this slowness to come to grips with reality was unavoidable. Not until the day of independence were the new rulers able to have access to the crucial files and administrative information which could elucidate their true economic and political position.

However all this may have exactly been, there can be no doubt that something extremely real and important was certainly transferred.

This something real was the structural and economic *disorder* in which the colonial administrations—all or certainly most of them—were *already* involved and indeed became involved through colonial policies by that time many years old.

This disorder, this barely latent crisis of structure and relationship, was soon definable in a few major points. They are well enough known today but can bear repetition:

1. The impoverishing process of a prolonged adverse movement in the terms of trade. Subject to this process of wealth extraction, formerly prosperous countries were becoming steadily less prosperous.
2. More widely felt shortages of homegrown food, brought about over several decades by colonial concentration on rural production of export crops rather than on food for home consumption.
3. An explosion of urban or periurban populations through flight to the towns of rural communities suffering rural impoverishment. This had become an all-African phenomenon at least by the middle of the Second World War—a war which greatly enlarged the same processes of impoverishment.
4. An almost complete lack of investment in any form of systemic industrialism such as could have allayed the rapidly mounting problems of urban or peri-urban unemployment and, beyond that, launch an independent Africa toward a balanced economic viability.

And what we have seen over the past years has been the prolongation and extension of these same factors of generalized impoverishment: even while teams and relays of foreign advisers have continued to speak as though no such underlying impoverishment existed.

Thus the real inherited crisis—of structures, of systems, certainly of ideologies—was smuggled out of sight, even while most of the nationalist inheritors assumed the task of assisting in the process of camouflage. Why did they assume that task? Well, not everyone was getting poorer, not everyone was in crisis!

A few words on well-conned evidence will be enough to my purpose here.

Generally, since independence, the terms of trade have continued to move against African interests. If nothing else, the repeated fiascos of the UNCTAD [United Nations Conference on Trade and Development] conferences, designed to reverse the trend, are there to prove it. The trend has not been reversed.

We have witnessed a rapid hastening of impoverishment on a massive scale, above all, though not only, in the non-oil-producing countries. Meanwhile, the industrialized countries of the so-called developed world have stood by with arms folded and eyes wet with crocodile tears as major populations of the nonindustrialized world have limped toward starvation.

And this is no overstatement.

Non–oil producers such as Tanzania and Mozambique—but the examples are legion, for at least there is no shortage of statistics—have seen the purchasing-power value of their exports halved, or more than halved, in comparison with the early 1970s.

How do you survive when half your disposable wealth is removed by forces entirely outside your own control?

Debt incurred for purposes of development, or other purposes, has continued to soar over many past years. Here again we may be content with one single statistic, for it tells enough. It concerns the debt-service ratio: the percentage of export earnings, that is, which must be used to service foreign debt before exports can be used to pay for imports. At the outset of the 1970s, this debt-service ratio was at a perfectly manageable level: in 1974, for instance, it stood at an average of 4.6 percent. Yet by 1983, this same ratio had risen to a staggering average of more than 20 percent, and today is undoubtedly higher still.

Now these are factors governed largely by the outside world—by the "world economic order," as it is politely called.

But more properly *internal* factors have added their own painful impact.

Generally, the impoverishment of the rural areas has continued. The terms of trade between town and country, in other words, have continued to worsen against the interests of the countryside. No doubt the Sahel droughts have dramatized the consequences, but all of us know full well that the droughts are only part of the problem.

For whatever precise reasons, the fact remains that rural incomes have generally fallen when compared with urban incomes. In large regions—even here in your great country—the income position of rural producers today is almost certainly worse, and at times much worse, than in late colonial times.

The colonial pricing policy of state marketing boards—to go no further than that—was prolonged but also extended after independence, until it reached a point, by the late 1970s, at which average prices paid to rural producers were generally lower than they had been in the late 1950s. But wasn't independence supposed to relieve poverty, not deepen it?

The more obvious results have been plainly appalling. It may not be too much to say that pricing policy in Ghana, for example, has gone far to ruin what was once the world's greatest cocoa-producing industry. Another version of the same destructive strategy was adopted in Malawi, so often praised as a model economy on the road to a prosperous capitalism. But what do we actually find in Malawi? We find a consistent transfer of usable wealth from the poorest sectors of Malawian society—the rural producers, the village people, the peasants, if you wish—to the beneficiaries of the colonial legacy. This trend of wealth transfer from country to town had become quite patent by the late 1970s. In 1967, for instance, the Malawian government spent 14.7 percent of its revenue on the education of the majority of children, on public education; in 1979 it spent only 8.5 percent of a total government revenue not markedly larger than it had been in 1967. The president, Hastings Kamuzu Banda, used to be a physician—I knew him well during his London days, when he had a practice in Paddington and a house near Brondesbury Park, where I used to have tea with him—but in Dr. Banda's country today, twenty-two years after independence, medical conditions have not improved, but have worsened. The number of Malawians per physician was about 35,000 in 1960. It was more than 40,000 in 1977.

This consistently adverse bias against the interests of rural communities—against the majority of Africans, that is, in nearly all the countries of the continent—has been variously explained and glossed. But whatever explanation or excuse we may prefer, the consequences are not in doubt. Flight to the towns has continued, no matter if the towns can no longer absorb these new populations into gainful employment or civic society.

And so we come to another factor of continued impoverishment.

Food imports must increase at the cost of productive imports.

Your clearheaded fellow countryman, Dr. Adebayo Adedeji of the UN Economic Commission for Africa, has lately told us that, if present trends continue, most African countries may be spending by 1990—and that is only three years ahead—more on the import of wheat than they will be spending even on the import of oil.

We arrive at the truly daunting position in which a largely agrarian continent can no longer feed itself—a continent which, through countless centuries of the past, has been always able to sustain its peoples out of its own resources.

And why? But everyone knows the answer. It lies in the growing concentration of rural effort—from as early as the 1910s—on growing cash crops for export instead of food crops for home consumption. Everyone knows this, yet the pressure for still more cash-crop exports nonetheless continues, continues and grows stronger, whether individually from creditor countries or from organs such as the World Bank.

Foreign aid, no doubt, has continued to arrive, if with growing reluctance and rising rates of interest. But once more, everyone knows that foreign aid has failed to reverse the trend of impoverishment, whether comparative or absolute. To the contrary: David Fieldhouse [professor of imperial history at Cambridge University] has lately reminded us of the World Bank's calculation of 1981 that "it would be necessary to double official aid to African countries in the 1980s if any substantial growth (of their economies) was to be achieved." No such doubling has occurred, and the consequences are painfully obvious.

The crisis of late-colonial Africa has not been solved or stopped by the years of independence. All that has happened in this regard is that the crisis of late-colonial Africa has become manifest and undeniable. It has exploded into the consciousness of us all.

Very well—so where do we go from here?

It is happily no part of a historian's brief to chart the future.

Yet the history of the past twenty-five years and more is wonderfully rich in experience that is useful to the charting of the future. Historians will cultivate the experience of these years for a long time to come. I think they will reach some generally agreed conclusions.

Our historians in the future will agree, I think, that the nationalists who liberated Africa from foreign rule had no alternative, no other viable choice, than to accept the legacy of the colonial systems as well as the legacies of precolonial Africa itself.

They were stuck with these legacies. There was no way they could reject them.

Their duty, this being so, was to take power and to govern; and this, for the most part, is what they valiantly did—valiantly, because they had to bring order out of confusion, understanding out of ignorance, unity out of diversity. Above all, in the most backward, disadvantaged, or ravaged colonies, they had to build from the bare ground—modern systems of democracy, modern health services, perhaps most important, modern networks of public education.

It has become customary, at least among distant critics, to see the immediate postindependence years as years of a futile euphoria, of a groundless optimism, of a reckless eating of the seed corn. For myself, looking back on my convictions and impressions of those early years of independence, it is rather the reverse that seems true. Often against worldwide currents of patronizing prejudice, the pioneering leaders of that Africa forced the world to take Africans seriously and on their own terms, on terms of a hitherto unknown acceptance of equality. They deserve great historical merit. They will receive it.

But then, of course, the problems came quickly home to roost, as they were bound to do.

Here in West Africa, I suppose that the turning point arrived around the middle of the 1960s. The same turning point arrived in all Africa's regions, if at varying dates of onset.

With the power-political gap between urban and rural communities continuing to widen to the benefit of the towns, the politics of nationalism narrowed increasingly to the politics of the towns.

With the parliamentary models adopted at independence from the very different history of Western Europe now beginning to reveal their incapacity and inadequacy, there arose an outright rivalry for group gains, and even for personal gains; and this rivalry invaded the whole political arena with devastatingly adverse effects.

Before independence there had been much genuine debate about basic ideological options and perspectives; and there are those among you tonight, ladies and gentlemen, who joined in that debate and often led that debate. Yet after the middle 1960s there was less of such debate, and soon there was none of that debate. Censorship and repression bored into the daily scene. Prisons began to fill with dissidents. Mouths were shut by force or by corruption.

And with power increasingly paralyzed at the center, there opened a corresponding vacuum of public decision and initiative, and into this vacuum there now stepped the only group which still had real power to impose itself. There came the time of the military—as I have called it, justly or not, the time of the warlords.

And with the coming of the warlords, the space for constructive and radical debate—and what debate is ever constructive if it fails to be radical?—again terribly narrowed.

Some of the military rulers—and I certainly need not say this in the country which produced, for example, Murtala Muhammed and Oluse-gun Obasanjo, with others who supported them—wrestled with honesty and courage to find a creative road ahead. But elsewhere too many military rulers—warlords in the real sense of the word—became crimi-nals and bandits from whom nothing but disaster came or ever could have come—until we reach the ultimate depths of the sinister buffoonery of the "Emperor" Jean-Bédel Bokassa, or the atrocious antics of Idi Amin.

We have had to stand by and watch years when the Africa of hope became the Africa of despair, when the multiparty state became an unbridled hunt for sectional or personal gains at the cost of the commu-nity, and when the one-party state, all too often, degraded into the dictatorship of the no-party state.

We have had to witness years when the new rulers of Africa have come to seem, for most of the peoples whom they have claimed to rule, or misrule, in no way preferable and in some ways worse than the colonial rulers of the past.

Now it is easy for a historian of socialist convictions—such as I, as you know, have always been and still remain—to find the root of this conti-nental decline and degradation in an attempt to build systems of an independent capitalism. That had not been, of course, the perspective of the colonial legacy: the colonial legacy was intended to ensure that Africans, becoming politically independent, should build subsystems of subcapitalist *dependency*. The nationalists, however, hoped to do better than this: they hoped to build independent capitalist systems based on deepening class stratification and bourgeois hegemony.

Today it is starkly obvious that with one or two partial exceptions—among which Nigeria with its great size and potential wealth may con-ceivably turn out to be one—that this effort to build indigenous capitalist *systems* has met with frustration at every turn, and will continue to do so.

This failure, I suggest, was again unavoidable. Not because of factors such as corruption—far from it. The history of the building of a capitalist system in my own country, to go no farther afield, has amply proved that no system of capitalism can possibly be built without a large and even dominant element of corruption—what old Marx, in his ancient wisdom, called "primitive accumulation." Those stately fathers of British Victo-rian morality were no more, in truth, than the gamekeepers, in the field of sacred property, whose own fathers and grandfathers had been the poachers and the thieves.

All that, it seems, is historically clear and barely controversial.

The conviction that the capitalism attempted in Africa over the past twenty-five years and more will not work—will not work for any process of general improvement and development—can arise from the very manifest fact, plain for all to see, that *it has not worked*. This conviction can also arise from the fact that the times, generally, have passed when any form of independent capitalism can be constructed in the world of transnational capitalist monopoly and oligopoly in which we live today.

We have to find other solutions than those of this capitalism. Yet historians in the future will equally find that the alternative option, the socialist option, as attempted here in Africa by borrowing or adapting from a number of different foreign models, has also failed to work. We have seen various forms of that option attempted here: some of them merely ridiculous, others very serious, but none of them, as yet, proven capable of reversing the decline and moving forward once more.

The old masters of socialist revolutionary thought used to assert that revolutions are not for export; and it has appeared, time and again, that they were right.

In this field, again, our historians in the future will be able to examine a rich field of African experiment. They will spend little time, I feel, in considering the merely verbal or rhetorical forms of socialism practiced in Kenya, for example, or the Cameroonian socialism adumbrated under the late dictatorship of Ahmadou Ahidjo, or the Islamic socialism of this or that self-appointed prophet in the north.

They will make short work of the supposedly Marxist-Leninist project unfolded in Ethiopia after the overthrow of the old imperial regime headed by Haile Selassie. They will point out, in this connection, that the new military rulers of Ethiopia merely presided over a revolutionary land reform which the peasants of Ethiopia made for themselves and which, in fact, they could not be stopped from making. They will note that these same military rulers have utterly failed to address themselves to an absolutely central problem of Ethiopian democratic reconstruction: the displacement of imperial autocracy, that is, by a systemic devolution of power and initiative to the principal constituent nationalities of which Ethiopia consists, and among which the ruling Amhara are only one, and not the largest.*

Far from recognizing at least the historic *right* to secession—as the Bolsheviks, whom they claim as their mentors, recognized it in 1917 and

---

*They will also note that this Soviet-promoted dictatorship was overthrown in 1990 by a regime of decentralization.

made good in the test case of Finland—these would-be modern Bolsheviks in Ethiopia have persisted in an attempt to transform the old
Ethiopian empire into a new Ethiopian empire. Bloodshed and destruction, so far, have unfailingly gone with them.

Our historians in the future will look, but this time with care and
respect, at other socialist experiments in Africa. They will look at those
in Angola and Mozambique, serious projects of which we today cannot
yet judge the outcome. And we cannot judge their probable outcome for
the sufficient reason that Angola and Mozambique have had to face, and
still face now, the crippling and ruthless aggression and subversion of the
armed forces and the armed agents of racist South Africa.

But it is here too that we reach another major and most positive trend
of the past twenty-five years: the step-by-step reduction of the regimes of
racist imperialism in the southern subcontinent of Africa. What has come
about there was indeed unthinkable when I was young. That whole vast
region—from the southern borders of what was then the Belgian Congo
to the Cape of Good Hope itself—lay within the power and reach,
directly or indirectly, of the British Empire. And even after the upheavals
of the Second World War, it still seemed that British power would give
way to another power that would be much the same in its effect for
Africans—to the racist hegemony of apartheid South Africa, with its
many partners in North America and Europe.

And yet we have seen, and we are seeing now, a very different outcome:
we see that the legatees of British imperial power are not to be other
imperialists, but the derided and oppressed peoples of the region itself.
What a dramatic change! And how quickly, given the huge obstacles that
lay across its path, has this different outcome taken shape!

Twenty-five years ago, in 1961, the armies of the Portuguese dictatorship—in Angola and in Mozambique—stood supreme in their power, as
it seemed, to crush all African aspirations. Around their frontiers those
Portuguese racists had built what my friend and your friend, Amílcar
Cabral, described as "a wall of silence," and the silence, within those walls
twenty-five years ago, was for many the silence of the dead. Our British
Baptist missionaries in Angola estimated, in that year of 1961, that at least
20,000 Angolan men and women were massacred in the wild furies of
Portuguese fascist repression, and no subsequent evidence has shown that
this estimate was wrong. The frenzied fist of repression appeared then to
have beaten down all hope of change.

And yet, against huge obstacles and difficulties, the cause of liberation
has prevailed, and the fist of colonial fascism has been itself struck down.
With the emergence in 1975 of the independent republics of Angola and

Mozambique, there came a major shift in the whole balance of subcontinental power and influence, to the direct disadvantage of the apartheid regime in South Africa. And this, we may remind ourselves in this present time of depression, was a conspicuously African victory over the dead hand of the past. The great powers of Western Europe and America stood to the very last in support of the Portuguese dictatorship, supplied it with arms, fueled it with money, furnished it with diplomatic and political aid and comfort, and continued to believe—yes, to the very last—that the African peoples of the region could not prevail.

But prevail they did.

And here, if I may, I want to pay my own tribute of homage to those Nigerians who, with courage and statesmanlike foresight, took up the southern African struggle and made it their own—made it their own at no more crucial and decisive a moment, ladies and gentlemen, than during November 1975, when the federal government of Nigeria stood firmly by its own independence and recognized the newly born republic of Angola, ensuring, with this, that Angola would not remain alone with its then handful of friends.

After the eviction of racist rule from the Portuguese-defined territories, and their independence, there followed the eviction of racist rule from Rhodesia and the emergence of an independent Zimbabwe. The tides of anticolonial liberation now lapped strongly at the very frontiers of racist power: South Africa, with its imprisoned territory of Namibia.

So we are now immersed in the hardest struggle against the imperialist past in this continent. All the problems of the colonial legacy come together and combine, right across the subcontinent, in this challenge to South African militarism and dictatorship. Yet this is another struggle which Africa has been winning and may expect to continue to win, if slowly, painfully, and at sore cost of every kind.

Only success in this harsh enterprise can unlock the barriers which stand across any path to progress and peace in half this continent. The children of Soweto, the defenders of Angola and Mozambique, the new national forces of Zimbabwe and all their allies, hold in their hands the keys to the unlocking of those barriers. That will be difficult. Yet even the closest foreign friends of apartheid South Africa begin now to have their doubts of this regime's possible survival, begin to hedge their bets and withdraw their capital, begin to confirm, however hesitantly, that the cause of racist oppression is lost.

One other aspect should claim our attention. This has been the awakening of many other African peoples—alas, as yet, not of all African governments—to the crucial significance of this southern conflict. It is not so long ago, after all, that we heard influential African voices, including some West African voices, raised in support of a kind of dialogue, as they named it, with this South African regime, a dialogue all too clearly aimed at calling off the pressures against apartheid and its system. We no longer hear them now. Even this regime's last-ditch African supporters—even President Banda himself—sing a soft tune now.

Greed and stupidity have, as usual, been present in this historic confrontation, but they too have not prevailed. *Radix malorum est cupiditas*; but the evil, as it seems, can nonetheless be rooted out.

Other positive trends have begun to emerge from the conflicts and confusions of these past years. Or so it seems to me; and here, of course, I embark on controversial ground where historical analysis can also be the victim of bias or misunderstanding.

Many ardent debates are now going on about the means through which Africa can solve its problems, emerge from its institutional crises, and find reliable routes to stability and social expansion. These debates, I suggest, reveal the influence of past years above all in one conclusion, a tentative conclusion which nevertheless appears to win an ever wider assent, or at least attract an ever wider interest.

This conclusion starts from the familiar point that none of the range of institutional models offered to Africa by the outside world—neither the Western range of models, nor the Eastern range of models—is going to offer viable solutions, reliable routes of escape. They are the fruits of a different history.

Africa's recovery will have to be, essentially, the fruit of Africa's own history. This has been said before, as we know, and can mean little more than pious hope and a libation to the ancestors. But the last years have seen two new trends in play—not always easy to perceive, by no means mature, and yet visibly emerging from the history of those years.

The first of these trends is one which has demanded, in various ways and definitions, far-reaching devolutions of power. It has arisen, I think, from one increasingly powerful perception. This perception has been, and is, that the strongly centralized state systems of the colonial legacy have failed to prosper, or even to hold coherently together, because, more than anything else, they have not been *counterbalanced* by a systemic devolution of power to communities, above all rural communities, at the grass roots of society and the base of the social pyramid.

Countless rural communities have appeared to feel themselves powerless and abused. The stiffly centralized and authoritarian colonial state has been reproduced in African hands.

A specifically insistent feature of historical African political practice—

what we may call *local* government, local power of *self*-government—has either ceased to exist or has secured no effective presence. This new trend, now observable in many countries, more clearly here and less clearly there, is manifestly aimed at a reduction of this centralized monopoly of power.

Countries deep in institutional crisis—whether, for example, the Ghana of today or, still more recently, the Uganda now striving for peace under President Yoweri Museveni—have turned or appear increasingly to mean to turn in this direction—toward effective *participation* of and by people "at the base," toward creation of local organs of self-government, organs which can bring rural communities back into a national consensus and loyalty, above all by counterbalancing the powers of central government.

This trend toward mass participation in self-government seems to me to have become a genuine manifestation of Africa's capacity to find and apply its own solutions.

A second trend reinforces this first trend. This second trend, another very recent one, has emerged from a resurgence—if under different guise and in very different circumstances—of the old ideas and values of African unity, of what used to be considered Pan-African solidarity.

The reproduction of the colonial partition, of separate and isolated states within colonial frontiers, has come increasingly under challenge—at various levels. At the official level, for instance, in the formation of ECOWAS [Economic Community of West African States] in 1975 and, nearly a decade later, at the formation of SADCC [Southern African Development Coordination Conference], the one combining the aspirations of most of West Africa, the other of most of central and southern Africa.

It barely needs pointing out that these remain cautious instruments of intergovernmental policy and aim. As such, they are instruments of regional unification at an elementary stage, at a stage of declaration rather than of reality. But we may not be far off the truth if we conclude, from the evidence, that these purely governmental instruments begin now to gather the force of public opinion behind them, and that public opinion, if often in unexpected and even unwelcome ways, begins to believe that the frontier grids laid down by the colonial partition are no longer patterns which can serve constructive ends.

If this is so, then these trends of past years will mature into movements of unification in which peoples as such, peoples in their parties and their organizations, will take part and take over.

Here we are on delicate ground. And yet there surely is a sense today, and not a small one, in which peoples *already* are involved in forms of transfrontier—suprafrontier, one might say—movements of common effort. There may be few frontiers in Africa today, certainly in West Africa, across which, day by day or night by night, people do not take themselves and their goods in more or less complete defiance of the constitutional law. It might even be thought that the peoples of Africa are voting with their feet for some kind of unification.

Mr. Chairman, you will not think, I know, that I am recommending smuggling as a laudable and patriotic course of action—far from it!

Yet the sheer scale of this denial of the inherited frontiers is bound to recall, for a historian, the old economic unities and amenities of precolonial Africa, of the times before colonial partition.

In those times Africa possessed its own forms of regional unity, however limited by local rules and taxes. Precolonial West Africa, for one example, had its own widely recognized currency zones, its own far-reaching networks of interterritorial trade, its own intraregional dependencies and solidarities. However deplorable from a legal standpoint, the massive smuggling of today can nonetheless be seen as an equally massive, if perversely directed, vote for regional unities of the kind, precisely, which the fathers of African nationalism advocated and hoped one day to see in practice. Is it perhaps the Pan-Africanism of ordinary people, a kind of "peoples' Pan Africanism"?

Here I must stop—and with apologies to you for speaking at such length, and yet so briefly, on such great issues. Allow me a few concluding words.

I remain most unrepentently an optimist, an observer convinced of the grandeur of Africa's self-transformation to a real and useful equality with the rest of the world. This is not from sentimental reasons, even if such reasons may also exist. It is because the balance of the evidence, even in the distress and misery of today, still speaks for optimism.

This has to be, I believe, the central lesson of the whole experience of the past twenty-five years and more: the lesson, above all, of the dour and repeated failure to find salvation in the models and prescriptions of overseas peoples with a different history.

It may be no rhetoric to affirm the arrival on the scene, no matter how tentatively, how experimentally, of trends and attitudes which can at last, across the colonial divide and all its divisive legacy, link the Africans of yesterday to the Africans of tomorrow.

THE POLITICS OF RESTITUTION

I

I VENTURE TO SPEAK HERE ON WHAT I THINK OF AS A POLITICS OF restitution, meaning by this a politics for Africa that may be able to move toward restoring what has been taken away, toward restoring the perspective of an Africa that chooses its own options, solves its own problems, and thus behaves as Africa behaved, for better or for worse indeed, before the onset of the imperialist dispossessions of a century ago.

We are told, of course, that solutions tried and applied before the colonial dispossessions have neither relevance nor value for Africa in the modern world. We are told this above all, one can't but note, by persons who have only the faintest grasp of predispossession history. Harking back to the ideas and moralities of precolonial times can be, in their view, no more than a gesture of romanticism, a vain attempt to make history turn back upon itself and retrace its steps. Certainly, that would be foolish. Yet there is another way in which looking back to the past, even learning from the past, can be the reverse of foolishness. It may be useful, even very useful, to look at the ideas and moralities of the past, the practical solutions that were found, the structures that were built and the rationality of those structures, as though these were *not* entirely severed from the history of the present.

That the principles of governance in Africa have been thus severed

This essay was originally delivered, in somewhat different form, in 1992 at a conference of the African Centre for Development and Strategic Studies (ACDESS) held at Dakar, Senegal.

from the time of dispossession, severely and irreversibly severed, has been, as we know, the common coin of political discourse for very many years—a severance so complete, it is claimed, as to be seen to be beyond sensible discussion. And really this is strange. For of no other major branch of humanity has it been said that the past has no instructive value for the present or the future. No one in my country, so far as I have ever heard, has wished to affirm that the ways in which the British govern themselves, and consider that they should be governed, draw no essential guide or inspiration from the struggles against Plantagenet feudalism, from the struggles against Stuart autocracy, from the struggles for universal suffrage and the rule of constitutional law. Does anyone in France imagine for a moment that the revolution of two centuries ago has no relevance to the society of France today? Has anyone in Japan been heard to affirm that the Meiji Restoration of the nineteenth century offers no perspectives on the nature of modernizing development among the Japanese since then? And so on.

That kind of evidence is copious no matter where one looks, and it all points in the same direction: it all confirms that the problems and solutions of today have to be envisaged within a historical framework, an *indigenous* historical framework, no matter what contributions an external world may have made. Except, we have been told, in and for Africa. Here we have been confronted with a denial that appears to be unique. All those many plans and proposals for Africa's salvation—for what nowadays is called development—take their stand and draw their frames of reference from a history which begins around the year 1900, a history which begins with dispossession. All of them suppose a total disjunction between the Africa that was dispossessed and the Africa, this other Africa, an Africa without a history of its own. Read or reread, if you will, any of these great schemes for adjustment and readjustment—and how many there have been!—and you will be reminded that they all assume that useful or usable history in this continent starts from the colonial takeover. Before that? A void, a tumult, a panoply of ornamental titles at best or a fruitless confusion at worst. So we find, in a characteristic example of the literature, a solemn essay by an academic authority, American in this case, who tells us that "in building the newest nations, most of the population [of Africa] cannot be taught overnight, or even in a few generations, the skills necessary to participate meaningfully and effectively in politics."[1] That was said, I have to add, in the full light of modern political science and less than thirty years ago. Blandly sweeping aside the historical evidence of centuries, it comes to one as a statement of the absurd but, nonetheless, a statement widely accepted and believed and one, moreover, buttressed and confirmed for countless commentators by the evidence of political collapse that seems to lie on every hand today.

Africans, it was generally affirmed when I was not so old as I am now, would never command the wisdom and moral maturity to be able to govern themselves in peace and progress. That was the theme song of all those who were against decolonization, and who held that decolonization must end in ruin—a common view in my country, and, I think, by no means an uncommon view nowadays in Africa as well. For now, after all these years since colonial withdrawal, we are directed to the grim result: in the words of a source whose judgment and qualifications we rightly respect, today "the bald fact is that in Africa we have squandered almost thirty years with ineffective nation-building efforts," because "our policies were far removed from social needs and developmental relevance."[2] And it would be easy, as we all know, to lay alongside that severe self-judgment many others to the same effect. Generally, since independence from foreign rule, Africa's politics has been a politics of failure. And now we are asked to explain *why* this has been, and *what* should be a politics of success?

Your lecturer today does not have the answer; moreover, if the answer can be found, it will not in any case be found except by Africans. Development comes from within or it does not come at all; the essential failure is above all a failure of *non*-African legacies of dispossession. I do not say this to excuse Africans from any part or hand in that failure. On the contrary, their part and hand in failure has been pervasive and persistent. The fact remains that the essential failure derives from dispossession; both economists and political scientists seem agreed upon this, even if they phrase it differently. Are the world terms of trade a cause of continuing loss to Africa, a continuing transfer of wealth from Africa to other continents? Does the outcome of this situation impose an intolerable burden of foreign debt? Yes, of course; and the reasons for this, just as clearly, are to be found in the "world economic order" into which a colonized Africa was decolonized. Dispossession has been the culprit.

This line of thought has not been popular. It goes against a very general assumption, almost a fixed belief, that colonization was good for Africa, and decolonization accordingly gave Africans the best possible start to renewed independence. Being thought to have inherited no valid concepts of self-governance of their own, they were given the institutions of Britain and France. And when these are seen not to have worked, the blame is put not on the institutions but on the persons who have failed to make them work. And so the old colonial thesis comes back again, to the point, even, that salvation has to be found in new adjustments and readjustments imposed and controlled by those, across the seas, who know better. It is as though Africa's own history had never occurred at all. It is as though the old colonial thesis—of European trusteeship, of inherent European superiority—had after all been true.

How could this reversal have come about?

II

SETTING ASIDE ANY NONSENSE OF A RACIST SORT, THE IDENTIFIABLE CAUSE of crisis is institutional; and the institutions which have failed are precisely those set in place, and accepted with more or less goodwill, at the time of decolonization. This was done, with some protests and exceptions, exactly as though Africa itself could provide no historical experience or inspiration from which modernizing institutions could be evolved. For present in the minds of all those busy in devising institutions for a decolonized Africa was this disjunction, this acute cutoff between the centuries of predispossession self-development on one side, and on the other side this Africa of today, the decolonized Africa into which development was to be introduced for the first time in history.

And, unavoidably, the new institutions were fitted into the only legacy thought to be available: a colonial legacy that was authoritarian, invariably centralist, necessarily bureaucratic, and thus concerned above all with top-down forms of governance. Yet the enormous contradiction thus involved—between the rules of parliamentary self-government and the rules of bureaucratic centralism, of an acute and convinced centralism—seems in my recollection not to have been admitted, or perhaps even noticed. But a contradiction remains a contradiction even when denied, and the outcome of *this* contradiction has been what General Olusegun Obasanjo has vividly called "squandered years."

Among the consequences, these nation-statist structures produced a disastrous pair of options. Either there would be a situation in which clientelism—so-called tribalism—would scramble for the power, or else, this scramble becoming intolerable, the power would pass back to some new dictatorship. Familiar ground—but it is still worth recalling what may be the locus classicus of this nation-statist frustration. Somalia today offers a scene of self-destruction almost beyond description. Somali society has torn itself in pieces, not only because the institutions set in place in 1960 gave play to the rivalries of a clan-structured society but, worse, impelled these rivalries with new methods and resources. So that within a few years of independence, this Somalia claimed to possess no fewer than sixty parliamentary parties, none of which was or in reality could become more than a mask for clientelist rivalries. Massive corruption unavoidably followed, at which point, in 1969, there ensued a military takeover greeted with public relief, scarcely a single shot being fired by the soldiers.

At that time there was ardent and intelligent discussion on a possible alternative to a tiresome and wasteful clientelism on one side or, on the other, a relapse into authoritarian rule no more tolerable because exercised by African dictators and not by European dictators. And this discussion on an alternative such as might be made to yield genuine forms of social development did produce, in those earlier 1970s, some very positive results—entirely forgotten now, long since swept into oblivion, but undoubtedly real at the time. I mention one of these results. This was the reduction in 1972 of spoken Somali into written Somali. The great opportunities this gave for the launching of literacy among adults and, still more useful, of primary-school education in that brief moment between 1972 and 1976 resulted in some progress. Modern forms of Somali self-development flickered into life. It even seemed possible that clan-structured rivalries might be overcome. But the violence of recent history at once overtook and ruined this infant alternative. Interstate warfare opened doors to one degradation after another until, today, there is really left alive no such entity as a Somali nation.

Elsewhere, and widely, we have seen the same failure of institutions drawn from the legacies of dispossession, and the same forms of violent degradation—to the point that the rule of the gun can seem altogether to have displaced the rule of constitutional law. And here, it seems to me, we can usefully make an end to fruitless arguments on the virtues of capitalism or of socialism. In real terms the failure in Africa of what was called "actually existing socialism"—essentially, a reflection of the acute centralism practiced in the former Soviet Union—was made finally clear in the ferocious effort to impose that socialism on the Ethiopian empire ruled by the Amharic dictatorship of Mengistu Haile Mariam, an effort now happily brought to an end. I myself think that history in due course may still evolve valid forms of socialism. But we have not seen them yet.

Yet it is as well to remind armchair critics in distant lands that the socialist forms so far attempted in Africa were attempted, precisely, because an alternative was felt to be needed—an alternative to an "actually existing capitalism," if I may use the term, which has likewise failed to deliver prosperity or even peace. And at this point one is bound to notice, in this realm of commentary, a strange superficiality of debate.

The failure of institutions within this "actually existing capitalism" is referred not to the nature of those institutions, and the context within which they are expected to work, but to the people who have tried to make them work. The single-party state evolved because the multiparty state, within this capitalist dispensation, was found wanting; and the single-party state then became odious and intolerable, whereupon, we are told, Africa should simply turn upon its tracks and reestablish the old multiparty state which had been found wanting. It is rather as though these distant critics imagine democracy as being contained in some kind of magic bottle from which it can be poured at will. And yet this kind of superficiality comes not only from know-nothing purveyors of popular wisdom, but also from great institutions and learned think tanks.

Let me look briefly at another recent drama, one again that continues, and on a much larger scale than that of Somàlia. You find it in the vast central region of Africa known as Zaire. Here, in contrast with Somalia, or with what once was Somalia, there has been since independence no thoughtful effort to find an alternative to "tribalism" or dictatorship. And again in contrast with Somalia, independence in Zaire produced an immediate uproar and confusion. The reasons for this are clear in the record. Perspectives on unity and therefore on democracy died almost at once with the murder of Patrice Lumumba and the ruin of his like-minded colleagues in the Congolese national movement. These crimes were committed in the name of the Cold War and of the obfuscations of corporate greed, so that in 1965 a new and postcolonial dictatorship could be installed, about which, as befits tact and good taste, I will here say no more. All that needs to be said about it, perhaps, is what is obvious and beyond argument: that this dictatorship installed in 1965 by external influence, and maintained by external influence, has been completely characteristic of the physical decay and moral degradation which have accompanied all such neocolonial types of surrogate colonialism, whether they be supposedly capitalist or supposedly socialist.

If this may seem to strike a note of intolerant exaggeration, let me offer a single statistic from many analyses produced over recent years by various researchers into the condition of Zaire, most of them, as it happens, American in origin.[3] It was found that the usable road network of Zaire has shrunk in size from about 88,000 miles in 1960 to about 12,000 miles in 1985, and, of these remaining 12,000 miles, no more than 1,400 miles were paved. Vast rural areas from which no exportable wealth could easily or any longer be extracted, whether for the financial benefit of the dictatorship or its clients and foreign investors, were by all accounts abandoned to their own devices, and, again by all accounts, remain so to this day. Outside relatively narrow areas of export profitability, whether in the mining provinces or those concerned with plantation agriculture, there appears to have been no more than the most minimal state investment in any form of socioeconomic development; and in this neglect and degradation—denied, so far as I am aware, by no competent authority—widening hunger and social dislocation were evident as early as the 1970s.

One cannot be surprised. So long as mining wealth could be sold for food imported to feed the dictatorship and the state—its bureaucracy, its clients, its towns, its army, and its police to put down rebellion—there could be no profit in helping peasants in cooperatives or other forms of self-development. "The forests and savannahs outside that state might fester in their brooding solitudes. They might revert to the control of village governments, or shelter clans of rebellious guerrillas, or simply provide a refuge for 'masterless men' adapted to one piracy or another. But who should care? The aircraft of the state and its beneficiaries flew high above the forests and savannahs; passengers would not even notice that the roads below were drowned in all-engulfing vegetation."[4]

Hunger emerged, and hunger has spread. Dividends on mining shares might continue to be satisfactory; a large fragment of these people were nonetheless reduced to near-starvation or else to networks of smuggling and other forms of what is politely called "parallel trade." But "parallel trade" thrives only on clientelism, so that Zaire has come to suffer from a double disaster deriving on the one hand from a severely personalist dictatorship and on the other from an almost limitless clientelism. But this, after all, has been another instance of "actually existing capitalism," Zaire having been saved from any threat of "actually existing socialism" by its foreign guardians; and the outcome is what we see in Zaire today. And what then ensues? In 1991 the degradation of Zaire leads to the degradation of the dictatorship itself, and there is the prospect of a return to political development. And then, within a few months, Zaire is found to have come into possession of no fewer than 230 political parties, or bodies claiming to be such, not one of which, unhappily, can claim the legitimacy which derives from political mobilization and national purpose.

So the problem becomes clear. It is not to seek some more effective elaboration of systems evolved elsewhere, outside Africa, in very different historical circumstances. It is to discover and follow a path that avoids the curse of this postcolonial centralism, whether of a personal tyranny or of a bureaucratic apparatus, a path which can lead toward a restitution of legitimacy, of moral and political accountability, of structures in which rulers and ruled can and do sufficiently trust and respect one another. The conclusion is scarcely in doubt, and others have said this with greater authority than I can. The colonial state was illegitimate because it was a conquest state and, with its dictatorial centralism, remained a conquest state. But can it be said that the nation-state which emerged from the colonial state has been able to achieve a greater legitimacy?

In the recent words of a distinguished spokesman for Africa, it is now the case that "no one now disputes the centrality of popular participation and the human factor as the only viable development paradigm for Africa."[5] So far as I have heard, no disinterested opinion has denied this. Participation, mass participation in one form or another, is ever more widely seen as the answer to this centralism copied from the colonial state. One may add, if one wishes, that it is quite untrue that no one disputes this centrality. All manner of interested parties do in fact dispute this: clientelist politicians and their bureaucratic partners, so-called strong men and their servants, many hopeful members of extended families down to the third and fourth generation—all these and many more may well reject the sovereign value of democratic participation as a means of self-government. Any number of elected committees bent on making mass-participation work can find themselves packed, according to the evidence, with energetic persons bent on preventing any such thing. It remains that the displacement of centralized force and fraud, by development of genuine structures of election and control, is now agreed to be the only prospect that wins, and will win, mass support and serious purpose.

III

STRUCTURES OF GENUINE PARTICIPATION—BUT HOW TO ACHIEVE THEM AND make them grow? If the problem is clear, the solution appears less so. It lies along a route which has to be new, but which also has to call upon the wisdoms of the past. If Africa needs to restructure its institutions— and I speak here with even more hesitation than usual—then Africa needs to reinvent itself. The essential solution, if my argument holds, is to abolish the acute disjunction, between the history of the past and the history of the present, that was imposed by the dispossessions and their consequences. It is to renew the flow of history, of indigenous self-development, that was broken by the dispossessions. As far as an outsider can judge of such complexities, no solutions here will be valid and enduring unless they can make good the moral dislocations—the moral wounds—that were inflicted by dispossession on the fabric of community, on vital dimensions of self-esteem and therefore of self-confidence. And if this is so, then it may follow that a route to a genuinely democratic participation calls in turn for a reassessment of the lessons of the past. Not, let it be emphasized, in order to make any futile attempt to renew the past, but to reconsider what the past can say about valid and enduring forms of governance.

The forms that Europe has fostered here seem neither valid nor enduring. Rather do they now appear as an apparatus of helpless alienation in which creative potential is hard to find. Yet go back in time and think about the past; and then there appears the outline of a historical process and procedure which, in those circumstances, had undoubtedly known how to control the use and the abuse of power. There is the outline—and here I quote from an authority far more qualified than I could ever be, the Asiwaju of Ijebu-Ode—the outline of "a society where the monarch reigned rather than ruled, where there was decentralisation of power, public accountability, and economic and political empowerment," where, in short, effective participation could achieve a valid form of governance. That kingdom of Ijebu, along with others in its time and place, may have known nothing of modern "political parties, of the institutional voting system of the Western world, of the press as we know it today," and so on. "Yet democracy which involved the participation of the people in their governance prevailed"; and "government rested on consent and consensus." There was here a community, in brief, altogether opposed to the "totalitarianism in government" which came later from abroad.[6]

It may easily be seen today—and exactly in the light of its "totalitarianism in government"—that the postcolonial nation-state, as the inheritor of the colonial state, has proved a disastrous failure. At the same time, the history of more than a century is not to be wished away. Moving beyond this nation-state can only be a gradual process; and this process will need to draw whatever encouragement it can from Africa's own experience. Here then is one proposal in the context of the search for alternatives. It is that Africa's own historical experience be taken seriously. Not, of course, with any idea of returning to the past, but looking to those principles and attitudes and moralities of power control, and of power sharing in community, that proved repeatedly valuable wherever they were applied, or left failure behind them wherever they were not.

People remake their own history, or nothing useful happens. And if one turns from all the externally cogitated plans and planifications, and looks at the evidence on the spot—no matter in whatever unexpected shapes or forms—there do appear to be signs, in Africa now, that people are at grips with the challenge of remaking their own history. One finds the striving of countless individuals and collectives toward new types of self-organization—perhaps one should rather say self-defense—aimed in one way or another at operating outside the bureaucratic centralism of the neocolonial state. One comes upon associations of cultivators; cooperatives of one provenance or another; peasant assemblies; all manner of original initiatives, even new types of self-expression deriving from new advances in literacy. The spur and inspiration of all these have come from local needs and resources. And if "democracy which involves the participation of the people in their own governance" is what is required, then all these initiatives have to be relevant and interesting.

Participation means a genuine devolution of power, while moving beyond the colonial-type nation-state means moving toward relationships and attitudes of one federalizing pattern or another. Surely the difficulties are obvious; and the experience of the Economic Community of West African States, for one example, has told much about these difficulties. The risks are barely less obvious. They too certainly exist. Europe today has much to show on that score, even if the awful spectacle of Yugoslav self-destruction may be largely specific to itself. Yet in times of dire crisis these may be risks which have to be taken; and it is in considering these risks associated with possible surrenders of centralized power, and a corresponding strengthening of devolved power, that the African Centre for Development and Strategic Studies has surely found a major task and obligation. To that end, Professor Mahmood Mamdani over in East Africa was saying the other day, and very well, what is required. "We must question," he said, "the assumption that 'self-determination' must mean, in the final analysis, independent states."[7]

The centralisms of the postcolonial state have stood invariably upon the assertion that nothing constructive can be found at the grass roots of African community. The facts as they come to hand today propose a different conclusion. These facts suggest that there was and there remains, in the ethos of African community, a fountain of inspiration, a source of civility, a power of self-correction, and that these are qualities that may yet be capable, even in the miseries of today, of vital acts of restitution.

SOUTHERN AFRICA: PROGRESS OR DISASTER?

Returning from a visit made more than half a century ago, George Bernard Shaw described the South Africa that he had seen as a "slave state." Though this would be an overstatement even for the South Africa of today, the limited rights and freedoms of the black majority which prompted him to make that remark have since been reduced even further. South Africa is not a slave state; it is a state of organized servitude. But this condition of South Africa is no longer, as it was in Shaw's time and indeed much later than that, a matter of serious contention; it is the somber view of every serious observer.

What then can one usefully add to these judgments or to the immense quantity of factual evidence upon which they are based? In accepting the honor of giving this Canon Collins Memorial Lecture, I confess to having found myself in a contradictory state of mind. On one side there is the opportunity—in several ways unique, and much appreciated—of expressing some of the thoughts and conclusions which John Collins, as I believe, would have wished to hear expressed at this time—a time of rising violence in the subcontinent of southern Africa, a time of potent threat of worse to come. On the other side there is a situation, in the key country of South Africa, that does no more than repeat itself, yet each time in a scenario more brutal and more apparently hopeless than the last. Where, in that scenario, is there anything *new*, anything to set against the drift to further brutality and disintegration? Haven't all the crucial decisions long been taken?

This essay was originally delivered in 1983 in London as the first Canon Collins Memorial Lecture at the invitation of the British Defence and Aid Fund for Southern Africa.

Thirty-one years ago, in 1952, in a book which I called *Report on Southern Africa*, I allowed myself a prophecy. I said that the white minorities of the subcontinent faced an urgent choice. This choice—and forgive me for quoting myself—was between "waging bitter and perhaps bloody struggles as the Africans step-by-step assert their rights: or of conforming intelligently to the needs of those social and economic forces which white civilisation has itself forced into motion."

Without exception, the white minorities chose the first course, and, in the last two decades, have brought more violence and destruction to this whole wide region than ever before seen in history.

Things being as they now are, it is easy to forecast still more misery and destruction, and tempting to forecast nothing else. One is therefore bound to feel uneasy, and perhaps vulnerable to a charge of irresponsibility, in proposing that progress in southern Africa remains, even now, even at this late hour, a real alternative to the disaster which seems imminent on every hand.

All the same, my own belief is that progress—by which I mean a process of far-reaching and therefore constructive change—is not only possible today, but has, in practical fact, become possible for the first time since the shaping of modern South Africa more than a hundred years ago. This is a claim that rests on no wishful-thinking illusion. But to measure its reality one needs to stand back a little from the day-to-day unfolding of events and consider the scene within a longer timescale.

I

HISTORIANS KNOW THAT THE VARIOUS PARTS OF THE SUBCONTINENTAL region that we call southern Africa—roughly all the lands of the central-southern plateau and its coastal peripheries down to the Cape of Good Hope—have possessed since remote times an underlying unity of culture and economy. At any rate since the fourth century of our era, all the habitable zones of the region were mastered for human development, for community development, by a combination of stock raising, hoe farming, and mineral extraction. Those preindustrial societies had evolved a balance with nature that enabled them to survive and prosper at a slow but steady rate of growth of population. Though living within many political entities, they clashed little with each other until new circumstances arose in the eighteenth century, or, when they clashed, their wars were little more serious than a throwing of spears, by chosen champions, among countless communities spread thinly across the skylines of uncounted hills.

But from about the middle of the eighteenth century, all that began to be changed by new pressures coming from the outside world. Those pressures reached their own resolution, essentially, with the establishment of British overlordship; and by 1902—the termination of a prolonged struggle between Britain and the Boer republics—the effective outcome was one of British hegemony over the whole subcontinent. The old unities of culture and economy were now reshaped in terms and meanings that were new and drastically different. Throughout all these territories the same colonial policies were applied: the taxation of rural Africans so as to extract migrant labor for mines and plantations; the expropriation of land for the benefit of white settlers; and the concomitant denial of any political power, or share in power, to the black majorities. This was the realization of Cecil Rhodes's dream: that British enterprise and British capital should find all doors open and no frontiers closed. The Portuguese might have won large territories, but it made no difference. Southern Mozambique became an extension of the imperial economy of South Africa, while British concession companies of one kind or another secured control of as much of the rest of Mozambique as they might wish for, and other companies moved into Angola. South-West Africa, the Namibia of today, became in all essential ways a South African colony as soon as the Germans were ousted during the First World War.

This brief historical excursus may be enough to define what must be our starting point in looking at the situation of today. That starting point lies in perceiving the irreversible interdependence of all these lands and peoples to the south of the Congo Basin. No matter what incidental conflicts may divide them, their inherent unity of common interest is what, for good or ill, must govern their future. However many cultures and loyalties they may possess, their hopes for progress—or their fears of disaster—arise on common ground. All have been drawn into a world economy structured by the imperialism of the twentieth century, and all face the same basic problems.

What has changed, in this context, is that Britain has ceased to be the crucial arbiter. The central issue now is about the identity and nature of the next arbiter. More exactly, will the next arbiter be an expression of the autonomous power of these peoples, however crystallized in federal or confederal or some other organically cooperative union? Or will it be another form of colonial or paracolonial imposition, exercised directly by racist South Africa, and indirectly by the overseas beneficiaries of that racist regime? Behind the façades of nationalism, this is the real contention within the struggles of the past decades and of today.

White South Africans have generally believed that the imperial succession must pass to them by virtue of their economic strength and political cohesion. Just on two decades ago, the then South African prime minister, Hendrik Verwoerd, called confidently for the formation of a Southern African Common Market in which the white minority, embodied in South Africa, would gradually assume economic control of all the lands to the north, as far as the Congo Basin; and Balthazar Vorster, coming after Verwoerd, echoed the same ambition. Each seemed then to speak from unassailably strong ground.

On the one hand, black protest within South Africa was almost silenced in the 1960s, beaten down, imprisoned, killed. On the other hand, the long economic boom begun in the 1930s, enlarged during the Second World War, and continuously expanded since then by huge new inflows of British, American, and other capital into South Africa, seemed to have no end in sight. South Africa produced some 30 percent of the continent's total income, nearly one-third of its mineral output, twice as much electrical power and six times as much steel as the entire remainder of the continent. What could challenge that strength? There would arise, it was said, a constellation of more or less dependent states revolving around the sun of Pretoria in a system as evidently natural as it would be certainly convenient. From all these lands the industries of South Africa would draw every mineral or other raw material that could be useful or essential, while the peoples of these lands would provide an ever larger but always captive market for the manufactured exports of South Africa. The apartheid system would have realized its continental destiny.

That vision of the 1960s was one of an inexhaustible honeypot secured by South African investment and political influence, or, at need, military intervention; and for many it seemed far better than a vision. Having reviewed the scenario in 1970, as well-informed and powerful a body as the National Security Council of the United States government, in its memorandum number 30 of that year, concluded that the *status quo* of white domination would hold firm and that the USA should therefore continue to support the then existing regimes. It was further held that the drive for African independence and self-development would soon lose its power and forfeit its appeal. For "as the rest of Africa becomes disillusioned" with the outcome of their nationalism, Prime Minister Vorster had promised in 1967, those new nations "would turn their eyes towards South Africa." Dr. Banda's Malawi, after all, had already shown the way.

II

IT TURNED OUT DIFFERENTLY. BANDA'S MALAWI SOON PROVED TO BE SINGU-
larly isolated in its acceptance of white South Africa's role as continental
leader; while disillusionment with nationalism has not been with the aims
of independence but with the failure of governments to realize those aims.
When popular uproar overturned Banda's only companion on the road to
Pretoria, President Philibert Tsiranana of Madagascar, it was not because
Tsiranana had embodied the aims of independence; it was because he was
seen to have betrayed them.

But that proved only a minor prelude to the unexpected dramas of the
1970s. Against all official predictions, the colonial wars of Portugal were
not being won. The drive and appeal of anticolonial nationalism were not
being lost or forfeited. And in 1974 a generally astonished world beheld
the collapse of the whole Portuguese regime, whether in Africa or in
Europe, as its comparatively enormous armies accepted defeat and African movements of national liberation carried their campaigns to a remarkably complete success.

Colonial administrations, in every way convenient and in many ways
subservient to Pretoria, were swept away and regimes of radical nationalism took their place. By the end of 1975 the balance of political influence,
and even the balance of political power, had moved sharply to South
Africa's disadvantage. The prospects for South Africa's subcontinental
honeypot were badly shattered.

Zimbabwe followed; and even in Namibia the cause of an effective
decolonization was greatly reinforced by this change in the balance of
forces. Meanwhile, within the apartheid state itself, the silence of the 1960s
was broken by black protests and upheavals on an unprecedented scale,
and by a challenge to apartheid in many fields of action, ranging from
illegal but successful black strikes in manufacturing industries to outright
acts of sabotage of communications and oil refineries—again on a rising
scale of success—by the military wing of the African National Congress
of South Africa, Umkhonto we Sizwe. By the early 1980s, it was clear that
the giant of white South African military and industrial power was under
siege in ways that had not been thinkable ten years earlier.

An incident in September 1982 may be enough to illustrate the potentials of this great turnaround in the perspectives of the 1960s. The venerable king of Swaziland was joined to his ancestors with appropriate
ceremonial. Among the many official guests who attended that funeral

were the foreign and defense ministers of the South African republic. They represented racist South Africa. But with them in the same row of seats, coming from exile, but no less honored, was President Oliver Tambo of the African National Congress.* He represented nonracist South Africa. I doubt if Foreign Minister Roelof Botha or Defense Minister Magnus Malan had much to say to President Tambo, whom they would certainly have flung into prison if they could have got their hands on him; but their conjoint appearance in that arena had, nonetheless, to be accepted by them.

III

YET THAT LITTLE TRUCE, IF SUCH IT WAS, MARKED ONLY A MOMENT. ANY careful analysis of South African policy since 1974—since, that is, the collapse of the Portuguese empire—will find it directed to two aims. One aim is to safeguard the apartheid system in all its essentials, and I will come back to this. The other is to recover South Africa's power, whether actual or potential, to dominate the subcontinent along the lines projected by Verwoerd and Vorster during the 1960s.

This second aim can be seen most easily in the military field. It has produced an increasing and now far advanced militarization of the South African state, in a minor and almost incidental way, so as to add to the regime's already formidable armory of *internal* oppression, but much more, and in a major way, so as to wield the power to undermine and eventually destroy antiapartheid regimes in Angola, Mozambique, Zimbabwe, or elsewhere. This truly obsessive process of militarization was publicly admitted for the first time in a government White Paper of 1977, and seems now to envisage a South Africa embattled against all of Africa and, if necessary, against all of Africa's friends.

While the full facts are unknown, notably in respect of recent armaments imports and of South African nuclear-warfare capacity, even the published facts appear conclusive. In 1974, direct military expenditure in South Africa—not counting police and other security services—was R707 million. By 1983 the year's military spending had risen to R3.093 million, while official projections indicate that it has continued to rise since then. And these huge sums have been spent on weapons, and on the expansion of military manpower, that have also been used inside the country in an

*Acting president while Nelson Mandela was still in prison.

attempt to crush urban protest. Their major targets, however, can only lie outside South Africa, whether in actual or potential use of fighter and fighter-bomber aircraft, or in the high-level conscription of white and now even of black manpower, or eventually, of course, in nuclear-weapons capacity.

The South African invasion of the infant Republic of Angola late in 1975, and early in 1976, failed in the face of Angolan and Cuban resistance. That was a moment too when the policies of U.S. Secretary of State Henry Kissinger, disastrously mistaken in this arena, were rejected by Congress; and South Africa felt obliged to retreat. Yet new aggressions followed two years later, and in all ways save that of formal declaration, South Africa has been continuously at war with Angola since 1978.

South African troops and aircraft invaded southern Angola and seized possession of a belt of Angolan territory from which their raiding parties could attack civilian as well as military targets far inside the country. Such raids have been carried out, whether by land, sea, or air, with a ruthless intensity of destruction which has constantly tried to provoke an Angolan declaration of war or the direct involvement of Angola's Cuban allies. Meanwhile, in Mozambique, the use of black mercenaries was rising. Like the so-called UNITA "troops" of Jonas Savimbi in South African service in eastern Angola, these mercenaries were presented to the world as patriotic nationalists fighting for freedom, when in fact they were really fighting for the freedom to transform Angola and Mozambique into satellites of Pretoria.

These aggressions were said to be justified by Pretoria's need, as it was claimed, to strike at the rear bases of SWAPO, the Namibian independence movement, and of the South African ANC and its military wing. But any such pretense soon failed to convince; even a summary list of the targets attacked shows it to be patently false. A prime target of South African-backed raiding and sabotage in Angola has been, for example, the trans-Angolan railway from the central African Copperbelt to Lobito, as well as the ports of Benguela and Mossâmedes; while corresponding aggressions in Mozambique, whether in the central or southern provinces, have clearly had nothing to do, even indirectly, with strikes against the South African ANC. On the contrary, all have combined in a varied and extremely sinister effort to undermine the state structures of Angola and Mozambique, and thereby destroy their independence.

By late in 1983 it was clear that South African violence had weakened the newly founded republics of Angola and Mozambique, but had failed to destroy their independence. Floods or drought had meanwhile added to the economic and social problems of both countries and each, in any case, was in desperate need of peace after the long years of Portuguese colonial warfare from which they had so lately emerged. They welcomed agreements for peace with their new adversary, so long as these threatened neither their independence nor their continued political and diplomatic support for the black majorities in South Africa and Namibia; and Pretoria, for reasons of its own, moved to meet them early in 1984.

These South African reasons have not been admitted in public, but are not very hard to penetrate. One was that the cost of continual aggressions on Angola and Mozambique had begun to prove disagreeably high, even for a state as wealthy as South Africa. Another was that the maintenance of South Africa's white minority on what was practically a war footing had begun to prove increasingly unpopular with that minority. And there appears to have been a third reason. President Ronald Reagan of the United States was by this time the only leader of the Western world who still felt able to declare a clear preference for white South Africa against black Africa, and to give white South Africa direct and open support. Exit Reagan, and racist South Africa's isolation would at once become painful.

So the beginning of 1984 showed that there were fairly narrow limits to the further development of Pretoria's long-term plans for subcontinental hegemony, while, at the same time, proving once again that those plans remained dangerous and perfectly capable of "reactivation."

Pretoria's stance in Namibia has never been anything but militantly violent. Illegal by international law, universally condemned, South Africa's continued occupation of Namibia has been maintained by military force; a relatively huge force, perhaps as large as 100,000 troops, occupied the country as early as 1981, partly deployed against SWAPO national-liberation units but also, and in large measure, to maintain the levels of South African military intervention in southern Angola.*

Here again one sees that the all-embracing militarization of South Africa arises in no primary way from that country's internal situation—fraught with violence though that situation is—and much less from any conceivable danger of Soviet pressure, a merely propagandist bogey—but from a determination to regain an effective hegemony abroad while making no concessions at home. An independent Namibia could offer no kind of threat to the safety of South Africa. It would nonetheless signal another defeat for the policy of the 1960s. And luckily for Pretoria,

---

*I was too pessimistic about Namibia, which achieved its independence in March 1990. This was achieved, indirectly, by financial sanctions applied on South Africa by a Democratic (anti-Reaganite) U.S. Congress. Nothing less would have induced Pretoria's withdrawal.

President Reagan's so-called linkage—between progress toward Namibian independence and the withdrawal of Cuban troops from Angola—has enabled Pretoria to frustrate every recent effort to end South Africa's occupation and to bring peace. For without American insistence on this "linkage"—roundly condemned, most recently, by the prime ministers of the Commonwealth assembled in Delhi—Pretoria would face international pressures that it could no longer resist.

The result of all this becomes clear enough. What we have seen in action is a South African policy of unlimited confrontation—whether by political, economic, or military means—with every trend that works or speaks for the development of African progress and the postcolonial restructuring of African economies. Along *this* route—however interrupted by "truces" or maneuvers undertaken for temporary or tactical reasons—there appears ahead only widening poverty, political instability, and moral confusion throughout the subcontinent; and the further ravages are likely to be measured in terms of still greater misery and despair. I doubt if there are words to convey the depths of disintegration, and the consequent spread of an uncontrollable violence, that could be expected to ensue.

So much for the prospects of disaster. They are large, and they are many—and, at the moment, they are dominant.

IV

YET THE PROSPECTS OF PROGRESS—AGAINST POVERTY, AGAINST INSECURITY, against confusion—nonetheless exist, even if, at times, they may be hard to see.

They are, above all, hard to see because the management of the world economy, wherever it bears on the subcontinent outside the privileged economy of white South Africa, goes in the same direction of disaster. Consider only the case of Tanzania, largely symptomatic of the wider subcontinental condition. It is often said that Tanzania represents a non-capitalist experiment which has failed. However that may or may not be, one may well wonder what different policy could have succeeded in Tanzania in these recent years.

In 1982, Tanzania was obliged to spend about 60 percent of export earnings on essential imports of oil, having none of its own. Another 15 percent had to be earmarked for the service of foreign debts incurred largely for developmental purposes. To pay for everything else that

Tanzania needed—spare parts, road and rail maintenance, the completion of development projects, even the servicing of completed projects—
there remained only 25 percent of export earnings, entirely insufficient
even for elementary needs. This is where the "north-south" conflict of
interest, embodied above all in worsening terms of trade for the "south,"
has reached truly dramatic proportions; and no expert advice of which I
am aware has so far offered the least prospect of relief.

Tanzania is thus threatened by a downward spiral of decay for which
its government and people are not responsible, and against which, on
their own, they can make no sufficient defense.

Something of the same can be said of Zimbabwe. There, indeed, the
gains of ending a racist dictatorship are very evident to anyone who
knows that country, even if that ending had to come with a legacy of
inherited troubles. Some of these troubles, the less important as it happens, have derived from precolonial history and will need some years of
responsible self-government to assuage. But most of the troubles and by
far the most disturbing derive from colonial history; and one example
may be enough to demonstrate the intractable nature of this inheritance.

There are probably, today, about 4.5 million inhabitants of the least
fertile areas of Zimbabwe that were once labeled native reserves and more
recently as tribal trust lands. Those areas, it appears generally agreed, can
support about 2.5 million people at a level of acceptable poverty; but to
ensure even this modest level it will be necessary to remove upward of 2
million people to lands elsewhere, or else to crowd still more jobless
peasants into already overloaded towns. In a large measure this would
mean—as in Kenya during the 1960s—either buying out or expropriating a
substantial proportion of the still-existing European farming community.

Expropriation is forbidden by the Lancaster House settlement which
gave birth to Zimbabwe, while, at the same time, British and other finance
was promised for a program of purchase. Little of that money has become
available, and Zimbabwe cannot find it from its own resources. Yet expropriation, the only alternative to rising rural discontent, would be condemned by the very powers which promised the purchase money. Here
is another case in which the problems of the colonial inheritance pass
beyond the capacity of the country in question.

The prospects of progress become distinctly brighter when one turns
to Angola and Mozambique.* Let me say at once that this has little or

---

*Here I was too optimistic. Foreign-supported banditries were to continue to ruin these
countries, and this was still the case in 1994 when military supplies were still being
channeled to these banditries.

nothing to do with an ideological argument. The real choice in these countries—all ideological labels apart—lies only between building new economies on new foundations or accepting an otherwise unavoidable chaos. To see these countries as members of the Soviet bloc is to misinterpret the anticolonial movements which carried them to independence.

These countries inherited nothing from Portuguese rule that was workable in terms of structure, system, or even day-to-day administration. Their wars of liberation had swept away a rigidly racist and constrictive dictatorship. The self-induced panic of several hundred thousand Portuguese settlers, fleeing to Portugal under the influence of guilt and malicious rumor, had removed almost all personnel with any technical experience or qualification. A real degree of literacy was possessed by much less than 3 percent of the African populations of Angola and Mozambique, and most of this tiny proportion of literates were junior civil servants whose lifestyle had long absorbed the paper-crazy attitudes of their Portuguese masters.

V

THE LIBERATION MOVEMENTS HAD TO TAKE OVER WHAT AMOUNTED TO A vacuum of administrative structure and of economic system. They had to build on new foundations, and these foundations had to be different in kind from any associated with the system they had overthrown. They had to be, or to try to be, noncapitalist—or, if you wish, potentially socialist— in structure and intention. Anything else would simply return them to a new colonial dependence. Their former dependence had reduced them to an acute poverty.

They have met with encouraging success in building on new foundations against huge difficulties, much worsened in the last few years by South African aggressions. Their long-term prospects have become unusually good. That is partly because of their success in building new structures of a potentially strong independence. It is also because they are potentially rich countries, perhaps among the richest in the so-called "Third World," with large and largely untapped resources in minerals and in soils capable of growing a wide range of crops for food or for industrial purposes.

Yet they remain, in the short run, acutely deprived of economic infrastructure and available capital. In spite of their advantages, they too cannot succeed on their own. Whether to safeguard their independence or to advance their development, they need to become part of a regional system capable of maximizing their conjoint resources and of attracting large amounts of developmental investment.

To that end, in 1979, they took the lead in forming—with Zimbabwe, Zambia, Tanzania, Malawi, Swaziland, Botswana, and Lesotho—a body called the Southern African Development Coordination Conference, or SADCC, with headquarters in Botswana. So far, SADCC can represent little more than a statement of intentions and a means of launching common action. Potentially, however, it points to the possibility of a very different future, downgrading and eventually blurring the frontiers of the colonial partition and presenting to the world a major zone of internal cooperation. This, in short, is the outline of a blueprint for a postcolonial future.

Yet the greatest source of potential investment is missing: the economy of South Africa. That economy is largely the product of vast international investment over many decades—a foreign investment said to exceed some £20 billion in current values—but its rulers, as we have also seen, remain the declared enemies of almost all the other countries in the region. So the crucial component of South Africa's economic contribution is missing; and it will remain missing as long as the apartheid system holds.

I therefore turn now to South Africa itself, truly the key to all the fundamental problems of the subcontinent.

VI

A MORE OR LESS RIGID DISCRIMINATION AGAINST BLACK PEOPLE HAS BEEN the instrument of white rule in South Africa ever since that state came into being, and has rested, after formation of the Union in 1910, on a few basic legal weapons. One of these was the Native Land Act of 1913, which (with the later Act of 1936) restricted African land ownership to some 13 percent of the land surface. Another was the Urban Areas Act of 1923, which likewise established a regime of strict physical segregation and discrimination within the 86.3 percent of the land surface reserved to white ownership: within, that is, the so-called white areas.

The meaning of "separate development"—of what has since become the still more rigid system called apartheid—was in fact set down in clear words by the official Stallard Commission of 1921, even before the Act of

1923 was passed. This explained that the black man "should only be allowed to enter urban areas, which are essentially the white man's creation, when he is willing to enter and to minister"—"minister," the word is worth reflecting on—"to the needs of the white man, and he should depart therefrom when he ceases so to minister."

With that, the almost limitless prosperity of white South Africa was well assured. Capital inflows from the outside world, before the 1950s primarily from Britain, were guaranteed a more than ample supply of captive black labor, available in every zone of South Africa where capital could be profitably invested.

The position today is no more than a painful—though painfully complex—elaboration on that of fifty or forty years ago. Within the so-called white areas of total discrimination—86.3 percent of the land surface since 1936—there are approximately 46 percent of all Africans in the country, or nearly half a total African population of some 22 million.

These Africans live on sufferance, "ministering" to the needs of white employers—without rights of citizenship, without freedom of movement, without the hope of any evenhanded protection by the law. Nor do they have any constitutional rights of residence, even though these "white areas" may be the lands of their remote ancestors. Since the 1960s the juggernaut of apartheid doctrine has dragged more than 3 million people from their homes and driven them into new zones of segregation, often in zones of open bush with no facilities for human habitation and no chances of employment.

Grotesquely bland advertisements in British newspapers may claim that white South Africa is building a society of equal rights and duties. The harsh reality is precisely the reverse. A few cosmetic reforms notwithstanding, the rigors of segregation do not become less. They simply become more elaborate, and, in becoming more elaborate, they become more oppressive.

VII

IT HAS SOMETIMES BEEN SAID THAT THIS SOUTH AFRICAN OPPRESSION IS essentially the product of Boer or Afrikaner prejudice. This is at best a very partial truth: others also have their ample share in the profits of captive land and labor. Total British investment was competently estimated, in January 1982, as amounting to £11 billion, and total U.S. investment at £10 billion, with lesser totals for West Germany, France, Sweden, and other countries. And capital, as we know, goes where it can find its best return.

Put crudely, the returns on investment in South Africa have been generally far higher than the world average for profitable use of money. Economists working for the Economic and Social Council of the United Nations have lately shown that returns on direct British investment in South Africa stood at an average of 18 percent in 1979, compared with 10 percent elsewhere; or, in 1980, 21 and 9 percent respectively. American companies seem to have done even better: the same investigations revealed, for 1980, an average profitability of 29 percent for American-based companies operating in South Africa, compared with 18.4 percent elsewhere; or, for 1981, 19 percent in South Africa and 14.4 percent elsewhere.

The primary reason for this relatively high rate of profit has been the payment to black labor of low or very low wages. It would be easy to show this in exhaustive detail; briefly, the apartheid system has guaranteed a level of black wages—whether paid to Africans, to Coloreds, or to Indians—which, more often than not, has stood near or below the officially admitted starvation line. Successful black protest, chiefly in the manufacturing industries, began somewhat to improve that situation early in the 1970s; and today, it is claimed officially, the volume of money paid out in black wages is considerably larger than twelve years ago. Yet it seems more than probable that numerical growth in the black population has canceled any average improvement in real wages, given too that there is now heavy black unemployment in the towns and, outside the towns, widespread black destitution among millions who have been, in the jargon of apartheid, "re-located."

VIII

OFFICIAL PROPAGANDA LIKEWISE CLAIMS THAT APARTHEID PROVIDES FOR THE development of Africans inside their own "homelands"—inside, that is, the old native reserves—some 13.7 percent of the land surface—now known as Bantustans. Again, the facts speak a different language.

Census estimates of 1980 showed that 54 percent of Africans—perhaps 12 or 13 million people—were living in the Bantustans. But these so-called homelands scattered about the country within an otherwise meaningless jigsaw of boundaries are no more viable today than they used to be when they were native reserves. They have long been little better than rural slums; in the words of a government White Paper of 1936, when their condition was better than today, they are—and I quote—"congested, denuded, overstocked, eroded, and for the most part, in a deplorable condition."

It will be no exaggeration to say that a substantial part of their populations exist in a condition of living death, and survive at all only because another substantial part of the population regularly "commutes" to employment in the "white areas" and sends wages home. The average rate of death of children under ten in the Transkei, largest of the Bantustans, is competently estimated at around 40 percent; other such estimates confirm a desperate mortality.

Annual levels of production over recent years suggest that only about 3 percent of South Africa's gross domestic product has been produced in these "black areas" or "homelands," where, with few exceptions, there is no industry, no investment, and very little soil left for cultivation. It is in any case clear that the Bantustans are able to produce no more than an insignificant fraction of South Africa's GDP, although more than half the African population lives in them, or is supposed to live in them.

That is the reality of "separate development"; as was said as long ago as 1944, by the African scholar Z. K. Matthews, this dispensation is "the separation of black and white, not with the idea of protecting each group in regard to its basic interests, but the separation of the groups in order to facilitate the subordination of one group to the other—the exploitation of one group by the other." The "independent homelands" are an organic part of that exploitation. Their acute and often helpless poverty is another guarantee of an ample supply of black labor for the "white economy," another contribution to the profits of overseas investors. To suggest that these "black areas" are zones of development is to propound a grim absurdity.

IX

SUCH IS THE SYSTEM. CAN IT CHANGE? OR, RATHER, CAN IT CHANGE ITSELF?

I was once among those who thought that it could and indeed would. I thought that the sheer expansion of the white economy must call for ever larger supplies of skilled labor, substantially black skilled labor, and that this would break through industrial color bars, bans on black enterprise, and all the various barriers of apartheid. Many other observers thought and have continued to think like this, but they ceased to include me a long time ago.

Such optimism may be convenient to those who like to have their cake and eat it: to pocket their profits, that is, while expressing disapproval of the system. The record shows it is baseless. The record shows that with every expansion of the South African economy—since 1910, but more especially since the long boom began in the 1930s, and above all since the 1950s—there has come a further tightening of the screws of an instrumental racism embodied in an enormously long list of laws, decrees, and administrative actions. The number of black skilled workers has certainly increased, but pari passu, along with that, the color bars and other weapons of discrimination have sharpened and grown heavier. Something like the embryo of a black "middle class" has come into existence, but only as the helpless puppet of an immensely more powerful white "middle class," as may be seen today in the wretched stooges who run the Bantustans.

In 1970 an industrialist as authoritative as Mr. Harry Oppenheimer of the Anglo-American Corporation and De Beers could sadly conclude that "there is no evidence so far that economic integration has led to any improvement in political or social integration." Everything that has happened since 1970—not least this latest constitutional referendum of 1983—has confirmed that Mr. Oppenheimer was right.

So far, in short, the system has revealed, within itself, no self-correcting mechanism capable even of beginning the dismantlement of apartheid. Much has been said lately about reforms. The past decade has seen a major extension of the organization of black workers, and with it have come gains in terms of trade-union rights. These gains have been made in the face of continued and vicious repression. Pressure has been brought to bear by the regime in an attempt to impose new controls and to confine union activists to a narrow sphere of activity.

Steps have been taken to reduce some of the minor aspects of discrimination in matters such as the segregation of telephone kiosks or benches in parks. More white people than before accept that the system spells disaster for themselves as well as for blacks; they remain, at best, an exiguous minority.*

Nothing has been done, or promised, or even discussed at the govern-

---

*International sanctions, chiefly financial, against the apartheid regime have begun to change this prospect. Thanks to nonwhite pressure for change much was done after 1989 to undermine apartheid. But white racist resistance remained strong.

mental or National Party level, which in any way dismantles the overall system. That may be seen most strikingly, behind the blandishments of official propaganda, in this year's constitutional referendum. A white parliamentary assembly is to be "partnered" by an Indian assembly and a Colored assembly, but all effective power will remain with the white assembly. The 10 or 11 million Africans in the "white areas" remain utterly disenfranchised, and, by the laws relating to the Bantustans, are now denied any rights of citizenship in 87.3 percent of the country. Nothing, in any essentials, has changed.

X

THERE MAY STILL BE THOSE WHO THINK THAT THE APARTHEID SYSTEM WILL fall apart from its own internal contradictions, even from its own inherent absurdity. Even today, when the black majority numbers some 25 million, a white domination of fewer than 5 million people can pursue apartheid only by brute force, and sustain it only by ever more painful laws and practices of oppression. Within a generation there will be upward of 45 million black people in South Africa; and one may well wonder what conceivable system of organized servitude will be able to contain them.

Yet to imagine that this system will fall apart of itself—or even, of its own volition, change against itself—is to fall into the illusion which held, years ago, that expansion of the economy would be enough to reduce and eventually to end apartheid.

The system will not fall apart of itself.

It must be made to fall apart. That being so, the course of wisdom must be to make it fall apart in such a way that the violence of the system is displaced, as rapidly as possible, by movement toward a democracy of genuinely equal rights and duties.

To that end, only two pressures can be real factors on the scene.

The first and decisive pressure is that of the black community. To the extent that black people struggle for a real freedom to participate fully in representative institutions with real powers—political parties, national parliament and government, trade unions, integrated types of education, and the rest—they will be able to open the way for a democratic and therefore peaceful country.

This, of course, is what the representative organs of black opinion, and most comprehensively the African National Congress, have asked for and urged since the very foundation of modern South Africa. For decade after

decade they have relied on peaceful argument and passive protest or
resistance—always, invariably, in vain.

Now they are reduced to illegality or legal subjection, and they have
turned as a last resort, as did the black peoples of the Portuguese colonies
and of Rhodesia, to an armed struggle of counterviolence to the violence
of the system. We should deplore that counterviolence if it were a black
racist response to the provocations of white racism. But all the evidence
shows that it is nothing of the kind, and that it is aimed not at replacing
one apartheid by another, but precisely at winning a society of equal
rights and duties.

This being the case, I do not see how governments or peoples who
condemn apartheid can fail to support the African National Congress and
its companions. To tolerate a system of violence while rejecting the
planned and restrained use of counterviolence—of course, as only one
means of securing change—is morally untenable.

The militant wing of the African National Congress has hit successfully and hard at the confidence and security of the apartheid state, and
possesses every legitimate reason to expect understanding and support
from antiapartheid trends outside South Africa. This is a part of the
picture of renewed protest and demand for change within South Africa;
and most of that picture, since 1976, has shown a wide and widening
resurgence of political and moral support for the broad political aims of
the ANC and other antiapartheid bodies.

Nothing so forcefully reveals the falsity of the regime's claims for its
own success, in "winning hearts and minds," than this astonishing resurgence. Astonishing, as it must be, for by 1983 the ANC had been outlawed
for twenty-three years, all known sympathizers pursued with the ferocity
of repressive laws, and all its best-known leaders banned, jailed, dead, or
driven into exile. And yet ANC-inspired opposition to the regime has
become stronger than ever.

Listen, for example, to a report in the highly orthodox American
journal *Foreign Affairs* (Winter 1983–84), which cannot be suspected of
polemical bias toward antiapartheid South Africa. It is by Professor
Thomas Karis of the City University of New York. Professor Karis is no
newcomer to the study of South Africa, and his scholarly work has long
received due recognition. His words carry the weight of a long and careful
scrutiny of South African realities.

"Although outdoor meetings have been banned since 1976," he writes
of African political protest, "15,000 to 20,000 people at a time have attended funerals of prominent ANC personalities. There, at meetings

indoors and at trials, supporters display ANC flags and colors of black, green and gold. They shout ANC slogans, give black power salutes, and sing freedom songs. Church bells tolled throughout Soweto, the sprawling black area near Johannesburg, in the early hours of June 9, 1983, when three ANC guerrillas were hanged."

And 1983 brought another and potent development of this political resurgence. On August 20–21, near Cape Town, a meeting of some 12,000 people rose in standing ovation for a powerful message of defiance sent them from prison by the ANC leader Nelson Mandela and other ANC leaders. Having done this, the people at the meeting went on to launch a new vehicle of mass solidarity, a new means of working for unity and joint action across all communities, and they named it the United Democratic Front (UDF). And having done that, they dispersed to the tasks of building the UDF into a countrywide framework for democratic action and discussion among all antiapartheid persons and organizations, whether African or white, Colored or Indian.

First brought into nominal existence during January 1983 and despite the repressive measures used against some of its leaders, the UDF has since flowered into a national reality. Though obliged to operate within the narrow jaws of apartheid legislation, the UDF has grown into a movement based on several hundred existing organizations, such as trade unions, church bodies, youth and other associations which represent all the "racial" communities, with black organizations in a large majority.

Its broad aims recall the older Freedom Charter of the ANC. Three of its presidents are veteran ANC activists: Albertina Sisulu (wife of Walter Sisulu, the ANC's imprisoned secretary-general), Archie Gumede, and Oscar Mpetha, while its publicly acknowledged patrons include Nelson Mandela, Walter Sisulu, and Govan Mbeki, all now in prison, as well as other well-known ANC personalities.

If that were all, it might be thought that the regime could move rapidly and easily to suppress the UDF, as it has long tried to abolish the ANC. But the UDF has aimed, and with increasing success during its first year of life, at bringing together many strands of antiapartheid opinion. In fact, the earliest call to form the UDF came from Dr. Allan Boesak, who is president of the World Alliance of Reformed Churches, supported by the Reverend Beyers Naude, another prominent Afrikaner and leader of the banned Christian Institute; while the voice of democrats of English origin is stubbornly represented by Andrew Boraine, former president of the English-speaking National Union of South African Students. Among Africans, meanwhile, the Black Consciousness movement is likewise

present in the UDF in the person of the Reverend Smangaliso
Mkhatshwa, secretary-general of the Catholic Bishops' Conference, as
well as other Black Consciousness veterans such as Mosiuoa Lekota.

"We, the freedom-loving people of South Africa," runs the Declaration
of the UDF, "say with one voice to the whole world, that we

- cherish the vision of a united, democratic South Africa based
  on the will of the people;
- will strive for the unity of all people through united action
  against the evils of apartheid, economic and all other forms of
  exploitation.

And in our march to a free and just South Africa, we are guided by
these noble ideals

- we stand for the creation of a true democracy in which all
  South Africans will participate in the government of our
  country;
- we stand for a single non-racial unfragmented South Africa. A
  South Africa free of bantustans and Group Areas;
- we say, all forms of oppression and exploitation must end."

How then, in the light of all this—and much more could be added to
the same effect—can the Western world continue to excuse its inaction
or indifference on the grounds that the apartheid state alone speaks for
South Africa? How can the Western world continue to hide behind bland
statements of hope in some eventual "change of heart" on the part of the
ruling racist minority? What usefulness remains in mere statements of
good intention?

Surely we have had enough statements of good intention. Today,
parodying an earlier wit, it may be said that we are all against apartheid.
Conservative statesmen, for example, say now about South Africa and its
regime what they have not said before.

On May 23, 1983, Mr. Francis Pym, certainly a Conservative but also a
statesman, warned that "there is a desperate need to break the vicious
circle where violence begets violence, and to seek peaceful solutions to
the region's problems."

Even the U.S. administration of President Reagan, whose proapartheid
stance remains a major source of strength for the apartheid regime, now
adds to the chorus of alarm. Thus Mr. Lawrence Eagleburger, when U.S.

under secretary of state, told a San Francisco audience on June 23, 1983, that "a cycle of violence has begun: unless it is reversed, the interests of the region and the West will be severely damaged." Even the International Monetary Fund has said that it is worried.

If such attitudes are more than pale hypocrisy or tactical vote catching, they demand action.

Antiapartheid action by the outside world is the second and supporting force that can make for removal of the system which is the origin, maker, and motivator of this "cycle of violence" so rightly deplored by Mr. Pym and Mr. Eagleburger.

This means whatever appropriate action may be possible to support and encourage the opponents and critics of apartheid inside South Africa, whether these be Africans, Coloreds, Indians, or whites.

It means positive action to reinforce the independence of the nine SADCC countries and, very urgently, to help protect them from the aggressions of Pretoria, so that they can pursue a national and regional development to which, eventually, a democratized South Africa could bring its skills and wealth.

It means a combined program—far more effective than any so far envisaged—of what may be called negative action—initially, to isolate the apartheid regime and its components and press them to accept democratic transformation.

And this in turn means a comprehensive program of sanctions against apartheid—political, military, and, above all, economic.

Compelling sanctions were long dismissed by governments and parliaments as beyond realization or likely to be unproductive. No competent opinion holds that view today.

On the contrary, there is substantial agreement across a widening spectrum of political opinion that real sanctions are not only desirable but very realizable. Late in 1983, for example, the U.S. Congress voted sanctions against further American investment in apartheid South Africa.*

We cannot know exactly what a postapartheid South Africa would be like. But we do know that apartheid South Africa is an intolerable blot and misery; and we know as well that antiapartheid forces exist, inside South Africa, which stand for peace, progress, and a stability which cannot exist now. We can act, in everyone's interest, to support those forces.

---

*These and other economic sanctions were undoubtedly the decisive factor in forcing reforms on Pretoria. I leave these last pages unchanged because they accurately show how just and valid were the arguments for sanctions.

Without such action, there will remain the certainties of disaster.

But with such action, concerted and determined—undertaken now, and undertaken to succeed, and to succeed as rapidly as may be possible—there will be good prospects for the whole subcontinent: far better prospects, indeed, than at any time in the past hundred years or more.

ARGUMENTS

ALTHOUGH OF A MILD AND TOLERANT NATURE, I HAVE FAILED TO AVOID getting into arguments during these many years—I mean into controversies rather than debates, sometimes very heated controversies. However differently in ways or circumstance, these controversies have to do with a burning issue of our times, an issue from which the study of history can barely think to remain distant. They have to do with aspects of the culture of imperialism in its instrumentalist essence, with its forcing of humanity into rigid hierarchies in which certain social groups, countries, "races," have become the systemic victims of others. In short, they have to do with the origins and mind-sets of racism.

Much of our world, as everyone knows, has been confined by this process of reduction; and dense fogs of mystification have puffed around the process to the point that humanity's having thus become divided against itself may even seem—has often seemed—perfectly right and natural. Yet the culture of postimperialism, as it now gets itself together, has begun to tear holes in the mystification and unveil the realities behind. We see that the motivating force of racism has had little to do with the superstitions of ignorance, or with the provincialisms of antiquated prejudice, or with misguided belief. All those make the fog denser. But the motivating force has been severely practical, extremely realist. Its power has been drawn from the hard-and-fast economics of exploitation.

This power can be both subtle and pervasive. A modern African example of its pervasiveness springs to mind. For some thirty years until 1990 the repressive power of Ethiopian imperialism was used unsparingly, even mercilessly, to insist on a factual supremacy—conceived and used as a "racist" supremacy—of the Amharic nationality over the other and more numerous nationalities within the Ethiopian empire-state. This domination spawned conflicts, and the conflicts spawned hatreds, until it could appear that these conflicts and hatreds were somehow natural and inherent to these various nationalities. These peoples, it began to be said, could not live without loathing each other.

Within the empire-state, as it fell out, the Eritrean people struggled to assert and liberate their historic rights and cultures, including the public use of their languages. They were duly presented to the world by Amharic spokespersons and other imperial dependents as contumacious rebels, violent troublemakers, careerists seized by ambitions that were evil. Yet the outcome has displayed these rebels, and no few of their neighbors, in a different light. Having made good their right to decide their own identity and future, they have appeared as peace-minded peoples concerned to participate in a reorganization of the vast region of the Horn on postimperialist lines.

And they will be able to promote this desirable reorganization, they say—and here I am quoting their foremost statesman, Issaias Afwerki, a veteran of their long anticolonial struggle—because "there is no inherent hatred among our peoples which cannot be erased by a just distribution of powers and rights." Lift off oppression or the fear of oppression, and "natural and inherent" conflicts will resolve themselves. But insist on that oppression, and those conflicts will quickly live again. After 1990 the case of Eritrea forcefully illuminated these truths in Africa, just as, in Europe, renewed oppressions in Yugoslavia demonstrated precisely the reverse.

In the slow but steady development of modern imperialism, of a directly racist imperialism, the haunting legacy of Christopher Columbus can still benefit from discussion. For if "discovering America" was one thing, it remains that installing racism was quite another, and this is the aspect of the Columbian saga that still calls for examination.

What were the nature and influence of ancient Egyptian civilization on the rest of the world, above all on the rise of the classical civilization of Greece? Was there any such influence and, if so, was it African? Such questions derive from a modern controversy which dates back, essentially, to the 1830s. That was when the colonial enclosure of Africa by Europe—for example, of Algeria by France—gained momentum. This is another controversy concerned with racism, although in quite another context than the voyages of Columbus. Of this often acute controversy the most recent and by far the most interesting analysis has appeared in the masterfully erudite writings of Martin Bernal. His has been, and is, a profoundly liberating work because it clears the ground of muffling mystifications spread around during the 1830s and ever since. The weight of

Bernal's findings, and of their implications for the study of history, will be felt far ahead.

They will be felt, however indirectly, in the great and challenging project that lies before the world at this time: the shaping and safeguarding of a postimperialist future, of a future within which hatreds and conflicts between peoples can lose their domination, and can give way, as Issaias Afwerki has said, to reconciliations which come from a just sharing of powers and rights.

THE ANCIENT WORLD
AND AFRICA:
WHOSE ROOTS?

I

To a television series about the history of the Africans which I lately had the good fortune to be able to present to a wide public in many countries, there were of course some protests and objections. Surprisingly, however, these were fewer than I had expected. They came mostly from persons of evidently fixed opinions who clearly knew little or nothing of the subject of the programs, and who made up for their astonishment at being shown that Africans have a history of their own by accusing me of bias, exaggeration, or sentimental frailty. A few objections were from white South Africans in Britain or former Rhodesian settlers, foreseeably couched in the kind of gutter language one has learned to expect from such quarters. And several were from otherwise sympathetic viewers who had oddly convinced themselves that black history could be written only by a black historian. One of these even went so far, although politely, as to suggest that the series in question should have been presented by my late friend and colleague Cheikh Anta Diop, who was certainly a notable historian but who spoke no English.

None of these objections has seemed to me to warrant serious argument, but there was another, far more solidly based in European culture, which undoubtedly does warrant such argument and in which, I think, one can find some of the crucial origins of established or intellectual denial of value to the cultures of Africa. This objection, heard from a number of viewers in Europe and North America, was against a central

This essay originally appeared in 1987 in *Race and Class*. Reprinted with permission.

theme in the series. This theme portrayed Egypt of the pharaohs, ancient Egypt before conquest by the Arabs in the seventh century A.D., as a country of black origins and population whose original ancestors had come from the lands of the great interior, and whose links with inner Africa remained potent and continuous. To affirm this, of course, is to offend nearly all established historiographical orthodoxy. The ancient Egyptians, by that orthodoxy, were not only not black—in whatever pigmentational variant of nonwhite that nature may have provided—but they were also not Africans. To say otherwise must be so mistaken, one has gathered, as to be patently absurd.

But isn't Egypt, other issues apart, quite simply a part of Africa? That, it seems, is a merely geographical irrelevance. The civilization of pharaonic Egypt, arising sometime around 3500 B.C. and continuing at least until the Roman dispossessions, has been explained to us as evolving either in more or less total isolation from Africa or as a product of West Asian stimulus. On this deeply held view, the land of ancient Egypt appears to have detached itself from the delta of the Nile, some fifty-five hundred years ago, and sailed off into the Mediterranean on a course veering broadly toward the coasts of Syria. And there it apparently remained, floating somewhere in the seas of the Levant, until Arab conquerors hauled it back to where it had once belonged.

Now what is one to make of this unlikely view of the case, coming as it has from venerable seats of learning? Does its strength derive from a long tradition of research and explanation? Is it what Europeans have always thought to be true? Have the records of ancient times been found to support it? As Martin Bernal has now most ably shown in his *Black Athena*, the remarkable book about which I am chiefly writing here, the answer to such questions is plainly and unequivocally in the negative. That the ancient Egyptians were black (again, in any variant you may prefer)—or, as I myself think it more useful to say, were African—is a belief which has been denied in Europe since about 1830, not before. It is a denial, in short, that belongs to the rise of modern European imperialism and has to be explained in terms of the "new racism," specifically and even frantically an antiblack racism, which went together with and was consistently nourished by that imperialism. I say "new racism" because it followed and further expanded the older racism which spread around Europe after the Atlantic slave trade had reached its high point of "take-off" in about 1630. Was there no racism, then, before that? The point is complex and can be argued elsewhere; essentially, however, the answer to this is also in the negative. Before the Atlantic slave trade, and before its capitalism, there was plenty of ancient xenophobia, fear of "blackness," association of blackness with the Devil, and so on and so forth; but none of this was the racism that we know.

The racism that we know was born in Europe and America from the cultural need to justify doing to black people, doing to Africans, what could not morally or legally be done to white people, and least of all to Europeans. To justify the enslavement of Africans, in short, it was culturally necessary to believe, or be able to believe, that Africans were inherently and naturally less than human, were beings of a somehow subhuman, nonhuman, nature. That was the cultural basis, in this context, of the slave trade and of the modern imperialism in Africa which followed the slave trade. The racism that we know, accordingly, was altogether different from ancient xenophobia or superstitious "fears of the dark": its core and motivation were to act as a weapon of dispossession and exploitation. And its success in this dehumanizing project needs no demonstration here, for it is obvious in our culture to this day.

The consequences of this need to condemn Africans as less than human—and how otherwise justify enslaving and then invading them?—have been many and various. Among these consequences, logically enough, has been a denial of the Africans' possible possession of histories of their own, and thus of common humanity with other peoples elsewhere. Not surprisingly, this denial began to be heard from eminent spokesmen in Europe as soon as Europe's modern imperialism imposed a corresponding need to structure and systematize its attitudes to overseas conquest and imperialist enclosure. In the year that France invades Algeria, for example, we find Hegel appropriately lecturing at Jena on this very subject. He knows nothing of Africa, has never been there, is oblivious to all the older sources of African knowledge that were extant then as now. Never mind; in 1830 he is able to say, in a course of lectures which were celebrated for generations after they were given, that "the Negro . . . exhibits the natural man in his completely wild and untamed state . . . for [Africa] is no historical part of the World; it has no movement or development to exhibit." And one grave academic after another, one belaureled explorer after another returning to the plaudits of a Grateful Nation, went on duly to explain that Africans had no history because Africans were insufficiently human. They were grown-up children who had failed to develop into adulthood. There was something missing in the frontal lobes of the African brain. They might seem to copy but could not invent, and even their copying was a masquerade. Such stereotypes filled book after book.

Then what about Ancient Egypt, universally held before the 1830s to be African, and the source of Europe's own civilizing process by way of the Greeks? How could that belief be squared with the "grown-up children" stereotypes? The questions were heard and briskly dealt with. After the 1830s ancient Egypt ceased to be seen as part of Africa, and pharaonic civilization ceased to be an aspect of Africa's development and initiative. As for the ancient Egyptians, the builders of the pyramids and of the greatest civilization of High Antiquity, they were steadily reduced to the status of a rather feeble bunch of mystics and magicians.

This operation, consciously or not in the minds of those who made it, was the required adjunct of another. It flowed from the need—as we can see it now, the racist-motivated need—to overthrow the hitherto accepted version of Europe's civilizing origin and process. This Ancient Model, as Bernal calls it, had accepted as self-evident that European civilization, launched from classical Greece in the sixth century B.C., was essentially and inseparably, though not exclusively, the product of older civilizations, above all those of Egypt and Phoenicia. This Ancient Model, as Bernal is careful to insist, gave full credit to the moral and intellectual achievements of classical Greece, but it still saw these as being initially derived from Egypt, and to a lesser extent from the centers of Phoenician civilization. It taught that the founding beliefs of classical Greece, like the mathematics and astronomy of classical Greece, had for the most part come from Egypt. And Egypt being accepted as an African country, they had thus come from Africa.

Such had been the traditional view of the matter. It had been questioned by no sufficient need to dehumanize Africans, at least until late in the seventeenth century when the slave trade began to prick at Christian consciences, and even as late as that it remained a view of history which was scarcely questioned. And this was not surprising, for the Ancient Model was based on solid historiographical evidence. This evidence was no other and no less than what the historians of classical Greece had themselves accepted as fact. Without exception, so far as surviving texts can show, every Greek thinker of the Classical Age looked to Egypt for inspiration and guidance, and accepted the cultural primacy of Egypt.

The philosophers and propagandists of the new imperialism could obviously not accept such views. They set about constructing a new model of Europe's civilizing process, an Aryan Model (again, Bernal's useful term). This proposed, and increasingly asserted with an intellectual arrogance perfectly in tune with the new imperialism, that classical Greece had been the pure and original source and creator of all that was civilized in Europe: all the arts of government and the values of freedom, all the gods that men should worship and the teachings they should follow. These nineteenth-century proponents of racism, of racist discrimination as a systemic weapon of oppression, were thus obliged to shove whatever the ancient Greeks had thought and written about African origins right under their academic carpet and lose it there. As Bernal says in his illuminating treatment of this operation, "the more the nineteenth century admired the Greeks, the less it respected their writing of their own history."

But if this newly created Aryan Model of Europe's civilizing origins responded to European nineteenth-century needs, it was not, of course, entirely mistaken. Linguistic studies duly showed that the language of the classical Greeks, as of modern Greeks, is one of a wide language family which linguists know as Indo-European: speakers of one or another derivative of "original Indo-European" had ranged from an "Aryan heartland," never quite fixed but supposedly in Eastern Europe or western Asia, right across the continent to the shores of the Atlantic, the Celtic languages being those that have survived farthest to the west. It was further found to be true, moreover, that speakers of the Indo-European parent of Greek had entered Greece in large numbers at some time before the emergence of classical civilization. The simplicity of the Ancient Model, which had derived Greek civilization from Egyptian and Phoenician exemplars as well as from Egyptian and Phoenician settlements in preclassical Greece, had therefore become clearly insufficient. Bernal deals with all this in lucid fashion and great detail, and proposes a Revised Ancient Model; this maintains the essence of the Ancient Model while accommodating the Indo-European evidence.

My brief foray here into this subject of vast complexity is concerned primarily to draw attention to *Black Athena*, Bernal's far-ranging treatment; and indeed, I know of no other work of such value. Bernal asks us to follow him through difficult terrain, but the effort is well repaid. Traveling with Bernal seems to me to offer the same kind of impact, for everyone involved in the problems of race and class, as another moment held for me, long ago, when at last I reached the iron-slag mounds of Meroe and knew that everything the books had taught me about history in Africa would have to be thought anew.

I I

AS HIS TITLE INDICATES, BERNAL'S OVERALL OBJECTIVE IS TO REESTABLISH the place of Egypt, and thus of Africa, in the moral and cultural development of classical Greek civilization in which Europe has seen, and generally persists in seeing, its founding parentage. He does this with an immense erudition, respect for sources, and notable linguistic scholarship, and I shall make no effort here to track the route he follows. As he himself remarks, any attempt to summarize "the complications of this vast and extraordinarily ramified theme can best be described by the Chinese expression 'looking at flowers from horseback.' " Even so, some of the flowers along the way are enough to make one pause and dismount.

To begin with, there is the evidence of what the Greeks themselves thought; and this is really very awkward for our racists. The Greeks all agreed upon the cultural supremacy of pharaonic civilization, and the ways in which they wrote about this clearly show that they would have thought it absurd to advance a contrary opinion. Herodotus of Halicarnassus in Asia Minor, for example, was born around 490 B.C. and wrote his great world histories some forty years later. Several of his nine books, but especially the second, have much to say on Egypt and Africa, and were composed after the long sojourn in Egypt which all Greek scholars of that time thought desirable or entirely necessary.[1] And they thought this, one may remark in passing, for the most persuasive reason that Egyptian civilization enjoyed a towering prestige and influence, and seemed of immemorial weight and value. Their grasp of exact historical chronology could not be as good as ours, but they were perfectly alive to Egypt's immense time dimension: not surprisingly, for two thousand years had passed since the building of the pyramids at Gizeh, or as much time—even if they knew it less precisely than we do—as has passed for us since the threshold of the Christian era. For the Greeks of the Classical Age, Egypt was where one went to learn history.

The same writers likewise took it for well-established fact that the Greeks had learned their civilization from the same source, and that this had come about, in some degree, because Egyptians had formed settlements in Greece in earlier centuries. Herodotus simply assumed that his readers would know this. "How it happened," he wrote, "that Egyptians came to the Peloponnese [southern Greece], and what they did to make themselves kings in that part of Greece, has been chronicled by other writers. I will therefore add nothing but proceed to mention some points which no one else has yet touched upon." For example, "the names of nearly all the gods came to Greece from Egypt." Moreover, "it was only, if I may so put it, the day before yesterday that the Greeks came to know the origin and form of the various gods . . . for Homer and Hesiod, the poets who composed our theogonies and described the gods for us . . . lived, as I believe, not more than four hundred years ago."

The philosophers and mathematicians were in full agreement. Pythagoras spent no fewer than twenty-one years in Egypt. Aristotle said that "Egypt was the cradle of mathematics." Eudoxus, Aristotle's teacher and a leading mathematician of his time, had likewise studied in Egypt before teaching in Greece. Isocrates and Plato were profoundly influenced by Egyptian philosophy. Euclid, again, learned mathematics in Egypt before applying them elsewhere. And who could be surprised? For the pyramids and temples of the Nile were not built by guesswork or rule of thumb. They were built by the use of mathematical propositions which the Egyptians had discovered and proven. How otherwise could it have come about that the difference in length between the shortest base side of the Great Pyramid at Gizeh (ca. 2600 B.C.) and the longest side (756.08 inches) is no more than a surprisingly accurate 7.9 inches? Herodotus and the men of his time did not know this, but they did know that the Great Pyramid was only one of innumerable mathematical marvels to be found in the land of the pharaohs.

Yet the Greeks of the Classical Age went further. They also affirmed that pharaonic culture had derived from inner Africa, from the lands of the "long-lived Ethiopians," as Herodotus wrote, meaning not the people of the country we nowadays call Ethiopia but in general the country of the blacks. This was another Greek belief that went back to the remote origins of Greek culture. Homer's *Iliad* had said it long before, when recounting the visit of Zeus and the rest of the Greek gods to the annual banquet given for all the gods by the gods of the blacks:

> For Zeus had yesterday to Ocean's bounds
> Set forth to feast with Ethiop's faultless men,
> And he was followed there by all the gods . . .

Many histories written by the classical Greeks have long been lost to us. But another which has not been lost is the world history composed by Diodorus Sikeliotes, Diodorus of Sicily, in about 50 B.C. "Now the Ethiopians [that is, the black peoples of Africa], as historians relate, were the first of all men," writes Diodorus in his second book, "and the proofs of this statement, they [that is, these same Greek historians] say, are manifest."[2] As for the people of Egypt, adds Diodorus from the same sources, they "are colonists sent out by the Ethiopians" after, as he explains, the steady annual accumulation of Nile silt had raised the land of Egypt above the level of the waters. "And the larger part of the customs of the Egyptians, [these historians] hold, are Ethiopian, the colonists still preserving their ancient manners." Allowing for all the differences of conception that separate us from Diodorus, this is an astonishingly exact statement of what archaeologists now affirm: i.e., that the cultures of the lower Nile, of Egypt proper, were initially derived from Neolithic cultures, and that these first took shape in the then green Sahara of the fifth millennium B.C. and earlier. Just as Egypt had been the gift of the Nile, in the splendid phrase of Herodotus, so also was inner Africa the cultural begetter of the peoples who accepted the gift. By a marvelous if infinitely diffuse process of social evolution, the cultures of the Saharan Neolithic led on to those of the pharaonic Nile. In the amazing harvests of pharaonic achievement that followed, there was no doubt a place for other formative elements, including several from the Near East and Mesopotamia. But the primary heritage from inner Africa seems to come ever more clearly from the archaeological record.

Yet consider the version offered for so long by our schools and universities. Here we have been presented with another Aryan Model, likewise very dear to imperialism. This has preached that any signs of past progress detectable among the black peoples must have been the fruit of outside intrusion, of northern intrusion: in a word, of "white" intrusion. This supplementary form of the Aryan Model, so handy for the "civilizing mission" of Europe in Africa, went into countless books and lectures. It was best enunciated in a "scientific" guise by a British anthropologist of the 1920s, C. G. Seligman, in his *Races of Africa*, published in 1929.

Maintained as proven truth, this view asserted that a people or peoples known as "Hamites" were responsible for any process of history that might be identifiable in Africa, because the "Negroes" were too primitive to be able, on their own, to embark on any such process. Apart from relatively recent Semitic influence, Phoenician or Arab, Seligman taught that "the civilisations of Africa are the civilisations of the Hamites." And who were and are these pioneering and indispensable Hamites? No problem for Seligman: the Hamites were and are not really Africans at all. They "are Caucasians, i.e., belong to the same great branch of mankind as almost all Europeans." Or again, just to make sure: "The incoming Hamites were pastoral Caucasoids—arriving wave after wave—better armed as well as quicker witted than the dark agricultural Negroes." Seligman was following a well-beaten trail. Years earlier in 1912, for example, the German anthropologist Carl Meinhof had explained that "in the course of [African] history"—at least he admitted that there had been some!—"it has repeatedly happened that the Hamitic peoples have subjugated and, as a ruling people [*Herrenvolk* in Meinhof's original German], have governed dark-pigmented Negroes who spoke languages different from that [*sic*] of the Hamites."

Seligman, in fact, was reflecting the imperialist culture of his times; and this was as pervasive in academic circles as it was passionately advanced. Thus we have H. E. Egerton, when professor of colonial history at Oxford early in the 1920s, publishing a book in which he defends colonialism as "the right way . . . of dealing with the native problem." With colonialism, he says, "what had happened [was] the introduction of order into blank, uninteresting, brutal barbarism"; and one may note in passing just how passionately the adjectives pile up. That was in 1922, and the same theme continued to be sounded loud and clear. So we have Egerton's successor at Oxford, Reginald Coupland, sounding it again late in the twenties. History in Africa, with him, has to wait to begin until the arrival there of the missionary-explorer David Livingstone. "A new chapter in the history of Africa began with David Livingstone. . . . So far, it might be said, Africa proper had had no history." Ancient Egypt and All That, presumably, was "Africa improper"? In any case, until the middle of the nineteenth century, "the main body of Africans . . . had stayed, for untold centuries, sunk in barbarism. Such, it might almost seem, had been Nature's decree. . . . So they remained stagnant, neither going forward nor going back. . . . The heart of Africa was scarcely beating." And so it continued—and these men, after all, were the opinion makers of their time—until well after the Second World War and the beginnings of anticolonial change in Africa. Even then, there was a rearguard action, notably signaled by Hugh Trevor-Roper (today Lord Dacre) who, when Regius Professor of History at Oxford in 1963, found it perfectly right to provide his own version of Hegel's nonsense of 130 years earlier.

III

NOW THIS EXTENSION OF THE EUROPEAN ARYAN MODEL TO AN ENTIRELY comparable African version—to an African Aryan Model for all of Africa beyond Egypt—has not been Bernal's concern in this present volume, although he is manifestly well aware of it and of its racist origins and uses. Yet it remains entirely relevant and cognate to Bernal's thesis that this African Aryan Model, as I think he will allow me to call it, has been very largely overthrown during the past thirty years or so. No serious Africanist of today would think of taking Egerton or Coupland or Trevor-Roper for a moment seriously when they speak of Africa's lack of history; and the breakthrough point here can probably be dated to Onwuka Dike's thesis of 1956 (*Trade and Politics in the Niger Delta*), as well as, in a large archaeological sense, to Willard Libby's demonstration of the early 1950s that the C-14 isotope of carbon can be used to provide approximately probable dates of organic materials in archaeological sites otherwise undatable.

No serious Africanist, by the same token, any longer believes in the "Hamitic hypothesis" of progress in ancient Africa, or even in the existence, now or in the past, of any people properly definable as Hamites. By a nice coincidence of 1963, as it happens, the abolition of the Hamites—however "Caucasoid" and "quicker witted," as Seligman had reassured his readers—began with the publication in that year of J. H. Greenberg's essential *Languages of Africa*,[3] and has continued ever since. The Hamites were a myth: "Even the linguistic use of the term Hamite," wrote Greenberg with an authority unchallenged in this context, "should be abandoned." Likewise, the then fashionable term "Hamito-Semitic" for major languages in northern and northeastern Africa should be dropped as misleading. For these languages Greenberg coined a new term, "Afroasiatic," and this has since come into general acceptance, being also used by Bernal in this volume. Yet Afroasiatic can also be misleading for the nonspecialist, though certainly less so than Hamito-Semitic, for the Asiatic element in Greenberg's classification applies only to one of the five major groupings in this linguistic family, that of the Arabic, which became current in northeastern Africa only after the middle of the seventh century. The other four linguistic elements in Afroasiatic, as Greenberg lists them, are Egyptian (extinct today), Berber, Kushitic in its five derivative variants, and Chadian—all of them, as you see, thoroughly African. But the Hamites and their Caucasoid "quicker wits" have in any case vanished from the scientific scene.

So have other stereotypes of the racist model. The scholarship of the last thirty or forty years has simply tipped them into the dustbin of exploded fantasies. This was not achieved easily or without a lot of stubborn effort, but it has now been achieved beyond any possibility of reversion. It may even be claimed that this achievement is among the most significant intellectual advances of the twentieth century. Bernal's treatment of this important aspect of his own subject is disappointingly deficient, since it is little more than an afterthought at the end of his book. No doubt he has it in mind to expand on this in a later volume. As it is, reading his pages in this respect must leave one without any indication of the fact that the study of African history and humanity, in many disciplines, has become the concern of manifold colleges and universities in all the continents, not least in Africa itself. One could not guess that whole libraries of books and papers are now available in one or another field of Africa-centered and Africa-directed research and debate. Bernal refers very briefly only to two or three American historians apart from Cheikh Anta Diop. This is, again, surprising in a writer as conscientious as Bernal, for African studies in the USA, where Bernal teaches, had also become impressively wide in their range and distinguished in their level at least by the middle 1960s. Valiantly toppling the Aryan Model for Europe, this sympathetic writer has not yet had time to notice that its counterpart in Africa has meanwhile bitten the dust.

Has bitten the dust, that is to say, among all serious students of Africa: not yet, by any means, with the nonspecialized serious public and much less with any "general public" in Europe or North America. Hence the objections to the television series mentioned earlier. The news has evidently yet to get through; but there are explanations for this outside any question of inherited prejudice. One of them concerns our almost total ignorance of the developmental relationship which came to exist between the civilization of the pharaohs and the peoples of inner Africa, the peoples of "the land shadowing with wings which lies beyond the rivers of Ethiopia."

Here is a subject from which historians and archaeologists have tended to shy away, no doubt because of the formidable influence of schools of Egyptology which have had no interest in the question and which, more or less ferociously, have resisted any "Africanizing" of their field of work. Yet it is now a subject which needs tackling if Aryan mythologies of the Hamitic sort are to be finally dismissed. Given, for example, that the origins of pharaonic civilization are traceable to the remote Neolithic of the green Sahara, as they increasingly appear to be, what was the manner and the movement of the civilizing "feedback" by that civilization, in due course of its astonishing development, to the peoples of the continental interior? Or, if peoples in western Africa possess symbols and beliefs which have been parallel to those of the ancient Nile—to mention only two, the serpent and the ram—who acquired them first? Or if people in southern Africa have used headrests comparable with those of ancient Egypt, has this been mere coincidence of "separate invention," or, if not, how is it to be explained?

And so on. Remote African history is alive with such taunting questions, and very possibly they will never win sufficient answers. Yet it seems to me that their importance in this whole story calls urgently for provisional and tentative answers, and, furthermore, that such answers now begin to be possible. Working suppositions which I believe that many specialists now accept, or more or less accept, are that the geographical locus of all or most of Africa's ramifying cultures lay, as I remarked above, in the long unfolding of the Saharan Neolithic[4]; that these cultures manifestly achieved their greatest elaboration and success in pharaonic Egypt; and that, in one elusive way or another, the consequential "feedback" was shuttled to and fro but became ever more tenuous as desiccation after ca. 2500 B.C. severely continued in the lands to the south and west of the Nile. However one may conceive this process, what emerges today is that one has to think of all these African cultures, those of the Nile certainly included, as belonging to the same capacious arena of this continent's history.

This is a view of the matter which is still found shocking by the orthodox. That is easily understandable because, like Bernal's Revised Ancient Model, it calls for the radical and therefore painful rethinking of many received opinions. It asks for the healing of more than one neurosis in the field of "race relations," above all (at least within Europe, but I suspect elsewhere as well) of the neurosis which has to see black humanity as inherently "less"—add any substantive that you may wish—than white humanity. Here in Britain it remains so widely spread that we shall have to work away at removing it for a long time before its fevers fall.

I V

To THAT END, IT SEEMS TO ME, ONE CANNOT SUFFICIENTLY INSIST THAT ALL such racist opinions and neuroses are relatively new—older than Bernal's Aryan Model, and yet not so very much so. Shakespeare's *Othello*, for example, was written before the great onset of racism in northern Europe, and it is not a racist play. It is a play about sexual jealousy, careerism, and hatred of competitive foreigners; and if the Moor was certainly black, he was still the powerful and admired commander of the armies of the Venetian Republic, then the strongest of the city-states of the Mediterranean, and greatly trusted by the masters of that republic. At most, *Othello* in 1603 can be interpreted in a racist sense as foreshadowing the coming racism of the Atlantic slave trade in northern Europe (a racism which appeared somewhat earlier in Portugal). Yet before that? Here is one case, to round off these notes on *Black Athena*, which offers a suggestive answer.

What did Europeans think about black people before the rise of racism? How did they estimate the values of black humanity? There are countless indications in the pictorial arts. Think only of the noble portraits of the black monarch among the three kings who journeyed to salute the birth of Christ. Think of the work of the great masters of the Renaissance who painted black persons. Think of Rembrandt, Velázquez, many more. Each

of them, without exception, painted black persons from the same standpoint as they painted white persons, whether either of these, white or
black, were kings or merchants or ambassadors or servants. Yet none of
these paintings, even so, has seemed to me to possess as much persuasive
and explanatory power as a medieval statue in the Magdeburger Dom,
the majestic thirteenth-century cathedral of the German city which was
then the capital of the Holy Roman Empire. This is the statue of a
crusader figure, sculpted life-sized and wearing the chain-mail armor of
the period.

The statue in fact is of St. Maurice, patron saint of Magdeburg, made
for the cathedral in about 1240. That in itself is not in the least surprising,
for St. Maurice was well known to the Middle Ages as a great military
saint, and was in this respect the companion of St. George. Whether or
not he was a real historical person rather than a pious legend, he was
widely revered. Said to have been martyred as a Christian legionary
commander of late Roman times—for having refused an imperial order
to kill one in ten (that is, *decimate* in the Roman meaning of the word) of
the soldiers of another legion which had gone into revolt—St. Maurice
was always referred to as St. Maurice of Thebes. This was the Thebes of
Egypt, not of Greece, but Maurice nonetheless had always up to now
been portrayed as white. Innumerable icons in the churches of Europe
had shown him as being as white as any European saint.

Yet here at Magdeburg in 1240, something new occurred. Overnight, as
it were, St. Maurice became black. He became an African beyond any
doubt, even down to the lineage cuts upon his forehead. Facing his stern
and yet warmly protective gaze, you know that you are looking at a
crusader in the chain mail likewise worn in Nubia then, but a Nubian,
moreover, very clearly regarded as a friend and ally. Now what had
happened, and why was this?

A few years before this remarkable statue was carved—so manifestly
from the life—and placed in the cathedral of Magdeburg, the Holy
Roman emperor Frederick II had led the sixth of the Christian Crusades
to recover the Holy Land and Egypt from their Muslim rulers. From his
point of view Frederick managed rather good results from this Crusade
of 1227–29, although the pope bitterly denounced him for not managing
better; ten years of peace ensued in Palestine and a treaty with the sultan
of Egypt, warfare being renewed only in 1239. In any case, it was altogether
understandable that the Crusade should be commemorated in the emperor's principal place of worship, the cathedral of Magdeburg. And what
could be more natural, one may ask, than that it should be commemorated
in such a way as to celebrate the Crusaders' only religious allies in the

distant lands to which they had gone? For the twin kingdoms of Nubia, due south of Egypt, were bastions of Christianity in the early thirteenth century, and had been so for more than six centuries.

These Nubian Christian kingdoms have been largely erased from memory since the fifteenth century, engulfed as they were by Islam after about 1450. But in the time of Frederick II they were an integral part of the Eastern Christian Church and, as such, had been sporadically at war with the Saracen rulers of Egypt for more than a hundred years. What more probable, even if precise proofs are lacking, than that the Christian Nubians were in fighting alliance with the Crusaders from the West? (Very suggestive evidence to this effect is in fact available, but I will not go into it here.) What more to be expected, then, than that the Crusaders of Magdeburg should wish to celebrate their distant ally? What more understandable than that the citizens of Magdeburg, rededicating their newly rebuilt cathedral of the late 1230s to St. Maurice, should honor their patron saint as black, as Nubian?

This, in any case, is exactly what they did. And from then on the cult of this black St. Maurice spread far and wide across Europe. Black icons of the saint supplanted earlier white icons. And it has seemed to me that there could be no more dramatic and instructive an illustration of the mental abyss, in the whole matter of "white-black relations," which divided the consciousness of the Middle Ages from the racism of later times.

As it happens, there is an unnoticed English footnote to this German illustration of preracist attitudes to powers and persons who were black. Let me at least mention it here. Medieval England, as everyone knows, shared in the continental European influence and appeal of the Crusades. Knights trekked in from the most remote fiefdoms, and in due course the churches of the period became rich in the effigies of knights who had taken part in the crusading venture. As in many other places, this is what happened in the medieval churches of remote Herefordshire in western England (where, simply to explain, I lately lived). Among these churches is that of the forgotten little parish of Brinsop.

There in Brinsop you will find a superb east window in which the stained glass of the Middle Ages has wonderfully outlived the assaults of time. And in the center of this thirteenth-century Brinsop splendor, you will see the portrait figure of a knight in armor. About that, in itself, there is again nothing to be surprised—*except* that the face of the knight is as black as the face of the Magdeburg Maurice. Given the historical context, the conclusion appears so obvious as to be undeniable. No doubt; and yet Brinsop Church is not dedicated to St. Maurice, much less to a black St. Maurice, nor is there any mention of Maurice in any aspect of the building. The church is dedicated to St. George, a very white saint, while the heraldic banner woven by nineteenth-century Herefordshire ladies, and proudly displayed in the nave, is careful to portray the saint in the window as a saint most properly white. Thus does history get stood upon its head.

Now it cannot be proved that Brinsop Church was originally dedicated to St. Maurice, nor that the black saint in the east window is an echo of the black Maurice of Magdeburg. But the contrary cannot be proved either, the records being lost, and we are simply left with the anonymous face of a black saint. So much, after all, has gone beyond recall. The churches of medieval Herefordshire, like others elsewhere, have many Crusaders' effigies; seldom or never can any name be assigned to them. One certain fact at Brinsop is that the saint in the east window has a completely black face, even though his features have long since blurred away. Another certain fact is that the blackness of this saint, in racist times, has been utterly ignored, just as if it were not there at all.

Now, a black St. Maurice could in no way have shocked or astonished the congregations of the Middle Ages, as so many black icons are there to show. But in racist times any such icon became unthinkable; and the unthinkability continues. Even the devotedly conscientious Nicolaus Pevsner, in the Herefordshire volume of his monumental *Buildings of England,* has nothing to say on the subject. Having examined every feature of Brinsop Church with his always exacting care and expertise, Pevsner passes in silence over the blackness of the saint in question, and simply notes that Brinsop's east window has panels of medieval glass, depicting "especially a St. George." St. George, that is, with a black face—and yet no comment. Pevsner himself was not, of course, a racist; on the contrary, he was a refugee from racism in Nazi Germany. On this occasion he was simply reflecting, however unconsciously, the racist culture of the times in which he lived and in which we still live. That is another small example of how racism has been a weapon, even when innocently used, to stand history upon its head.

Bernal's book is an attempt, a major attempt, to help old history back upon its feet again so that we may better understand later history and our own history. It is a profoundly liberating work because it cuts through the murk of racism, academic or otherwise, that has obscured and confused our conceptions of intercontinental history, just as racism, consciously or not, does this still. I hope that Bernal's book will be very widely read and pondered. One need not consent to everything advanced by this remarkable author. One can find some of his arguments insufficient, and some of his arrows wrongly aimed. His is a book to argue with as well as to agree with; and it is indeed in this sense that he tells us he has written it. But his main target—*that* he strikes with powerful and unfaltering skill.

THE CURSE OF COLUMBUS

I

THE MAN HIMSELF SEEMS TO HAVE BEEN DRIVEN BY AN OVERWEENING personal ambition and a truly monstrous greed, as strange and violent in character as the ends he sought and the adventures he invited. His cautious biographer in the *Encyclopaedia Britannica* explains that the "discoverer" of the Caribbean possessed a mind that was "lofty and imaginative, and so taut that his actions, thoughts and writings do at times suggest a man just this side of the edge of insanity." But not, perhaps, so very far "this side," while in behavior this Cristóbal Colón, as he usually called himself (being in any case of dubious Genoese extraction), may stand in history as a worthy leader of the plunderers and tyrants who hastened to follow him across the seas. All this is well known, even while one need not be surprised that the five hundredth anniversary of his initial voyage should have become an occasion for rejoicing in some parts of the Americas. Here I want to look "behind Columbus" at what our world today may more widely regard as his greatest achievement: his first opening of a "New World" to be "developed" by the merciless use of chattel slaves.

Chattel slavery has to be seen from the start as inseparable from the Columbus project, and certainly in Columbus's own mind. He himself insisted that it was. "He raised crosses everywhere," recalls his encyclopaedic biographer, "but he kept his eye on the material value of things even to the extent of seeing men as goods for sale." He lost little time, moreover, in getting into the business of sending Caribbean captives back

This essay originally appeared in 1992 in *Race and Class*. Reprinted with permission.

for sale in Spain. The dates on the calendar tell the essential story and deploy its ferocious implications. Aside from the enslavement of Caribbean peoples, the enslavement of imported Africans in the Caribbean, and soon elsewhere, was in full swing within a dozen years or so. The Spanish government's earliest proclamation of laws concerned with the export of enslaved captives to the other side of the ocean—mainly, at this date, to the island of Hispaniola (Haiti and Santo Domingo)—came as early as 1501, only nine years after Columbus's first voyage. Some of these earliest victims were white: but already how many were black—were African—may be glimpsed in a complaint of 1503 sent back to Spain by the governor of Hispaniola, Nicolás de Ovando. He told the Crown that fugitive "Negro" slaves were teaching disobedience to the "Indians," and could not be recaptured. It would, therefore, be wise for the Crown to desist from sending African captives; they would only add to troubles already great enough. But the Crown, naturally, did no such thing. Even by now, there was too much money at stake.

These early slaves, like others later on, proved incurably rebellious. Huge African revolts shook island after island, and the records are copiously eloquent on the incapacity of settlers and garrisons to put them down. Never mind—the project set moving by Columbus continued to prosper. In 1515 there came the first shipment of slave-grown West Indian sugar back to Spain, and three years later, another date to be remembered, the first cargo of captives from Africa to be shipped to the West Indies, not by way of Spain or Portugal (then under the same Crown), but directly from an African port of embarkation. With this, the long-enduring and hugely profitable "triangular trade" had its inception: trade goods from Europe to Africa for the purchase of captives from African merchants; purchased captives sold into enslavement across the ocean; and sugar (chiefly, sugar) back to Europe. Such was the potent value of this trade that millions of African captives would be dispatched along that *via dolorosa*, and centuries would pass before it could be stopped.

In this perspective, then, Columbus was the father of the slave trade to the Americas; and this trade, far more than any other consequence attached to his name, may be seen—it seems to me without the least manipulation of the evidence—as composing the true and enduring curse of Columbus. Should Columbus then be seen, as well, as the father of the racism which was to excuse or justify this massive work of enslavement? Was this racism of the slave trade in any case a new thing, or was it simply an elaboration of earlier justifications for medieval forms of bondage? When can one say, with some solidity of judgment, that racism in the modern sense—the plain and directly instrumental sense of crude exploitation—actually began? The argument here is that it began with the early consequences of Columbus.

Of course, slavery was nothing new in Europe; far from it. In medieval Europe it had long depended on supplies of captives from pre-Christian Slav lands and then from Muslim lands in northern Africa or farther east; and, at least in Mediterranean Europe, a trade in captives was both permanent and pervasive. Papal prohibitions on the enslaving of Christians made little difference, and the Genoese were not the only Europeans in the business to shrug off excommunication for persisting in the trade of selling Christians. It remains that none of this slavery was chattel slavery, mass slavery, plantation slavery; rather, it took the form of what may perhaps be called "wageless labor"—coerced, but in no way subject to any kind of "market law." Slaves were bought and sold after their capture, and prices varied with the times, but a market in wages had still to come into existence. Demand was overwhelmingly for domestic labor of one kind or another and, in general, only the rich and privileged could afford to buy and maintain this labor. This was a slavery that could involve great pain and misery, but rather seldom was it a hopeless Calvary: the relatively high cost of slaves helped to limit the persecutions they were otherwise liable to suffer.

The point is worth emphasis. Throughout the High Middle Ages (roughly, the tenth through the thirteenth centuries), in S. D. Goitein's authoritative summary, slavery "was neither industrial nor agricultural. With the exception of the armies, which were largely composed of mercenaries who were legally slaves, it was not collective but individual. It was a personal service in the widest sense of the word, which, when the master served was of high rank or wealthy, carried with it great economic advantages as well as social prestige. . . . In and out of bondage, the slave was a member of the family."[1] No doubt there were exceptions, but I am not concerned with exceptions here; I am concerned with the general run of things. I have read quite a few accounts of plantation slavery in the Caribbean, most lately the horrible and revolting memoirs of Thomas Thistlewood, and I have found in them nothing that remotely resembles the domestic slavery of medieval times.

If that was the general situation in lands around the Mediterranean, it was just as true of tropical African lands farther south. Absorbed into extended-family structures, slaves in Africa—and, here again, the records are copious and unequivocal—could expect with a fair confidence to accede to full family rights without long delay. They could marry into their owner's families. They could inherit their owner's wealth. They could make careers in the public service; and wherever slaves acquired

military training, armaments, and corresponding disciplines or connections, they could (and quite often did) seize state power, govern as kings,
and even found dynasties of kings. I am not here putting in a good word
for slavery, any more than for dynasties of kings. I am only emphasizing
the differences between modes of enslavement. Not surprisingly, these
different modes gave rise to different ways of thinking about slaves—to
different ideologies, as the academics would say.

In Spain and Portugal, for example, there was also a large number of
slaves before the New World was discovered by Columbus. But there
were very few chattel slaves, and no sensible owner would have considered that his or her slaves were of a naturally and inherently inferior kind
of human being. There was, in short, no ideology of instrumentalist
racism. By the fifteenth century most such slaves in Iberia were from
North Africa. They lived hard lives, and yet, so far as the evidence goes,
a good deal less hard than the "free workers" who toiled alongside them.
"Slaves—as all servants—of wealthy and powerful men were [in those
times] better off materially, and before the courts, than were free labourers. If their work was not domestic"—tied to the home, that is—"they
might travel the country or live apart from their masters"; sometimes they
could benefit, if they wished (and it is not at all clear that many would
have wished), from early manumission.[2] The point here, may I be allowed
to insist, is that this was a servitude, however much otherwise to be
deplored, which did not foster, because it did not have to foster, the
ideology that slaves were slaves because they belonged to an inherently
inferior humanity, to a humanity, as it was going to develop in the
mentality of the slave trade, that could be "set apart" as being barely
human at all. To grasp the nature of the medieval relationship of bondage,
as it appears generally to have been, one can usefully study the medieval
iconography of slaves, including slaves from Africa. They are seen and
shown as servants like other servants, but valuable servants, costly servants, even cherished servants. They were no more inherently inferior
than they were easily expendable.[3]

II

Was there, then, no racism before the major onset of the Atlantic
slave trade? It is a teased issue because the words in general use are vague,
but overall the answer is in the negative. There was vast misunderstanding, gross abuse, bewildered superstition. But there was no racism in the

instrumentalist sense in which the term is rightly used today. Broadly, in those days when the "known world" was so very small and narrow, human deviation from the norm was believed to grow with physical distance (yet is it, really, so very different today?). Neighbors were entirely "normal" and "nondeviant," even if distrusted or disliked. Near-neighbors might also be fairly normal. But peoples far away began to become exceedingly strange until, as imagined distance widened, they altogether ceased to be human like you and me. The locus classicus of this view of life is probably a passage in the histories of Herodotus (ca. 450 B.C.) where he relates that "Aristeas, son of Caystrobius, a native of Marmora" in nearby Asia Minor (Turkey today) "journeyed to the country of the Issedones." These lived a long way off, but were still reasonably human. Yet "beyond the Issedones live the one-eyed Arismaspians," clearly deviant in having only one eye apiece, "and beyond them the griffins who guard the gold"; and the griffins, whatever exactly they may have been, were obviously much more than deviant.[4] So it was, in medieval times, that distant peoples were confidently reported as "having heads that grow beneath their shoulders," or a single eye in the middle of their chests, or, if they were women—as the Florentine Malfante was reporting back from the central Sahara in 1447—as being able to habitually produce up to five children at a birth. In those times, when the earth was so flat that you could risk falling off the edge, anything was possible.

Such beliefs seem to have been universal in one form or another, and they long persisted among peoples beyond the reach of the "known world." Less than half a century ago, for instance (but the instances are many), the Lugbara of Uganda (numbering then some 200,000 souls) were found to believe in all good faith that people became hostile, strange, and "upside down" in the measure that they dwelt farther away or far from the Lugbara homeland. Of the most distant strangers known to the Lugbara, even if known only by hearsay, there were creatures who habitually walked on their heads or hands, and indulged in other habits which the Lugbara thought perverse and wicked.[5] Distance multiplied deviation; and all this bespoke customary superstition, distrust of foreigners, various onslaughts of xenophobia, and so on. But it did not bespeak racism.

The transition from beliefs such as this to all that superstructure of instrumentalist justification of mass enslavement, of racist enslavement, which began with the Columbian voyages was an often complex and contradictory process in the European mind. But it can first be seen at work in the case of the Portuguese, if only because their active involvement in mass enslavement, plantation enslavement, came at least half a century, or even longer, before that of other European peoples (in some

degree with the exception of the Spanish). Beginning with the import of
a few hundred trans-Saharan captives (mostly Berbers of the desert) in
the 1440s, they found a home market which rapidly demanded more.
These early African captives were sold on the open Iberian market for the
most part as domestic servants who would also, if they revealed a talent
for learning and literacy, serve as clerks and trusted commercial agents.
Their small numbers in the fifteenth century were merely added to the
much larger number already in the country and in Spain, and their arrival
called for no rethinking of Portuguese attitudes to the status and condition of slavery.

But all this changed after 1500, and so did much else. The earth would
soon cease to be flat, the stars no longer hang fixed immutably in space,
and even the sun would stop revolving and stand still, until much that
yesterday had seemed sacred and unquestionable was due to be thrust
aside, forgotten, or derided. Ferocious times lay ahead such as even the
Middle Ages, with its racks and thumbscrews, had not envisaged, and
whole continents would feel their impact and bleed from their destruc-
tions. This is the context of that elusive ideological transition to the
mentalities of the slave trade and plantation slavery. It is reported, for
example, that the first auction of African captives imported into Portugal
in the 1440s "was interrupted by the common folk, who were enraged at
seeing the separation of families of slaves."[6] All such attitudes were
rapidly swept away, and every humanist reaction was engulfed in a rising
tide of greed. On all this the records are unrelievedly grim. Of the
Portuguese who were looting India, wrote in 1545 the Christian missionary who was to become St. Francis Xavier, "there is here a power which
I may call irresistible, to thrust men into the abyss where, besides the
seductions of gain and the easy chance of plunder, their appetites for gain
will be sharpened by having tasted it."

The New World, beginning with the Caribbean, already lay in the pain
of that abyss by 1545, and there were men in Europe, peering over its edge
into what they saw below, who were shocked into protest. Merchants in
Portugal and Spain—and, afterward, merchants elsewhere as well, above
all in England and France—had now to deal with the pricks of an uneasy
conscience at the consequences of their booming trade in chattel slaves.
The polemics of the time are clear on that; but they are also clear that
ideological balm was quickly found and applied. And in this process, in
this "transition," one may see how and where the bedevilments of racism
now began.

III

THE ARGUMENTS USED TO JUSTIFY THE MASS REDUCTION OF CAPTURED
Africans to the subhuman status of chattel enslavement show a clear
trajectory of moral degradation. These arguments began in the Most
Catholic Kingdoms of Spain and Portugal as presenting a means of
spreading Christianity, of giving the means of salvation to pagans otherwise condemned, ineluctably, to the fires of hell. It could not be long, of
course, before this kind of evangelism was lost in the verbiage of hypocrit-
ical claptrap; and this claptrap was to echo down the years until it reached
its deafening chorus in the writings of Liverpool and Bristol merchants of
the 1770s. But it was meager stuff at best, and almost from the start it was
seen that something more was needed if the slave trade was not to be
threatened by abolition.

These captives, it was therefore soon being said, were fitted for enslavement because they lacked the capacities to know and use freedom:
they belonged in truth to an inferior sort of humanity; in short, they were
"primitives" whom it was practically a mercy to baptize and enslave. Even
before the middle of the fifteenth century, the Portuguese royal chronicler Zurara was able to assure the court in Lisbon that West Africans then
being imported were "sinful, bestial, and, because of that, naturally servile."[7] And with *this* application of the idea that "distance widens deviation from the norm," there appeared and rapidly flourished all that
farrago of disgusting nonsense that was to take shape as the ideology of
racism, whether in high-minded academic "explanations" or the yobbery
of saloon-bar gossip.

No doubt this ideology of justification for doing to blacks what Christianity and law alike forbade Europeans to do to whites came in many
ingenuities and subtleties of gloss. There is no need in these pages to
enlarge upon them. The point here is that the ideology of this justification
grew and developed in the measure that the overseas slave trade from
Africa became enlarged from a trickle to a flood. After that, moreover, it
was enlarged again when the overseas slave trade, in itself the product of
a protocolonial relationship between Europe and Africa, was transformed
into the imperialism of the nineteenth century. Racism had been useful
to the justification of mass enslavement. It was to be still more useful to
the justification of invading and dispossessing Africans in their own lands,
Africans at home, at a time when invading and dispossessing Europeans
in their own lands, Europeans at home, was stridently deplored as an act

of barbarism. Everyone knows this now, even if they seldom like to admit to knowing it, and there is again no need for me to insist upon the point. But I would like to look a little further into those crucial years when the "racism" of superstition, of "deviance," became transformed into the racism—without quotation marks—of hard cash.

I V

WHEN, IN 1603, KING JAMES VI OF SCOTLAND AND I OF ENGLAND FOLLOWED Elizabeth to the throne of what was not yet Britain (insofar, that is, as "Britain" has ever become a cultural reality), it could not be said that the English were a racist people. As it happened, they were not even a particularly superstitious people in the sense that superstition feeds racism; after the 1540s, the Reformation had increasingly seen to that. They were going to become a racist people in the fullest "hard cash" meaning of the term, but that was going to take some time to happen. The case of *Othello,* surely one of Shakespeare's greatest plays, is there to suggest some of the complexities along this route of transition. Written in 1603 or 1604, just when the Elizabethan age was passing away, *Othello* was played to London audiences for whom the slave trade in captives seized in Africa— to the extent that those audiences could have been aware of the trade— was the work and monopoly of England's mortal enemies Spain and Portugal (the latter being then part of the Spanish realm). It was not a trade in which English venturers, then, can have wished to have any but a marginal or purely piratical part. But times were changing.

England would become expansionist, would carve out colonies in the Caribbean, would embark upon the slave trade, would eventually become the greatest slaving power of all. And for all this, the necessary mental transitions were already under way. This is what we see and hear in *Othello.* The play itself, as C. L. R. James used rightly to insist, is in no substance a racist play, and to see it as such is to have misunderstood the motives of the drama, motives concerned above all with careerism, distrust of foreigners, and sexual jealousy: the "classic" motives, in short, of the Elizabethan theater when dramatizing the frailties of humankind. Yet the motives of racism have already edged their way into the scenario. Othello is the mighty general of the armies of the Republic of Venice, and entrusted by the rulers of Venice with the defense of their interests and empire in the Mediterranean Sea. Even the traitorous Iago has to admit "the Moor—howbeit that I endure him not—is of a constant loving noble

nature." And while Iago dies as a despised traitor, Othello meets—at least
in the Elizabethan view—a most honorable death. But the Moor's features
and physique are nonetheless made to serve Iago's purpose. Racism is on
the way and, in England, will begin to flourish within less than half a
century.

A. C. de C. M. Saunders is entirely right when he says in his most useful
book (to which I would like to draw attention here) that "the introduction
of black slaves into Portugal marks a turning point in the history of
slavery." It marks this turning point not because that introduction, in
itself, brought anything new to the scene. It does so because it led directly,
and within a handful of years, to the massive export of captives from
Africa for chattel enslavement in the Americas. And this was made possible, in turn, because Christopher Columbus had "discovered America."
That is why this "history of slavery" is, no less, the history of modern
imperialism, for without the slave trade, the "conquests" across the Atlantic must soon have withered for lack of the labor to exploit them. Without
mass enslavement, in short, there would have been no transatlantic European empires save for the initial looting and sacking of material wealth.
The track followed by the maturity of capitalism would have been a
different one, and very conceivably a less ruthless and destructive one.

Anyone who cares to toil through the archives of the partition of Africa,
and its consequences after 1900, when that partition was made more or less
complete, will soon find reason to ponder all this. For the partition of
Africa and other such activities in the history of modern imperialism all
lead back to the birth of an instrumentalist racism. The dead hand of
Columbus, clutching in its icy grasp the "certainties" of white superiority
in one guise or another, and therefore the destinies of black subjection, is
there to shake its ghastly warning as surely as did Banquo's ghost at
Macbeth's triumphal feasting and to evoke Macbeth's response:

> *Avaunt, and quit my sight! Let the earth hide thee!*
> *Thy bones are marrowless, thy blood is cold . . .*

And yet we know with what malignant power the bones and blood of this
racism could operate. Calling up this Banquo's ghost at the festivities in
celebration of Columbus may be tactless, even in poor taste. Yet I have
the hope that some awareness of the curse that Columbus labored to lay
upon humankind may occur at this time, and induce—what shall I say—a
certain sobriety, even a sense of shame.

Notes

THINKING ABOUT AFRICA

1. Edward W. Said, *Culture and Imperialism* (New York: Knopf; London: Chatto and Windus, 1993), pp. xiii and *passim*.

2. Basil Davidson, "Ideology and Society," in Hamza Alavi and Teodor Shanin, eds., *Introduction to the Sociology of "Developing Societies"* (London and New York: Macmillan, 1982), p. 450.

3. Bishop William George Tozer, *Pastoral Letters* (Zanzibar: U.M.C.A., 1904), p. 189.

4. W. W. Rostow, *The Stages of Economic Growth: A Non-Communist Manifesto* (Cambridge: Cambridge University Press, 1968), pp. 4ff.

5. I am borrowing here, I hope without misrepresenting him, from Bloch's *Apologie pour l'Histoire* (Paris: Armand Colin, 1967), pp. 9ff.

6. L. Mottoulle, *Politique sociale de l'Union Minière . . .* (Brussels: Institut Royal Colonial Belge, 1946), p. 5.

7. Shula Ramon, "Man and his Shadow: Models of Normality and Non-Normality," in Teodor Shanin, ed., *The Rules of the Game* (London, 1972), p. 110.

8. John Middleton, "Witchcraft and Sorcery in Lugbara," in Middleton and E. H. Winter, eds., *Witchcraft and Sorcery in East Africa* (London: Routledge and Kegan Paul, 1963), pp. 257ff.

9. S. D. Goitein, *A Mediterranean Society,* Vol. 1: *Economic Foundations* (Berkeley: University of California Press, 1967), pp. 130ff.

10. Baker's writings are full of such remarks; this gem is from his *Albert Nyanza* (London: Macmillan, 1898), p. 153.

11. I owe much to Robin Horton's writings on the Kalabari, as do all Africanists. See, e.g., "The Kalabari World View: An Outline and Interpretation," *Africa* (quarterly) XXXII, no. 2 (1962).

12. J. B. King, in *Journal of the Royal Geographical Society* (London), 1844, p. 260; quoted here from E. Isichei, *The Ibo People and the Europeans* (London: Faber and Faber, 1973), p. 81.

13. Roberto Battaglia, *La Prima Guerra d'Africa* (Turin: Einaudi, 1958), pp. 123–24.

CLAIMS

THE SEARCH FOR AFRICA'S PAST

1. For critical references on one side or the other of this claim, see comments and notes in Bruce Williams, "Forebears of Menes in Nubia: Myth or Reality?," *Journal of Near Eastern Studies* 46, no. 1 (1987).

2. I have discussed these matters at length in *The African Genius* (Boston, 1969); U.K. title: *The Africans* (London, 1969). There is a rich bibliography; its European aspects are best explored in E. H. Kantorowicz, *The King's Two Bodies* (Princeton, 1957), *passim*.

3. M. W. Young, "The Divine Kingship of the Jukun," *Africa* XXXVI, no. 2 (1966).

4. See S. D. Goitein, *A Mediterranean Society*, Vol. 1: *Economic Foundations* (Berkeley, 1967), *passim*.

5. See E. Lévi Provençal, *Histoire de l'Espagne Musulmane*, vol. 3 (Paris, 1967), pp. 243 and *passim*.

6. My debt to the masterworks of Marc Bloch will be obvious. See especially some of his papers published in *Land and Work in Mediaeval Europe* (*Mélanges Historiques* in the original) (London, 1967), notably in this connection, "The Problem of Gold in the Middle Ages." I was able to dramatize some of these ideas about the importance of medieval gold in my TV series of 1984 entitled *Africa* (no. 3 of the series).

AFRICA AND THE INVENTION OF RACISM

1. Even a summary list of relevant works would be immensely long; here I offer an introductory guide.

The written sources bearing on Africa before and around 1600 are copious in Arabic and several European languages. As to the Arabic sources, many remain in need of publication or of retranslation, but a notable beginning has been made by a number of authors in French and English, and lately sponsored by the International Academic Union with its *Fontes Historiae Africanae (Series Arabica)* under the general direction of J. O. Hunwick; while 1981 saw the publication of its *Corpus of Early Arabic Sources for West African History* (Cambridge University Press) with English translations of sixty-five authors down to al-Maqqari (b. Tlemcen, 1591; d. Cairo, 1632). For al-Masudi, a precious (Cairene) source for East African history in the tenth century (A.D.), we now have Charles Pellat's admirable revision of an earlier French translation of al-Masudi's only surviving work: *Les Prairies d'Or*, 2 vols. (Paris: C.N.R.S., 1982). For the Cordoban annalist al-Bakri (uniquely valuable for the history of the Western Sudan down to the 1060s, non-Arabists must still rely on a French translation of 1913 reprinted by Maisonneuve, Paris, 1965; and the same is true for two great chronicles completed in Timbuktu in the 1650s, *Tarikh al-Sudan* and *Tarikh al-Fattash*, trans. Houdas, reprinted by Maisonneuve, 1964, for the first, and Houdas and Delafosse likewise for the second, also reprinted in 1964. An entirely new English translation and scholarly edition of the *Tarikh al-Sudan* will soon (1994) be available from J. O. Hunwick, Evanston, Ill. Of al-Wazzan ("Leo Africanus"), Ramusio's 1550 version of his *Description of Africa* (in Italian) became available in 1978 in vol. 1 of a superb series published by Einardi, Turin; there is also a sound French translation by Epaulard, published by Maissonneuve, Paris, 1956. These and other such works provide essential starting points.

For European sources down to 1600 (and indeed after), a few excellent anthologies may be mentioned, notably Hodgkin, *Nigerian Perspectives*, rev. ed. (Oxford, 1975), and Fyfe, *Sierra Leone Inheritance* (Oxford, 1964); and perhaps I may add my own anthology, *The African Past: Chronicles from Antiquity to Modern Times* (London: Longman, 1964; Trenton,

N.J.: Africa World Press, 1991). Indispensable for the early "contact period" is a whole list of reports and memoirs published in English by the Hakluyt Society, London, notably a collection edited by Blake, *Europeans in West Africa, 1450–1560,* 2 vols. (London, 1942); and to these should be added Mauny's seminal inquiry into the maritime possibilities of that period, entitled *Les Navigations mediévales sur les Côtes sahariennes Antérieures à la Découverte portugaise (1434)* (Lisbon: Centro de Estudos Históricos Ultramarinos, 1960).

For the importance of the African gold trade and its consequences, the right beginning is with Goitein's pathfinding studies of the Jewish trading documents of Fatimid Cairo (the so-called Geniza Archive), notably *A Mediterranean Society,* vol. 1: *Economic Foundations* (Berkeley: University of California Press, 1967), where the significance of the *dinar* minted from West African gold is explored in riveting detail. For consequences in Western Europe, see Marc Bloch's "Problem of Gold in the Middle Ages," repr. in *Land and Work in Medieval Europe: Selected Papers,* with English trans. by Anderson (London: Routledge, 1967); beyond which, especially for the sixteenth century, there are valuable commentaries in Braudel, *La Méditerranée et le Monde méditerranéan,* 2 vols. (Paris: Colin, 1966).

Correspondence between sixteenth-century kings of Portugal and Kongo was published in Lisbon in 1877: Visconde de Paiva-Manso, *História do Congo (Documentos);* while the famous *regimento* of 1512 will be found in various books, including Cuvelier's *L'Ancien Royaume de Congo* (Brussels: Brouwer, 1946). Most of Ultzheimer's writings appear to have perished long since, but such as we have (initially printed in 1878–79) is to hand in Andrea Josua Ultzheimer, *Warhaffte Beschreibung Ettlicher Reisen....* (Tübingen and Basel: Erdmann, 1971). Vasco da Gama's logbook is readily available in an English trans. by Ravenstein (London: Hakluyt Society, 1898); while Duarte Barbosa is similarly available in English trans. by Dames, 2 vols. (London: Hakluyt Society, 1918).

We now have several good surveys of Swahili civilization, above all John Middleton's *World of the Swahili* (New Haven: Yale University Press, 1992), and a few indispensable archaeological surveys, notably Chittick's *Kilwa,* 2 vols. (Nairobi: British Institute in Eastern Africa, 1974) while the best general account of the Zimbabwe Culture now available is Garlake's *Great Zimbabwe* (London: Thames and Hudson, 1973).

2. The page references in my essay refer, in order, to:

C. Meillassoux, "The Role of Slavery in the Economic and Social History of Sahelo-Sudanic Africa," in J. E. Inikori, ed., *Forced Migration* (London: Hutchinson, 1982).

M. A. Zouber, *Ahmad Baba de Tombouctou: Sa Vie et Son Oeuvre* (Paris: Maisonneuve et Larose, 1977).

H. Kjekshus, *Ecology Control and Economic Development in East African History* (London: Heinemann, 1977).

M. Bloch, *supra.*

F. Braudel, *supra.*

W. E. von Eschwege, *Journal von Brasilien* (Weimar, 1818).

C. L. R. James, " 'Othello' and 'The Merchant of Venice,' " *Spheres of Existence: Selected Writings* (London: Alison and Busby, 1980).

RESCUING AFRICA'S HISTORY

1. *The Historian in Tropical Africa:* Studies presented and discussed at the Fourth Seminar of the International African Institute, Dakar, 1961. Edited by J. Vansina, R. Mauny, and L. V. Thomas (Oxford, 1964), p. 27.

2. R. G. Collingwood, *The Idea of History* (Oxford, 1946), p. 53.

3. Quoted in Eric Williams, *British Historians and the Caribbean* (Port-of-Spain, 1964), p. 131.

4. R. Coupland, *Kirk on the Zambezi* (Oxford, 1928), p. 3.

5. W. Y. Adams, "Post-Pharaonic Nubia," *Journal of Egyptian Archaeology* 50, p. 114; "An Introductory Classification of Meroitic Pottery," *Kush* 12, p. 126.

6. ———, "An Introductory Classification of Christian Nubian Pottery," *Kush* 10, p. 115.

7. *Annales d'Ethiopia*, vols. for 1955 on. For an authoritative but concise statement of the present position, consult J. Leclant, "Frühäthiopische Kultur," *Christentum am Nil*, International Arbeitstagung zur Austellung "Koptische Kunst" (Essen, 1963).

8. G. Camps, *Aux Origines de la Berbérie: Monuments et Rites funéraires protohistoriques* (Paris, 1961).

9. M. G. Smith, "The Beginnings of Hausa Society, AD 1000–1500," in *The Historian in Tropical Africa*, p. 339.

10. Y. Person, "En Quête d'une Chronologie ivoirienne," in *The Historian in Tropical Africa*, p. 322.

11. J. D. Clark, "The Prehistoric Origins of African Culture," *Journal of African History* 2 (1964), p. 181.

12. R. G. Armstrong, *The Study of West African Languages* (Ibadan, 1964).

13. Reprinted in E. E. Evans-Pritchard, *Essays in Social Anthropology* (London, 1962), p. 23.

14. *Ibid.*, p. 64.

15. E. H. Carr, *What Is History?* (London, 1961), p. 114.

16. Clark, *loc. cit.*

17. F. Hintze, *Studien zur Meroitischen Chronologie* (Berlin, 1959), p. 24. See also F. Hintze, "Nubien und Sudan—ihre Bedeutung für die alte Geschichte Afrikas," Festbrief in *Spektrum*, Mitteilungsblatt für die Mitarbeiter der Deutschen Akademie der Wissenschaften zu Berlin, 1964.

18. For relevant C-14 datings, consult lists compiled by B. M. Fagan, *Journal of African History* 2, no. 1; 4, no. 1; and 6, no. 1.

19. al-Idrisi, *Kitab Nuzhat al-Mushtag fi'Khtiraq al-Afaq*, trans. S. Maqbul Ahmad (Leiden, 1960), p. 13.

20. H. F. C. Smith, "The Islamic Revolutions of the 19th Century," *Journal of the Historical Society of Nigeria* 2, no. 2, p. 176.

21. S. J. Patel, "Economic Transition in Africa," *Journal of Modern African Studies* 1, no. 3, p. 319.

AFRICANISM AND ITS MEANINGS

1. Ajala, Adekunle. *Pan-Africanism: Evolution, Progress, and Prospects.* London, 1973.

Davidson, Basil. *Africa in History.* 385. Rev. ed. London, 1984.

Dike, K. Onwuka. *Trade and Politics in the Niger Delta.* Oxford, 1956.

Elias, T. Olawale. *The Nature of African Customary Law.* xii + 318. Manchester, 1956.

Greenberg, J. H. "The Languages of Africa." *International Journal of American Linguistics* 29, no. 1 (January 1963)

Hayford, J. E. Casely. In M. J. Sampson. *The West African Leadership.* Ilfracombe, England, 1951.

Hegel, G. W. F. *The Philosophy of History.* New York, 1944, p. 99.

Kouyaté, T. G. Letter to W. E. B. Du Bois, dated April 29, 1929, quoted here from J. Ayodele Langley, *Pan-Africanism and Nationalism in West Africa.* Oxford, 1972, p. 312. Kouyaté himself died in Nazi-occupied France during the Second World War in circumstances never sufficiently explained.

Levtzion, N., and J. F. P. Hopkins. *Corpus of Early Arabic Sources for West African History.* Cambridge, 1981.

Mokhtar, G., ed. *UNESCO General History of Africa.* Vol. 2. London and Berkeley, 1981.

Montgomery, James. *Poetical Works of* . . . Vol. 1. London, 1841, p. 177.

Ogot, B. A. *History of the Southern Luo.* Vol. 1: *Migration and Settlement 1500–1900.* Nairobi, 1967.

Proceedings of the First International Congress of Africanists, 1962. Edited by Lalage Bown and Michael Crowder. ix + 369. London, 1964.

Seligman, C. G. *The Races of Africa.* London, 1930.

Thompson V. Bakpetu. *Africa and Unity: The Evolution of Pan-Africanism.* xix + 412. London, 1969.

Vansina, J. *De la Tradition Orale,* Annales du Musée Royal de l'Afrique Centrale, Sciences Humaines No. 36, 1961. English ed., *Oral Tradition.* London, 1965.

ANTIPATHIES

THE ROOTS OF ANTIAPARTHEID

1. Benson, M. *The African Patriots.* London: Faber and Faber, 1963.

Bulletins of Statistics (and *South African Statistics*), South African Government Printing Office, relevant years.

Bunting, B. *The Rise of the South African Reich.* Harmondsworth and Baltimore: Penguin, 1964; rev. ed., 1969.

Davidson, B. *Report on Southern Africa,* London: Jonathan Cape, 1952.

———. *Africa in Modern History.* London: Lane/Penguin, 1978.

Kadalie, C. *My Life and the ICU.* London: Cass, 1970.

Karis, T., and G. Carter, *From Protest to Challenge: A Documentary History of African Politics in South Africa.* Vol. 2. Stanford: Hoover Institution, 1973.

Luthuli, A. *Let My People Go.* London: Collins, 1962.

Mbeki, G. M. *South Africa: The Peasants' Revolt.* London and Baltimore: Penguin, 1964.

Oosthuizen, O. O. *A Guide to Politics for Young and Old.* Pretoria: United Party, 194?.

Simons, H. J. and R. E. *Class and Colour in South Africa, 1850–1950.* Harmondsworth and Baltimore: Penguin, 1969.

Smit, D. L., et al., *Report of the Inter-Departmental Committee on the Social, Health, and Economic Condition of Urban Natives.* Pretoria: Government Printer, 1945.

Tingsten, H. *The Problem of South Africa.* London: Gollancz, 1955.

van der Horst, S. T. *Native Labour in South Africa.* Oxford, 1942.

Wilson M., and L. Thompson, eds. *Oxford History of South Africa, 1870–1966.* Vol. 2. Oxford: Oxford University Press, 1971.

PLURALISM IN COLONIAL AFRICAN SOCIETIES

1. Leo Kuper, "Plural Societies: Perspectives and Problems," and M. G. Smith, "Institutional and Political Conditions of Pluralism." In discussion of this paper, which I have modified at several points in the light of what was said, there repeatedly emerged a need for further work on (a) the closer definition of various types of pluralism as parts of a wider spectrum of sociopolitical typology, and (b) the possible points of transition and linkage between "conflict" models and "equilibrium" models.

2. J. S. Furnivall, *Colonial Policy and Practice* (London: Cambridge University Press, 1948), esp. p. 310.

3. For both, cf. R. Meinertzhagen, *Kenya Diary, 1902–1906* (Edinburgh: Oliver and Boyd, 1957), p. 31: In 1902 the high commissioner, Sir Charles Eliot, "envisaged a thriving colony of thousands of Europeans with their families, the whole of the country from the Aberdares and Mount Kenya to the German border [i.e., of Tanganyika] divided up into farms; the whole of the Rift Valley cultivated or grazed, and the whole country of Mumbwa, Nandi to Elgon and almost to Baringe [i.e., right across into Uganda] under white settlement. He intends to confine the natives to reserves and use them as cheap labor on farms. . . ." This striking testimony comes all the more convincingly in that it was noted at the time by a man whose aunt, Beatrice Webb, was a friend of Eliot's: Eliot was talking within the family circle. Mutatis mutandis, the same plans were made, and carried out, for Southern Rhodesia.

4. Smith, "Institutional and Political Conditions of Pluralism."

5. There are useful extracts from J. dos Santos, *Ethiopia Oriental* (Convento de S. Domingos de Evora, 1609), in Eric V. Axelson, ed., *South African Explorers* (London: Oxford University Press, 1954), p. 19.

6. A. C. P. Gamitto, *King Kazembe* (1854), trans. I. Cunnison. 2 vols. (Lisbon: Junta de Investigacões do Ultramar, 1960).

7. B. M. Fagan, *Southern Africa During the Iron Age* (London: Thames and Hudson, 1965), esp. p. 65. For latest summaries, see Fagan, "The Later Iron Age in South Africa," and D. W. Phillipson, "Early Iron-Using Peoples of Southern Africa," papers presented at the Lusaka conference on the history of southern Africa, 1968.

8. L. H. Gann, *The Birth of a Plural Society* (Manchester: Manchester University Press, 1958), p. 165: "In 1906 he [Moore] was able to start a newspaper of his own, the *Livingstone Mail*, preceded by the *Livingstone Pioneer and Advertiser*, which he subsidized from the profits of his shop. He was able to use this journal as the vehicle of his political views, and since his was the only newspaper in the country it made Moore a prominent person." This is a little ungenerous to Moore; what really made him a prominent person, newspaper or no, was the intelligence and determination of this unusual man.

9. J. W. Davidson, *The Northern Rhodesian Legislative Council* (London: Faber and Faber, 1948).

10. The best account is in the masterly review by George Shepperson and Thomas Price, *Independent African* (Edinburgh: University Press, 1958).

11. E. Roux, *Time Longer Than Rope* (London: Gollancz, 1948), pp. 161–205.

12. See R. I. Rotberg, *Christian Missionaries and the Creation of Northern Rhodesia, 1880–1924* (Princeton: Princeton University Press, 1965).

13. Recounted in L. H. Gann, *A History of Northern Rhodesia: Early Days to 1953* (London: Chatto and Windus, 1964), pp. 64, 68.

14. Kuper, "Plural Societies: Perspectives and Problems."

15. Audrey I. Richards, "The Political System of the Bemba Tribe," in M. Fortes and E. E. Evans-Pritchard, eds., *African Political Systems* (London: Oxford University Press, 1940), p. 86.

16. John D. Omer-Cooper, *The Zulu Aftermath* (London: Longmans, Green, 1966), chap. 8.

17. Smith, "Institutional and Political Conditions of Pluralism."

18. Mahmoud Kati, *Tarikh el-Fettach*, trans. O. Houdas and M. Delafosse (Paris: E. Leroux, 1913), pp. 209–10.

19. See the introductory pages to M. G. Smith, *The Plural Society in the British West Indies* (Berkeley and Los Angeles: University of California Press, 1965), esp. pp. vii–xii.

20. Text of concession treaty in Gann, *The Birth of a Plural Society*, p. 215.

21. Noted in A. J. Hanna, *The Story of the Rhodesias and Nyasaland* (London: Faber and

Faber, 1960), p. 114. Of the part played by missionaries in securing these concession treaties, there is a useful description in Rotberg, *op. cit.*, p. 21. Cf. pp. 25–26: "The Lozi felt that their country had been unfairly seized by a commercial group under the pretext of British protection. They had been prepared to become vassals of a great white queen, but the interposition of the Company had denied them such an opportunity." Not unexpectedly, "Coillard [François Coillard of the Paris Missionary Society, who had reached Lealui, the Lozi capital, in 1885, and played a crucial part in helping Lochner] was regarded as a traitor, and members of his society suffered indignities and occasional physical harm as a result of their role in helping to secure the treaty."

22. Gann, *History of Northern Rhodesia*, p. 92.

23. *Ibid.*, p. 93.

24. M. Gelfand, *Northern Rhodesia in the Days of the Charter* (Oxford: Basil Blackwell, 1961), p. 140. There is an interesting study to be made on the social composition of these and other settlers. This too had its mythology and appropriate attitudes which had their various effect. In the period between the wars it was somewhat unkindly said, in British colonial circles, that the settlement after 1918 was carried out on the principle of "Officers to Kenya, NCOs to the Rhodesias." There was possibly something in it. The Rhodesias had no Lord Delamere.

25. Census figures quoted in Gann, *The Birth of a Plural Society*, p. 175.

26. *Ibid.*, p. 166.

27. *Ibid.*, pp. 164–65.

28. Kenneth D. Kaunda, *Zambia Shall Be Free* (London: Heinemann, 1962), p. 17.

29. Hanna, *op. cit.*, p. 194.

30. *Debates of the Northern Rhodesian Legislative Council* (hereafter cited as *Legislative Council Debates*), July 20, 1927, col. 143 of appropriate volume (issued annually).

31. The "childishness" of colonized Africans was a theme rather more favored by the French and the Belgians, though the British were also impressed by it. See, for example, a Belgian Katanga veteran writing in 1946: "The colonizer must never lose sight of the fact that the Negroes have the spirits of children who are molded by the methods of the educator: they watch, listen, feel—and imitate" (L. Mottoulle, *Politique Sociale de l'Union Minière du Haut Katanga pour sa Main d'Œuvre indigène et ses résultats au cours de vingt années d'application* [Brussels: Van Campenhout, 1946], p. 5). *Sous entendu*, invariably, was the implication that the process could be nothing if not exceedingly slow.

32. *Legislative Council Debates*, June 6, 1939, col. 501.

33. *Ibid.*, March 7, 1932, col. 437.

34. Gelfand, *op. cit.*, p. 1: "So great was the loss of [European] life that at the turn of the century men in England believed that Northern Rhodesia was a black man's country only and that it would not be advisable for the European to settle there as he had in South Africa and even Southern Rhodesia. . . . [But] by the time the Colonial Office became responsible for the administration of Northern Rhodesia in 1924, it could be claimed that the European had successfully defeated the environment and that he could survive in this climate."

35. See Richard Gray, *The Two Nations* (London: Oxford University Press, 1960), and esp. chap. 2 by P. Mason on land policy in the Rhodesias and Nyasaland. The ideology of "reserves"—of removing African homes from the vicinity of African cash employment—had been well defined, in other circumstances, by the British Poor Law Commissioners in the England of 1834, who remarked: "We can do little or nothing to prevent pauperism; the farmers will have it; they prefer that the laborers should be slaves; they object to their having gardens saying: 'the more they work for themselves the less they work for us' " (*ibid.*, p. 47).

36.   A. J. Willis, *An Introduction to the History of Central Africa* (London: Oxford University Press, 1964), p. 290: "In fact the standard of living of Africans in the rural areas was declining during the inter-war period. . . . The publication of Dr. Audrey Richards' *Land, Labour and Diet in Northern Rhodesia* in 1939 revealed the decay of rural life among the Bemba.... Frequently more than half of the men would be away from the village at one time, creating an atmosphere of decay and frustration." See also G. St. J. Orde-Browne, *Labour Conditions in Northern Rhodesia* (Col. Office 150, 1938). Such statements can be generalized for the whole of settler Africa, and probably for the whole of colonial Africa, in the interwar period; see my *Which Way Africa?* (Baltimore: Penguin Books, 1967), chaps. 6, 7, for further evidence.

37.   Gray, *op. cit.*, p. 85.

38.   C. H. Thompson and H. W. Woodruff, *Economic Development in Rhodesia and Nyasaland* (London: Dobson, 1954), p. 53. I have not been able to find the figures for farms in 1936.

39.   Nor, incidentally, were their farming methods particularly inefficient. Commenting on this shifting subsistence agriculture, known as *chitemene*, the *Economic Survey of the Colonial Territories* for 1951 commented that "research has . . . so far failed to find an alternative for Chitemene methods for poorer soils which is practicable within the extremely limited resources of the cultivators" (quoted in Thompson and Woodruff, *op. cit.*, p. 54). Cf., for forest regions, a comment by soil scientists P. H. Nye and D. H. Greenland, noting that "even now, after a quarter of a century of experiment in the African tropics, we have failed to introduce to the forest regions any method of staple food production superior to the system of natural fallowing used in shifting cultivation" (*The Soil Under Shifting Cultivation*, Commonwealth Bureau of Soils, Technical Communications 51 [1960]).

40.   Gray, *op. cit.*, p. 39.

41.   See R. S. Hall, *Zambia* (London: Pall Mall, 1965), p. 259, for a good potted account of copper mining expansion.

42.   As late as 1954, Northern Rhodesian mining companies were still paying local tax at a rate of 25 percent while gold-mining companies in South Africa were paying 50 percent (see B. Davidson, *The African Awakening* [London: Jonathan Cape, 1955], p. 243).

43.   Gray, *op. cit.*, p. 133.

44.   *Ibid.*

45.   H. Kitchen, ed., *The Educated African* (New York: Praeger, 1962), p. 223.

46.   *Legislative Council Debates*, June 6, 1939, col. 501.

47.   Furnivall, *op. cit.*, p. 310.

48.   *Legislative Council Debates*, Nov. 18, 1930, col. 40.

49.   Cf. the Passfield restatement of the "doctrine of Native paramountcy" dating from 1923, and pp. 167–68, above.

50.   *Legislative Council Debates*, March 21, 1939, col. 332.

51.   Hall, *op. cit.*, p. 131.

52.   Shepperson and Price, *op. cit.*, p. 163.

53.   Gray, *op. cit.*, p. 148.

54.   *Legislative Council Debates*, March 13, 1931, col. 7.

55.   In this context it is worth looking at the *Report* of the Royal Commission of Rhodesia and Nyasaland, under Lord Bledisloe, which inquired into the state of opinion regarding amalgamation, and published its findings in 1939 (Cmd. 5949 of that year).

56.   *Legislative Council Debates*, May 4, 1936, cols. 70–71.

57.   J. Lewin, *The Colour Bar in the Copper Belt* (Johannesburg: South African Institute of Race Relations, 1941), p. 4.

58.   *Ibid.*

59. *Ibid.*

60. B. Davidson, *Report on Southern Africa* (London: Jonathan Cape, 1952), pp. 249–50. Average African underground wages in 1953 had become 130s. 5d., and wages for surface work, 119s. 7d., an enormous increase over figures quoted for 1940 by Lewin, *op. cit.*, and Thompson and Woodruff, *op. cit.*, p. 73.

61. In discussion of this paper it was argued that the pluralist structure of Northern Rhodesia, in order to become fully meaningful, would have to include many extraterritorial influences and pressures behind all its communities, whether European, African, Indian, or Colored.

62. *Legislative Council Debates,* Nov. 18, 1930, col. 30.

63. Charles Dickens, *Bleak House* (London: Oxford University Press, 1948), pp. 34–37.

64. Gray, *op. cit.*, p. 5.

65. *Indians in Kenya,* Cmd. 1922 (1923), p. 10, quoted in Gray, *op. cit.*

66. *Memorandum on Native Policy in East Africa,* Cmd. 3573 (1930).

67. Kuper, "Plural Societies: Perspectives and Problems." I make here a distinction between a *system* of differential incorporation and a *society,* supposing the latter to have the organic characteristics of common values, or of evolving common values which the former does not have.

68. The UNIP was in fact the successor to another movement called the Zambian African National Congress. This had been formed in 1958 by Kaunda and his colleagues as a breakaway movement from the Northern Rhodesian African National Congress (NRANC). The reason for this breakaway was a conviction that the leadership of the NRANC had lost both courage and conviction, which later events were to confirm. By all the evidence the break had not been made without some heart searchings. In a letter to friends and supporters in London, dated December 2, 1958, Mr. Kaunda remarked: "No one denies the fact that [the ANC leader] has done something to arouse mass consciousness among the African people of Northern Rhodesia, but since the last two years it has been growing clearer every day that the two months he spent with me in Her Majesty's Hostel were more than enough for him, for he has spoken openly that he was not prepared to go to prison. . . . Other people think [he] has looked so despondent politically because he does not see how Africans could get through their present set of problems. Whichever is correct he has brought us all to a standstill . . . ," and hence a clean break was required.

69. Cf. *Voice of Zambia* for December 1963–January 1964: "It is unfortunate that although UNIP had extended the hand of friendship to the European electorate, in the result it was totally rejected, though the small majority of 121 by which Sir John Moffat [a well-known liberal for the European electorate standing on the UNIP side] was defeated shows that there was in fact considerable support for the UNIP among the Europeans. However, Dr. Kaunda has made it clear that he will not tolerate the perpetuation of a divided nation by these reserved seats [reserved, that is, for Europeans] and has declared that they will be abolished as soon as independence is achieved." There was a good deal of bitterness among UNIP supporters because the European electorate, but for the tiny handful, had vehemently rejected every chance of electoral reconciliation during the period leading up to independence.

70. Smith, "Institutional and Political Conditions of Pluralism."

71. J. K. Nyerere, *Democracy and the Party System* (Dar es Salaam, 1963), p. 15.

72. After the Southern Rhodesian rebellion of November 11, 1965, and its repercussions across the Zambezi, the enhanced recalcitrance of a part of the European minority— mainly on the Copperbelt—began to threaten an as yet fragile structure of crosscutting loyalties between Europeans and Africans; and there began to appear—unwished, it must be said, by UNIP—the old colonial situation in reverse: the situation in which one

community (now the Africans) were "the community" while the rest (now the Europeans) were outside it. It could be expected that a defeat for the rebellion would also be a defeat for this "denationalization" of the Northern Rhodesian Europeans, while the rebellion's success would probably confirm the trend.

73. Kuper, "Plural Societies: Perspectives and Problems."

74. With the appalling war that followed, however, any such outcome was clearly to be long delayed.

SYMPATHIES

1. D. K. Fieldhouse, "How Africa Lost Its Past," *Times Literary Supplement* (London), December 18, 1992.

2. For background here, see my *Black Man's Burden: Africa and the Curse of the Nation-State* (New York: Times Books; London: James Currey, 1992).

3. Fieldhouse, *loc cit.*

AFRICAN PEASANTS AND REVOLUTION

1. Angola: 481,351 square miles with an estimated approximate population in 1973 of about 5 million Africans (not counting several hundred thousand Angolan refugees in Zambia and Zaire) and 350,000 white civilians, mostly Portuguese. Guiné: 13,948 square miles with (similarly guessed) populations of 800,000 Africans and 3,000 white civilians. Mozambique: 302,328 square miles with about 8 million Africans and perhaps 200,000 white civilians.

2. By 1973 the Lisbon regime had committed to active service in these territories a total metropolitan force of about 130,000 (as well as local black and white levies). These are the largest forces ever raised in Portuguese history, and, on a per capita basis of comparison of population sizes, would be equivalent to 3,250,000 U.S. troops, or more than six times the largest U.S. army ever committed to South Vietnam.

3. If anglophone writers have seldom wished to define rural Africans as peasants, this may be because the word in English contexts refers to historical categories which have long since vanished from the English scene. One finds no such hesitation with francophone writers: with them, moreover, the word "peasant" is commonly applied to many rural French people, although it is a very long time since a French peasant's household has been "characterised by the nearly total integration of the peasant family's life with its farming enterprise." Or is it merely that definitions applied to Africans "have to be" different from those applied to Europeans, or at least to Englishmen—as, for example, with the familiar English reference to "African tribes" when writing of communities whose type and history, self-consciousness and coherence, would have long since earned them in Europe the name of "nations"?

4. I have elsewhere discussed Portuguese secondary sources for overseas history in Africa, and this is not the place to discuss primary sources, except perhaps that one should mention, as a guide to their wealth Ryder (1965), listing 997 documents housed in Lisbon and elsewhere. For recent non-Portuguese sources (with bibliographies), see especially Birmingham (1966), Boxer (1963), Duffy (1959), Wheeler (in Duffy, 1959, pt. 1), and Pélissier (1971).

5. E.g., Vansina (1966), Birmingham (1966), Wheeler (in Duffy, 1959, pt. 1), and various papers including "Origins of African Nationalism in Angola" in Chilcote, ed., 1972; and,

above all, in the matter of Euro-African interaction a pathfinding and highly relevant study of the Zambesian *prazos:* A. F. Isaacman (1972). For a recent work on the nationalist movements and their history, see Mondlane (1969), Davidson (1969a and 1972), with their bibliographies, and J. S. Saul (1973).

6. For a recent study of this attitude in a "classical" case, C. Coquéry-Vidrovitch (1972); there one may see how the French state was content to make its effort merely on behalf of concessionary companies, always provided, of course, that the cost of the effort was paid for by local taxation. The comparison with Angola is especially interesting.

7. I described the contractual system in Angola in *The African Awakening* (1955), and have since reviewed it in a general way in Davidson (1972), and bibliographies.

8. Notably in his Decree 137 of 1921; see Davidson (1972, p. 128).

9. Now, at last, beginning to be studied in detail. See, e.g., E. de S. Ferreira (forthcoming). In 1960 the proportion of *assimilados* was around 2 percent of the whole population in Angola, rather less in Mozambique, and less than 0.3 percent in Guiné. The offshore islands (Cape Verdes, Sao Thomé, and Principe) were, at least in principle, subject to a different categorization.

10. E.g., F. Nogueira (when Portuguese foreign minister during the 1960s): "We alone, before anyone else, brought to Africa the notion of human rights and racial equality. We alone practised the principle of multiracialism, which all now consider to be the most perfect and daring expression of human brotherhood and sociological progress. . . . Our African provinces are more developed, more progressive in every respect than any recently independent territory in Africa south of the Sahara, without exception" (Nogueira, 1967. pp. 154–55). One can only marvel at such verbiage, said at a time, moreover, when large parts of all three "provinces" were engulfed in war.

11. The leaders of African nationalism in these territories, or those at least who could rightly claim to be authentic, had long since grasped the nature of Portugal's weakness by the time the wars began. For them Portugal was and is in no real sense an imperialist power but only the "ideologized agent" of other and genuine imperialist powers. Thus Amílcar Cabral in 1965: "Ce qui caractérise fondamentalement de nos jours le colonialisme portugais est un fait très simple: le colonialisme portugais, ou si vous le préférez, l'infrastructure économique portugaise, ne peut pas se donner le luxe de faire du néo-colonialisme. C'est à partir de ce point que nous pouvons comprendre toute l'attitude, tout l'entêtement du colonialisme portugais envers nos peuples. Si le Portugal avait un développement économique avancé, si le Portugal pouvait être classé comme pays développé, nous ne serions sûrement pas aujourd'hui en guerre contre le Portugal" (1965, p. 152). Nothing, in short, could be hoped from Portuguese reformism save a more or less meaningless manipulation of the status quo; hence the compensation for the pains and sufferings of these wars to overthrow the status quo lies, for the nationalists, in the avoidance of a reformist "neo-colonialism."

12. That it has so spread is what the Portuguese authorities, of course, deny. Yet the whole trend over the past few years, as defined in a large body of evidence from many different and contrasting sources, stands at variance with the Portuguese claim, and not least the size of their present armed forces fighting in Africa.

13. So-called because they do not use the name itself, this being a Portuguese colonial usage borrowed from their western neighbors, the Ovimbundu. Their main components are Luvale, Luchazi, Chokwe, and Mbunda, with numerous subgroups. When immigrants in Zambia, these peoples often refer to themselves as Ma-Wiko, the "people of the west," which, when in Zambia, is what they geographically are.

14. 3° *Recenseamento Geral de Populaçao: Prov. de Angola,* Luanda, vol. 3.

15. Not to be confused with Mbundu (Ovimbundu), and still less with the Kimbundu.

16. Ministry of Colonies (1942), but written of the decades of Pôrto's experience in Angola (1847–90).

17. Based on information collected shortly before the First World War: Diniz (1918), esp. pp. 65, 84, 92.

18. Walking that way in 1970 with guerrillas of the Angolan nationalist movement, the MPLA—most of that little detachment being Mbunda—I was shown the site of the house "where Mwene Bando ruled," and it was clear, from this and other incidents, that the memory of precolonial independence was still a warm one. Here, after all, it had existed only fifty years earlier.

19. See Davidson (1969b) for extended discussion of "ancestral charters."

20. Galvão (1934 [but written in 1930], p. 303). An experienced Angolan administrator, Galvão was well qualified to know what he was talking about and, of course, had access to primary administrative sources until his opposition to the regime became active, leading to his imprisonment and later escape abroad.

21. Founded clandestinely in Luanda late in 1956.

22. In "National Liberation and Culture": address delivered at Syracuse University, Syracuse, New York, in commemoration of the late Eduardo Mondlane, the Mozambican leader who was assassinated by a parcel bomb delivered in January 1969.

23. All of them have had to contend with more or less serious crises caused by the falling away of individuals or of groups who have thought that the time had come to negotiate peace with the colonial power and get whatever minor concessions the colonial power might be ready to offer; or who have preferred a limited ethnic-group advantage, or hoped-for advantage, over national aims; or who have taken concealed service with the colonial power against promises of personal advantage. Some of these have not stopped short of assassination, as with the killing of Amílcar Cabral in January 1972, and a reportedly comparable plot against the MPLA leader, Agostinho Neto, in that same month.

24. The depth of General Spínola's political understanding may perhaps be gauged by one of his recent statements when replying to a question from a South African journalist about the origins of "guerrilla subversion in Africa." For General Spínola, it is all a question of outside machination and invasion, and goes back to the victory over the Nazi-Fascist coalition in the Second World War. "The last war," he said, "ended with the triumph of a political and social ideology which, under the guise of humanity and respect for the individual human's rights, was based on political premises deliberately extended to a mankind that, because of its cultural heterogeneity, cannot naturally assimilate it." If only Hitler had won! Quotation in Venter (1973, p. 185).

25. Formed in 1964 with an original nucleus of 900 men, this army has been much expanded since. See Davidson (1969a) for extended record and discussion.

26. The passage comes from an address delivered in Havana in 1966.

27. "My own view," he said in 1967, "is that there are no real conflicts between the peoples of Africa. There are only conflicts between their élites. When the people take power into their own hands, as they will do with the march of events in this continent, there will remain no great obstacles to effective African solidarity. Already we see in our own case how the various peoples of Guiné are finding cooperation more and more possible and useful as they free themselves from attitudes of tribal strife—attitudes that were encouraged, directly or indirectly, by colonial rule and its consequences." Quoted in Davidson (1969a, p. 139).

28. Or any implications deriving from Fanonist ideas about "the inherent virtues of violence."

29. Quoted in *Socialist Register* (London: Merlin Press, 1970), p. 237.

30. A point that would take us too far here; but consider, for example, the defections from FRELIMO in 1968–69, and the manifestly greater strength and solidarity that FRELIMO has since displayed.

31. Whether in the guerrilla-type movements of the Second World War in Europe, in China and Southeast Asia (the well-known Malayan case being the one that failed to win a widening participation, and was defeated), very obviously in Latin America, and now in the African colonies of Portugal.

32. Birmingham, D. 1966. *Trade and Conflict in Angola*. Oxford: Clarendon Press.

Boxer, C. R. 1963. *Race Relations in the Portuguese Colonial Empire 1415–1825*.

Cabral, Amílcar. 1965. *La Lutte de la Libération nationale dans les Colonies portugaises*. Algiers: CONCP.

————. 1966. Havana address.

————. 1969a. "National Liberation and Culture," address delivered at Syracuse University, Syracuse, New York.

————. 1969b. *Revolution in Guinea*. London: Stage One.

Caetano, M. 1954. *Os Nativos na Economia Africana*. Coimbra.

Chilcote, Ronald, ed. 1972. *Protest and Resistance in Angola and Brazil*. Berkeley: University of California Press.

Coquéry-Vidrovitch, Catherine. 1972. *Le Congo au temps des Grandes Compagnies Concessionaires 1898–1930*. Paris: Mouton.

Davidson, Basil. 1955. *The African Awakening*. London: Jonathan Cape.

————. 1969a. *The Liberation of Guiné*. Harmondsworth: Penguin.

————. 1969b. *The Africans*. London: Longman.

————. 1972. *In the Eye of the Storm: Angola's People*. Garden City, N.Y.: Doubleday; London: Longman.

Diniz, J. de O. Ferreira. 1918. *Populaçoes Indigenas de Angola*. Coimbra.

Duffy, J. 1959. *Portuguese Africa*. Cambridge: Harvard University Press.

Ferreira, F. de S. *Portuguese Colonialism: Its Effects on Education*. UNESCO (forthcoming).

Galvão, H. 1934. *Historio de Nosso Tempo: João de Almeida (sua obra e acção)*. Lisbon.

Isaacman, A. F. 1972. *Mozambique*. Madison: University of Wisconsin Press.

Marcum, J. 1969. *The Angolan Revolution*. Vol. 1: *The Anatomy of an Explosion 1950–1962*. Boston: MIT Press.

Ministry of Colonies. 1942. *Viagems e Apontamentos de Uma Portueunse em Africa*. Lisbon.

Mondlane, E. 1969. *The Struggle for Mozambique*. Harmondsworth: Penguin.

Nogueira, F. 1967. *The Third World*.

Pélissier, R., and D. L. Wheeler. 1971. *Angola*. New York: Praeger.

Ryder, A. F. C. 1965. *Materials for West African History in Portuguese Archives*. Institute of Historical Research, University of London.

Saul, J. S., with G. Arrighi. 1973. *Essays in the Political Economy of Africa*. New York: Monthly Review Press.

Shanin, Teodor. 1972. *The Awkward Class*. Oxford: Clarendon Press.

Vansina, J. 1966. *Kingdom of the Savanna*. Madison: University of Wisconsin Press.

Venter, A. J. 1973. *Portugal's War in Guiné-Bissau*. Pasadena: California Institute of Technology.

Verhaegen, B. 1967. *Rebellions au Congo*. Vol. 1. Brussels: C.R.I.S.P.

THE LEGACY OF AMÍLCAR CABRAL

1. Private source. If the circumstances of this necessarily clandestine congress, in its bearings on Portugal's colonies, have found publication, this is unknown to me.

2. Compare this with the development of practice and policy by EPLF, Eritrea; ZANU, Zimbabwe; ANC, South Africa; and others.

3. So much was evident, in the days immediately following the coup, from many statements of the coup makers: from their rabid accusations of Cape Verdean domination; from their initial release and acceptance of the turncoat PAIGC leader, Rafael Barbosa, who had made himself a leading tool of the colonial regime in its war against the PAIGC; from the jubilation of anti-PAIGC "circles" and groups in Lisbon and elsewhere outside the country; and from much else to the same effect. I can myself easily imagine Cabral's scalding contempt for these "new leaders" who then said, repeating the propaganda of the defeated colonial regime, that the people of Guinea-Bissau had been colonized by those of Cape Verde. I can as well picture his rage at seeing the institutions of democratic control, notably the national council of the PAIGC in Guinea-Bissau (of which the principal coup maker had long been the chairman) pushed aside and then abolished by militarist action. I can also think that Cabral would have taken, in 1978–79, certain steps that were not taken, and would have acted against other steps that were taken. For some initial discussion of the background and consequences of the November 1980 coup, see Rudebeck (1983), Dowbor (1983), and Davidson (1981, preface).

4. I can recall several conversations in which he insisted on the sincerity of that homage. It was all the more convincing because he had been well aware of Nkrumah's limitations while in power in Ghana, and admired Nkrumah's personal development during the last years of exile.

5. References:

Cabral, Amílcar. 1969a. "Brief Analysis of the Social Structure in Guiné." In selected writings, *Revolution in Guiné*. Translated by Richard Handyside. New York. Monthly Review Press.

———. 1969b. "Foreword by Amílcar Cabral." Pp. 9–15 in Basil Davidson, *The Liberation of Guiné*. Harmondsworth: Penguin.

———. 1969c. "Resistência cultural." Seminar paper at PAIGC conference of cadres, November 19–24.

———. 1971. *Our People Are Our Mountains*. (Available from MAGIC, 34 Percy Street, London W1P 9FG.)

———. 1979. *Unity and Struggle*. Translated by M. Wolfers. New York: Monthly Review Press. (Also published in London by Heinemann, 1980, and in Paris as *Unité et lutte* by Maspero, 1975, in 2 vols.)

Chaliand, Gérard. 1969. *Armed Struggle in Africa*. New York: Monthly Review Press.

Davidson, Basil. 1969. *The Liberation of Guiné*. Harmondsworth: Penguin; republished in enlarged ed., *No Fist Is Big Enough to Hide the Sky*. London: Zed, 1981.

———. 1976. "The Politics of Armed Struggle." In B. Davidson et al., eds., *Southern Africa*. London: Penguin.

———. 1978. *Let Freedom Come*. Boston: Little, Brown (Also published as *Africa in Modern History*. London: Penguin.)

———. 1981. *No Fist Is Big Enough to Hide the Sky*. London: Zed. (A republication of *The Liberation of Guiné* with additional chapters.)

Dowbor, Ladislau. 1983. *Guiné Bissau: a busca da independência económica*. São Paulo: Brasiliense.

Evans-Pritchard, E. E. 1962. *Essays in Social Anthropology.* London: Faber and Faber.

Hodgkin, T. 1981. *Vietnam: The Revolutionary Path.* New York: Macmillan.

Hydén, G. 1980. *Beyond Ujamaa in Tanzania.* London: Heinemann.

"MFA na Guiné." 1974. *Boletim Informativo* 1 (June 1).

Rudebeck, Lars. 1974. *Guinea-Bissau.* Uppsala: Scandinavian Institute of African Studies.

————. 1983. "The class basis . . . in Angola, Guinea-Bissau and Mozambique." Uppsala.

Urdang, Stephanie. 1979. *Fighting Two Colonialisms: Women in Guinea-Bissau.* New York: Monthly Review Press.

DEBATES

1. John Lonsdale, "States and Nations," *Journal of African History* 34 (1993), pp. 143–79.

2. The argument at length, and in historical detail, is in my *Black Man's Burden* (New York: Times Books; London: James Currey, 1992).

3. Lonsdale, *loc. cit.*

4. As argued in *The Black Man's Burden,* what is required are new constitutional "containers" for national consciousness.

5. In *Bulletin* of ACDESS (African Centre for Development and Strategic Studies; Ijebu Ode, Nigeria), November 1992, p. 8.

6. Adebayo Adedeji, in a statement quoted here from *West Africa* (London, weekly), November, 11, 1991.

7. In this connection I would mention, of my own work in this field, two relevant books from these years. One is Lionel Cliffe and Basil Davidson, eds., *The Long Struggle of Eritrea* (Trenton, N.J.: Africa World Press; Nottingham, England: Spokesman, 1988); the other is Basil Davidson, *The Fortunate Isles: A Study in African Transformation,* a history of the Cape Verde Islands and Republic (Trenton N.J.: Africa World Press, 1989; London: Hutchinson, 1989). The latter may be particularly useful in relation to the theory and practice of participation; see esp. app. 2, p. 205.

NATIONALISM AND ITS AMBIGUITIES

1. V. L. Grottanelli, "Sul significato della scultura africana," Lugard Memorial Lecture, 1961; repr. in *Africa,* October 1961.

2. P. Walshe, *The Rise of African Nationalism in South Africa* (London, 1970), p. 1.

3. The best short discussion of the philosophical and practical meanings of religion in Africa that is known to me is R. Horton, "African Traditional Thought and Western Science," in *Africa* XXVII, no. 2 (1967). I have reviewed the subject at some length in *The Africans* (London: Longman, 1969; Harmondsworth: Penguin, 1974). The U.S. title is, *The African Genius* (Boston: Little, Brown, 1969, and many reprints).

4. See especially, in this context J. F. A. Ajayi and M. Crowder, "West Africa 1919–1939: The Colonial Situation," in their (with other contributors) *History of West Africa,* vol. 2 (London: Longman, 1974), pp. 514ff.

5. For a detailed discussion of these forms of participation and commitment, see B. Davidson, "The Politics of Armed Struggle," in R. Segal, ed., *Southern Africa: The New Politics of Revolution* (Harmondsworth: Penguin, 1976).

6. Quoted in B. Davidson, *In the Eye of the Storm: Angola's People* (Harmondsworth: Penguin, 1974), p. 273.

7. Réunion d'Experts sur les notions de race, identité et dignité, UNESCO, Paris, July 3–7, 1972.

8. A. Cabral, "Sur le rôle de la culture dans la lutte pour l'indépendance" (UNESCO, July 1972), pp. 9 and 25.

9. Alas, all this in Somalia was swept away after 1978.

THE POLITICS OF RESTITUTION

1. W. J. Foltz, "Building the Newest Nations," in K. W. Deutsch and W. J. Foltz, eds., *Nation-Building* (New York: Atherton, 1963), p. 117.

2. Olusegun Obasanjo in address to OECD Conference, Paris, April 17, 1990.

3. For some of these, see D. Rothchild and N. Chazan, eds., *The Precarious Balance: State and Society in Africa* (Boulder and London: Westview, 1988).

4. B. Davidson, *The Black Man's Burden: Africa and the Curse of the Nation-State* (New York: Times Books, 1992), p. 258; (and London: James Currey).

5. Adebayo Adedeji, quoted here from *West Africa* (London), November 11, 1991.

6. The Asiwaju of Ijebu-Ode, in preface to *The Anglo-Ijebu War of 1892,* and *passim* (Ijebu-Ife, Nigeria: Adeyemi Press, 1992).

7. Mahmood Mamdani, "Africa: Democratic Theory and Democratic Struggles," *Dissent,* Summer 1992, p. 317.

ARGUMENTS

THE ANCIENT WORLD AND AFRICA: WHOSE ROOTS?

1. The *Histories* of Herodotus are available in English in an excellent modern translation by Aubrey de Selincourt (Harmondsworth: Penguin Books, 1954).

2. English translation in twelve volumes by C. H. Oldfather, *Diodorus of Sicily* (London: Heinemann; Cambridge: Harvard University Press, 1967).

3. J. H. Greenberg, *The Languages of Africa* (Bloomington: Indiana University Press, 1963).

4. For a useful recent summary on the Saharan Neolithic, with a large specialized bibliography, see Marianne Cornevin, "Les Néolithiques du Sahara Central et l'histoire générale de l'Afrique," *Bulletin de la Société Préhistorique Française* 79, nos. 10–12 (1982).

THE CURSE OF COLUMBUS

1. S. D. Goitein, *A Mediterranean Society,* vol. 1: *Economic Foundations* (Los Angeles, 1967), pp. 130–31.

2. A. C. de C. M. Saunders, *A Social History of Black Slaves and Freedmen in Portugal 1441–1555* (Cambridge, 1982), introduction and chap. 1 *passim.*

3. All this is made clear from an analysis of the relative costs of purchase and maintenance of slaves in medieval times, an aspect of "labor history" that is much in need of detailed synthesis. We find, for instance, that in medieval Cairo, according to Goitein *(op. cit.)* working from contemporary documents, "In and out of bondage, the slave was a member of the family" (p. 145), while "the acquisition of a male slave was a great affair, on which a man was congratulated almost as if a son had been born to him. No wonder, for a slave fulfilled tasks similar to those of a son" (p. 132).

4. Herodotus, *The Histories,* in the translation by Aubrey de Selincourt (Harmondsworth, 1954), p. 247.

5. John Middleton, *Lugbara Religion* (Oxford, 1960), especially pp. 230ff.

6. Saunders, *op. cit.*, p. 35.

7. *Ibid.*, p. 39, relying largely on Zurara's contemporary chronicle and other contemporary sources.

Index

Abomey, 76

Adams, W. Y., 67

Adedeji, Adebayo, 251, 272

Affonso, king of Kongo, 186

Africa: colonial frontiers of, 240, 242, 266–69, 279–80; cultural unity of, 67, 69, 82, 93, 279; development of technology and institutions of, 13, 38–39, 41, 46, 51–59, 77–78, 88, 100, 144, 254–55, 264, 283, 292, 325–26; equality in early European contacts with, 12–13, 56–64, 329–32; kingdoms of, 19–41, 46–50, 55, 257; political unity in, 79–80, 267; in sixteenth century, 42–64; slavery within, 31, 187, 336–37

African-Americans, 80

African Awakening, The (Davidson), 101, 179

African history: advances in study of, 3–14, 253–54, 263–64; archaeological evidence of, 6, 20, 21, 37, 54, 67–69, 71–72, 92, 100, 143, 264, 325, 326–27; beginning of, 70; "ethnohistory" and, 4, 5, 69, 70; Europeans' denial of, 13, 67, 99–100, 250, 255, 264, 283–84, 320, 325–26; linguistic evidence of, 69, 92, 327; nationalism and, 9, 254; oral sources of, 23, 30, 45, 68, 90–91, 143; "otherness" in, 7–8; periodization in, 65–78; Portuguese and, 185–86, 190; "prehistory" and, 69, 70; regions in, 65;

sources on, 90, 178–79; writing of, 65–78

Africanism, meanings of, 79–93

African Mineworkers' Union, 162

African National Congress (ANC) (South Africa), 107–8, 109, 122–24, 295, 296, 297, 307, 308–9

African studies, 7, 80, 84–93, 97–102, 328–29

Afrikaners (Boers), 41, 43, 149, 293; in South Africa, 98, 111–12, 113, 114, 115–16, 117, 118, 127, 128, 129, 303–4, 309

Afwerki, Issaias, 316, 317

agriculture: cash crops in, 269, 272; in postcolonial Africa, 269, 271–72, 287; precolonial development of, 39, 53–54, 144, 292

Ahidjo, Ahmadou, 275

Ahmad Baba, 49

Ajayi, Ade, 258, 268

Akan, 30, 39, 75, 251

Algeria, 26, 185, 228; as French colony, 81, 316, 320; war of independence of, 184

All-African People's Conference (1961), 227

Almeida, Francisco d', 56

Almeida, Joao de, 190

Alves, Pascoal, 205, 206, 207

Americas, 83, 334–35; *see also* North America

Amhara, 275, 285, 315–16

A NOTE ABOUT THE AUTHOR

Basil Davidson was born on November 9, 1914, in Bristol and is today an internationally recognized historian and expert on African affairs. Three times decorated, he served with the British Army during the Second World War in the Balkans, Italy, and North Africa. He has been diplomatic and foreign correspondent to major British daily and weekly papers, including *The Economist* (1938–39), *The Times* (1945–49), and the *New Statesman* (1950–54). He has held academic posts at the universities of Ghana (1964), California (1971), and Edinburgh (1972), holds honorary doctorates at the universities of Ibadan and Edinburgh, and has been a national sponsor of the London-based Anti-Apartheid Movement since 1969. In 1972, he was elected Corresponding British member of the Académie des Sciences d'Outre-Mer, Paris; in 1975, he won the Haile Selassie Award for African Research, and, in 1976 the Medalha Amílcar Cabral.

Basil Davidson has written more than twenty books on Africa, published in twenty-two countries. They include: *The African Slave Trade*, *The Lost Cities of Africa*, *The African Genius*, and *The Black Man's Burden: Africa and the Curse of the Nation-State*, which was named a Notable Book of the Year by *The New York Times* in 1992.